www.wadsworth.com

wadsworth.com is the World Wide Web site for Wadsworth Publishing Company and is your direct source to dozens of online resources.

At *wadsworth.com* you can find out about supplements, demonstration software, and student resources. You can also send e-mail to many of our authors and preview new publications and exciting new technologies.

wadsworth.com
Changing the way the world learns®

Ethics in Crime and Justice

Dilemmas and Decisions

Third Edition

JOYCELYN M. POLLOCK
Southwest Texas State University

West/Wadsworth
I⊤P® An International Thomson Publishing Company

Belmont, CA • Albany, NY • Bonn • Boston • Cincinnati • Detroit • Johannesburg • London • Madrid
Melbourne • Mexico City • New York • Paris • Singapore
Tokyo • Toronto • Washington

Criminal Justice Editor: Sabra Horne
Assistant Editor: Claire Masson
Editorial Assistant: Kate Barrett
Project Editor: Angela Mann
Marketing Manager: Mike Dew
Print Buyer: Karen Hunt
Copy Editor: Donald Pharr
Permissions Editor: Peggy Meehan
Cover Designer: Liz Harasymczuk
Compositor: Thompson Type
Printer: The Maple-Vail Book Manufacturing Group/Vail-Ballou Press

Printed in the United States of America
4 5 6 7 8 9 10

For more information, contact Wadsworth Publishing Company, 10 Davis Drive, Belmont, CA
94002, or electronically at http://www.wadsworth.com/wadsworth.html

International Thomson Publishing Europe
Berkshire House 168-173
High Holborn
London, WC1V 7AA, England

Thomas Nelson Australia
102 Dodds Street
South Melbourne 3205
Victoria, Australia

Nelson Canada
1120 Birchmount Road
Scarborough, Ontario
Canada M1K 5G4

International Thomson Publishing GmbH
Königswinterer Strasse 418
53227 Bonn, Germany

International Thomson Editores
Campos Eliseos 385, Piso 7
Col. Polanco
11560 México D.F. México

International Thomson Publishing Asia
221 Henderson Road
#05-10 Henderson Building
Singapore 0315

International Thomson Publishing Japan
Hirakawacho Kyowa Building, 3F
2-2-1 Hirakawacho
Chiyoda-ku, Tokyo 102, Japan

International Thomson Publishing
Southern Africa
Building 18, Constantia Park
240 Old Pretoria Road
Halfway House, 1685 South Africa

Library of Congress Cataloging-in-Publication Data

Pollock-Byrne, Joycelyn, M., 1956–
    Ethics in crime and justice : dilemmas and decisions / Joycelyn M.
Pollock. — 3rd ed.
        p.   cm.
    Includes bibliographical references and index.
    ISBN 0-534-50793-X
    1. Criminal justice, Administration of—Moral and ethical aspects.
    2. Criminal justice, Administration of—United States.   I. Title
HV7419.P65   1997
364.973—dc21   97-22962

To my son,
Gregory James Byrne

"The real education teaches us to be whole human beings."

Vimala McClure, *The Tao of Motherhood*

Contents

Preface

The ethics of criminal justice practitioners continues to be an important and growing topic in the media and academic venues. In this third edition of *Ethics in Crime and Justice: Dilemmas and Decisions,* I have updated the 1993 edition and also responded to student and reviewer comments in an effort to provide an extensive and pedagogically sound text.

To aid students in comprehension and retention of the diverse ethical issues, I have added many pedagogical tools. Chapter Objectives and Chapter Outlines have been added to aid instructors in organizing a syllabus around chapter topics. I have added "Queries?," which are discussion questions or to be used to spur thoughtful analysis of the relevant issues, "Quotations," which are of interest but not essential to the discussion, and "Literary Perspectives," which are longer paragraphs and often fiction. I changed the back-of-the-chapter questions to content-review questions, which can be used for testing purposes, changed some of the ethical dilemmas and added "Selected Readings," which are primarily new material.

In an effort to more fully develop the ethical dilemmas in each area of the criminal justice systems, I have significantly increased the chapter contents. The first chapter has substantial changes: I added a first section, Why Study Morals?, and added a section on analyzing ethical dilemmas. The second chapter has an expanded discussion of ethics of virtue, relativism, and I have added a new section on situational ethics. The chapters on justice and law in the second edition have been combined to form one chapter in this edition. The chapters on ethics for law enforcement practitioners, legal professionals, and correctional practitioners have all been divided into two chapters each, increasing the total number of chapters to eleven. The law enforcement chapter, especially, has been substantially revised. The last chapter has also been substantially revised, adding sections on policy-making and myths in criminal justice, as well as expanding the section of "Why Be Ethical?" The book has increased in length by over 100 pages, reflecting new material and updated examples of ethical issues. Prevalent themes are emphasized, such as the role of all criminal justice professionals as public servants and their role in preserving due process and civil liberties.

Unfortunately I was unable to provide the American Bar Association Model Rules in appendices, as was done in the last edition because the ABA would not allow reprinting. I apologize to those instructors who made use of those appendices in the classroom. Most of the changes made were in response to reviewers' comments. I would like to thank the following reviewers: Bradley S. Chilton, The University of Toledo; Lee Colwell, The University of Arkansas Little Rock; James Houston, Appalachian State University; Mark Jones, East Carolina University; Nicholas Meier, Kalamazoo Valley Community College; Thomas E. Reed, Eastern Kentucky University; Emilio Viano, The American University; and Miki Vohryzek-Bolden, California State University Sacramento. Their comments and suggestions for additional sources were extremely helpful. I have had the advantage of excellent feedback in the last several years and thank everyone who has corresponded with me or discussed the book with me at national conferences. I would like to encourage readers to continue letting me know what they like and don't like about the book.

Unfortunately there is always new material to add when writing an ethics text. Questionable practices in law enforcement, the court system, and corrections continue to occur. It is also important to recognize, however, that while we focus on the few who violate ethical standards, the majority of practitioners in the criminal justice system are honest, hardworking, and attempt to live up to the ethical standards of their profession.

Joycelyn M. Pollock
San Marcos, Texas
JP12@SWT.EDU

1

Morality, Ethics, and Human Behavior

Why Study Ethics?

Defining Terms
Morals and Ethics
Making Moral Judgments
Duties
Values

Morality and the Law
Regulations, Standards, and Ethics

Morality and Behavior

Analyzing Ethical Dilemmas

Conclusion

Review Questions

Ethical Dilemmas

Suggested Readings

Chapter Objectives

Become familiar with the major arguments supporting the importance of studying ethics in the criminal justice field.

Understand the vocabulary of ethics—i.e., morals, ethics, values, ethical codes, ethical standards, and dilemmas.

Understand how to analyze an ethical dilemma.

Become sensitive to the types of ethical dilemmas faced in one's professional life.

You are a police officer patrolling late at night and see a car weaving back and forth across lanes of traffic. You turn on your siren, and the car pulls over. The driver stumbles out of the car, obviously intoxicated. There is no question that the driver meets the legal definition of intoxication. He also happens to be your father. What would you do?

WHY STUDY ETHICS?

The above dilemma places the reader in a situation where a decision must be made. Either one does one's duty as a police officer and issues a ticket, or one doesn't issue a ticket based on some rationale of familial loyalty, mercy, or care. You may have had difficulty resolving the dilemma, or you may have quickly and easily decided the "right" thing to do. Learning how to determine the "right thing to do" is the central purpose of this book.

The approach taken in this exploration of ethics is that criminal justice professionals, whether they work in law enforcement, the courts, or corrections, are placed in a unique position to protect or violate the rights and privileges of citizens. This special position, or public trust, requires that those who have this type of power be especially sensitive to the ethical issues that may arise in their professional lives.

Legislators have the power to define activities as illegal and punishable. They do so usually on some rationale of public safety, but also employ moral definitions for deciding which behaviors should be legal and which should be illegal. For instance, no one could argue that state prohibitions against same-sex marriages are supported by a public safety rationale; the only argument against same-sex marriages is a purely moral one. Other laws are also written based on lawmakers' definitions of morality (e.g., abortion, drug laws, gambling, prostitution, and liquor sales on Sunday). When there is disagreement about the "rightness" or "wrongness" of certain actions, legislators have the power to define, and ultimately that definition leads to deprivations of rights.

(For example, although you may not believe there is anything morally wrong with small amounts of marijuana, you act on that belief at your peril.) Thus, one might question how legislators use their great discretion and how they balance the rights of all people. Chapter 4, on law and justice, explores these questions in more detail.

Police officers have the power to deprive people of their liberty (through arrest), they have the power to decide which individuals to investigate and perhaps target for undercover operations, and they have the power to issue a ticket or provide "mercy" and let a driver off with a warning. They serve as the interface between the awesome power of the state and the citizenry governed. In some countries, police operate as a fearsome coercive force for a controlling political body. In this country, some see police operating in a similar way; however, we do enjoy constitutional protections against untrammeled police power. In Chapters 5 and 6, on law enforcement, the ethical use of police discretion will be discussed in more detail.

Prosecutors probably face the least public scrutiny of all criminal justice professionals, which is ironic since they wield incredible power in their discretion in deciding what and how to prosecute. They decide which charges to pursue and which to drop, they decide which cases to take to a grand jury, they decide how to prosecute a case, they decide whether to pursue the death penalty in homicide cases, and so on. They often make general decisions about the types of crimes to pursue, affecting police officers' decision making regarding enforcement. They have ethical duties to pursue "justice" rather than conviction, but one might argue that, at times, their decision making may seem to be more political than "just." Judges also hold incredible power, typically employed through decision making in accepting plea bargains, decisions regarding rules of evidence, and decisions about sentencing. Chapters 7 and 8 deal with the ethical issues of legal professionals in the criminal justice system.

Finally, correctional officials also have immense powers over the lives of certain citizens. Probation officers make recommendations in presentence reports and violation reports that affect whether an individual goes to prison or not. Prison officials decide to award and take away "good time," and make decisions regarding placing inmates into segregation—in both types of decisions, the individual's liberty is affected. The discretion of parole officials is similar to that found in probation. All correctional professionals have a great deal of discretion over the lives of those they control. The issues involved are discussed in Chapters 9 and 10.

All the professionals discussed above have several elements in common:

1. They each have discretion, meaning the power to make a decision. While the particular decisions are different, they all involve power over others and potential deprivation of life, liberty, or property.

2. They each have the duty of enforcement of the law. While this concept is obvious with police, it is also clear upon reflection that each of the professionals mentioned has a basic duty to enforce all laws; they serve the law in their professional lives.

3. In addition, they all must accept that their duty is to protect the constitutional safeguards that are the cornerstone of our legal system, specifically, due process and equal protection. Due process protects each of us from error in a governmental deprivation of life, liberty, or property. We recognize the right of government to control and even to punish, but we have certain protections against arbitrary or inaccurate use of that power. Due process protects those interests. We also expect that government's power will be used fairly and in an unbiased manner. Equal protection should ensure that what happens to us is not determined by the color of our skin, our gender, nationality, or the religion we practice. Laws are for everyone, and the protection of the law extends to all of us. Although there is a fair amount of evidence to indicate that different treatment does exist, the ideal of equal protection is an essential element of our legal system and should be an operating principle for everyone working in this system.

4. They are public servants. That is, their paychecks come from the public purse. Public servants possess more than a job; they have taken on special duties involving the public trust. Individuals such as legislators, public officials, police officers, judges, and prosecutors are either elected or appointed guardians of the public's interests. Arguably, they must be held to higher standards than those they guard or govern. As Delattre (1989: 82) notes,

> Part of what is needed is a public sense of what Madison meant by wisdom and good character: balanced perception and integrity. Integrity means wholeness in public and private life consisting of habits of justice, temperance, courage, compassion, honesty, fortitude, and disdain for self-pity.

Temptations are many, and often it seems we find more examples of *double* standards, where public servants take advantage of their positions for special favors, rather than *higher* standards of exemplary behavior. Therefore, all professionals in the criminal justice field must be sensitive to ethical issues. These issues may involve their relations with citizens and others over whom they have power, their relationships with their agency, or their relationships with one another.

Obviously, the law governs many of the decisions public servants make, but because of the discretion that exists at every step of the criminal justice process, there is always the possibility of an unethical use of such discretion. Understanding the ethical issues involved in one's profession may help to guide such discretion and prevent abuse.

This section is titled "Why Study Ethics?" Felkenes answered the question ten years ago:

1. Professionals are recognized as such in part because "profession" . . . normally includes a set of ethical requirements as part of its meaning. . . . Professionalism among all actors at all levels of the criminal justice system depends upon their ability to administer policy effectively in a morally and ethically responsible manner.

Principles of Public Service Ethics

1. **Public Service.** Public servants should treat their office as a public trust, only using the power and resources of public office to advance public interests, and not to attain personal benefit or pursue any other private interest incompatible with the public good.
2. **Objective Judgment.** Public servants should employ independent objective judgment in performing their duties, deciding all matters on the merits, free from avoidable conflicts of interest and both real and apparent improper influences.
3. **Accountability.** Public servants should assure that government is conducted openly, efficiently, equitably and honorably in a manner that permits the citizenry to make informed judgments and hold government officials accountable.
4. **Democratic Leadership.** Public servants should honor and respect the principles and spirit of representative democracy and set a positive example of good citizenship by scrupulously observing the letter and spirit of laws and rules.
5. **Respectability.** Public servants should safeguard public confidence in the integrity of government by being honest, fair, caring and respectful and by avoiding conduct creating the appearance of impropriety or which is otherwise unbefitting a public official.

SOURCE: Josephson Institute of Ethics.

2. Training in critical ethics helps to develop analytical skills and reasoning abilities needed to understand the pragmatic and theoretical aspects of the criminal justice system.

3. Criminal justice professionals should be able to recognize quickly the ethical consequences of various actions, and the moral principles involved.

4. Ethical considerations are central to decisions involving discretion, force, and due process which require people to make enlightened moral judgments.

5. Ethics is germane to most management and policy decisions concerning such penal issues as rehabilitation, deterrence, and just deserts.

QUOTATION

Raise the salaries [of public servants], we are encouraged, and then you can expect better. I doubt it. . . . Raise the salaries if the jobs merit higher pay but not in expectation of buying integrity. Nobody sells that. People who have it give it for free.

SOURCE: Delattre, E. "Ethics in Public Service: Higher Standards and Double Standards." *Criminal Justice Ethics* 2 (Summer/Fall 1989): 78–83.

6. Ethical considerations are essential aspects of criminal justice research. (Felkenes, 1987: 26)

In answer to a similar question, Braswell (1996a) explains the five goals of a study of ethics:

1. Become aware and open to ethical issues.
2. Begin developing critical thinking skills.
3. Become more personally responsible.
4. Understand how the criminal justice system is engaged in a process of coercion.
5. Develop "wholesight" (which roughly means explore with one's heart as well as one's mind).

The comprehensive nature of these two lists requires no additions. We will simply reiterate some basic points. First, we study ethics because criminal justice is uniquely involved in coercion, which means there are many and varied opportunities to abuse such power. Second, almost all criminal justice professionals are public servants and, thus, owe special duties to the public they serve. Finally, we study ethics to sensitize the student to ethical issues and provide tools to help resolve the ethical dilemmas that individuals may be faced with in their professional lives.

DEFINING TERMS

The words *morals* and *ethics* are often used in daily conversations. For instance, when public officials use their offices for personal profit or when politicians accept bribes from special interest groups, they are described as unethical. When an individual does a good deed, engages in charitable activities or personal sacrifice, or takes a stand against wrongdoing, we might describe that individual as a moral person. Very often, *morals* and *ethics* are used interchangeably. This makes sense because they both come from similar root meanings. The Greek word *ethos* pertains to custom (behavioral practices) or character, and *morals* is a Latin word with a similar meaning.

Morals and Ethics

Morals and *morality* refer to what is judged as good conduct. (*Immorality* is, of course, bad conduct.) The term *moral* is also used to describe someone who has the capacity to make value judgments and discern right from wrong (Souryal, 1992: 12). *Ethics* refers to the study and analysis of what constitutes good or bad conduct (Barry, 1985: 5; Sherman, 1981: 8).

There are several branches or schools of ethics. *Metaethics* is "the highly technical discipline investigating the meaning of ethical terms including a critical study of how ethical statements can be verified" (Barry, 1985: 11). *Normative ethics* and *applied ethics* are concerned with the study of what constitutes right and wrong behavior in certain situations. Normative ethics determines

---

QUERY

- Should we be concerned with a politician who has extramarital affairs? Drinks to excess? Gambles? Uses drugs? Abuses his or her spouse?
- What about if the person was a police officer? Judge?
- Should a police officer be sanctioned for drinking to excess in public and making a spectacle of himself or herself in a bar?

---

what people ought to do and defines moral duties. Applied ethics is the application of ethical principles to specific issues. *Professional ethics* is an even more specific type of applied ethics relating to the behavior of certain professions or groups.

To many people, ethics has come to mean the definition of particular behaviors as right and wrong within a profession. Very often, in common usage, morality is used to speak of the total person, or the sum of a person's actions in every sphere of life, and ethics is used for certain behaviors relating to a profession, and is an analysis of behavior relevant to a certain profession. For instance, the medical profession follows the Hippocratic Oath, a declaration of rules and principles of conduct for doctors to follow in their daily practices; it dictates appropriate behavior and goals. In fact, most professions have their own set of ethical standards or canons of ethics.

Even though professional ethics typically restricts attention to areas of behavior relevant to the profession, these can be fairly inclusive and enter into what we might consider the private life of the individual. For instance, doctors are judged harshly if they engage in romantic relationships with their patients, as are professors if they become involved with students. These rules are usually included in codes of ethics for these professions. We are very much aware of how politicians' private behavior can affect their career in politics. When politicians are embroiled in controversial love affairs or are exposed as spouse abusers, these revelations have definite effects on their future. It is clear that, in some professions anyway—typically those involving public trust such as politics, education, and the clergy—there is a thin line between one's private life and one's public life.

It does not make a great deal of difference for our purposes whether we use the formal or colloquial definitions of *morals* and *ethics*. This text is an applied ethics text, in that we will be concerned with what is defined as right and wrong behavior in the professions relevant to the criminal justice system and how people in these professions make decisions in the course of their careers. It is also a professional ethics text, because we are primarily concerned with professional ethics in criminal justice.

Making Moral Judgments

We make moral or ethical judgments all the time: "Abortion is wrong." "Capital punishment is just." "It is good to give to charity." "It is wrong to hit your spouse." These are all judgments of good and bad behavior. We also make decisions when faced with behavioral choices. I chose to stay home from work today even though I wasn't sick. You might give back extra change that a clerk gave you by mistake. I choose not to tell a friend that her husband is having an affair. The police officer in the dilemma that begins this chapter must choose whether to arrest his or her father for DWI. Do all behavioral choices involve questions of ethics? Are all judgments we make ethical or moral judgments? Obviously not. In order to more specifically draw the boundaries of our ethical discussion, we need to know what sorts of behavioral decisions might be judged under ethical standards.

Act   First of all, we must have some act to judge. For instance, we are concerned with the act of stealing or the act of contributing to charity, rather than an idle thought that stealing a lot of money would enable us to buy a sailboat or a vague intention to be more generous. We are not necessarily concerned with how people feel or what they think about a particular action unless it has some bearing on what they do. The intention or motive behind a particular behavior is an important component of that behavior; for instance, in ethical formalism (which we will discuss in Chapter 2) one must know the intent of an action in order to be able to judge it as moral, immoral, or neither. However, one must have some action to examine before making a moral judgment.

Only Human Acts   Second, judgments of moral or ethical behavior are directed specifically to human behavior. A dog that bites is not considered immoral or evil, although we may judge careless pet owners who allow their dogs the opportunity to bite. Nor do we consider drought, famine, floods, or other natural disasters immoral, even though the death, destruction, and misery caused by these events are probably greater than that caused by all combined acts that humans have perpetrated on their victims. Behaviors of animals or events of nature cannot be judged in the same way as actions performed by human beings. The reasons we view them differently may become apparent in the next paragraph. Morality (or immorality) has been applied only to humans because of their capacity to reason. Because only humans have the capacity to be "good," which involves a voluntary, rational decision and subsequent action, only humans, of all members of the animal kingdom, have the capacity to be "bad."

Free Will   In addition to limiting discussions of morality to human behavior, we also usually further restrict our discussion to behavior that stems from free will and free action. Culpability is not assigned to persons who are not sufficiently aware of the world around them to be able to decide rationally what is good or bad. The two groups traditionally exempt from responsibility in this sense are the young and the insane. Arguably, we do not judge the morality of their behavior because of a belief that they do not have the capacity to reason and therefore cannot choose to be moral or immoral. Although we may punish a two-year-old for hitting a baby, we do so to educate or socialize, not to punish, as we would an older child or adult. We incapacitate the mentally ill to protect ourselves against their violence and strange behavior, but we consider them sick, not evil. This is true even if their actual behavior is indistinguishable from that of other individuals we do punish. For example, a murder may result in a death sentence or a hospital commitment, depending on whether the person is judged to be sane or insane, responsible or not responsible.

Admittedly, at times we have difficulty in deciding whether behavior originates with free will, or we do not care whether it does. Historically, the insane and even those with physical illnesses such as epilepsy and leprosy were punished in the belief that they suffered these afflictions because of their own sinfulness. Even today we seem to exhibit mixed opinions. For instance, some believe that alcoholism and drug addiction are serious illnesses; therefore, the person cannot be morally culpable for actions caused by the addictions, but others believe that drinking and drug abuse are caused by moral weakness.

We continue to imprison and even execute those who show obvious signs of mental illness, despite our legal tradition of holding only "rational" people legally culpable. Miller and Radelet (1993) discuss the long history of excusing the mentally ill, a practice that dates back to medieval times. The supporting rationales for such excuses are as follows:

1. Humanitarian reasons.
2. Fair play (they can't help themselves).
3. Retributive goals are not met (because they don't appreciate their suffering).
4. They can't spiritually prepare for death.
5. Deterrence is not served because others identify only with premeditated acts, not those borne of insanity.
6. They can't help in their own defense, calling into question the accuracy of guilt. (1993: 2–4)

Even so, there are many examples of individuals who were not only prosecuted but convicted and executed, arguably because of the extreme nature of their crimes, rather than a belief that their actions stemmed from rational thought.

QUERY

- Do you agree that a child before the legal age of reason is not morally culpable for his or her actions? Why or why not? What should the age of reason be?
- What are some situations in which the individual cannot be considered rational or, alternatively, is not acting from free will? Is the behavior that results moral or immoral?

QUOTATION

[An expert witness discusses Albert Fish, who killed and ate children and engaged in other bizarre practices such as sticking needles in his body, eating his own feces, and setting fire to his rectum.]

Well, a man might for nine days eat that [human] flesh and still not have a psychosis. There is no accounting for taste.

SOURCE: Quoted in Miller and Radelet, 1993: 7.

Several states have passed laws that create a "guilty but insane" conviction rather than the previous acquittal "by reason of insanity." Thus, they need no legal fiction of "sanity" in order to punish. Individuals are housed in forensic facilities until (or unless) they are "cured," at which time they are transferred to penal facilities for punishment.

Attitudes toward the *age of reason* and when a child is said to have reached it also seem to be changing. Many states are now revising their laws regarding the trial and punishment of juveniles because of changing beliefs regarding the age of rationality and responsibility. Several states have reduced the age at which a child is considered an adult or have developed procedures allowing youngsters who have committed serious crimes, such as murder, to be remanded to adult courts for trial and sentencing. The United States is one of the few countries in the world that will execute seventeen-year-olds, a distinction shared by such countries as Iran, Iraq, and Nigeria (Miller and Radelet, 1993: 8).

Part of the impetus for this harsher treatment of juveniles has been a public perception that juvenile crime is increasing and is becoming more violent. Since lawmakers respond to public pressure, public perceptions affect laws. In the case of juvenile crime, facts do seem to support the conclusion that juvenile crime is increasing and becoming more violent, but whether harsher sentences will alleviate or exacerbate the situation remains to be seen.

Careless actions, such as driving while intoxicated or playing with a loaded weapon, are judged as less "bad" than those actions performed with deliberation and intent. An individual who has weighed the consequences and knows the outcome and all the ramifications of the action and then proceeds has greater moral culpability than someone who has proceeded without such deliberation, albeit with a negligent disregard for potential or probable consequences.

The moral culpability of an actor is not necessarily equivalent to legal culpability, although we have used the legal terms *negligence* and *recklessness*. *Mens rea*, or "guilty mind," refers to the mental element of a crime. The four levels of legal culpability (relating to the degree of mental blameworthiness) are negligence, recklessness, knowing, and intentional. These concepts are useful for us in moral judgments, yet we should not be misled that moral judgments and legal judgments are always the same. One might not be guilty of a crime and still be considered morally culpable. One might be guilty of a crime and be considered morally blameless. The differences between the law and morality will be discussed in a later section.

Intent and free will presuppose voluntary control over behavior. However, there is an argument that some actions are caused by life circumstances and are therefore are not completely voluntary. For instance, if someone came from an impoverished background and was exposed only to criminal role models, is this person responsible for his or her subsequent delinquency? Do all people truly have freedom of choice? It is illegal for a rich man or a poor man to steal a loaf of bread, but a rich man doesn't have to, nor does he usually engage in armed robbery even though he might be guilty of tax evasion, toxic waste dumping, or embezzlement. We are all bound by limitations (or opportunities) of birth and circumstance. If we were to analyze moral culpability on the basis of life choices, it might be that, because of their respective life positions, some people who commit serious crimes are less blameworthy than others who come from better backgrounds and commit less serious crimes. For instance, the embezzler who already makes a good salary might be considered more blameworthy than the mugger who has no job and steals because it is the only thing he or she knows how to do.

Affects Others Finally, we usually discuss moral or immoral behavior only in those cases where the behavior significantly affects others. For instance, throwing a rock off a bridge would be neither good nor bad unless you could possibly hit or were aiming at a person below. If no one were there, your behavior is neutral; if someone were below, however, you might endanger that person's life, so your behavior would be judged as "bad." All the moral dilemmas we will discuss in this book involve at least two parties, and the decision to be made affects the other individual in every case. In reality, it is difficult to think of an action that does not affect others, however indirectly. Even self-destructive behavior is said to harm the people who love us and who would be hurt by such actions. We sense that this is an important aspect of judging morality when we hear the common rationale of those who, when caught, protest, "But nobody was hurt!" Indeed, even a hermit living alone on a desert island may engage in immoral or unethical actions. Whether he wants to be or not, the hermit is part of human society; therefore, some people would say that even he might engage in actions that could be judged immoral if they degrade or threaten the future of humankind, such as committing suicide or polluting the ocean.

QUERY

- Are poor thieves less blameworthy than rich thieves?
- Can you think of any action that does not affect other people?
- Do you believe the state should regulate behavior that arguably "doesn't hurt anyone else," such as motorcycle or bicycle helmet laws? Prostitution? Gambling?

One's actions toward nature might also be defined as immoral, so relevant actions include not only actions done to people, but also to animals and to nature. To abuse or exploit animals can be defined as immoral—judgments can be made against cockfighting, dog racing, laboratory experimentation on animals, and hunting. The growth of environmental ethics reflects increasing concern for the future of the planet. The rationale for environmental ethics may be that any actions that harm the environment affect all humans. It may also be justified by the belief that humankind is a part of nature—not superior to it—and part of natural law would be to protect, not exploit, the world of which we are a part.

Thus far, we know morality and ethics concern the judgment of behavior as right or wrong. Furthermore, such judgments are directed only at voluntary human behavior that affects other people, the earth, and living things.

We can further restrict our inquiries regarding ethics to those behavioral decisions that are relevant to one's profession in the criminal justice system. For instance, an argument might be made to look only at those decisions that may result in infringements on the liberty or privileges of others. So ethical discussions regarding police officers would concern only those decisions that affect the freedoms of others. This is somewhat of an incomplete approach, however, since many decisions that do not affect liberties are arguably also ethical issues—e.g., whether to sleep on duty, whether to call in sick when one wants to play golf or go fishing, or whether to lie on an expense sheet. In the box provided, a variety of ethical issues is presented, and one sees that decisions fall into major categories of effects on citizenry, effects on other employees, and effects on the organization one works for.

Duties

Another comment we should make about behavior and morality is that philosophers distinguish between moral duties and *superogatories*. Duties refer to those actions that an individual must perform in order to be considered moral. For instance, everyone may agree that one has a duty to support one's parents if able to do so, one has a duty to obey the law (unless it is an immoral law), and a police officer has a moral and ethical duty to tell the truth on a police report. These duties exist in one's personal life, and unique ethical duties exist in every profession.

Other actions, considered superogatories, are commendable but not required. A Good Samaritan who jumps into a river to save a drowning person, risking his or her own life to do so, has performed a superogatory action—there is no moral condemnation of those who stood on the bank, because the action was above and beyond anyone's moral duty. Of course, if one can help save a life with no great risk to oneself, then a moral duty does exist in that situation, and police officers may have an ethical duty to get involved in certain life-threatening situations that others do not. There are also what are called *imperfect duties*. These are general values that one should uphold, but without specific application to when or how. For instance, most ethical sys-

---

Inventory of Ethical Issues

The Individual and the Organization:
work ethic
petty theft
overtime abuse
gifts and gratuities
falsifying reports
misuse of sick days
personal use of supplies or equipment
personal demands interfering with work performance
other: _____

The Organization and Employees:
sexual or racial discrimination
sexual or racial harassment
discouraging honest criticism
unfair decisions
inadequate compensation
no recognition of good performance

inadequate training
unrealistic demands
other: _____

The Individual and Other Employees:
"backstabbing" and lack of support
gossip
sexual or racial harassment
lying to cover up blame
taking credit for other's work
other: _____

The Individual and the Public:
misuse of authority
inadequate performance of duty
sexual, racial, ethnic harassment
special treatment
lack of expertise in profession
other: _____

---

tems would support a general duty of generosity, but there is no specific duty demanding a certain type or manner of generosity.

Values

Values are defined as elements of desirability, worth, or importance. Values, and judgments of worth, are often equated with moral judgments of goodness. We see that both can be distinguished from factual judgments, which can be empirically verified. Note the difference between the factual judgments "He is lying" and "It is raining" and the value judgments "She is a good woman" or "That was a wonderful day." The last two judgments are similar to the moral judgments we will be discussing in later chapters. Both can be distinguished from factual judgments in that "facts" are capable of scientific proof whereas values and moral judgments are not. Some writers indicate that value judgments and moral judgments are indistinguishable since neither can be verified (Mackie, 1977; Margolis, 1971). Just as some believe that there are no universal moral standards, some also feel that values are relativistic and individual. For these people, values are not universal and are subjective rather than objective; thus, they are not "truth," but rather something closer to opinion (Mackie, 1977: 22–24). Values and morals are very similar, but while values merely indicate relative importance, morals prescribe or proscribe behavior. The value of honesty is conceptually distinct from the moral rule against lying.

Individual values form value systems. All people prioritize certain things that they consider important in life. Behavior is generally consistent with values. For instance, some individuals may believe that financial success is more important than family or health. In this case, we may assume that their behavior will reflect the importance of that value and that these persons will be workaholics, spending more time at work than with family and endangering their health with long hours, stress, and lack of exercise. Others may place a higher priority on such values as religious faith, wisdom, honesty, and/or independence than other values such as financial success or status. Their lives would be lived largely in accordance with such values.

Discussions concerning values imply a choice or judgment. If, for instance, you were confronted with an opportunity to cheat on an exam, your values of academic success and honesty would be directly at odds. The choice you make in that particular situation may be decided by your value system. Some individuals value success above all other factors and will lie, cheat, and steal to achieve the standard of success to which they aspire. Others may hold honesty so dear that they would not steal even if they were starving and there were no other way to obtain food. Very often we live our lives without taking a close look at the value system that influences our behavior.

Values and morals are somewhat related, since one's values help to form one's moral beliefs. Moral standards derive from the value one places on such things as honesty, integrity, and trust. However, universalists would not hesitate to add that all values are not equal. Valuing money over life, for instance, would be wrong, as would valuing pleasure over charity. An explicit value system is a part of every ethical system, as we will see in Chapter 2. Certain values hold special relevance to the criminal justice system. Such values as privacy, freedom, public order, justice, duty, and loyalty are all values that will come up again and again in later discussions. Typically, the values involved in most

---

Value Exercise

Rank the following "values" in order of importance, with #1 representing the most important value to you, and so on.

Achievement	Friendship	Power
Altruism	Health	Recognition
Autonomy	Honesty	Religion
Beauty	Justice	Success
Creativity	Knowledge	Wealth
Duty	Love	Wisdom
Emotional Well-Being	Loyalty	
Family	Pleasure	

ethical systems are the values of life, respect for the person, and the continued survival of society.

MORALITY AND THE LAW

Our laws legislate many aspects of our behavior. Laws, in the form of statutes and ordinances, tell us how to drive, how to operate our business, and what we can and cannot do in public and even in private. They are the formal, written rules of society. Yet they are not comprehensive in defining moral behavior. There is a law against hitting one's mother (assault) but no law against financially abandoning her, yet both are considered morally wrong. We have laws against "bad" behavior, such as burglarizing a house or embezzling from our employer, but we have very few laws prescribing "good" behavior, such as helping a victim or contributing to a charity. The exception to this would be the "Good Samaritan laws" that exist in some states and are quite common in Europe. These laws make it a crime to pass by an accident scene or witness a crime without rendering assistance.

We have so many laws that not all of them are enforced regularly, so people routinely break them and go unpunished. Some actions prohibited by law are thought to be private decisions of the individual and not especially wrong or harmful. Many people object to sodomy laws and other laws regulating sexual behavior because they feel this is private behavior and outside the parameters of social control; others object to speed limits. When laws prohibit behaviors that are not universally condemned, such as laws prohibiting alcohol, drugs, and prostitution, enforcement is more subject to criticism and, not incidentally, more prone to corruption because the ability to rationalize under-enforcement or preferential treatment is greater.

We have had laws in the past that were or are now considered immoral—for instance, the internment of Japanese Americans during World War II and pre–Civil War laws that mandated the return of runaway slaves to their owners. An important question in the study of ethics is whether one can be a good person while obeying a bad law. Civil disobedience is the voluntary disobedience of what is considered an unjust or immoral law. In Chapter 3, we discuss morality and immorality in relation to the legal system.

QUOTATION

Laws are just like spider's webs, they will hold the weak and delicate who might be caught in their meshes, but will be torn to pieces by the rich and powerful. (Anacharsis, 600 B.C.)

The more mandates and laws which are enacted,
The more there will be thieves and robbers. (Lao-Tze, 600 B.C.)

SOURCE: Quoted in Roth and Roth, 1989: 3.

Regulations, Standards, and Ethics

In addition to laws, we have a vast number of *regulations* governing the activities of occupations from physician to plumber and organizations from governmental agencies to private clubs. Regulations typically come from a governmental authority and often specify sanctions for noncompliance; *standards* may come from private or public bodies and are often used as a basis for some type of accreditation; *guidelines* may come from a professional group and are usually recommendations rather than directions. Distinctions can be made among these terms although they are often used interchangeably. These rules for behavior do not carry the formal sanctions of criminal law, but some may carry civil liabilities. Typically, the behavior in question is specific to that particular organization or occupation. Regulations and standards set down parameters of ideal behavior. Most regulations are from the state and federal governments. For instance, the Food and Drug Administration prescribes certain procedures and rules for pharmaceutical companies to follow in developing, testing, and distributing drugs. The Environmental Protection Agency watches over industry to make sure that safe methods for disposal of hazardous wastes are implemented.

Noncompliance with standards and regulations is not equated with immoral behavior as readily as is criminal lawbreaking. Although fines may be levied against the construction supervisor who ignores Occupational Safety and Health Agency standards or the automaker who violates standards of the Consumer Safety Board, ordinarily they are not considered criminals, even when these actions result in injury or death. Reiman observes the different reporting styles used to describe a mining accident and a murder:

> Why do 26 dead miners amount to a "disaster," and six dead suburbanites a "mass murder"? "Murder" suggests a murderer, while "disaster" suggests the work of impersonal forces. But if over 1000 safety violations had been found in the mine—three the day before the first explosion—was no one responsible for failing to eliminate those hazards? And if someone could have prevented the hazards and did not, does that person not bear responsibility for the deaths of 26 men? Is he less evil because he did not want them to die although he chose to leave them in jeopardy? Is he not a murderer, perhaps even a mass murderer? (Reiman, cited in Scheingold, 1984: 23)

In fact, sometimes superficial compliance or outright violation of standards is considered good business practice. Examples of businesses or individuals in business routinely violating standards and/or regulations include insider information trading on Wall Street, toxic waste dumping in industry, and marketing of unsafe products in manufacturing. One example of what was considered good business practice being redefined as illegal is the law prohibiting hiring illegal aliens. Many businesses had not been willing to follow standards against hiring illegal aliens because lower labor costs resulted in greater profits. Redefinition from a regulatory infraction to a crime sometimes occurs when the behavior is persistent or the public becomes enraged over a particular incident or accident. When rules or standards are violated, other relevant criminal charges may be imposed as well. For instance, if a company blatantly violates safety regulations by forcing employees to work with toxic chemicals, company officials may be charged with negligent manslaughter if a worker dies. However, this situation is extremely rare, and there is usually a great deal of difference between the sanctions related to a violation of regulations and criminal lawbreaking.

In addition to guidelines and standards, professions usually have a code of ethics or set of professional rules to educate and encourage their members to perform in accordance with an ideal of behavior. These may be fairly general or fairly specific; for instance, lawyers have extensive "rules," but police officers are often given the International Chiefs of Police "Code of Ethics," which is only a page. Laws, standards, regulations, guidelines, and codes of ethics are all designed to control and guide behavior.

It is interesting to observe that regulations and rules for behavior often seem to expand in inverse relation to the practiced ethics of a particular profession or organization. Frequently, when a breakdown in ethical behavior is detected, there is an attempt to bring people back in line by the use of rules. However, it seems that in any profession, the most effective ethical guides are not those that specify behavior, but rather those that are consistent with and support an organizational ideal. People can find many ways of violating the spirit of an administrative rule while complying with its exact wording. Current examples abound of politicians routinely engaging in behavior or contracts involving conflicts of interest, but without actually breaking any laws, and lawyers who get around their ethical responsibilities by complying with the letter but not the spirit of the rules. However, decision makers in organizations often feel it is necessary to give employees extensive lists of rules. In an office these may include injunctions not to take supplies, not to make personal telephone calls, and not to spend more than fifteen minutes on breaks. Enforcing rules is very different from promoting an ethical standard of honesty and integrity in the workplace. Where ethical standards are nonexistent, it is doubtful that multitudinous rules of behavior will be able to eliminate wrongdoing. In Chapter 5, we will discuss how impossible it is to specify all the ethical issues that police officers may confront in their careers, and the ethical code of police officers does not attempt to do so. Rather, it gives general guidelines for priorities and goals while expecting the individual to make the correct decision in a specific situation.

MORALITY AND BEHAVIOR

One of the most difficult things to understand about human behavior is the disjunction between morals and behavior. We all can attest to the fact that believing something is wrong does not always prevent us from doing it. Very often, in fact, we engage in acts that we believe are bad, such as lying, stealing, and cheating. In any group of people (such as a college class), a majority will have engaged in some type of wrongful act at least once.

Why do people engage in behavior they believe to be wrong? Criminology attempts to explain why people commit unlawful acts. Psychological experiments show that a large percentage of schoolchildren will cheat when given an opportunity, even though they know it is wrong (Lickona, 1976). More recent studies show that many people will keep found wallets or purses. Theories that endorse everything from learning and role modeling to biological predisposition abound, but we still haven't answered fundamental questions of causation. Even with all these scientific and philosophical attempts to explain human action, we are still left with troubling questions when we read or hear about people who kill, steal, or otherwise offend our sense of morality. Evil is still one of the great mysteries of life.

Ironically, our society seems to endorse one set of beliefs while glorifying just the opposite. Examples of this glorification include Al Capone and Jesse James, who are in some ways cultural heroes even though they were known criminals. We have also glorified business executives when their actions could be defined as exploitative, as in the movie *Wall Street*. We are dismayed by the amount of violence and crime in our society, yet the television programs that play on these themes are the most popular. We abhor lying, but politicians who tell the truth are rejected by voters. We profess to be a country that cherishes our Constitution and due process rights, but we clap and cheer in movie theaters when "Dirty Harry" types kill the "bad guys." Why do we idolize people who have done things we know and believe to be wrong? Some say we sublimate our wish for excitement and our greed through their exploits. Many of the ideals of success in this society involve aspects of ruthlessness and aggression, traits hard to reconcile with an ideal conception of the good person. At least in Western culture, a "good" person who upholds the ideals of honesty, charity, and selflessness is considered somewhat of a weakling. The fact that our society has mixed values regarding what is considered good and desirable is reflected both in our popular culture and in individual action.

ANALYZING ETHICAL DILEMMAS

Two general levels of ethical issues in criminal justice can be distinguished. The first might be called ethical or moral issues that are broad social questions, often concerning the government's social control mechanisms and the impacts on those governed—e.g., what laws to pass, what sentences to attach to certain crimes, the death penalty, and whether to build more prisons or use community correctional alternatives are broad social issues that one person typically does not have much control over. These are important issues and should be discussed, but are distinct from ethical dilemmas.

Ethical dilemmas are those situations in which one person must make a decision about what to do. Either the choice is unclear, or the "right" behav-

---

Moral Issues

   I. Punishment: Should someone be punished or not? Why? What is fair punishment?

   II. Property: Should someone give, take or exchange property or not? Why? What are property rights?

   III. Affiliation: Should someone help another or maintain the other's expectations in a personal relationship? Why? What are the motives and obligations of a good family member or friend?

   IV. Authority: Should someone obey or accept the authority of another person or of a government or rule-making group? Why? What are the characteristics of a good governor and a good citizen?

   V. Morality and Conscience: Should one follow one's moral opinion or conscience when it conflicts with law, love or self-interest? Why? What is the nature of morality and what is the basis of its validity?

   VI. Law: Should someone obey or maintain a law? Why? What are the characteristics of a good law?

   VII. Contract: Should someone violate or uphold the political, economic, and social rights of another person or group? Why?

   VIII. Truth: Should someone tell the truth or allow the truth to be disclosed or not? Why? What defines truth-telling and why is it valuable?

   IX. Liberties: What are the basic political, economic and social rights?

   X. Life: Should someone save a life or not? Why? What makes life valuable?

   XI. Sex: Should one have a sexual relationship or not? Why? What is the nature of a good erotic relationship and why is it valuable?

SOURCE: Kohlberg, L., Colby, A., Gibbs, J., Speicher-Dubin, B., and Power, C. *Assessing Moral Stages: A Manual.* (Cambridge, MA: Harvard University, Center for Moral Education, 1977.)

---

ior is difficult to choose. Ethical dilemmas involve the individual struggling with personal decision making, whereas ethical issues are those topics wherein one might have an opinion, but rarely a chance to take a stand that has any impact (unless one happens to be a Supreme Court judge or a legislator or president).

Personal ethical dilemmas occur when the individual is forced to choose between two or more choices of behavior. In order to analyze such dilemmas, one must discover all relevant information. The following analytical steps might be taken in order to clarify the dilemma:

1. First, review all the facts. Make sure that facts are what is known—not future predictions, not suppositions, not probabilities.

2. Identify all the potential values of each party that might be relevant. For instance, in the first dilemma presented at the end of this chapter, values of life, law, family, and self-preservation are at issue.

3. Identify all possible moral issues for each party involved. This is to help us see that sometimes one's own moral or ethical dilemma is caused by the actions of others. For instance, Brenda's predicament in the dilemma at

Literary Perspective

Both boys are crying hard as they are forced toward the scaffold, but since they are obviously just boys I think that they will be all right. They have been trying to smuggle tins of fish and a bottle of vodka into the ghetto, things that now fetch an unbelievable price. Like a charade, the boys are lifted up on stools and their hands are tied behind their backs and nooses are put around their necks. The scene is so ghastly and I hear Jews moaning because they know it will do no good to lift their voices in protest. . . . Then I hear my name being called and it is Kruger who sees me and orders me to come out of the crowd that has gathered. They are only boys I say with my head bowed and he strikes me with a riding crop on the face and I taste blood in my mouth. . . . "You are a member of the Judenrat, a leader of your people," he whispers to me. "Let me see you make the hard decisions, perform the action that wartime requires of all the servants of the Reich. For so long Jews have been parasites and leeches. You perform an act that will help rid the Reich of such vermin. You hang those two pieces of shit, piano player." . . . Then Kruger says to me—and these are the words that change something in me, Jack—he says, "If you do not hang them now, I will hang your pretty Sonia and all your pretty children on these same gallows tomorrow." With these words, I do not hesitate to act for a second. I walk up to those boys and with their father watching me in hatred I kick those stools from under those boys. Kruger holds my neck as I try to turn away. He makes me watch the boys twitch and struggle and die in agony. It takes much longer for the younger boy to die than it does for the older one.

SOURCE: Conroy, Pat. *Beach Music* (New York: Doubleday, 1995): 533–534. Copyright © 1995 by Pat Conroy. Used by permission of Doubleday, a division of Bantam Doubleday Dell Publishing Group, Inc.

the end of this chapter occurs because of the immoral actions of her captors. A police officer's ethical dilemma when faced with the wrongdoing of a fellow officer is a direct result of that other officer making a bad choice. It is helpful to see all the moral issues involved in order to address the central issue.

4. Decide what is the most immediate moral or ethical issue facing the individual. This is always a behavior choice, not an opinion. For example, the moral issue of whether abortion should be legalized is quite different from the moral dilemma of whether I should have an abortion if I find myself pregnant. Obviously, one affects the other, but they are conceptually very distinct.

5. Resolve the ethical or moral dilemma. In order to resolve the dilemma, think of ethical judgments as a pyramid, as indicated in Figure 1–1. The "tip" of the pyramid is the judgment itself. We make ethical judgments all the time. However, we may or may not provide reasons for these judgments. The rationale that supports such judgments makes up the body of the pyramid. If one asked the question "why?" the answer might take the form of "moral rules," which are general rules and standards of behavior. These rules, in turn, are supported by ethical systems, which will be covered in the next chapter. Some rules are inconsistent with some ethical

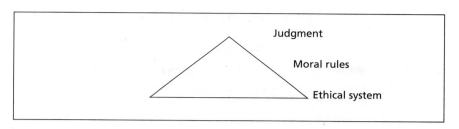

FIGURE 1–1 Ethical Judgments

systems; for instance, "one must always follow the law" may be consistent with ethical formalism and inconsistent with ethics of care.

These concepts will be clearer as we work through a number of ethical systems in the next chapter. Suffice to say for now that ethical judgments always have some rationale behind them. These rationales tend to be consistent with traditional and historical ethical systems. In Chapter 2, we will explore some of these traditional ethical systems.

CONCLUSION

In this chapter, we defined the terms *morals* and *ethics* as both relating to standards of behavior. It was noted that not all behaviors would be subject to ethical judgments—only those that are performed by humans who are acting with free will and affecting others. Professional ethics deals only with those behaviors relevant to one's profession. Our ethical judgments (what we consider right and wrong) are made using rationales derived from historical and traditional ethical systems. These ethical systems will be described in the following chapter.

This chapter closes with some review questions to answer in class or in a journal. Ethical dilemmas are also presented to encourage the reader to practice ethical analysis. Throughout the text, ethical dilemmas will be presented that are relevant to the topics discussed in each chapter.

REVIEW QUESTIONS

1. Why should we study ethics or morals?
2. Define *morals, ethics, values, duties,* and *ethical systems.*
3. What types of behaviors are judged under ethical criteria?
4. Do laws cover all moral rules? If your answer is no, explain why.
5. What are the steps in analyzing an ethical dilemma?

ETHICAL DILEMMAS

Situation 1

Brenda S. was a rich businessman's daughter. She had the best of everything all her life. Her future would have been college, a good marriage to a successful young man, and a life of comparative luxury, except that she was kidnapped by a small band of radical extremists who sought to overthrow the government by terror, intimidation, and robbery. After being raped, beaten, and locked in a small, dark closet for many days, continually taunted and threatened, Brenda was told she must participate with the terrorist gang in a bank robbery; otherwise, she and her family would be killed. During the course of the robbery, Brenda shot a bank guard. Was her action immoral? What if she had killed the guard? What if the terrorists had her mother or father, too, and told her if she didn't cooperate, they would kill her parents immediately? What would you have done in her place?

Situation 2

You are a sales representative for a large auto manufacturer. It seems to be a fairly common practice for the merchandising agents of distributors to receive large sums of money in return for contracts. You have been asked by one such agent for a $10,000 "fee" for a $1 million contract with his company. Would you pay him? Is it ethical, given the fact that everyone else is doing it? What if the contract were essential for the survival of your company (and your job)? What if you were doing business in another country and it was the standard practice to bribe public officials in that country in return for government approval?

Situation 3*

In Europe, a woman is near death from a special kind of cancer. There is one drug that the doctors think might save her. It is a form of radium that a druggist in the same town has recently discovered. The drug is expensive to make, but the druggist is charging ten times what the drug cost him to make. He paid $200 for the radium and is charging $2,000 for a small dose of the drug. The sick woman's husband, Heinz, goes to everyone he knows to borrow the money, but he can get together only about $1,000, which is half of what he needs. Heinz tells the druggist that his wife is dying and asks him to sell the drug cheaper or let him pay later. The druggist says, "No, I discovered the drug and I'm going to make money from it." Heinz is desperate and considers breaking into the man's store to steal the drug for his wife. Should he steal the drug? Why or why not? If Heinz doesn't love his wife, would this make a difference in your answer? Why or why not?

---

*SOURCE: Kohlberg, L. *The Psychology of Moral Development.* (San Francisco: Harper & Row, 1984): 186.

Situation 4

You are taking an essay exam in a college classroom. The test is closed book and closed notes, yet you look up and see that the person sitting next to you has hidden a piece of paper filled with notes under his blue book, which he is using to answer some questions. What would you do? Would your answer change if the test was graded on a curve? What about if the student was a friend? What would you do if the student was flunking the course and was going to lose the scholarship he needed in order to stay in school?

SUGGESTED READINGS

Braswell, M. 1996. "Ethics, Crime and Justice: An Introductory Note to Students." Pp. 3–9 in Braswell, M., McCarthy, B., and McCarthy, B. (eds.), *Justice, Crime and Ethics,* 2d Ed. Cincinnati: Anderson.

Felkenes, G. 1987. "Ethics in the Graduate Criminal Justice Curriculum." *Teaching Philosophy* 10(1): 23–36.

Miller, K., and Radelet, M. 1993. *Executing the Mentally Ill.* Newbury Park, NJ: Sage.

Schmalleger, F., and McKendrick, R. 1991. *Criminal Justice Ethics: An Annotated Bibliography.* Westport, CT: Greenwood.

Souryal, S., and Potts, D. 1993. "What Am I Supposed to Fall Back On? Cultural Literacy in Criminal Justice Ethics." *Journal of Criminal Justice Education* 4, 15–41.

2

✤

Determining Moral Behavior

Chapter Objectives

Become familiar with the major ethical systems
and the criticisms leveled against each.

Understand the controversy between
relativism and absolutism.

Become familiar with how the major ethical
systems have relevance to issues in criminal justice.

Learn how to apply the major
ethical systems to ethical dilemmas.

E ach of us has opinions about social issues such as abortion, adultery, and capital punishment. We also judge the morality of actions—both our own and those of others. We usually do not make decisions about right and wrong haphazardly or arbitrarily. Whether we recognize it or not, we all have moral or ethical systems that help us make decisions regarding specific behaviors. For instance, when someone asks us our views on any of the subjects just mentioned, we respond by judging the action as right or wrong, moral or immoral. Our response is not a factual statement, as it would have been if the person had asked us whether the action were legal or illegal. We may use facts to help us decide issues, and very often discussions get caught up in factual rather than moral questions. For instance, in judging the morality of abortion, a relevant fact is when, on average, a fetus can survive outside the womb. Although this fact is important, it is not the same thing as the concept of life. The fact of viability can be proven, but the concept of life cannot—for what is life? What is death, for that matter—cessation of brain activity? Can someone be dead and then come back to life through medical technology, and, if so, where does that leave traditional definitions of life and death? There is no agreement on when life begins or when it ends, but one's concept of life affects one's moral beliefs about abortion and the use of "life-supporting" technology.

In any discussion, it is important to identify and agree upon facts. Concepts and values may or may not be agreed upon but are also important to identify. For instance, one's values of duty, friendship, and loyalty are usually at the heart of professional ethical dilemmas that involve whistleblowing. These values, as well as honesty and integrity, affect one's moral and ethical decision making. A moral judgment is one that probably was made with the help of basic moral rules that are embedded in ethical systems. This chapter presents descriptions of a number of ethical systems.

ETHICAL SYSTEMS

Our principles of right and wrong form a framework for the way we live our lives. But where do they come from? Before you read on, answer the following question: If you believe it is wrong to steal, why do you believe this to be so? You probably said it is because your parents taught you or because your religion forbids it or maybe because society cannot tolerate people harming one another. Your answer is an indication of your *ethical system*. Ethical systems are the source of moral beliefs. They are the underlying premises from which you make judgments. Typically, they are beyond argument. That is, although ethical decisions may become the basis of debate, the decisions are based on fundamental "truths" or propositions that are taken as a given by the individual employing the ethical system.

C. E. Harris (1986: 33) refers to such ethical systems as "moral theories" or "moral philosophies," and defines them as a systematic ordering of moral principles:

> The order of reasoning from moral judgments, through more general moral principles, and finally to a basic moral principle, gives the outline of any moral theory. A moral theory has three levels: The level that you eventually arrive at when you trace your moral convictions back to your most basic moral principles is the moral standard. The intermediate moral principles are moral rules. The moral statement that begins the discussion is a moral judgment.

To put this discussion into our terms, an ethical system is a *moral theory* or basic set of principles of right and wrong. We don't consciously think of ethical systems, but we use them to make judgments. For instance, we may say that a woman who leaves her children alone to go out drinking has committed an immoral act. That would be the *moral judgment* Harris refers to. Moral rules that underlie this judgment might be "Children should be looked after," "One shouldn't drink to excess," or "Mothers should be good role models for their children." These basic moral rules are derived from an infrastructure of moral principles that is at the heart of all moral decision making. The ethical judgment pyramid provided in Chapter 1 is a visual representation of this discussion (Figure 2–1).

In this chapter we will not discuss all possible ethical systems, nor will we claim that the short descriptions here are enough to give the reader a total picture of each of the systems mentioned. A reader would be well advised to consult texts in philosophy and ethics for more detail. However, we will explore some of the most prevalent views on ethics; specifically, ethical formalism (Kantism) and utilitarianism are presented as the clearest examples of deontological ethics (based on the intent of an action) and teleological ethics (based on the consequences of an action). Religious ethics, natural law, the ethics of virtue, the ethics of care, and egoism are also presented.

All ethical systems generate moral rules; for instance, in the example just given, we might say, "Children should be looked after," because the utility derived from caring for children is a relative good for all of society and

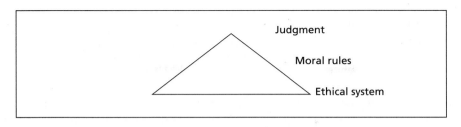

FIGURE 2–1 Ethical Judgments

outweighs the individual utility (or good) that might be derived from the mother's very transitory pleasure. In this case, our ethical system would be utilitarianism. The moral rules of utilitarianism are consistent with the premise that what is good is that which results in the greatest utility for the greatest number.

Ethical systems have been described as having the following characteristics (Baelz, 1977: 19):

1. They are prescriptive; certain behavior is demanded or proscribed. They are not just abstract principles of good and bad, but rather have substantial impact on what we do.

2. They are authoritative; they are not ordinarily subject to debate. Once an ethical framework has been developed, it is usually beyond question.

3. Moral considerations arising from ethical systems are logically impartial or universal. If something is considered wrong it is wrong for everyone. Relativism has no place in an ethical framework.

4. They are not self-serving. They are directed toward others; what is good is good for everyone, not just the individual.

Notice that in the last instance, ethical frameworks are described as "not self-serving." We will discuss one ethical system, egoism, that is indeed self-serving; in fact, it is the very basis of the system that what is good for the individual is good in itself. Although egoism is included in this chapter, it should be noted that it is widely rejected as an ethical system. In fact, some authors prefer to view egoism as the lack of an ethical system and as an example of ethical relativism. However, it should also be noted that "objectivism," a philosophical system exemplified by the writings of Ayn Rand, is a type of egoism that has many adherents. This system is similar to our description of enlightened egoism.

DEONTOLOGICAL AND
TELEOLOGICAL ETHICAL SYSTEMS

A deontological ethical system is one that is concerned solely with the inherent nature of the act being judged. If an act is inherently good, then even if it results in bad consequences, it is still a good act. Teleological systems are interested in the consequences of an act. An act may look "bad," but if it results

Literary Perspective

All I really need to know about how to live and what to do and how to be I learned in kindergarten. Wisdom was not at the top of the graduate-school mountain, but there in the sandpile at Sunday School. These are the things I learned:

Share everything.

Play fair.

Don't hit people.

Put things back where you found them.

Clean up your own mess.

Don't take things that aren't yours.

Say you're sorry when you hurt somebody.

Wash your hands before you eat.

Flush.

Warm cookies and cold milk are good for you.

Live a balanced life—learn some and think some and draw and paint and sing and dance and play and work every day some.

Take a nap every afternoon.

When you go out into the world, watch out for traffic, hold hands, and stick together.

Be aware of wonder. Remember the little seed in the Styrofoam cup: the roots go down and the plant goes up and nobody really knows how or why, but we are all like that.

Goldfish and hamsters and white mice and even the little seed in the Styrofoam cup—they all die. So do we.

And then remember the Dick-and-Jane books and the first word you learned—the biggest word of all—LOOK.

SOURCE: Fulghum, Robert. *All I Really Needed to Know I Learned in Kindergarten* (New York: Villard Books, 1986): 6. Copyright © 1986, 1988 by Robert Fulghum. Reprinted by permission of Villard Books, a division of Random House, Inc.

in good consequences, then it can be defined as good under a teleological system. The clearest examples of these two approaches are ethical formalism and utilitarianism.

Ethical Formalism

Immanuel Kant (1724–1804) believed moral worth comes from doing one's duty (Kant, 1949). Just as there is the law of the family (father's rule), the law of the state and country, and the law of international relations, there is also a universal law of right and wrong. Morality, according to Kant, arises from the fact that humans, as rational beings, impose these laws and strictures of behavior upon themselves. People, as flesh and spirit combined, are in constant dynamic conflict over base desires and morality; only by appealing to higher reason can they do what is right. Kant's *categorical imperative* states that "man must act only according to the maxim whereby one can at the same time will that it should become a universal law." At all times one is obliged to behave in a manner one would hope all people would follow. This is an absolute command. According to Kant, *hypothetical imperatives* are commands that designate certain actions to attain certain ends; an example is "*If* I want to be a success, *then* I must do well in college." A categorical imperative, by contrast, commands action that is necessary without any reference to intended purposes or consequences (Kant, 1949: 76):

> This imperative is categorical. It concerns not the material of the action and its intended result but the form and the principle from which it results. What is essentially good in it consists in the intention, the result being what it may. This imperative may be called the imperative of morality.

In Kant's view, pure reason demands that one must abide by moral dictates—the categorical imperative—to avoid chaos. Moral laws come from within, and their expression places the person in the true order of the universe.

Ethical formalism is a *deontological* approach because the important determinant for judging whether an act is moral is not its consequence but only the motive or intent of the actor. Ethical formalism judges the intent of the actor. According to Kant, the only thing that is intrinsically good is a *good will*. If someone does an action from good will, then even if it results in bad consequences, it can be considered a moral action. On the other hand, if someone performs some activity that looks on the surface to be altruistic but does it with an ulterior motive—for instance, to curry favor or gain benefit—then that act is not moral. For instance, Gold, Brasswell, and McCarthy (1991) offer the example of a motorist stranded by the side of the road; another driver who comes along has a decision to help or pass by. If the decision is made to stop and help, this would seem to be a good act. Not so, according to ethical formalism, unless it is done from a good will. If the helper stops because he or she expects payment, wants a return favor, or for any other reason other than a good will, then the act is only neutral—not moral. Only if the help springs from a good will can we say that it is truly good. A consequentialist would say the act is good because the result is good for all. For an action to be moral, then, the actor must perform it from a good will and the action must not violate the categorical imperative.

A system such as ethical formalism is considered an absolutist system—if something is wrong, it is wrong all the time, such as murder or lying. To assassinate evil tyrants like Hitler or Idi Amin might be considered moral under a teleological system because of the action's consequence of ridding the world of dangerous people. However, in the deontological view, if the act and intent of killing is wrong, it is always wrong; thus, assassination must also be considered immoral in all cases. Even lying is deemed to be immoral in this system, despite some good arguments for the case that, at times, lying might be beneficial. For instance, Kant used an example that if someone asked to be hidden from an attacker in close pursuit and then the attacker asked where the potential victim was hiding, it would be immoral to lie about it. This seems wrong to many and serves to dissuade people from seeing the value of ethical formalism. However, according to Kant, lying or not lying is not the determining factor in that scenario or in any other. An individual cannot control consequences—only actions—therefore, one must act in a moral fashion without regard to potential consequences. In the example, the attacker may not kill

QUERY

- Are there any situations in which lying is acceptable?
- Can you think of any acts that result in bad consequences but should still be considered good acts?
- Do people do things solely for altruistic reasons, or are there always hidden motives and egoistic agendas operating?

the potential victim; the victim may still be able to get away; the attacker may be justified—the point is that no one person can control anything in life, so the only thing that makes sense is to live by the categorical imperative.

Kant also defends his position with semantics—he distinguishes untruths from lies with the explanation that a lie is a lie only when the recipient is led to believe or has a right to believe that he or she is being told the truth. The attacker in the previous scenario or an attacker who has one "by the throat" demanding one's money has no right to expect the truth; thus, it would not be immoral to not tell this person the truth. Only if one led the attacker to believe that one were going to tell the truth and then did not would one violate the categorical imperative. In other words, Kant distinguishes untruths from lies. To not tell the truth when the attacker doesn't deserve the truth is not a lie, but if one intentionally and deliberately sets out to deceive, then that is a lie—even if it is being told to a person who doesn't deserve the truth (Kant, 1981).

The following are some of the principles of Kant's ethical formalism (Bowie, 1985: 157):

1. Act only on that maxim through which you can at the same time will that it should become a universal law. In other words, for any decision of behavior to be made, examine whether that behavior would be acceptable if it were a universal law to be followed by everyone. For instance, a student might decide to cheat on a test; but for this action to be moral, the student would have to agree that everyone should be able to cheat on tests. In the situation involving Heinz and the expensive drug (see Chapter 1, p. 22), for one to approve of Heinz's stealing one would have to agree that it would be morally acceptable for everyone in similar situations to steal.

2. Act in such a way that you always treat humanity, whether in your own person or that of any other, never simply as a means but always at the same time as an end. In other words, one should not use people for one's own purposes. For instance, suicide might be considered immoral if one has the goal of making relatives or other people feel guilty and hurt. This would be contrary to Kant's second principle because the person would be using his or her own body as a means to an end. Another example would be offering a gift to someone in the hope that they will do something in return; this would also be using them as a means for one's own ends. Even otherwise moral actions, such as giving to charity or doing

charitable acts for others, would be considered immoral if done for ulterior motives such as self-aggrandizement.

3. Act as if you were, through your maxims, a lawmaking member of a kingdom of ends. This principle directs that the individual's actions should contribute to and be consistent with universal law. Also, because we freely choose to abide by moral law and these laws are self-imposed rather than imposed from the outside, they are a reflection of the higher nature of humans.

Additional elements of Kant's philosophy include the idea that one must freely perform acts consistent with the categorical imperative in order for those actions to be moral. This relates to our earlier discussion of free will, where we questioned whether unintended action or irrational action can ever be moral. Kant proposed that an action can only be moral when there is free will and intent; otherwise, the action is only neutral. Finally, Kant repudiated the idea that actions are moral because they make people happy or even that a moral life will make the individual happy. Kant believed that although a moral life may make a person happy, that is not a certainty, nor the reason to be moral (Borchert and Stewart, 1986: 212).

This ethical framework is somewhat difficult to understand, but it follows very simply from the beliefs that an individual must follow a self-imposed moral law and that one is capable of using reason to determine right actions since one can evaluate any action using the principles just listed.

Applying Kant's principles, let us see whether ethical formalism can help us solve some ethical dilemmas. We can use the abortion example again. The first principle states that one must act in such a way that the behavior could be universal. If we believe abortion to be morally acceptable, we have to agree to abortion rights as a universal law.

The second principle states that we must not treat others as a means to an end. We might consider that the mother is treating the unborn fetus as a means since the removal of the fetus would result in the end of the inconvenience or problems caused by the pregnancy. On the other hand, most ethical formalists would probably not consider the unborn as persons with inherent rights; thus, we might decide that the mother is being treated as a means to an end if she is denied an abortion since she is treated only as the means for the baby's birth. This interpretation obviously depends on one's definition of life. This illustrates a situation in which facts and concepts are important in deciding moral dilemmas. Most anti-abortionists would argue that the unborn fetus is already a living human deserving of respect. Most pro-choice advocates argue that life begins at some later point than conception, often in the second trimester or the fifth month, or at the point of viability. The Catholic church used to hold the view that human life begins at the moment of "quickening," or when the woman first feels the movement of the fetus in her womb. One's concept of life determines when the fetus is deserving of respect when applying the second principle, which is important to the resolution of the dilemma.

The third principle might be interpreted to mean that all of our behavior must be autonomous and freely chosen to be judged as moral or immoral. We would have to make a decision freely in order for it to be moral. If a person was frightened into having a baby or pressured into aborting it, neither of these actions would be judged in moral terms.

Turning to the situation of Heinz, the third dilemma in Chapter 1, the categorical imperative would probably judge stealing the drug to be immoral. We would be unlikely to accept a universal law allowing theft of things we can't afford. Furthermore, remember that Kant was not concerned with the consequences of the action; therefore, the drug's use in keeping Heinz's wife alive is irrelevant in deciding the morality of the theft. According to ethical formalism, it is pure luck that she is sick in the first place, and stealing the drug will not ensure her survival since she may be hit by a bus the day after she takes the drug, or the drug may not work, or Heinz may get killed stealing the drug. One cannot justify an otherwise immoral act because of the good consequence that may result.

Criticism is directed at the Kantian view that morality is limited to duty. One might argue that duty is the baseline of morality, not the highest aspiration of it. One could also argue that this system does not help us resolve issues of conflicting duties. For instance, Heinz has a duty to his wife as well as the duty to obey the law. A police officer has a duty to enforce the law but also a duty to respect his father; therefore, in the dilemma involving the police officer who stops his father for DWI, how should those conflicting duties be resolved?

Another problem with the Kantian view is the priority of motive and intent over result. It may be seriously questioned whether the intention to do good, regardless of result or perhaps with negative result, is always moral. Many would argue that the consequences of an action and the actual result must be evaluated to determine morality (Maestri, 1982: 910). In the most difficult ethical dilemmas, ethical formalism often requires a harsh application of law and little emphasis on individual need, mercy, or caring.

Other writers present variations of deontological ethics that do not depend so heavily on Kant (Braswell, McCarthy, and McCarthy, 1996). The core elements of any deontological ethical system are the importance placed on intention and basing morality on a predetermined set of principles rather than looking to the consequences of the act to determine goodness.

Utilitarianism

Utilitarianism is a teleological ethical system: what is good is determined by the consequences of the action. Jeremy Bentham (1748–1832), one proponent of utilitarianism, believed that the primary determinant of the morality of an action is whether the action contributes to the good of the majority. According to Bentham, human nature seeks to maximize pleasure and avoid pain, and a moral system must be consistent with this natural fact.

The "utilitarian doctrine asserts that we should always act so as to produce the greatest possible ratio of good to evil for everyone concerned" (Barry, 1985: 65). That is, if you can show that an action significantly contributes to the general good, then it is good. In situations where one must decide between a good for an individual and a good for society, then society should prevail, despite the wrong being done to an individual. This is because generally the utility or good derived from that action outweighs the small amount of harm done (because the harm is done only to one whereas the good is multiplied by the many who benefit). For instance, if it could be shown that using someone as an example would be an effective deterrent to crime, whether or not the person was actually guilty, then the wrong done to that person by this unjust punishment might be outweighed by the good resulting for society. This assumes that citizens would not find out about the injustice and lose respect for the authority of the legal system, which would be a negative effect for all concerned.

Bentham did not judge the content of utility. He considered pleasure a good whether it derived from vice, such as avarice or greed, or from virtue, such as charity and kindness. Later utilitarians, primarily John Stuart Mill (1806–1873), recognized and placed a value on the type of pleasure and utility. Some kinds of utility are judged better than others. For instance, art offers a different utility for society than alcohol. On the other hand, who is to determine what utility is to be ascribed to these pleasures? A value judgment is certainly being made, but the question is whose criteria should be used (Borchert and Stewart, 1986: 190).

In one widely used hypothetical moral dilemma, a woman and her children are hiding in a cabin that is being attacked by Indians. If one of the babies starts crying, should the woman suffocate the baby to save the rest of the children and herself? Ethical formalism would condemn the action because the baby's death would be a means to an end (survival) and the universal law (that everyone should act in the same way under similar circumstances) could not be applied since it is unlikely anyone would agree that babies should always be sacrificed to save others. Remember, if Kant were forced to defend the view that the woman should risk the lives of the other children, he would say that she doesn't know for sure that they will be killed if she does not suffocate the baby and she doesn't know whether they may be killed even if she does suffocate the baby—maybe the cabin will be burned down and they will all perish.

QUOTATION

Nature has placed mankind under the governance of two sovereign masters, pain and pleasure. It is for them alone to point out what we ought to do, as well to determine what we shall do. On the one hand, the standard of right and wrong, on the other the chain of causes and effects, are fastened to their throne. They govern us in all we do, in all we say, in all we think; every effort we can make to throw off our subjection, will serve but to demonstrate and confirm it. In words, a man may pretend to abjure their empire: but in reality he will remain subject to it all the while. The principle of utility recognizes the subjection, and assumes it for the foundation of that system.

SOURCE: Bentham, quoted in Borchert and Stewart, 1986: 183.

Religious ethics would also probably not support such an action; God's will may be hard to understand in this scenario, as in many others when individuals are faced with severe hardships. Arguably, no Christian religious ethical system would support the sacrifice of an innocent baby; however, religious ethics might also support forgiveness or redemption for the mother.

Utilitarianism, on the other hand, may very well provide the basis for defining that action as moral since the good derived from the baby's death would be the survival of the rest of the children. Of course, some might interpret the situation differently. For instance, the baby's death might result in a callousness toward human life among those involved and thus in the long term result in more negative results than positive utility.

Act Versus Rule Utilitarianism Utilitarianism has two forms: act utilitarianism and rule utilitarianism. The basic difference between the two can be summarized as follows: in *act utilitarianism,* the basic utility derived from an action is alone examined. We look at the consequences of any action for all involved and weigh the units of utility accordingly. In *rule utilitarianism,* one judges that action in reference to the precedent it sets and the long-term utility of the rule set by that action. We might use the example of Heinz again to illustrate this point. Act utilitarianism would probably support stealing the drug because the utility of his wife's survival would outweigh the loss to the druggist, who could always make up more of the drug. Therefore, the greater utility of the theft would lead to a judgment that the theft was moral. On the other hand, rule utilitarianism would be concerned with the effect that the action would have if made into a rule for behavior. The rule that anytime an individual could not afford a drug he or she could steal it would result in a state of lawlessness and a general disrespect for the law. Such a rule would not result in the greatest utility for the greatest number. With rule utilitarianism, then, we are not only concerned with the immediate utility of the action but also with the long-term utility or harm if the action were to be a rule for all similar circumstances. If we reject Heinz's proposal to steal the drug, it may result in his wife's death, but in the long term, laws against theft, which provide general good for all, will be protected.

These differences are also apparent in a utilitarian argument about the morality of abortion. Act utilitarianism might evaluate the obvious harm to the fetus against the positive utility to the mother. The long-term harm to the fetus if it were born into a hostile and poverty-stricken family would also need to be considered. In act utilitarianism, then, we would be concerned with the total utility to the fetus, to the mother, and to society compared with the disutility to all. It may very well be the case that abortion is judged moral for one woman and immoral for another, because of different situational elements and consequences. Rule utilitarianism would evaluate the long-term utility derived if we were to translate the action into a general rule. Would a situation in which all women could obtain abortions on demand result in a net gain of happiness and utility for society or a net loss? However one answers that question, it is clear that this is a different decision-making process than that described for act utilitarianism.

Criticism of the utilitarian framework centers on the difficulty of measurement and implementation. How does one measure the pleasure derived from an action? No measuring device exists to help us; therefore, the equation determining what is good is hypothetical at best. Further, as discussed earlier, pleasure is not defined, and it is unclear whether pleasure must be the same for all people or can be individually defined. Another argument against utilitarianism focuses on the assumption that happiness is derived from pleasure. As other systems indicate, it may be that happiness derives from something else, such as doing one's duty, altruistic sacrifice, or productive achievement (Maestri, 1982: 6).

Another problem with the implementation of utilitarianism is the difficulty of predicting the consequences of any action. In the Heinz dilemma, only by artificially providing the consequences (the drug will save her) does the hypothetical create the persuasive balance of utility. In actuality, there are no certainties—the drug might save her, or Heinz might get shot as an intruder. In any dilemma, the individual can only guess what the consequences of any action might be. In the opening police officer dilemma, the individual may decide that the greatest good for all concerned would be to drive his father home rather than give him a ticket; then, the very next night, the father kills himself or someone else. We simply cannot determine what consequences might result from any action we take, thus undermining the whole basis of the utilitarian framework.

Also, and importantly, there is little concern for individual rights in utilitarianism. Note this is extremely inconsistent with natural law and ethical formalism. In both natural law and ethical formalism, it is presumed that each individual has inherent rights and must be treated with respect and not be used as a means to an end. However, under utilitarianism, the rights of one individual may be sacrificed for the good of many. For instance, Churchill allowed Coventry to be bombed in World War II so the Germans would not know the Allies had cracked the Germans' secret military radio code. Several hundred English people were killed in the bombing raid. It was a calculated risk for greater long-term gains: bringing the war to an end sooner. This could be justified under utilitarianism but not under ethical formalism.

In the well-known "lifeboat" dilemma, five people are in a lifeboat with enough food and water only for four. It is certain that they will survive if there are only four; it is also certain that they will all perish if one does not go overboard. What should be done? Under Kantian ethics, it would be unthinkable to sacrifice an innocent even if it means that four others may live. Under utilitarian ethics, it is conceivable that the murder might be justified. Again, however, this hypothetical points out the fallacy of the utilitarian argument. In reality, it is not known whether any will survive. The fifth may go overboard just before a rescue ship appears on the horizon. The fifth may go overboard, but then the remaining four are still eaten by sharks. Only in artificial hypotheticals is it ever clear what the outcome of decisions will be.

In summary, utilitarianism holds that morality must be determined by the consequences of an action. Society and the survival and benefit of all are more important than any individual. This is a functional theory of right and

Cesare Beccaria: Utilitarian or Retributivist?

In two articles arguing that Beccaria has been widely misunderstood, David Young presents the contradictions in Beccaria's work and the historical evidence that his retributivist (deontological) views were misinterpreted, mistranslated, suppressed, or deemphasized in favor of his utilitarian principles.

On Crimes and Punishments does contain a strong dose of utilitarianism. Its author's propensity for calculating pleasure and pain in mathematical terms, for instance, probably endeared him to Bentham. But side-by-side with this emphasis on utility are other emphases of a retributivist nature. Like Kant, Beccaria stressed the human rights of offenders, rights which no consideration of utility could override. His attacks on judicial torture and on the death penalty are replete with such arguments. (1984: 156)

Individuals, argued Beccaria, give up only the "least possible portion" of their liberty in order to enjoy the remainder more securely. In Beccaria's eyes, laws ought to be regarded as the terms of the social contract, the conditions on which people unite. Further, they should be seen as having been willed by all members of a community. Coercion is justifiable only against someone who violates these conditions from which everyone benefits. (1983: 319)

Beccaria had indeed employed utilitarian arguments against the death penalty, holding that it is not an effective deterrent, among other things. However, he had in fact asserted that the state does not have the right to kill a citizen, except perhaps in cases of open rebellion or treason. The right to inflict capital punishment, said Beccaria, could not possibly arise from the social contract. For Beccaria, the question of the death penalty was a matter of justice at least as much as it was a matter of utility. (1984: 163–164)

On several occasions, Beccaria addressed himself to the question of natural (or human) rights, notably the right of self-defense. His case against judicial torture and against compelling prisoners to testify against themselves was largely based on the contention that such proceedings violate the natural right of every person to preserve his own being. Likewise, his most compelling argument against the death penalty rested on grounds of right, not utility. The state's right to punish, he maintained, is based upon the surrender of liberty made in the original social contract, and any punishment which exceeds this is a violation of the rights of the criminal. (1983: 321–322)

Proponents of a deterrence model of criminal justice can find much to admire in On Crimes and Punishments. Bentham's praise and Kant's criticisms, however, should not blind the modern reader to the deep, underlying foundation of retributivism on which Beccaria's work rests. (1983: 324)

SOURCE: Young, David, "Cesare Beccaria: Utilitarian or Retributivist?" *Journal of Criminal Justice* 11 (1983): 317–326. "Let Us Content Ourselves with Praising the Work While Drawing a Veil Over Its Principles: Eighteenth-Century Reactions to Beccaria's *On Crimes and Punishments*." *Justice Quarterly* 1, 2 (1984): 155–171. All notes omitted.

wrong—something is right when it benefits the continuance and good health of society. Rule utilitarianism may be closer to the principles of Kantism, since it looks at general universal laws; the difference between the two is that the laws themselves are judged right or wrong depending on the motives behind them under ethical formalism, whereas utilitarianism looks to the long-term consequences of the behavior prescribed by the rules to determine their morality.

OTHER ETHICAL SYSTEMS

Some of the ethical systems discussed below can be described as teleological. For instance, egoism is definitely teleological because it is concerned solely with the "good consequences" of any action for the individual. The ethics of virtue has also been described as teleological. However, since utilitarianism and ethical formalism are arguably the two best representatives of the contrast, they have been discussed separately above.

Religion

Probably the most frequent source of individual ethics is religion. Religion might be defined as a body of beliefs that addresses fundamental issues such as "What is life?" and "What is good and evil?" A religion also provides moral guidelines and directions on how to live one's life. For instance, Christians are taught the Ten Commandments, which prohibit certain behaviors defined as wrong. The authority of *religious ethics,* in particular Christian ethics, stems from a willful and rational god. For believers, the authority of God's will is beyond question and there is no need for further examination because of this perfection. If God's character is perfection, or perfect good, what is said to be right or good cannot be questioned as long as it comes from the authority of God. The only possible controversy comes from human interpretation of God's commands. Indeed, these differences in interpretation are the source of most religious strife.

However, the other major element of religious ethics is love, which encompasses believers and nonbelievers, saints and sinners alike. Forgiveness, mercy, and charity, as opposed to harsh condemnation, can be found in many interpretations of Christianity.

Religious ethics is, of course, much broader than simply Christian ethics. Religions such as Buddhism, Confucianism, Judaism, and Islam also provide a basis for ethics, since they provide explanations of how to live the "good life" and also address other philosophical issues, such as "What is reality?" Pantheistic religions, those of primitive hunter–gatherer societies, promote the belief that there is a living spirit in all things. A basic principle follows from this belief that life is important and one must have respect for all things, including trees, rivers, and animals. However, there must be a willful and rational god or god figure before there can be a judgment of right and wrong, and thus before a religion can serve as the basis for an ethical system. Those religions that do have a god figure consider that figure to be the source of principles of ethics and morality.

> **QUOTATION**
>
> *I have set an example, that you should do as I have done to you. . . .*
>
> *I give you a new commandment: love one another.*
>
> *As I have loved you, you are to love one another.*
>
> ─────────
>
> SOURCE: John 13:15.

It is also true that of the religions we might discuss, many have very similar basic moral principles. Many religions have their own version of the Ten Commandments; in this regard, Islam is not too different from Judaism, which is not too different from Christianity. The Golden Rule of "Do unto others as you would have them do unto you" is echoed in Hinduism ("Do naught to others which, if done to thee, would cause thee pain: this is the sum of duty"), in Buddhism ("In five ways should a clansman minister to his friends and familiars . . . by treating them as he treats himself"), in Confucianism ("What you do not want done to yourself, do not do unto others"), and in Judaism ("Whatsoever thou wouldest that men should not do unto thee, do not do that to them") (Reiman, 1990: 147). However, while what is right and wrong stems always from the authority of God and the basic rights and wrongs are not too different, particular tenets of behavior may vary from religion to religion because of different interpretations of God's will. Dancing may be immoral to some; drinking, working on Sunday (or Saturday), abortion, and so on are all viewed differently by various religions.

One issue in Western religious ethics is how to determine God's will. Some believe that God is inviolable and that positions on moral questions are unchanging. This is a legalist position. Others feel that God's will varies according to time and place—the situationalist position. According to this position, situational factors are important in determining the rightness of a particular action. Different decisions may be made about behavior as a result of the situation surrounding it (Borchert and Stewart, 1986: 157).

According to Barry (1985), human beings can "know" God's will in three ways. The first is through individual conscience. That is, an individual's conscience is the best source for discovering what God wants one to do. If one feels uncomfortable about a certain action, it is probably wrong. The second way we might discover God's will is by referring to religious authorities. They can interpret right and wrong for us and are our best source if we are confused about certain actions. The third way is to go directly to the Bible, Koran, or Torah as the source of God's law. Some believe that the written word of God holds the answers to all moral dilemmas (Barry, 1985: 51–54).

Strong doubts exist as to whether any of these methods are true indicators of divine command. Our consciences may be no more than the products of our psychological development, influenced by our environment. Religious authorities are, after all, only human, with human failings. Even the Bible, as we know, seems to be used by various groups, all of whom disagree yet can find support within its pages. For instance, some may conclude that capital punishment is prohibited by religious ethics ("Vengeance is mine saith the Lord"); however, others might use other references from the Bible to support capital punishment ("an eye for an eye").

The question of whether people can ever know God's will has been explored through the ages. Thomas Aquinas (1225–1274) believed that human reason was sufficient not only to prove the existence of God but also to discover God's divine commands (Borchert and Stewart, 1986: 159). Others feel that reason is not sufficient to know God and that it comes down to unquestioning belief, so reason and knowledge must always be separate from faith. These people believe that one can know whether an action is consistent with God's will only if it contributes to general happiness, because God intends for us to be happy, or when the action is done through the "holy spirit"—that is, when someone performs the action under the influence of true faith (Borchert and Stewart, 1986: 164–171).

These two positions—that one can use reason to understand God and that one must rely on faith—do not help us much when we have a sincere confusion over what to do or what is right. Some who argue on the basis of religious ethics do so from a legalist view: what is considered wrong is always wrong. An example is the Catholics' absolute condemnation of suicide. Others may argue from a situationalist perspective: God's will may depend on situational circumstances. For instance, lying may be wrong unless it is to protect an innocent, or stealing may be wrong unless it is to protest injustice and to help unfortunates. In fact, some would say it is impossible to have an *a priori* knowledge of God's will because that would put us above God's law since we ourselves would be "all-knowing"; rather, for any situation, if we are prepared to receive them, we can know God's divine commands through faith and conscience.

The example of abortion illustrates how an ethical system based on religion might resolve a moral dilemma. The Catholic church has stated unequivocally that abortion is wrong. This judgment, based on the interpretation of God's will, condemns those who usurp God's power over life and death. If one accepts the Pope as the true and only representative of God on earth, there is no choice to be made regarding abortion. This is a legalist view based on religious authority. Other religions and disaffected Catholics base their arguments on God's will also; the difference is in interpretation. If one uses evidence from the Bible to support a pro-choice stand, the basis of the belief is still a religious ethical system. There are others who do not deny that religious doctrine forbids abortion yet support it anyway based on other ethical systems, such as the ethics of care, utilitarianism, or egoism, with the accompanying belief that God is merciful and would forgive the abortion. Obviously, this stand is still influenced by a religious ethical system because of the belief that God would condemn the action while also forgiving it.

Very often, issues are not as clear-cut as the abortion question seems to be. For instance, given the moral dilemma of Heinz in Chapter 1, could one make a choice using religious ethics? You will recall that Heinz had to make a moral

Other Major World Religions

Islam

One of the newest yet largest religions is Islam. Like Christianity, this religion recognizes one god, Allah. Jesus and other religious figures are recognized as prophets, as is Muhammed, who is considered the last and greatest prophet. Islam has the Koran, which is taken much more literally as the word of Allah than the Bible is taken by most Christians. There is a great deal of fatalism in Islam: *Im Shallah,* meaning "If God wills it," is a prevalent theme in Moslem societies. On the other hand, there is recognition that if people choose evil, they do so freely. The five pillars of Islam are (1) repetition of the creed *(Shahada),* (2) daily prayer *(Salah),* (3) almsgiving *(Zakah),* (4) fasting *(Sawm),* and (5) pilgrimage *(Has).* One of the other features of Islam is the idea of the holy war. In this concept, the faithful who die defending Islam against infidels will be rewarded in the afterlife (Hopfe, 1983).

Buddhism

Siddhartha Gautama (Buddha) attained enlightenment and preached to others how to do the same and achieve the release from suffering. He taught that good behavior is that which follows the "middle path" between hedonistic pursuit of sensual pleasure and asceticism. Essentials of Buddhist teachings are ethical conduct, mental discipline, and wisdom. Ethical conduct is based on universal love and compassion for all living beings. Compassion and wisdom are needed in equal measures. Ethical conduct can be broken into right speech (refraining from lies, slander, enmity, and rude speech); right action (abstaining from destroying life, stealing, and dishonest dealings, and helping others lead peaceful and honorable lives); and right livelihood (abstaining from occupations that bring harm to others, such as arms dealing and killing animals). To follow the "middle path," one must abide by these guidelines (Kessler, 1992).

Confucianism

Confucius taught a humanistic social philosophy that included central concepts such as *Ren,* which is human virtue and humanity at its best as well as the source of moral principles; *Li,* which is traditional order, ritual, or custom; *Xiao,* which is familial love; and *Yi,* which is rightness, both a virtue and a principle of behavior—that is, one should do what is right because it is right. The doctrine of the mean exemplifies one aspect of Confucianism that emphasizes a cosmic or natural order. Humans are a part of nature and are included in the scheme of life. Practicing moderation in one's life is part of this natural order and reflects a "way to Heaven" (Kessler, 1992).

Hinduism

In Hinduism, the central concept of *Karma* can be understood as consequence. Specifically, what one does in one's present life will determine what happens in a future life. The goal is to escape the eternal birth–rebirth cycle by living one's life in a moral manner so that no bad Karma will occur (Kessler, 1992). People start out life in the lowest caste, but if they live a good life, they will be reborn as members of a higher caste, until they reach the highest Brahman caste, and at that point the cycle can end. An early source for Hinduism was the Code of Manu. In this code are found the ethical ideals of Hinduism, which include pleasantness, patience, control of mind, nonstealing, purity, control of the senses, intelligence, knowledge, truthfulness, and nonirritability (Hopfe, 1983).

choice between his wife's life and breaking the law. If one decides that Heinz should steal the drug, can this answer be supported by religious ethics? For instance, some religions hold that cure is in the hands of God and that humans should not interfere. If one was raised with this religious belief, it would be simple to decide that it was God's will whether Heinz's wife should live or die and that therefore it would be wrong for him to steal. Other religions might hold that life is more important than law or that a person is God's instrument and that God shows intent by a sign. In this case Heinz might decide that God intended for him to get the drug—otherwise, the druggist would not have been able to invent it—therefore, he must act out God's will by stealing it.

Many ethical issues are not as difficult. Stealing from your place of employment is obviously wrong; one need look no further than the Ten Commandments to determine that issue. Putting in a day's honest work for a day's pay is also dictated by religious ethics because to do otherwise would be a type of stealing. Basic values of charity and humility are also prescribed by religious ethics.

Religion, even while serving as a guide for good behavior, has also been the cause of much human suffering throughout history. From the systematic destruction of all early nativistic religions, to the Crusades, to the more recent religious wars and practices that condemn and destroy other cultures, including their particular belief systems, religion has been used as the rationale for destruction.

Thus far, we have concentrated mostly on Christianity, although we mentioned that other religions can also serve as the basis of a religious ethical system. In fact, Christianity is not the most prevalent religion in the world, nor is it the oldest. Islam, Buddhism, Confucianism, and Hinduism each present fundamental truths about what is good and the nature of morality.

To summarize, the religious ethics system is widely used and accepted. The authority of the god figure is the root of all morality; basic conceptions of good, evil, right, and wrong come from interpretations of the god figure's will. Many people throughout history have wrestled with the problem of determining what is right according to God, and current controversies within and between religious groups illustrate the unresolved difficulties that continue to exist.

Natural Law

In the *natural law* ethical system, there is a universal set of rights and wrongs that is similar to many religious beliefs, but there is no reference to a specific supernatural figure. Originating with the Stoics, natural law is an ethical system wherein no difference is recognized between physical laws—such as the law of gravity—and moral laws. Morality is part of the natural order of the universe. Further, this morality is the same across cultures and times. In this view, Christians simply added God as a source of law (as other religions added their own prophets and gods), but there is no intrinsic need to resort to a supernatural figure since these universal laws exist quite apart from any religion (Maestri, 1982).

The natural law ethical system presupposes that what is good is what is natural and what is natural is what is good. The essence of morality is what conforms to the natural world; thus, there are basic inclinations that form the core of moral principles. For instance, the preservation of one's own being is a basic, natural inclination, and thus is a basic principle of morality. Actions consistent with this natural inclination would be those that preserve one's own life, such as in self-defense, but also those that preserve or maintain the species, such as a prohibition against murder. Other inclinations are peculiar to one's species—for instance, humans are social animals; thus, sociability is a natural inclination that leads to altruism and generosity. These are natural and thus moral. The pursuit of knowledge or understanding of the universe might also be recognized as a natural inclination of humans; thus, actions that conform to this natural inclination are moral.

Another thread of this ethical system is that all of us have inherent rights by virtue of our mere existence. Souryal (1992) describes natural law as the "steward" of natural rights. This country's founders might be described as natural law theorists. In the Constitution, "natural rights" endowed by the creator are recognized. Natural law theory is either extremely pessimistic about the nature of humankind or optimistic. A pessimistic version of natural humanity is Hobbes's "war of all against all," and "the law of the jungle" is used to describe a natural state where the strong prey upon the weak. On the other hand, there is also the belief that humans are naturally more inclined toward altruism and sociability than aggression. In this view, the natural state of humankind is one of peaceful coexistence, and it is only when civilization thwarts natural impulses that we see negative and immoral behaviors emerge.

Natural law can be applied to the ethical dilemmas we have discussed thus far. In the example of abortion, natural law ethics would probably condemn the decision to abort unless it was to save the life of the mother, since it runs counter to a natural inclination to preserve life. In the Heinz example, one can see that it would be a natural response to help a loved one, consistent with the natural sociability characteristic. Natural law ethics would support stealing the drug.

Natural law theory defines good as that which is natural. The difficulty of this system is identifying what is consistent and congruent with the natural inclinations of humankind. How do we know which acts are in accordance with the natural order of things? What are the natural laws? These are the fundamental problems with this ethical system.

QUERY

- What are "natural rights"—rights that everyone has purely by virtue of being alive?
- What are the "natural" inclinations of human beings?

The Ethics of Virtue

Each of the foregoing ethical systems seeks to define "What is good action?" The *ethics of virtue* instead asks the question "What is a good person?" This ethical system rejects the approach that one might use reason to discover what is good. Instead, the principle that to be good, one must do good applies. Virtues that a good person possesses include thriftiness, temperance, humility, industriousness, and honesty. It is a teleological system because it is concerned with acting in such a way as to achieve a good end (Prior, 1991). The specific "end" is happiness, or *eudaimonia*. However, the meaning of this word is not the same as Bentham's. This translation of happiness did not mean simply having pleasure, but also meant living a good life, achievement, and moral excellence:

> As far as its name is concerned, most people would probably agree: for both the common run of people and cultivated men call it happiness, and understand by "being happy" the same as "living well" and "doing well." (Aristotle, quoted in Prior, 1991: 149)

The roots of this system are in the work of Aristotle, who defined virtues as "excellences." These qualities are what enable an individual to move toward the achievement of what it takes to be human. Aristotle distinguished intellectual virtues (wisdom, understanding) from moral virtues (generosity, self-control). The moral virtues are not sufficient for "the good life"; one must also have the intellectual virtues, primarily "practical reason."

Aristotle evidently was a learning theorist—he believed that we are, by nature, neither good nor evil but become so through training and the acquisition of habits:

> . . . the virtues are implanted in us neither by nature nor contrary to nature: we are by nature equipped with the ability to receive them and habit brings this ability to completion and fulfillment. (Aristotle, quoted in Prior, 1991: 156–157)

Habits of moral virtue are obtained through following the example of a moral "exemplar." They are also more easily instilled when "right" or just laws also exist. Moral virtue is a state of character in which choices are consistent with the *principle of the golden mean*. This principle states that virtue is always the median between two extremes of character. For instance, liberality is the mean between prodigality and meanness, proper pride is the mean between empty vanity and undue humility, and so on (Albert, Denise, and Peterfreund, 1984).

David Hume might also be considered as endorsing the ethics of virtue, since he believed that morality is a matter of cultivating character traits that give a person peace of mind and consciousness of integrity and that make a person good company to others (Baier, 1987). A current philosopher defines virtues as those dispositions that will sustain us in the relevant "quest for the good, by enabling us to overcome the harms, dangers, temptations and distractions which we encounter, and which will furnish us with increasing self-knowledge and increasing knowledge of the good" (MacIntyre, 1991: 204).

Catalog of Virtues

AREA	DEFECT	MEAN	EXCESS
fear	cowardice	courage	recklessness
pleasure	insensitivity	self-control	self-indulgence
money	stinginess	generosity	extravagance
honor	small-minded	high-minded	vain
anger	apathy	gentleness	short temper
truth	self-depreciation	truthfulness	boastfulness
shame	shamelessness	modesty	terror-stricken

SOURCE: Prior, 1991: 165.

Moral virtue comes from habit, which is why this system emphasizes character. The idea here is that one does not do good because one reasons out that the good action is using utilitarianism or ethical formalism; rather, one does good because of the patterns of a lifetime. If one has a good character, she or he will do the right thing; but if one has a bad character, she or he will usually choose the immoral path. In *Character and Cops: Ethics in Policing,* Edwin Delattre uses an excerpt from a police chief's biography to illustrate an individual who represents the ethics of virtue:

> One Friday, just before Christmas in 1947, Seedman helped lug into the Safe and Loft office dozens of cartons of toys that had been recovered from a hijacking case. There were dolls, teddy bears, stuffed animals of all kinds.
>
> Ray McGuire, busy overseeing the operation, suddenly looked up and saw that it was close to three o'clock. "I'm never going to get to lunch," he said. "I was going to stop at Macy's to pick up some toys for my girls." One of the detectives mentioned he had to do the same at Macy's. McGuire handed him a twenty-dollar bill. "Pick up a pair of dolls for me, will ya?" (Seedman and Hellman, 1974, cited in Delattre, 1989: 41)

It never even occurred to McGuire to take any of the dolls and toys surrounding him, because that would be stealing. As Delattre writes, "The habit of not even considering greedy behavior, of not speculating about ways to profit from vice, prevents such conduct from ever occurring to us" (1989: 41).

A Kantian ethicist might say that McGuire applied the categorical imperative to the situation and concluded that the action of taking a doll could not be translated into a universal law. A utilitarian formulation would have McGuire weigh the relative utilities of taking the doll or not. However, in the ethics of virtue, as Delattre indicates, if one has developed a habit of integrity, it may be that taking advantage of the situation never even occurs to that person. Under this moral system, those individuals who possess the necessary virtue will act morally and those who don't will act immorally. Unfortunately, not all police can be considered a "moral exemplar" as was the captain described by Delattre:

> A truck soon arrived and the [stolen television] sets were unloaded. Suddenly a plainclothes policeman—unrelated to the narcotics investigation—wandered into the store. He saw what was happening and he immediately called in a report to the local police headquarters. Within ten minutes there were fifty cops in the store arresting the owner and the hijackers. Then, within minutes, a fleet of private cars—Volkswagens, station wagons—arrived. Virtually all the policemen in the local precinct came in private cars and started loading TVs into their trunks and onto the roofs. The police were waiting in line to steal the hijacked TV sets. But there were more TVs than the local police could carry; so several began calling their friends at other precincts to tell them the good news.
>
> Unfortunately for the cops most of the calls were made from the telephone in the store—the phone was tapped. Each of these felonious calls was being recorded by Leuci's tape. [Leuci was Robert Leuci—"The Prince of the City"—who testified against fellow officers in corruption prosecutions.]
>
> SOURCE: Dershowitz, Alan. *The Best Defense.* (New York: Vintage Books, 1983): 338–339.

It should also be noted that some of us have some virtues and not others. There are many other virtues besides those already mentioned, including compassion, courage, conscientiousness, and devotion. Some of us may be completely honest in all of our dealings but not generous. Some may be courageous but not compassionate. Therefore, we all are moral to the extent that we possess moral virtues, but some of us are more moral than others. One difficulty is in judging the primacy of moral virtues. For instance, in professional ethics there are often conflicts that involve honesty and loyalty. If both are virtues, how does one resolve a dilemma in which one virtue must be sacrificed?

Let us see how this ethical system can be applied to the examples we have used thus far. One can see that it is more difficult to do so because this system is not a reasoning or formulistic approach. In the abortion dilemma, the ethics of virtue would not help us decide whether that act is moral or not. If a woman holds all moral virtues (or at least relevant moral virtues), then one must conclude that she will do what is right. In Heinz's dilemma, his action will depend on his choice between the virtue of honesty and the virtues of compassion or loyalty to his wife. Which virtue is more important?

Even with this difficulty, the ethics of virtue probably explains more of individual behavior than other ethical systems since most of the time, if we have developed habits of virtue, we do not even think about the possible "bad" acts we might do. For instance, most of us do not have to analyze the "rightness" or "wrongness" of stealing every time we go into a store. We do not automatically consider lying every time a circumstance arises. Most of the time, we do the right thing without thinking about it a great deal. However, when faced with a true dilemma—i.e., a choice where the "right" decision is unclear—the ethics of virtue may be less helpful as an ethical system.

The Ethics of Care

The *ethics of care* is another ethical system that does not depend on universal rules or formulas to determine morality. The emphasis is on human relationships and needs. The ethics of care has been described as a feminine morality since women in all societies are the childbearers and consequently seem to have a greater sensitivity to issues of care. Noddings (1986: 1) points out that the "mother's voice" has been silent in Western, masculine analysis: "One is tempted to say that ethics has so far been guided by Logos, the masculine spirit, whereas the more natural and perhaps stronger approach would be through Eros, the feminine spirit."

The ethics of care is founded in the natural human response to care for a newborn child, the ill, and the hurt. Carol Gilligan's work on moral development in psychology, discussed in more detail in Chapter 3, identified a feminine approach to ethical dilemmas that focuses on relationships and needs instead of rights and universal laws. She found that in their responses to ethical dilemmas, some women were resistant to solving the dilemmas given the restraints of the exercise. They wanted to know what would happen after the fact, they wanted to know what the person felt, and they wanted to know other elements that were deemed not relevant if one was applying ethical principles as predetermined by Kohlberg's moral development scale (also discussed in the next chapter). These women were ranked fairly low on the moral development scale, yet Gilligan proposed that theirs is not a less developed morality but rather a different morality. The most interesting feature of this approach is that while a relatively small number of women actually voiced these principles, no men did. She attributed this to the fact that in Western society, both men and women are socialized to Western ethics, which are primarily concerned with issues of rights, laws, and universalism (Gilligan, 1982).

Applying the ethics of care to the examples we've been using leads not to different solutions necessarily, but perhaps different questions. In the abortion example, the discussion has largely been phrased in terms of the rights of the mother versus the rights of the child. In an ethical system based on care, we would be concerned with issues of needs and care. What would happen to the mother if she chose the abortion, and what would happen if she did not? Would the child receive the care needed if born? Would it meet the needs of the mother to give birth and then put her child up for adoption? How could her needs be met? In Heinz's dilemma, the solution would probably be to steal the drug since the relationship with his wife is more primary than the relationship with the druggist, but the ethics of care would be concerned with how Heinz and the druggist might come to some understanding about payment, or some other means for both to get their needs met.

Other writers point to some eastern religions, such as Taoism, as illustrations of the ethics of care (Gold et al., 1991). In these religions, a rigid, formal, rule-based ethics is rejected in favor of gently leading the individual to follow a path of caring for others. In criminal justice the ethics of care is represented to some extent by the rehabilitative ethic rather than the just-deserts model. The interest in the motives and needs of all concerned rather than retribution is consistent with the ethics of care. In personal relationships, the ethics of care would promote empathy and treating others in a way that does not hurt them. In this view, meeting needs is more important than securing rights.

Recently, there have been several writers who have exemplified the "ethics of care" operating in criminal justice. Whether it is called feminine justice, "peacemaking justice," "restorative justice," or some other term, various authors are discussing alternative concepts to retribution and punishment that are distinct from treatment goals that characterized an earlier era. For instance, in a recent text Braswell and Gold (1996) discuss a concept called "peacemaking justice." They show that the concept is derived from ancient principles and concerns "care" as well as other concepts: "Peacemaking, as evolved from ancient spiritual and wisdom traditions, has included the possibility of mercy and compassion within the framework of justice" (1996: 23). They propose that the peacemaking process is composed of three parts: the first part, "connectness," has to do with the interrelationships we have with one another and all of us have with the earth; "caring" is similar to the concepts discussed above (they use Noddings as a source to discuss this idea that the "natural" inclination of humans is to care for one another); finally, "mindfulness" involves being aware of others and the world (1996: 27–31).

"Peacemaking" as a concept in corrections and criminal justice builds on the work of Lozoff (in corrections) and Braithwaite (in juvenile justice). For instance, several authors discuss the "family conference," an alternative to formal judicial processing in which a juvenile, all family members, the victim, the victim's family members, neighbors, and other interested parties meet to discuss the offense, the victim's needs, and the offender's needs. The approach is not concerned so much with punishment as with meeting needs.

Other authors also question traditional approaches to offenders. For instance, Snider (1995) questions whether "criminalization" can ever be a satisfactory response to domestic violence, arguing that a violent system (as the criminal justice system obviously is) can hardly teach nonviolence in family systems. What is needed, she argues, is a more inclusive, more educational approach, one that has in common much of what has been discussed under the "ethics of care" system.

Egoism

Very simply, *egoism* postulates that what is good for one's survival and personal happiness is moral. The extreme of this position is that all people should operate on the assumption that they can do whatever benefits themselves. Others become the means to ensure happiness and have no meaning or rights as autonomous individuals. *Psychological egoism* is a descriptive principle rather than an ethical prescription. Psychological egoism refers to the idea that humans naturally are egoists and that it would be unnatural for them to be any other way. All species have instincts for survival, and self-preservation and self-interest are merely part of that instinct. Therefore, it is not only moral to be egoistic, but it is the only way we can be, and any other explanations of behavior are mere rationalizations.

Enlightened egoism is a slight revision of this basic principle, adding that the objective is long-term welfare. This may mean that one should treat others as we would want them to treat us to ensure cooperative relations. Even seemingly selfless and altruistic acts are consistent with egoism, since these benefit the individual by giving self-satisfaction. Under egoism, it would be not only impossible but also immoral for someone to perform a completely selfless act. Even those who give their lives to save others do so perhaps with the expectation of rewards in the afterlife. This system completely turns around the priorities of utilitarianism to put the individual first, before anyone else and before society as a whole. As Harris (1986: 47) puts it,

> Egoism as a moral philosophy originated in ancient Greece, but the modern emphasis on the individual in competition with other individuals has given it special prominence. The egoistic moral standard states that actions are right if and only if they produce consequences that are at least as good for the self-interest of the egoist as the consequences of any alternative action. Each egoist must personally define self-interest and propose a hierarchy of goods within that definition. Most egoists will be concerned with the fullest realization of their self-interest over a lifetime rather than during only a short period of time.

Let us see how egoism would be used to solve the ethical dilemmas we have been discussing thus far. In the case of abortion, a morality of self-interest would evaluate the benefit to the woman. If it benefited the woman, it would be considered moral. The only case in which the abortion might be considered immoral under egoism is if the mental stress from the abortion would be long-standing and outweigh the benefit of having the abortion in the first place. In the case of Heinz, self-interest would obviously dictate that he steal the drug if his wife was dear to him and it was reasonably certain he would not be caught. However, a more difficult decision would exist if Heinz thought he would be punished for the crime. In that case, self-interest would support saving his wife as well as avoiding punishment. If Heinz loved his wife so much he could not live without her, then he would be willing to take the

---

The Major Ethical Systems

Ethical formalism: What is good is that which conforms to the categorical imperative.

Utilitarianism: What is good is that which results in the greatest utility for the greatest number.

Religion: What is good is that which conforms to God's will.

Natural law: What is good is that which is natural.

Ethics of virtue: What is good is that which conforms to the golden mean.

Ethics of care: What is good is that which meets the needs of those concerned.

Egoism: What is good is that which benefits me.

punishment; if he did not love his wife, self-interest would lead him to protect himself and let her die.

Obviously, egoism is rejected by many philosophers and laymen because it violates the basic tenets of an ethical system. Universalism is inconsistent with egoism, because to approve of all people acting in their own self-interest is not a logical or feasible position. It cannot be right for both me and you to maximize our own self-interests, because it would inevitably lead to conflict. Egoism would support exploitative actions by the strong against the weak, which seems wrong under all other ethical systems. On the other hand, psychological egoism is a relevant concept in natural law (self-preservation is natural) and utilitarianism (hedonism is a natural inclination). But if it is true that humans are *naturally* selfish and self-serving, one can also point to examples that indicate that humans are also altruistic and self-sacrificing. What is the true nature of humankind?

RELATIVISM AND ABSOLUTISM

Ethical relativism describes those moral systems in which what is good or bad changes depending on the individual or group. The generation of the 1960s encapsulated this belief in the saying "You do your thing and I'll do mine." What is right is determined by culture and/or individual belief; there are no universal laws.

There are two main arguments for relativism. The first is that there are so many moral standards of behavior. According to Stace, "We find that there is nothing, or next to nothing, which has always and everywhere been regarded as morally good by all men" (1995: 26). The second argument is that we do not know how to determine the absolute rules. Who is to say what is right and what is wrong?

One may look to anthropology and the rise of social science to explain the popularity of moral relativism. Over the course of studying different societies—past and present, primitive and sophisticated—anthropologists have found that there are very few universals across cultures. Even those behaviors often believed to be universally condemned, such as incest, have been institutionalized and encouraged in some societies (Kottak, 1974: 307).

Basically, *cultural relativism* defines good as that which contributes to the health and survival of society. For instance, societies where women are in ample supply may endorse polygyny, and societies that have a shortage of women may accept polyandry; hunting and gathering societies that must contend with harsh environments may hold beliefs allowing for the euthanasia of burdensome elderly, whereas agricultural societies that depend on knowledge passed down through generations may revere their elderly and accord them an honored place in society.

In criminology, cultural differences in perceptions of right and wrong are important to the subcultural deviance theory of crime, wherein some deviant activity is explained by subcultural approval for that behavior. The example

---

QUERY

■ Do you believe that there are no absolute moral truths and that morality is simply an individual's definition of right and wrong?

■ If you answered yes to the question above, then are you also saying that child molesters and cannibals have the right to decide which behaviors are acceptable for them?

---

typically used to illustrate this is that of the Sicilian father who kills the man who raped his daughter, because to do otherwise would violate values of his subculture emphasizing personal honor and retaliation (Sellin, 1970: 187). A recent case of subcultural differences involves a father who sold his fourteen-year-old daughter into marriage. Because he lived in Chicago, he was arrested; if he had lived in his homeland of India, he would have been conforming to accepted norms of behavior.

Although cultural relativism accepts the fact that different societies may have different moral standards, it also dictates that individuals within a culture conform to the standards of their culture. Therein lies a fundamental flaw in the relativist approach; if there are no universal norms, why should individuals be required to conform to societal or cultural norms? If their actions are not accepted today, it might be argued, they could be accepted tomorrow—if not by their society, perhaps by some other. An additional inconsistency in cultural relativism is the corresponding prohibition against interfering in another culture's norms. The argument goes as follows: since every culture is correct in its definitions of morality, another culture should not step in to change those definitions. However, if what is right is determined by which culture one happens to belong to, why then, if that culture happens to be imperialistic, would it be wrong to force cultural norms on other cultures? Cultural relativism attempts to combine an absolute (no interference) with a relativistic "truth" (there are no absolutes). This is logically inconsistent (Foot, 1982).

Cultural relativism usually concerns behaviors that are always right in one society and always wrong in another. Of course, what is more common is behavior that is judged to be wrong most of the time but acceptable in certain instances. For example, killing is wrong except possibly in self-defense and war; lying is wrong except when one lies to protect another. Occupational subcultures also support standards of behavior that are acceptable only for those within the occupation. For instance, certain types of police behavior may be considered acceptable by the police subculture even while being contrary to general societal morals. This is especially true of actions such as the use of force or the willingness to overlook a law. For instance, some police officers believe that it is wrong to break the speed limit unless one happens to be a police officer—even an off-duty one.

It must be noted that even absolutist systems may accept some exceptions. The *principle of forfeiture* associated with deontological ethical systems holds that people who treat others as means to an end or take away or inhibit their freedom and well-being forfeit the right to protection of their own freedom and well-being (Harris, 1986: 136). Therefore, people who aggress first forfeit their own right to be protected from harm. This could permit self-defense (despite the moral proscription against taking life) and possibly provide justification for lying to a person who threatens harm. Critics of an absolutist system see this exception as a rationalization and a fatal weakness to the approach; in effect, moral rules are absolute *except* for those exceptions allowed by some "back door" argument.

The biggest danger in relativism is the tendency to accept certain types of behavior, which then become the support for individuals to justify other behaviors. In many cases, relativism allows lines to be drawn, but these lines are purely arbitrary and subject to shift based on the person, the circumstance, or the time. For instance, many feel that it is acceptable for a police officer to accept gratuities but object to politicians accepting gifts from special interest groups. Or some may feel that police accepting free coffee and free dinners is fine, but would condemn police officers who take a squad car to all the businesses in a district to pick up "presents" (including cases of beer, cigarettes, and other goods) at Christmas to distribute them back at the precinct. Where is the line to be drawn? Only meals? Only on duty? Only under a certain dollar amount?

In another example, I might believe that lying for a good cause is moral and that small lies are also acceptable, but somewhere between small and large lies is a line; on one side the action is acceptable, and on the other it is wrong. Relativism allows for adaptation to specific circumstances, but universalists would argue that if moral absolutes are removed, subjective moral discretion leads to egoistic rationalizations.

TOWARD A RESOLUTION: SITUATIONAL ETHICS

Situational ethics is often used as a synonym for *relativism;* however, if we clarify the term to include the elements discussed below, it might serve as a resolution to the problems inherent in both an absolutist and a relativist approach to ethics. Recall that relativism is criticized because it must allow any practice to be considered "good" if it is considered good by some people; therefore, even human sacrifice and cannibalism would have to be considered moral, a thoroughly unpalatable (no pun intended) consequence of accepting the doctrine. Absolutism, on the other hand, is also less than satisfactory because we all can think of some examples where the "rule" must be broken; even Kant declined to be purely absolutist in his argument that lying isn't really lying if told to a person who is trying to harm us. What is needed, then, is an approach that resolves both problems. One solution might be a definition of situational ethics as follows:

1. There are basic norms or principles of human behavior.
2. These can be applied to ethical dilemmas and moral issues.

3. The norms may call for different results in different situations, depending on the needs, concerns, relationships, resources, weaknesses, and strengths of the individual actors.

Fletcher (1966: 26) proposes that "love" be one of the guiding principles or norms:

> The situationist enters into every decision making situation fully armed with the ethical maxims of his community and its heritage, and he treats them with respect as illuminators of his problems. Just the same he is prepared in any situation to compromise them or set them aside in the situation if love seems better served by doing so.

Situational ethics are different from relativism because there is a recognition of absolute norms whereas under relativism there are no norms. What are absolute norms? Natural law, the Golden Rule, and the ethics of care could help us fashion a set of moral absolutes that might be general enough to ensure universal agreement. For instance, we could start with the following propositions:

1. Treat each person with the utmost respect and care.
2. Do one's duty in such a way that one does not violate the first principle.

These principles would not have anything to say about dancing (as immoral or moral), but they would definitely condemn human sacrifice, child molestation, slavery, and a host of other practices that have been part of human society. Practices could be good in one society and bad in another—for instance, if polygamy was necessary to ensure the survival of society, it might be acceptable; if it was to serve the pleasure of some by using and treating others as mere objects, it would be immoral. Selling daughters into marriage to enrich the family would never be acceptable because that is not treating them with respect and care; however, arranged marriages may be acceptable if all parties agree and the motives are consistent with care.

To resolve the dilemma of the police officer who stops his father for DWI, one might argue that he can do his duty and still respect and care for his father. He could help his father through the arrest process, treat him with care, and make sure that he received help, if he needed it, for his drinking. Although this may not be enough to placate his father, and his father may still be angry with him, as would others, their reaction could then be analyzed: Are they treating the officer with care and respect? Is it respecting someone to expect him to ignore a lawful duty?

This system is not too different from a flexible interpretation of Kant's categorical imperative, a strict interpretation of rule-based utilitarianism, or an inclusive application of the Golden Rule. All ethical systems (except egoism) struggle with objectivity and subjectivity, along with respect for the individual and concern for society. Interestingly, situational ethics seems to be entirely consistent with the ethics of care, especially when one contrasts this ethical system with a rule-based, absolutist system. In the ethics of care, you will recall, each individual—both victim and offender—is considered in the equation of what would serve the interests of "justice." Deontological systems, such as ethical formalism, support punishment for punishment's sake, but teleological systems must find some "good" in punishment for it to be considered thus. The difference between utilitarianism and the ethics of care is that the utilitarian will sacrifice the individual for the good of society, and under the ethics of care the individual is never sacrificed.

The following schemata may help to isolate the differences and similarities between these concepts:

Absolutist	*Situational*
Rationality, law, rules, duty	Emotion, mercy, discretion
Natural law, ethical formalism	Religion, ethics of care, emotivism

Utilitarianism is arguably on the legal/rule side since the absolute rule of "the greatest utility for all" is often at the expense of the individual. Interestingly, the ethics of virtue, at least Aristotle's version, might be placed on the Situational side even though Aristotle believed that "practical reason" was more important than "moral virtues." This is because he recognized in the "Golden Mean" the concept of individuality. In other words, one person's "mean" of courage might be different from another's, and this would have to be taken into account before judging behavior.

Resulting Concerns

As mentioned previously, ethical systems are not moral decisions as such; rather, they provide the guidelines or principles to make moral decisions. It can happen that moral questions are decided in different ways under the same ethical system—for instance, when facts are in dispute. When there is no agreement concerning the accepted facts in a certain case, it is confusing to bring in moral arguments before resolving the factual issues. Capital punishment is supported by some because of a belief that it is a deterrent to people who might commit murder. Others believe that capital punishment is wrong regardless of its efficacy in deterrence. Most arguments about capital punishment get confused during the factual argument about the effectiveness of deterrence. "Is capital punishment wrong or right?" is a different question from "Does capital punishment deter?" The second question might be answered through a study of facts; the former can only be answered by a moral judgment.

Another thing to consider is that none of us are perfect—we all have committed immoral or unethical acts. Even when we know something to be wrong, we sometimes still perform the act. Very few people follow such strong moral codes that they never lie or never cause another person harm. One can condemn the act and not the person. There have been situations so horrible that behaviors, while perhaps not moral, are at least understandable and perhaps excusable.

Literary Perspective

Do you think you could throw you daughter Leah into a crematorium, Jack? Of course you do not. Your love for her is too great, correct? Let me starve you for a year. Let me beat you into submission. Let me kill everyone you love around you and work you until you drop. Let me humiliate you and fill your hair with lice and your bread with maggots. Let me test you to the limit and find out where civilization ends and depravity begins along the edges of your soul. Here's what they did to me, Jack. At the end of the war, I could have thrown the Messiah himself into the fires of the crematorium and I would have done it for an extra cup of soup. I could throw Ruth, Shyla, Martha, Sonia, my sons, Leah and everyone else into those fires and never think of it again. Here is the trick, Jack. You have to break a man down completely and then you own him. Let me break you like they broke me and I promise you would throw Leah into a fire, hang her by her neck, see her raped by a hundred men, then have her throat cut, and her bodily parts thrown to starving dogs in the street. I upset you. I am sorry. I tell you what I know. But know this: it is possible for you to kill Leah with your own hands because the world has come apart and God has hidden his face in his hands and you will think, by killing her, you are proving your love of Leah like never before.

SOURCE: Conroy, Pat. *Beach Music* (New York: Doubleday, 1995): 528. Copyright © 1995 by Pat Conroy. Used by permission of Doubleday, a division of Bantam Doubleday Dell Publishing Group, Inc.

Very few people are consistent in the use of one ethical system in making moral decisions. Some of us are fundamentally utilitarian and some predominantly religious, but we may make decisions using other ethical frameworks at times. Ethical systems help us to understand or analyze morality, but knowing them is no guarantee that we will always act morally and ethically.

CONCLUSION

In this chapter we have explored some of the major ethical systems. Ethical systems are ordered principles that define what is right or good. Each of these ethical systems answers the question "What is good?" in a different way. Sometimes the same conclusion to an ethical dilemma can be reached using several different ethical systems, but sometimes using different ethical systems may result in contradictory answers to the determination of goodness. Ethical systems are more complex to apply than they are to explain. For instance, utilitarianism is fairly easy to understand, but the measurement of utility for any given act is often quite difficult. Ethical formalism says to "do one's duty" but does not help us when there are conflicting duties. The ethics of care emphasizes relationships but is quite vague in providing the steps necessary to resolve ethical dilemmas. Relativism and absolutism are contrary principles but may be reconciled using the concept of "situational ethics."

REVIEW QUESTIONS

1. If you had to choose one ethical system, which one most closely conforms to your own beliefs? Be explicit.

2. Is there a universal truth relating to right and wrong, moral and immoral? If you answered yes, what are the principles of such a system?

3. Describe each of the ethical systems and provide a critique of each.

4. Discuss the arguments against and supporting relativism. Do the same for absolutism.

5. Explain the differences between situational ethics and relativism.

ETHICAL DILEMMAS

Situation 1

You are a Christian Scientist, as is your family. One of the teachings of this belief system is that medical science detracts from faith and that sickness can be cured through prayer and reliance on God. Christian Science nurses attend to the ill and practice some home remedies for maladies, and even at times agree to the intervention of medical experts, but most illness is treated with prayer. Your child is severely ill with high fever, vomiting, and convulsions. The representative of the church tells you that the illness is made worse because you do not believe that prayer is helping; thus, in order for the child to get better, you must pray more and not think about taking the child to the hospital. What would you do?

Situation 2

You are a manager of a retail store. You are given permission by the owner of the store to hire a fellow classmate to help out. One day you see the classmate take some clothing from the store. When confronted by you, the peer laughs it off and says the owner is insured, no one is hurt, and it was under $100. "Besides," says your acquaintance, "friends stick together, right?" What would you do?

Situation 3

You are in a lifeboat along with four others. You have only enough food and water to keep four alive for the several weeks you expect to be adrift until you float into a shipping lane and can be discovered and rescued. You will definitely all perish if the five of you consume the food and water. There is the suggestion that one of you should die so that the other four can live. Would you volunteer to commit suicide? Would you vote to have one go overboard if you choose by straws? Would you vote to throw overboard the weakest and most sickly of the five? If you were on a jury judging the behavior of four who did murder a fifth in order to stay alive, would you acquit them or convict them of murder?

SUGGESTED READINGS

Braswell, M., and Gold, J. 1996. "Peacemaking, Justice and Ethics." Pp. 22–39 in Braswell, M., McCarthy, B., and McCarthy, B. (eds.), *Justice, Crime, and Ethics,* 2d Ed. Cincinnati: Anderson.

Foot, P. 1982. "Moral Relativism." Pp. 152–167 in Meiland, J., and Krausz, M. (eds.), *Relativism: Cognitive and Moral.* Notre Dame: University of Notre Dame Press.

Gold, J. 1996. "Utilitarianism and Deontological Approaches to Criminal Justice Ethics." Pp. 9–23 in Braswell, M., McCarthy, B., and McCarthy, B. (eds.), *Justice, Crime, and Ethics,* 2d Ed. Cincinnati: Anderson.

Prior, W. 1991. *From Virtue and Knowledge: An Introduction to Ancient Greek Ethics.* New York: Routledge, Kegan Paul.

Snider, L. 1995. Towards Safer Societies. Unpublished manuscript. Dept. of Sociology, Queen's University. Kingston, Ontario.

Stace, W. 1995. "Ethical Relativity and Ethical Absolutism." Pp. 25–32 in Close, D., and Meier, N. (eds.), *Morality in Criminal Justice.* Belmont, CA: Wadsworth.

3

❖

Developing Moral
and Ethical Behavior

Chapter Objectives

Become familiar with the major theories regarding
the development of moral behavior, especially Kohlberg's
moral development theory and learning theory.

Become familiar with Gilligan's research
exploring gender differences in moral development.

Recognize the difficulty associated with understanding
the relationship between moral beliefs and behavior.

Become familiar with some of the applications of
moral development theory to criminal offenders.

Become familiar with some issues regarding
teaching ethics in criminal justice.

In the previous chapter, we explored a variety of philosophical definitions of morality. In this chapter, we will take a different approach and ask the question "How does an individual develop into a moral person?" As we have seen, philosophers have looked to God, natural law, reason, intuition, and emotion to determine morality. There are fundamental questions about the nature of morality—whether it is subjective and of human construction or whether it is apart from and only discoverable by humans, thus universal and objective. Philosophers are still debating these ancient questions while the more recent science of psychology helps us understand how individuals develop their own moral systems and definitions of morality.

PSYCHOLOGICAL THEORIES OF MORAL DEVELOPMENT

Psychology addresses such questions as "How does one acquire moral beliefs?" and "Do moral beliefs determine behavior?" The two most important contributions to this discussion are Lawrence Kohlberg's moral stage theory and behaviorism, or learning theory.

QUERY

Who has been the greatest influence on your moral development? Why? How?

Kohlberg's Moral Stages

The contributions of Jean Piaget and Lawrence Kohlberg have become essential to any discussion of moral development. Piaget believed that we all go through stages of cognitive, or intellectual, growth. These stages parallel moral stages of development, and together they describe a systematic way of perceiving the world. Piaget studied the rules that children develop in their play. These rules reflect the perceptions they hold of themselves and others and move from egocentrism to cooperativeness. Kohlberg carried on with Piaget's work and more fully described the stages each individual passes through in moral and cognitive development (Boyce and Jensen, 1978: 87–95).

Two-year-olds do not understand the world in the same way as twenty-year-olds do. This lack of understanding also affects their moral reasoning ability. The infant lacks sensitivity toward others and has a supreme selfishness regarding his or her needs and wants. Infants are not concerned with others because they are only vaguely aware of their existence. An infant's world is confined to what is within reach of his or her hands and mouth. Even a mother is only important as the source of comfort and food. Very slowly the infant becomes aware that others also have feelings and needs. This awareness leads to empathy and a recognition of right and wrong. At later stages, abstract reasoning develops, which leads to the ability to understand more difficult moral concepts.

The following are some characteristics of these cognitive and moral stages (Hersh et al., 1979: 52):

1. They involve qualitative differences in modes of thinking, as opposed to quantitative differences. The child undergoes dramatic changes in perceptions; for instance, in an early stage the realization occurs that what one does has an impact on others. An infant realizes that when she pulls someone's hair, the person reacts; when she cries, someone comes; and when she performs certain behaviors, she is praised.

2. Each stage forms a structured whole; cognitive development and moral growth are integrated. Perceptions of the world and the corresponding moral framework are similar among all individuals at that particular stage. Simplistically, this means that a child cannot be sensitive to larger issues such as world hunger until he is able to grasp the reality of such conditions.

3. Stages form an invariant sequence; no one bypasses any stage and not all people develop to the higher stages. In fact, according to Kohlberg, very few individuals reach the post-conventional level; the majority reach the conventional level and stay there.

4. Stages are hierarchical integrations; that is, each succeeding stage encompasses and is more comprehensive and complicated than the stage that precedes it.

Exercise

Talk to a child (four to eight years old) about a variety of moral issues—e.g., what is bad? What is good? Give the child a moral dilemma relevant to his or her world (make the characters children, the issue a familiar one). How does the child respond? Can you identify any moral principles? Can you identify which of Kohlberg's stages seems to describe the child's reasoning?

Kohlberg describes three levels of moral reasoning; included in each level are two stages. The levels and stages are described as follows (Barry, 1985: 14–16; Kohlberg, 1976):

Level A (Preconventional Level) At the preconventional level, the person approaches a moral issue motivated purely by personal interests. The major concern is the consequences of the action for the person. For instance, young children do not share toys with others because they see no reason to do so. They derive pleasure from them, so to give them to others is not logical. Even if the toys belong to others, there is a predisposition for children to appropriate them. Parents know the tears and tantrums associated with teaching a child that toys belonging to others must be given back. Young children at play first start sharing, in fact, when they perceive benefit to themselves, such as giving someone their doll in exchange for a game or a ball, or they grudgingly share because they fear punishment from an adult if they do not.

Stage 1 has a *punishment and obedience orientation*. What is right is that which is praised; what is wrong is that which is punished. The child submits to an authority figure's definition and is concerned only with the consequences attached to certain behaviors, not with the behavior itself.

Stage 2 has an *instrument and relativity orientation*. The child becomes aware of and is concerned with others' needs. What is right is still determined by self-interest, but the concept of self-interest is broadened to include others. Relationships are important to the child, and he or she is attached to parents, siblings, and best friends, who are included in the ring of self-interest. There is also the emerging concept of fairness and a recognition that others deserve to have their needs met.

Level B (Conventional Level) At the conventional level, people perceive themselves as members of society, and living up to role responsibilities is paramount in believing oneself to be good. Children enter this level when they are capable of playing with other children according to rules. In fact, games and play are training grounds for moral development, since they teach the child that there are defined roles and rules of behavior. For instance, a game of softball becomes a microcosm of real life when a child realizes that he or she is not only acting as self, but also as a first baseman, a role that includes certain specific tasks. Before this stage, the child runs to the ball regardless of where it is hit. Thus, in a softball game with very young children playing, one may see all the players run after the ball and abandon their bases, because they have difficulty grasping the concept of role responsibilities. Furthermore, although it would be more expeditious to trip the runners as they leave the base so they can be tagged out, the child learns that such behavior is not "fair play" and is against the rules of the game. Thus, children learn to submerge individual interest to conform to rules and role expectations.

Stage 3 has an *interpersonal concordance orientation*. The person performs conventionally determined good behavior to be considered a good person. The views of "significant others" are important to one's self-concept. Thus, individuals will control behavior so as to not hurt others' feelings or be thought of as bad. Stage 4 has a *law-and-order orientation*. The individual is concerned not just with interpersonal relationships, but also with the rules set down by society. The law becomes all-important. Even if the laws themselves are wrong, one cannot disregard them, for that would invite social chaos.

Level C (Post-Conventional Level) A person at the post-conventional level moves beyond the norms and laws of a society to determine universal good—that is, what is good for all societies. Few people reach this level, and their actions are observably different from the majority. For instance, Gandhi might be described as a person with post-conventional morality. He did not subscribe to the idea that laws must be obeyed, and he carried out peaceful noncompliance against the established law to conform to his belief in a higher order of morality. At this level of moral development, the individual assumes the responsibility of judging laws and conventions.

Stage 5 has a *social contract orientation*. The person recognizes larger interests than current laws. This individual is able to evaluate the morality of laws in a historical context and feels an obligation to the law because of its benefits to societal survival. The orientation of Stage 6 is *universal ethical principles*. The person who has reached this stage bases moral judgments on the higher abstract laws of truth, justice, and morality.

A Seventh Stage? Kohlberg has advanced the possibility of a seventh stage, which has been described as a "soft" stage of ethical awareness with an orientation of cosmic or religious thinking. It is not a higher level of reasoning, but qualitatively different. According to Kohlberg, in this highest stage individuals have come to terms with such questions as "Why be just in a universe that is largely unjust?" It is a different question from the definition of justice that forms the content of the other stages. In this stage one sees oneself as part of a larger whole and humanity as only part of a larger cosmic structure. This stage focuses on *agape*—a nonexclusive love and acceptance of the cosmos and one's place in it (Kohlberg, 1983; Power and Kohlberg, 1980; Kohlberg and Power, 1984).

Critics of Kohlberg

Some believe that Kohlberg's theory of moral development has several serious flaws. First, the stages tend to center too much on the concept of justice, ignoring other aspects of morality. Second, the stages, especially 5 and 6, may

---

Kohlberg's Stages

Level A: Preconventional

Stage 1: "Right is blind obedience to rules and authority, avoiding punishment, and not doing physical harm."

Stage 2: "Right is serving one's own or others' needs and making fair deals in terms of concrete exchange."

Level B: Conventional

Stage 3: "Right is playing a good 'nice' role, being concerned about other people and their feelings, keeping loyalty and trust with partners, and being motivated to follow rules and expectations."

Stage 4: "Right is doing one's duty in society, upholding the social order, and the welfare of society or the group."

Level C: Post-Conventional

Stage 5: "Right is upholding the basic rights, values, and legal contracts of a society, even when they conflict with the concrete rules and laws of the group."

Stage 6: "Right is guided by self-chosen ethical principles of justice, equality, and respect. Laws and social agreements are usually consistent with these principles."

SOURCE: Gibbs, J., Kohlberg, L., Colby, A., and Speicher-Dubin, B. "The Domain and Development of Moral Judgment: A Theory and Method of Assessment." In Meyer, J. (ed.), *Reflections on Values Education* (Waterloo, Ontario: Wilfrid Laurier University Press, 1976): 19–20.

---

be nothing more than culturally based beliefs regarding the highest level of morality: "Kohlberg assumes that the core of morality and moral development is deontological, that it is a matter of rights and duties as prescriptions" (Levine, Kohlberg, and Hewer, 1985: 95). Justice, rules, and rights are emphasized as higher values than are caring and relationships. Others say Kohlberg emphasizes reason in moral decisions and ignores emotional factors. In response, Kohlberg and his associates assert that the theory is a measurement of "justice reasoning," not an attempt to present the "total complexity of the moral domain" (Levine, Kohlberg, and Hewer, 1985: 99).

Other studies have found significant cultural differences in the age at which children reach the different stages of moral development. This criticism does not necessarily negate the validity of a stage sequence theory; however, it does call into question the specifics of movement through the stages (Boyce and Jensen, 1978). Still others criticize the lack of connection between reasoning levels and moral action in particular situations. There does not seem to be a strong correlation between one's moral stage, as measured by the interview format of Kohlberg's research or more recently devised paper-and-pencil tests of recognition, and how one will respond when faced with a situation allowing a choice to be honest or dishonest (Lutwak and Hennesy, 1985).

Kohlberg's research can also be described as sexually biased since he interviewed boys almost exclusively in early research. Subsequent studies have found that females tend to cluster in Stage 3 because of their greater sensitivity

---

Are Women More Ethical?

A recent study supports the premise that women in business are more ethical than men. A Baylor University study found that there were significant differences between females and males when asked to respond to different hypothetical scenarios, with women more often taking the ethical "high road." The study included 1,831 women and men from all 50 states who worked in professional and managerial positions. Women responded with more ethical responses to hypothetical situations involving exceeding legal pollution limits, bribery, corporate espionage, promotion practices, product safety, and executive salaries versus workers' salaries. Men responded more ethically to situations involving collusion in construction bidding and copying computer software. Researchers suggest socialization differences between men and women as a possible explanation for such differences.

SOURCE: Roser, M. A. "Business Study Finds Women More Ethical," *Austin American Statesman,* 26 Dec. 1996: A1, A11.

---

to and emphasis on human relationships. This is a relatively low level of moral development and lower than the law-and-order stage, where men tend to be clustered. Unless one believes that women are generally less moral or less intellectually developed than men, this is a troubling finding and one that calls into question the hierarchical nature of the theory.

Carol Gilligan (1982, 1987), one of Kohlberg's students, researched the apparent sex difference in morality and developed a theory that postulates that women may possess a *different* morality from men. Most men, it seems, analyze moral decisions with a rules or justice orientation (Stage 4), whereas many women see the same moral dilemma with an orientation toward needs and relationships (Stage 3). Gilligan labels this a "care perspective." A morality based on the care perspective would be more inclined to look at how a decision affects relationships and addresses needs whereas the justice perspective is concerned with notions of equality, rights, and universality. This ethics of care has been described in Chapter 2 as one of the ethical frameworks.

In Gilligan's study, although both men and women raised justice and care concerns in responses to moral dilemmas, among those who focused on one or the other, men exclusively focused on justice while half of the women who exhibited a focus did so on justice concerns and the other half focused on care concerns (Gilligan, 1987). It was also found that both male and female respondents were able to switch from a justice to a care perspective (or back again) when asked to do so; thus, their orientation was more a matter of perspective than inability to see the other side.

Another study of fifty college students (half men, half women) tested the subjects' orientation to three moral dilemmas, and the results were consistent with Gilligan's findings. However, the content of the dilemma evidently influenced whether or not care considerations would be found. The dilemmas involving interpersonal relationships were more likely to have care considerations than those without (Rothbart, Hanley, and Albert, 1986). It should also

QUOTATION

We all know, from what we experience with and within ourselves, that our conscious acts spring from our desires and our fears. Intuition tells us that is true also of our fellows and of the higher animals. We all try to escape pain and death, while we seek what is pleasant. We all are ruled in what we do by impulses, and these impulses are so organized that our actions in general serve for our self-preservation and that of the race. Hunger, love, pain, fear are some of those inner forces which rule the individual's instinct for self-preservation. At the same time, as social beings, we are moved in the relations with our fellow beings by such feelings as sympathy, pride, hate, need for power, pity, and so on. All these primary impulses, not easily described in words, are the springs of man's actions. All such action would cease if those powerful elemental forces were to cease stirring within us.

Though our conduct seems so very different from that of the higher animals, the primary instincts are much alike in them and in us. The most evident difference springs from the important part which is played in man by a relatively strong power of imagination and by the capacity to think, aided as it is by language and other symbolical devices. Thought is the organizing factor in man, intersected between the causal primary instincts and the resulting actions. In that way imagination and intelligence enter into our existence in the part of servants of the primary instincts.

SOURCE: Einstein, Albert. *Out of My Later Years* (New York: Philosophical Library, 1950): 15. Reprinted with permission.

---

be noted that other studies failed to find any differences between men and women in their responses to moral dilemmas (see reviews in Walker, 1986; Thoma, 1986).

A justice perspective arguably represents the dominant male Western philosophical position, exemplified by Kant's categorical imperative, rule utilitarianism, and even the Golden Rule. It also seems to be true that the care perspective seems more consistent with some Eastern philosophies that are less judgmental and more accepting of human failings. The fact that the justice perspective is the dominant one is not surprising given that Western philosophy has its roots in Platonic and Aristotelian philosophies, which were completely male-centered and defined the male perspective as representative of the human experience. Nor is it surprising that many women use the justice perspective in analyzing moral dilemmas, since they are socialized to these concepts from birth. What Gilligan points out in her research is that the care perspective completely drops out when one uses only male subjects—which is what Kohlberg did in his early research for the moral stage theory.

The importance of Kohlberg's work is the link he makes between moral development and reason. This concept originated with Kant and even earlier philosophers, but Kohlberg provides a psychological analysis that sheds light on *how* reason influences moral judgments. Also important in Kohlberg's work is the guidance it provides to education. According to the theory of moral stages, one can encourage movement through the stages by exposing the individual to higher stage reasoning. The procedures for encouraging moral growth include presenting moral dilemmas and allowing the individual to support his or her position. Through exposure to higher reasoning, one sees the weaknesses and inconsistencies of lower-level reasoning (Hersh et al., 1979). Kohlberg indicates clearly what is needed for moral growth; despite reservations about his descriptions of the moral stages, these guidelines to encourage moral development seem valid and are supported by other authorities.

Learning Theory and Behaviorism

Learning theorists agree that morality is cognitive but do not believe individuals go through stages of moral development. Rather, children learn what they are taught, including morals and values as well as behavior. In other words, right or wrong is not discovered through reasoning; rather, all humans are shaped by the world around them and form completely subjective opinions about morality and ethics. This learning can take place through *modeling* or by *reinforcement.*

In *modeling,* values and moral beliefs come from those one admires and aspires to identify with. If that role model happens to be a priest, one will probably develop a religious ethical system; if it happens to be a pimp or a sociopath, an egoistic ethical system may develop. If the identification is broken, moral beliefs may change. It is no surprise that when asked who has been important in their moral development, most people say their parents, since parents are the most significant people in one's life during important formative years. Although we may not hold exactly the same views and have exactly the same values as our parents, there is no doubt that they are influential in our value formation.

Another way learning theorists explain moral development is through *reinforcement.* Behaviors and beliefs that are reinforced (either through material rewards or through more subjective rewards, such as praise) are repeated and eventually become permanent. Since behavior is more easily stabilized and tends to come before permanent attitude change, it is often the case that behavior leads to the development of consistent beliefs—e.g., I am rewarded for sharing (by parental praise or the ability to borrow others' toys), and eventually I develop the belief that "sharing is good." Alternatively, I might be rewarded for being selfish and bullying others to gain what I want. On the playground, other children are afraid of me and I use the fear to demand toys or extra turns. No adults reprimand me or do so inconsistently, so the rewards far outweigh the negative consequences of such behavior. Eventually I may develop a "me first" and "every person for themselves is the way to live" philosophy of life.

When behavior is not consistent with beliefs, the discomfort that results is called *cognitive dissonance.* This leads to the development of attitudes to support one's behavior. The child who is told constantly to share toys and is disciplined upon refusal is learning not just the desired behavior, but also the values of cooperativeness and charity. In an adult, these values may be manifested by lending one's lawn mower to a neighbor or contributing to charities. On the other hand, if a child is never punished for aggressive behavior and instead is rewarded—for instance, by always getting the desired object—then aggressiveness and the accompanying moral principle of "might makes right" develops.

Bandura (cited in Boyce and Jensen, 1978: 123–124) states that there is a developmental approach to teaching, keyed to what the child is capable of understanding:

> According to the social learning view, people vary in what they teach, model and reinforce with children of differing ages. At first, control is necessarily external. In attempting to discourage hazardous conduct in children who have not yet learned to talk, parents must resort to physical intervention. . . . Successful socialization requires gradual substitution of symbolic and internal controls for external sanctions and demands. . . . Evidence that there are some age trends in moral judgment, that children fail to adopt opinions they do not fully comprehend, and that they are reluctant to express views considered immature for their age can be adequately explained without requiring elaborate stage propositions.

According to learning theorists, even the most altruistic behaviors provide rewards for the individual. For instance, acts of charity provide rewards in the form of goodwill from others and self-satisfaction. Acts of sacrifice are rewarded in similar ways. Honesty, integrity, and fairness exist only because they have been rewarded in the past and present and are part of the behavioral repertoire of the individual. The moral principles of "honesty is right," "integrity is good," and "fairness is ethical" come after the behavior has been stabilized, not before. This theory is very different from the view that moral principles influence actions.

There is little room in this theory for universalism, absolutism, or the idea that a moral truth exists apart from humans that is not of their construction but that awaits their discovery. The theory is completely humanistic in that morality is considered a creation of humans that explains and rationalizes learned behavior. Behavior is completely neutral; an infant can be taught any behavior desired and the moral beliefs consistent with that belief.

Much research exists to support a learning theory of moral development. For instance, it was found that large gains in moral maturity (as measured by paper-and-pencil tests of expression of beliefs) could be achieved by direct manipulation of rewards for such beliefs. Contrary to Kohlberg's view that an individual comes to a realization of moral principles through cognitive development, this theory proposes that one can encourage or create moral beliefs by reward (Boyce and Jensen, 1978: 143).

A more important question, however, is whether expressed beliefs would convert to behavior and long-term stability. Kohlberg believes that only when all the cognitions and values associated with a moral stage are internalized is there consistency between beliefs and behavior. For instance, schoolchildren who are ranked higher on moral stages are less likely to cheat when given the opportunity, and people who hold beliefs consistent with equality, fairness, and justice are more likely to protest injustice. There is also some evidence to indicate that compliance gained from external rewards is not stable until it becomes internalized, which involves adaptation to existing personality structures (Borchert and Stewart, 1978: 133–145). The question of when and why beliefs and values are internalized is not as easy to research. Even if ethical behavior could be ensured by providing rewards, this would not necessarily develop "moral character" or moral principles unless beliefs are somehow internalized.

In summary, both Kohlberg's theory of moral stages and learning theory explain how individuals develop moral beliefs. Kohlberg's moral stages would seem to place egoism and utilitarianism in lower levels of moral reasoning because of the concern for personal welfare and nonuniversalist reasoning. An alternative view is that Bentham's utilitarianism might actually be Stage 6 because of the concern with general welfare and universal laws regarding utility (Boyce and Jensen, 1978: 182). However, it is clear that according to a theory of moral stages, some ethical systems are more advanced than others. Learning theory, on the other hand, postulates that humans learn morality through reinforcement. It holds that morality is subjective and that humans do not discover moral laws through reason, but are taught moral beliefs and behaviors through rewards and punishment.

Other Approaches

The two theories above are not the only approaches to understanding moral reasoning and the development of moral behavior. Others have looked to biological "predeterminers," especially of aggressive behavior. Researchers who study the brain have discovered links between the brain and the predisposition to certain behaviors, as well as (potentially) the development of moral behavior. The frontal lobes seem to be the part of the brain implicated in feelings of empathy, shame, and moral reasoning. Individuals with frontal lobe damage display the following characteristics (Ellis and Pontius, 1989: 6):

1. Increased impulsiveness.
2. Decreased attention span.
3. Difficulty in logical reasoning.
4. Difficulty adjusting to new events.
5. Tendency toward apathy and erratic mood shift.
6. Tendency toward rude, unrestrained, tactless behavior.
7. Tendency to not be able to follow instructions even after verbalizing what is required.

Researchers present a theory postulating the frontal lobe and limbic system's influence on the individual's capacity for moral reasoning:

The three F-L-R network variables postulated in our model are as follows: (a) pro/antisocial emotions (primarily emanating from frontal–limbic functioning), (b) sensitivity to the environment (primarily residing in

---

QUERY

- Have you ever done something you knew to be wrong? Why did you do it?
- Do criminals have the same moral beliefs as others? Do they know that stealing is wrong?
- When can we predict individuals will perform unethical or immoral actions?

---

frontal–reticular functioning), and (c) goal setting and planning–monitoring activities (primarily performed by the prefrontal lobes themselves). Our model suggests that individuals who have frontal–limbic functioning which is lateralized toward the right hemisphere will be more antisocial than those who have lateralization toward the left hemisphere. Second, those with frontal–reticular functioning that is relatively insensitive to environmental input at a given intensity will be more antisocial than those with more sensitive frontal–reticular functioning. Third, individuals whose prefrontal lobes are disinclined to carefully devise long term goals and continuously monitor and fine tune strategies for achieving those goals will be more antisocial than persons with opposite prefrontal lobe tendencies. (Ellis and Pontius, 1989: 19)

The authors go on to discuss sex differences in brain activity. They discuss research presenting evidence that women are more inclined to empathy and sensitivity to human relationships. Over seventy studies found evidence that males are more antisocial, commit more serious types of offenses, and have serious childhood conduct disorders. There are also sex differences in delinquency, school performance, hyperactivity, impulsivity, and attention-deficit disorders. The authors propose that these differences are due to sex-linked brain activity, specifically in the frontal lobes and limbic regions. Males' sex hormones influence brain development prenatally and during puberty. While there is a great deal of overlap between male and female populations in brain development and activity, there are also distinct and measurable differences; specifically, these differences may influence the brain's ability to absorb "moral messages" or act upon them.

This approach indicates that biological elements must also be taken into account in our attempt to understand how individuals develop their moral beliefs.

ETHICS, BEHAVIOR, AND CRIMINALITY

Can one predict behavior from moral beliefs? Psychologists who have studied "immoral" behavior, such as lying and cheating among adults and children, have found it hard to predict whether or when people will perform these behaviors and have found little consistency between behaviors and beliefs.

Predicting Behavior

Some studies do find that beliefs and actions are somewhat consistent. In one study, "honesty scores" for people in three organizations were compiled from an attitudinal questionnaire about beliefs. It was found that the organization with the highest average honesty score had the least employee theft, and the organization with the lowest average honesty score had the most employee theft (Adams, 1981). However, Kohlberg cites the Hartshone and May study, which found no correlation between different tests of honesty, and another study in which a group of women prisoners were found to have the same rank orderings of vices as female college students. He uses these studies as support for the proposition that one cannot measure a trait in isolation and expect to find consistency between values and action (Kohlberg and Candel, 1984: 499–503).

Part of the problem is the difficulty in measuring moral beliefs and the validity of the instruments used. Kohlberg's work has been so influential in this field that it is difficult to find any measurement of morality that does not directly or indirectly use his stage definitions. If one attempts to examine whether or not "bad" behavior is associated with lower-stage scores, there is the assumption that lower-stage scores mean the person has less developed moral reasoning. We have previously discussed Gilligan's challenge of this conception, yet practically all studies that examine the correlation between behavior and belief continue to use stage scores as a measure of moral development.

Measurement of moral stages was accomplished in Kohlberg's work by interviews with subjects who were questioned using hypothetical moral dilemmas. Their responses were then rated by interviewers, with emphasis placed not necessarily on the answer given, but rather on the reasoning for the answer. What factors were emphasized, then, were used to place the person into the proper moral stage. This procedure is time-consuming and expensive, so paper-and-pencil tests have been devised, arguably measuring the same type of reasoning but through simpler, quicker means. Much criticism is directed at these so-called "recognition" tests, which require the subject merely to recognize and identify certain moral principles and agree with them, as opposed to "production" measures, which require the subject actually to reason through a dilemma and provide some rationale, which is then analyzed. It may be that recognition measures are less reliable in predicting behavior. Gavaghan, Arnold, and Gibbs (1983) reported that while production measures were able to distinguish between a group of delinquents and nondelinquents, recognition measures could not.

Those who subscribe to a stage theory of moral development would argue that inconsistent behavior merely means that the individual has not fully incorporated the higher-level reasoning. Learning theorists would look to immediate rewards. For instance, individuals who believe stealing is wrong may be influenced by immediate reward for wrongdoing if they have not internalized a strict sense of morality regarding stealing that would result in unpleasant feelings of guilt. In other words, all of us know that stealing is wrong, so we

---

Honesty

Reader's Digest conducted a nonscientific test of the public's honesty by dropping 120 wallets containing $50 and family pictures in various locales, including cities, suburbs, and small towns. They then watched who returned the wallets and who kept the wallets.

	Returned Wallet	Kept Wallet
Big Cities:		
Seattle	9	1
St. Louis	7	3
Atlanta	5	5
Suburbs:		
Los Angeles	6	4
Houston	5	5
Boston	7	3
Medium Cities:		
Greensboro, NC	7	3
Las Vegas	5	5
Dayton, OH	5	5
Small Towns:		
Meadville, PA	8	2
Concord, NH	8	2
Cheyenne, WY	8	2
Men (60)	37	23
(62% returned)		
Women (60)	43	17
(72% returned)		

SOURCE: Bennett, R. K. "How Honest Are We?" *Readers Digest* v.146–147 (December 1995) 49–56.

avoid the action because in the past we have been punished when we have stolen. Thus, stealing becomes associated with unpleasantness. In the past, this might have been pain (a spanking or parental scolding); in the present, it is associated with uncomfortable feelings of guilt. The immediate reward of money or material possessions will overpower a weak association between stealing and pain or guilt. Applying the same line of reasoning to professional ethics, one might assume that if the code of ethics is weak and there are immediate rewards for unethical behavior, then the individual will engage in unethical behavior.

Teaching Ethics

Many people believe that the general morality of this nation is declining. One of the reasons given for this perceived decline is that we have eliminated many of the opportunities for the teaching of morals. The community is not a cohesive force any longer, the authority of religion is not as pervasive as it once was, the family is weakening as a force of socialization, and educators have abdicated their responsibility for moral instruction in favor of scientific neutrality. It was not always this way.

In most colleges in the 1800s a course in moral philosophy was required of all graduates. This class, often taught by the college president, was designed to help the college student become a good citizen. The goal of college was not only to educate but also to help students attain the moral sensibility that would make them productive, ideal citizens. As it was taught, ethics involved not only the history of philosophical thought but also a system of beliefs and values and the skills to resolve moral or ethical dilemmas. Gradually, the general field of social science became more and more specialized. Each discipline carved out for itself an area of behavior or part of society to study, so today we have, among others, sociology, psychology, economics, history, and philosophy. The increasing empiricism of these disciplines crowded out the earlier emphasis on moral decision making. Only schools affiliated with religious denominations still routinely require courses that focus on one's moral character.

There is one small area in education in which moral instruction has reemerged, and that is in the teaching of professional ethics. As mentioned before, we commonly use ethics to describe good and bad behavior within the context of a profession or organization. Most professional schools today (law, medical, and business schools) require at least one class in professional ethics. Typically, these classes present the opportunity to examine the moral dilemmas that individuals may encounter as members of that profession and help students discover the best way to decide moral issues. Usually, there is a combination of moral discussion and moral instruction. Although some class time is devoted to letting students discuss their views, certainly part of the task is to train new members in what has been determined to be correct behavior. The alternative, of course, would be to ignore ethics in the learning phase of an occupation and let the person encounter ethical dilemmas on the job—for instance, when a prosecutor is tempted to ignore evidence to ensure an easy conviction, when a doctor must choose between two people who both need a heart transplant, or when a business executive is asked to accept a bribe to award a contract. In the rushed, pressure-filled real world, ethical decisions will be made in haste, with emotional overtones, and with peer and situational pressures heavily influencing the decision.

Administrators and managers may exert the strongest influence on the ethical climate of an agency. If leaders are honest, ethical, and caring, there is a good chance that those who work for these managers are also ethical. If administrators and/or managers are hypocritical, untruthful, and use their positions for personal gain, then workers often march in these same footsteps.

Research Applications

Research studies illustrate that the use of punishment and reward does change values and beliefs, at least for small children. For instance, in one experiment, children were told a hypothetical story in which an adult punished a neutral act, such as a child practicing a musical instrument; the children later defined that act as bad despite the intrinsic neutrality of the action. This indicates the power of adult definitions and punishment in the child's moral development. What is likely to be more effective in changing adults' and older children's moral beliefs is a method that forces them to think about their beliefs and provides exposure to other views (Boyce and Jensen, 1978: 133–170).

According to Kohlberg's theory, people develop at different rates of moral growth. He described the following criteria as necessary for moral growth (Kohlberg, 1976):

1. Being in a situation where seeing things from other points of view is encouraged. This is important because upward stage movement is a process of getting better at reconciling conflicting perspectives on a moral problem.

2. Engaging in logical thinking, such as reasoned argument and consideration of alternatives. This is important because one cannot attain a given stage of moral reasoning before attaining the supporting Piagetian stage of logical reasoning.

3. Having the responsibility to make moral decisions and to influence one's moral world. This response is necessary for developing a sense of moral agency and for learning to apply one's moral reasoning to life's situations.

4. Exposure to moral controversy and to conflict in moral reasoning that challenges the structure of one's present stage. This is important for questioning one's moral beliefs and forcing a look at alternatives.

5. Exposure to the reasoning of individuals whose thinking is one stage higher than one's own. The importance here is in offering a new moral structure for resolving the disequilibrium caused by moral conflict.

6. Participation in creating and maintaining a just community whose members pursue common goals and resolve conflict in accordance with the ideals of mutual respect and fairness.

People may become stuck at a certain point in moral development for several reasons, including not having sufficiently developed cognitive skills and/or living in a social environment that does not allow for role-taking opportunities or personal growth. For instance, a child growing up in a family that repeats basic moral views with little attempt to explain or defend them will learn to be closed to other viewpoints. A child who is never given responsibility or forced to take responsibility for his or her own actions will have difficulty developing moral reasoning skills and will not advance to higher stages. Such children will be, in a sense, stunted at the Kohlberg preconventional level of an infant constantly fed and cared for but not allowed to discover that other people exist and must be considered. As adults, if we surround ourselves only with people who think as we do, then it is very unlikely that we will ever change our moral positions or even consider others.

These principles are obviously based on the view that morality is associated with reasoning and that moral views can be discovered through intellectual development and rational argument. Learning theory would substitute a different approach—that systematically rewarding desired behaviors and values will achieve the desired result. Learning theory would propose that a more careful application of rewards would be beneficial. For instance, we should remove many mixed messages in society, such as the concurrent emphasis on the value of both peaceful resolution and military power. We also tend to ignore rather than reward good behavior, and this runs contrary to learning theory. For instance, in a classroom, the child who misbehaves usually gets more attention than the children who are quietly doing their work. Children who fight may be rewarded by special attention from important adults; the message is that adults pay attention only to those children who engage in negative types of behavior.

There is no doubt room for both approaches in any undertaking to improve ethical and/or moral behavior in children, employees, or any other group of people. Rewards can be effective tools in eliciting desired behaviors, and socio-moral reasoning opportunities, as well as the other elements suggested by Kohlberg, are probably necessary in one's ability to absorb and internalize the moral principles behind such behaviors.

Teaching Ethics in Criminal Justice

Many believe that it is much more effective to present moral or ethical questions to new members of a profession before the individual is faced with "real-life" dilemmas, such as in a law school or police academy. Of course, what often happens is that once students leave this setting they are usually told to forget what they've learned. This happens often in police academies, where cadets are taught "the book" and learn "the street" when they are paired with an older officer. This also happens when lawyers realize that the high ideals of justice they learned in law school have little to do with the bargaining and bureaucratic law of the courthouse.

It is often the case that the informal subculture in the workplace is at odds with the formal organizational value system. In the criminal justice system, police are sworn to uphold the law and protect and serve the public, yet the informal subculture supports a degree of illegal violence and a callousness to certain types of service calls considered "garbage calls." The occupational subculture, then, may have a set of ethics different from the official code of that profession. We will see that this is indeed the case with the criminal justice system. One enters a profession or occupation, becomes aware of the occupational ethics, and then must adopt them, adapt to them, or change them.

People respond to the discrepancies between official and subcultural ethics in a number of ways. They may ignore, participate in, or confront activities of their peers that they feel are wrong. It is difficult to ignore actions that run contrary to one's own value system, but very often employees establish complicated rationalizations to explain why it is not their business that others around them steal, perform less than adequately, or conduct illicit business during working hours. People often do not feel it is right to confront the immoral behavior of others even when their own behavior is consistent with accepted standards of morality.

Others are able to redefine their moral beliefs to accept the type of behavior practiced and approved of in the subculture. Chapter 5 discusses how police officers develop their "moral careers," which may include many types of otherwise immoral and unethical behavior.

Confronting the activities of one's peers typically involves a greater moral strength than most of us possess. An individual who confronts the indiscretions of others risks ostracism and even more serious sanctions. One must also resist the seductive rationalizations for the behavior that the subculture creates. Plea bargaining is completely incorporated into the system of courtroom procedure; lawyers who refuse to go along with this behavior must also be able to resist the rationalization that it is necessary for courtroom efficiency. Police officers who do not accept gratuities must usually argue against the explanation that the merchants truly want them to have the free or half-price meals. Correctional officers who challenge racial slurs will have to argue against the rationalization that no one is hurt by mere words.

One must also often sacrifice other values, such as loyalty or friendship, to confront wrongdoing. A dilemma faces individuals confronted with the choice of saying nothing and allowing corruption to continue or risk ostracism and censure from peers. *Serpico* (Maas, 1973) and *Prince of the City* (Daley, 1984) are two examples of police officers who chose to challenge the "blue curtain" of secrecy and testify against their fellow officers in corruption hearings. In *Prince of the City,* the officer agreed to testify only if he could protect his partners. Ultimately, he was unable to do so and had to live with the hatred, betrayal, and even suicide of past friends.

If one is interested in changing unethical behavior in an organization, the primary target might be new recruits, since those who have been engaging in unethical activities have built up comprehensive rationales for their behavior. Socio-moral reasoning opportunities could exist in classroom settings, such as academies. If new recruits explore moral questions ahead of time, they might have the opportunity to decide their views on moral issues before being faced with behavioral choices. On the other hand, we have already discussed the tendency to belittle academy or professional school information once on the street. Furthermore, knowing what is right may not translate into doing the

---

Literary Perspective

Some guys need a beating. In the street or the back of the precinct, there's a guy who needs a beating. And you got to do it. If you don't do it, the next situation that a cop runs into this character, it's going to be bad. It's hard for people to understand or believe that. But the fact of the matter is, if this guy runs into a cop, gets into a fistfight and really beats the shit out of him, he believes he can beat up all cops, if you arrest him without working him out. He's got to know that the next time he does this, he's going to get his ass kicked in. So I have no problem with that. Neither did any cop I've ever known have any problem with that. As long as you don't do it in public, as long as the guy really needs it, and as long as you don't carry it too far. . . .

SOURCE: Baker, M. *Cops* (New York: Pocket Books, 1985): 286. Copyright © 1985 by Mark Baker. Reprinted with permission of Simon & Schuster.

---

right thing in a corrupt setting. It is difficult, if not impossible, for a new worker to stand alone against a corrupt organizational subculture.

Learning theorists, on the other hand, might say that the most effective way to change the ethics of a profession is to make sure that behavior changes. According to learning theory principles, if one was sure to be punished for accepting bribes, lying, or performing other unethical behaviors, then the subcultural supports for such behavior and the moral apologia for it would disappear. However, only pure behaviorists would conclude that mere monitoring and application of consistent rewards and punishments would result in an ethical workforce. Others believe that although monitoring might result in a workforce that performed in an ethical manner, in order for ethical behavior to continue without monitoring, and for people to believe in principles of right and wrong, they must internalize an ethical system.

Teaching criminal justice ethics is simply one application of moral teaching. According to Sherman (1982: 17–18), the following elements are necessary for any ethics program relating to criminal justice:

1. Stimulating the "moral imagination" by posing difficult moral dilemmas.
2. Encouraging the recognition of ethical issues and larger questions instead of more immediate issues such as efficiency and goals.
3. Helping to develop analytical skills and the tools of ethical analysis.
4. Eliciting a sense of moral obligation and personal responsibility to show why ethics should be taken seriously.
5. Tolerating and resisting disagreement and ambiguity.
6. Understanding the morality of coercion, which is intrinsic to criminal justice.
7. Integrating technical and moral competence, especially recognizing the difference between what we are capable of doing and what we should do.
8. Becoming familiar with the full range of moral issues in criminology and criminal justice.

In ethics courses in the college classroom or law school there is time to analyze ethical systems and provide in-depth background in moral analysis. In the training academy or in-service training course, there is a need to cover quite a few issues in a short period of time. It is probably best to limit philosophical analysis to the extent that there is enough time to adequately address other issues. However, without some philosophical framework, ethics classes may run the risk of becoming simply "bull" sessions where everyone simply shares their views with no attempt at analysis or understanding. One problem in any ethics course is the tendency for students to assume that since there are a number of ethical systems that resolve ethical dilemmas differently, any approach is just as good as another. It is true that some hypotheticals reach different solutions under different ethical systems, but many other dilemmas that professionals face can be resolved similarly by different ethical systems. Further, any position or opinion presented in class should be supported by an ethical rationale. In most cases, it will be apparent to all concerned that the only ethical system that justifies blatant wrongdoing is the most shortsighted version of egoism.

In the study of criminal justice ethics, there are many ripe areas for inquiry. Issues include the definitions of justice and crime, the appropriate use of force, the relative importance of due process over efficiency, the ethical use of technology to control the populace, the variables used to determine responsibility and punishment, and the right of society to treat and the limits that should be placed on treatment.

Furthermore, there has been a wealth of excellent material published in the last several years, so the student or interested reader should be able to find sources that explore the issues above as well as others. Souryal and Potts (1993) propose that there is a standard body of knowledge available for those who want to become "literate" in the study of criminal justice ethics. In the box titled "Cultural Literacy in Criminal Justice" Souryal and Potts's sources are presented (see pages 78 and 79). The interested student would be well served to use this list to start a study of ethics.

Morality, Criminology, and Offender Populations

Even though criminology is directly concerned with behavior that can be judged immoral, it typically avoids moral definitions. Deviance is a sociological concept. Crime is simply unlawful behavior. These definitions alone do not necessarily make such behavior immoral, of course. Radical criminologists raise important points in their discussion of the way that certain behaviors are defined as criminal and who is allowed to do the defining. However, most criminal behavior—stealing, killing, assaulting, bribing, and so on—can also be defined as immoral or unethical. Whereas the field of psychology developed theories of moral development (studying expressed moral beliefs in response to hypothetical situations, and behaviors such as lying), the fields of sociology and criminology developed theories of deviance and criminality (focusing largely on environmental causes for criminal behavior). Interestingly, only recently have there been attempts to merge the two.

Two current attempts to explain criminality seem to indicate that theorists are moving back to developmental rather than social force theories of delinquency and crime. Tonry, Ohlin, and Farrington (1991) report on a long-term study of delinquency in which a cohort sample will be followed from birth to age twenty-five. Variables associated with delinquency will be studied. They include sex (males are more likely to be delinquent), low verbal intelligence, hyperactivity, unpopularity among peers, family history of crime and delinquency, discordant families (marital instability and harsh and erratic disciplinary practices), economic adversity, and living in a socially disorganized community. The authors cite three major theoretical perspectives that address the origins of delinquency—temperament, attachment, and social learning. After exploring the relative merits of these approaches, the authors postulate that temperament and attachment are interrelated in that the personality of the child may affect parental interaction, which, in turn, affects attachment. Alternatively, parents themselves may be poor or inconsistent caregivers, in which case attachment will be weak. Not rejecting any of the three perspectives, the researchers state that while parental child-rearing methods (attachment) may affect age of onset of delinquency, peer influence (social learning) may affect continuation or intensity of delinquency. These and many other hypotheses will be tested, but the general findings of the study thus far are that attachment and parental discipline are extremely important factors in delinquency.

In a similar vein, Gottfredson and Hirschi (1990) postulate that low self-control can explain deviance in general and that self-control, in turn, is learned primarily through family and school. If there is no one to care for the child, to identify wrongdoing and to discipline the child, then he or she will not develop self-control and will display a variety of deviant behaviors, including poor impulse control, aggression, alcohol and drug abuse, poor career motivation, and delinquency. Support for such theories can be found in studies that show associations between parental practices and delinquency.

Parental practices have also been identified as important in moral development in adolescents by Leahy (1981) and others:

> Several investigations have been concerned with the relationship between parental child-rearing practices and moral development. In support of this view, the use of affection and inductive discipline, rather than power assertion or love withdrawal, is associated with greater reliance on internal standards and the use of intention information in moral judgments. (Leahy, 1981: 582; notes omitted)

Although results are by no means clear, there does seem to be some type of association between parental practices and the development of moral standards. Leahy (1981) found that parental practices that emphasized unilateral respect (children should respect parents but not the reverse) or that were non-nurturant were related to a lower level of moral judgment (using a measurement device employing Kohlberg's stages). Whether the association of parental practices and moral development (as measured by paper-and-pencil tests) operates in the same way that parental practices influence delinquent behavior is a separate question.

Cultural Literacy in Criminal Justice

The Philosophy of Ethics

Adler, M. (1978).	*Aristotle for Everybody: Difficult Thought Made Easy*
Albert, E., Denise, T., and Peterfruend, S. (1988).	*Great Traditions of Ethics*
Bloom, A. (1987).	*The Closing of the American Mind*
Borchert, D., and Stewart, D. (1986).	*Exploring Ethics*
Campbell, K. (1986).	*A Stoic Philosophy of Life*
Keyes, C. D. (1978).	*Four Types of Value Destruction: A Search for the Good Through Ethical Analysis of Everyday Experience*
Lavine, T. Z. (1984).	*From Socrates to Sartre: The Philosophic Quest*
Porter, B. (1988).	*Reasons for Living: A Basic Ethics*
Thiroux, J. (1990).	*Ethics: Theory and Practice*
Warmington, E., and Rouse, P. (1984).	*Great Dialogues of Plato*

Moral Rules and Moral Judgment

Brink, D. (1989).	*Moral Realism of the Foundations of Ethics*
Carson, T. (1984).	*The State of Morality*
Cooper, N. (1981).	*The Diversity of Moral Thinking*
Fishkin, J. (1984).	*Beyond Subjective Morality: Ethical Reasoning and Political Philosophy*
Gert, B. (1970).	*The Moral Rules*
Goldman, A. (1988).	*Moral Knowledge*
Kekes, J. (1989).	*Moral Tradition and Individuality*
Lee, K. (1985).	*A New Basis for Moral Philosophy*
Singer, P. (1979).	*Practical Ethics*

Justice Theories

Cohen, R. (1986).	*Justice: Views from the Social Sciences*
Dworkin, R. (1977).	*Taking Rights Seriously*
Feinberg, J., and Cross, H. (1980).	*Philosophy of Law*
Hobbes, T. (1968).	*Leviathan*
Hochischild, J. (1981).	*What Is Fair? American Beliefs About Distributive Justice*
Lycos, K. (1987).	*Plato on Justice and Power*
MacIntyre, A. (1988).	*Whose Justice? Which Rationality?*
Rawls, J. (1971).	*A Theory of Justice*
Reiman, J. (1990).	*Justice and Modern Moral Philosophy*

Cultural Literacy in Criminal Justice *(continued)*

Ethics of Public Service

Beauchamp, T. (1975).	*Ethics and Public Policy*
Bok, S. (1978).	*Lying: Moral Choice in Public and Private Life*
Cleveland, H. (1985).	*The Knowledge Executive: Leadership in an Information Society*
Dubin, R. (1974).	*Human Relations in Administration*
Elliston, F., and Bowie, N. (1982).	*Ethics, Public Policy and Criminal Justice*
Herzberg, F. (1976).	*The Managerial Choice: To Be Efficient and to Be Human*
Nettler, G. (1982).	*Lying, Cheating, Stealing*
Regan, T., and Van DeVeer, D. (1982).	*And Justice for All: New Introductory Essays in Ethics and Public Policy*
Rohr, J. (1978).	*Ethics for Bureaucrats: An Essay on Law and Values*
Williams, J. D. (1980).	*Public Administration: The People's Business*

Ethics of Criminal Justice Agencies

Braswell, M., McCarthy, B., and McCarthy, B. (1991).	*Justice, Crime and Ethics*
Delattre, E. (1989).	*Character and Cops: Ethics in Policing*
Fleisher, M. (1989).	*Warehousing Violence*
Heffernan, W., and Stroup, T. (1985).	*Police Ethics: Hard Choices in Law Enforcement*
Lozoff, B., and Braswell, M. (1989).	*Inner Corrections: Finding Peace and Peace Making*
Pollock-Byrne, J. (1989).	*Ethics in Crime and Justice: Dilemmas and Decisions*
Schmalleger, F. (1990).	*Ethics in Criminal Justice*
Souryal, S. (1992).	*Ethics in Criminal Justice: In Search of the Truth*
Travis, L., Schwartz, M., and Clear, T. (1983).	*Corrections: An Issues Approach*
Whitehead, J. (1989).	*Burnout in Probation and Corrections*

SOURCE: Souryal, S., and Potts, D. "What Am I Supposed to Fall Back On? Cultural Literacy in Criminal Justice Ethics." *Journal of Criminal Justice Education* 4 (1993): 15–41. Reprinted with permission of S. Souryal and the Academy of Criminal Justice Sciences.

These approaches reject the subcultural deviance theory that delinquent or criminal behavior is learned in a subcultural group along with a different moral code that justifies such behavior. Rather, they view deviance as the absence of learning or incomplete socialization. In fact, when the individual does not develop self-control or internal standards of behavior, he or she will not make correct decisions when faced with opportunities to indulge in immediate gratification. Thus, criminals do not have different moral codes; rather, they know what is right, but simply are unwilling to conform their behavior to it because they were not taught to do so at a very early stage of development. These theories are very consistent with learning theory, although biological research sheds light on the interplay between family socialization and biological predispositions. Economic theories of criminality are almost completely rejected in the theories discussed in the previous paragraphs.

If the science of criminology has avoided questions of morality, there was no such hesitation in early corrections. Historically, criminality and sin were associated, and correctional practitioners were primarily concerned with reformation in a religious sense. Hence, early prisons were built to help the individual achieve redemption. There was a heavy dose of moral instruction in society's treatment of criminals; those who were said to lead dissolute and immoral lives were also targeted for reform. Society was much more tolerant of official attempts to intervene in individuals' lives to help them become moral and productive citizens. For instance, the juvenile court system was given the mission to reform and educate youth (primarily those from immigrant groups) in a manner consistent with societal beliefs (Platt, 1977). The orientation of corrections in the latter part of this century (1950s–1980s) became more scientific than religious, and intervention adopted the aim of psychological readjustment rather than personal redemption.

After the end of the rehabilitative ideal (1960–1970s), however, the rationale for corrections and punishment seemed to return to a moral orientation. Advocates of deterrence versus advocates for treatment set up arguments using distinctly moral terms and asking such questions as "Does society have the right to treat/punish?" and "What are the limits of punishment/treatment?" The "just deserts" position, covered in Chapter 9, is probably the clearest example of a moral perspective in criminal justice literature.

In the last twenty years or so, there have been various attempts to introduce offenders to "moral education." Hickey and Scharf (1980), who studied under Kohlberg, undertook an early attempt to apply moral development theory to corrections in their creation of a therapeutic community in a Connecticut prison. Eventually they had "just communities" for both men and women that were run according to principles of fairness, justice, and rights. Prisoners were exposed to moral analysis in discussions and group meetings. Increases in stage scores were measured as averaging one-and-one-half stages after prisoners had lived in the "just community."

It appears that simply offering moral discussion groups may also result in an increase in stage scores. Gibbs and his colleagues (1984) report on another intervention involving sixty incarcerated juvenile delinquents. Socio-moral reasoning improved significantly after eight weeks of discussion groups using moral dilemmas. Whereas 87.5 percent of the treatment group moved from Stage 2 to Stage 3, only 14.3 percent of the control group moved to Stage 3.

Wiley (1988) reports on a more modest application of moral development education in the Texas Department of Corrections. She reports that teacher style influenced gains in moral development scores. Specifically, inmate–students in prison classrooms where the teacher employed an interactive style (challenging and allowing active participation) showed significant gains in post-tests of moral development, unlike those inmate–students in classrooms where the teaching style was authoritarian and teacher-centered. Interestingly, the course content was less important. These were not "moral development" classes, but rather standard social science classes.

Arbuthnot and Gordon (1988) review findings from several studies that show that interventions with delinquents and adult offenders using socio-moral reasoning result in stage score improvement and also behavioral change. In one program for delinquents, for instance, subjects were monitored for one year, and significant differences in post-experimental problem behaviors existed between the experimental group and the control group. These authors also discuss some reasons why socio-moral reasoning development programs are not prevalent in corrections; specifically, they point to the need for organizational support, consistent organizational goals, the continuing need for expert consultation, an onsite champion of the program, and the careful selection and training of staff, among other factors.

Arbuthnot (1984) also discusses the interplay of environment and socio-moral reasoning programs. He points out that some prisoners find no rewards for expressing higher stage reasoning, much less acting upon such reasoning. Therefore, any gains made in reasoning through an intervention such as a moral analysis discussion group would be unlikely to result in changes in behavior unless the environment was more supportive of higher stages. It seems fairly clear that for such programs to work in prison, an isolated living situation must be created to insulate participants from the negative environment of the prison. Also, if the intervention is in the community, attention must be given to the social environment of the participants. If there are no social supports for stage improvements, the gains may not be expressed in behavioral choices. Arbuthnot's discussion, then, combines Kohlberg's stage theory with a type of reinforcement theory.

CONCLUSION

The two major theories of moral development are socio-moral stage theory and learning theory. These psychological approaches explain how humans come to formulate moral principles. Kohlberg's theory proposes a hierarchy of moral stages, with the highest stage holding the most perfect moral principles.

However, not everyone has the cognitive capacity or the proper exposure to discover these principles. According to Kohlberg, in the higher stages of moral development, ethical relativism must give way to universalism, and all those who reach the highest stages have discovered the true moral principles that are absolute and exist apart from humanity. Kohlberg's theory is consistent with religious ethics and ethical formalism and perhaps even utilitarianism, but probably not egoism since that theory is completely relativistic in what is considered good.

Learning theory, however, is relativistic in that it postulates human learning as neutral. There is no one true moral theory to discover; rather, the individual will adopt whatever moral theory has been rewarded. This is very consistent with egoism in that the individual is seen as engaging in behavior that provides maximum utility to the self. Egoism supports learning theory by indicating that not only do humans act in ways to benefit themselves and gain rewards, but also that behavior is defined as "good" and "moral" because of its utility to the individual.

If one believes that morals exist naturally and humans only discover their existence through reasoning ability, one might be more inclined to accept the developmental stage theory of moral development. If one believes that morals are simply what humans chose to define as such, then one might be more inclined to a learning theory perspective. However, the approaches to moral development presented in this chapter are not necessarily mutually exclusive. One can believe in a stage theory with the understanding that at lower stages, rewards are necessary to elicit moral behaviors (for example, rewarding young children for sharing). One might support learning theory but also accept the notion that there may be patterns of human beliefs occurring in later cognitive development that endorse certain moral principles resistant to reward contingencies. Thus, while small children may be fooled into thinking that practicing the piano is bad because someone was punished for it in a story, no older child or adult would be taken in by such a trick. Individuals in a totalitarian society may continue to believe in democratic ideals regardless of the lack of external rewards because of an internal cognitive stage that allows them to recognize intrinsic principles of morality.

REVIEW QUESTIONS

1. Explain Kohlberg's moral development theory. What problems do critics see with his theory?

2. Discuss learning theory as it applies to moral development. What problems do critics see with this theory?

3. How does one measure moral beliefs? What are the problems with such measurements?

4. What are the elements necessary for teaching ethics?
5. Describe some applications of moral training in corrections.

ETHICAL DILEMMAS

Situation 1

You are a rookie police officer and are riding with an F.T.O. During your shift the F.T.O. stops at a convenience store and quickly drinks four beers in the back room of the store. He is visibly affected by the beers and the smell of alcohol is very noticeable. What should you do?

Situation 2

You are a criminal justice student interning at a police department. One of the tasks you learn at the department is how to look up individuals' criminal histories on the computer. You are telling your friends about your experiences and they want you to look up their names to see what, if anything, is listed for them. You are pretty much left alone to do your work at the police department and it would be an easy matter to look up anyone. What would you tell your friends?

Situation 3

You are a senior getting close to graduation and have taken too many classes your last semester. You find yourself getting behind in classes and not doing well on tests. One of the classes requires a 30-page term paper and you simply do not have the time to complete the paper by the due date. While you are on the internet one day you see that term papers can be purchased over the internet on any topic. You ordinarily would do your own work, but the time pressure of this last semester is such that you see no other way. Do you purchase the paper and turn it in as your own?

SUGGESTED READINGS

Arbuthnot, J. 1984. "Moral Reasoning Development Programmes in Prison: Cognitive–Developmental and Critical Reasoning Approaches." *Journal of Moral Education* 13(2): 112–123.

Arbuthnot, J., and Gordon, D. 1988. "Crime and Cognition: Community Applications of Sociomoral Reasoning Development." *Criminal Justice and Behavior* 15(3): 379–393.

Gavaghan, M., Arnold, K., and Gibbs, J. 1983. "Moral Judgement in Delinquents and Nondelinquents: Recognition Versus Production Measures." *The Journal of Psychology* 114: 267–274.

Gilligan, C. 1982. *In a Different Voice: Psychological Theory and Women's Development*. Cambridge, MA: Harvard University Press.

Hickey, J., and Scharf, P. 1980. *Toward a Just Correctional System*. San Francisco: Jossey-Bass.

Kohlberg, L., and Power, C. 1984. "Moral Development, Religious Thinking and the Question of a 7th Stage." Pp. 311–372 in Kohlberg, L. (ed.), *The Psychology of Moral Development*. New York: Harper & Row.

4

❖

Justice and the Law

Chapter Objectives

Understand the origins and
components of the concept of justice.

Understand substantive and procedural justice.

Explore the relationship between justice and law.

Explore some of the rationales for and limits of law.

Understand the relationship between morality and law.

W hat is justice? What is law? Professionals in the criminal justice system serve and promote the interests of law and justice, and this chapter explores these concepts. An underlying theme will be that the ends of law and justice are different, perhaps even at times contradictory. Although law is often defined as "the administration of justice," it may very well be the case that law results in judgments that many would conclude are "unjust." Legal rights may be different than moral rights, rights may be different than needs, and needs may not be protected under either the law or some definitions of justice.

Definitions of justice include the concepts of fairness, equality, impartiality, and appropriate rewards or punishments. Justice "differs from benevolence, generosity, gratitude, friendship and compassion," according to Lucas (1980: 3). It is not something for which we should feel grateful but rather something upon which we have a right to insist. Justice should not be confused with "good." Some actions may be considered good, but not necessary for justice— for instance, the recipients of charity, benevolence, and forgiveness do not have a right to these things; therefore, it is not a question of justice to offer or

---

Definitions of Justice

- "the maintenance or administration of what is just especially by the impartial adjustment of conflicting claims or the assignment of merited rewards or punishments"
- "the administration of law; especially the establishment or determination of rights according to the rules of law or equity"
- "the quality of being just, impartial or fair"
- "the principle or ideal of just dealing or right action"

SOURCE: *Webster's Ninth New Collegiate Dictionary* (Springfield, MA: Merriam-Webster, 1984).

withhold them. Justice concerns rights and interests more often than needs. Although the idea of need is important in some discussions of justice, it is not the only component or even the primary one. It is important to understand that what is just and what is good are not necessarily the same. For instance, to give to charity is considered good, but not necessarily just. We know this because someone who is not inclined to contribute cannot be defined as unjust. Furthermore, if I contributed $100 to the American Heart Association and $1 to the Republican party, I could not be considered as acting unjustly even though I did not contribute equally to both of them. Even if the Republican party needed the money more than the American Heart Association did, it would not be an injustice to contribute less money to the Republicans, because they have no right to expect anything from me at all.

People can often be described as displaying unique combinations of generosity and selfishness, fairness and self-interest. Some writers insist that the need for justice arises from the nature of human beings and the fact that they are not naturally generous, openhearted, or fair. If we behaved all the time in accordance with those virtues, we would have no need for justice. On the other hand, if humans were always to act in selfish, grasping, and unfair ways, then we would be unable to follow the rules and principles of justice. Therefore, we uphold and cherish the concept of justice in our society because it is the mediator between people's essential selfishness and generosity; in other words, it is the result of a logical and rational acceptance of the concept of fairness in human relations (Hume, cited in Feinberg and Gross, 1977: 75).

Justice does not ordinarily regulate the sphere of private relations, only the rights and interests present in public interactions and in the interaction between the individual and the state. Justice does not dictate a perfect world, but one in which people live up to agreements and are treated fairly. Galston (1980: 282) described justice as follows:

> more than voluntary agreement, [but] . . . less than perfect community. It allows us to retain our separate existences and our self-regard; it does not ask us to share the pleasures, pains, and sentiments of others. Justice is intelligent self-regard, modified, by the requirements of rational consistency.

ORIGINS OF THE CONCEPT OF JUSTICE

Justice originates in the Greek word *dike,* which is associated with the concept of everything staying in its assigned place or natural role (Feinberg and Gross, 1977: i). This idea is closely associated with Plato's and Aristotle's definitions of justice. Even today, some writers describe justice as "the demand for order: everything in its proper place or relation" (Feibleman, 1985: 23).

According to Plato, justice consists of maintaining the societal status quo. Justice is one of four civic virtues, the others being wisdom, temperance, and courage (Feibleman, 1985: 173). In an ordered state, everyone performs his or her role and does not interfere with others. Each person's role is the one for which the individual is best fitted by nature; thus, *natural law* is upheld. Moreover, it is in everyone's self-interest to have this ordered existence continue because it provides the means to the good life—appropriate human happiness. Plato's society is a class system, based on innate abilities, rather than a caste system, which differentiates by accidents of birth.

Aristotle believed that justice exists in the law and that the law is "the unwritten custom of all or the majority of men which draws a distinction between what is honorable and what is base" (Feibleman, 1985: 174). Aristotle distinguished *distributive justice* from *rectificatory justice*. Distributive justice concerns what measurement should be used to allocate society's resources. Aristotle believed in the idea of proportionality along with equality. In Aristotle's conception of justice, the lack of freedom and opportunity for some people—slaves and women, for instance—did not conflict with justice, as long as the individual was in the role in which, by nature, he or she belonged. In other words, unequal people should get unequal shares.

In contrast, our form of government is founded on the idea of equality. Rights, privileges, and (supposedly) opportunities are afforded to all without regard to race, creed, sex, or wealth, as protected by the equal protection clause of the Fourteenth Amendment and referred to elsewhere in our Constitution. Although these ideals may not describe the reality of this country's treatment of women, minority groups, and the poor, no one doubts that the ideals themselves are part of this country's consciousness, history, and tradition.

Rectificatory justice, or *commutative justice,* concerns business deals where unfair advantage or undeserved harm has occurred. Justice demands remedies or compensations to the injured party. Aristotle's notions of justice, according to one writer, were primarily concerned with preserving an existing order of rights and possessions (Raphael, 1980: 80). Again, however, the problem of applying notions of fairness, proportionality, and equal treatment emerges. These elements of justice are still with us today.

COMPONENTS OF JUSTICE

Justice can be separated into distributive, corrective, and commutative justice (Feinberg and Gross, 1977: 53). *Distributive justice* is concerned with the allocation of the goods and burdens of society to its respective members. Rewards and benefits from society include wealth, education, entitlement programs, and health care. Because some people get less than others, it may be that these goods are not distributed fairly. Burdens and responsibilities must also be dis-

---

QUERY

Do you believe that "who you are" makes a difference in today's system of justice? Give examples.

tributed among the members of society; for instance, decisions must be made about who should fight in war, who should take care of the elderly and infirm, who should pay taxes, and how much each should pay. The difficulties in deciding how to divide these goods and burdens and what each person deserves form the discussion of distributive justice.

Corrective justice concerns the determination and methods of punishments. Again, the concept of desert emerges. In corrective justice, we speak of offenders getting what they deserve, but this time the desert is punishment rather than goods. The difficulty, of course, is in determining what are "just deserts."

Finally, *commutative justice* is associated with transactions and interchanges where one person feels unfairly treated. The process of determining a fair resolution—for example, when one is cheated in a business deal, or when a contract is not completed—calls into play the concepts of commutative justice. The method for determining a fair and just resolution to the conflict depends on particular concepts such as rights and interests.

A continuing theme in any discussion of justice—whether it be distributive, corrective, or commutative justice—is the concept of *fairness*. In the example concerning the Heart Foundation and the Republican party, giving to one and not to the other was not considered unjust because neither group had a right to expect anything. However, other distributions are scrutinized under a "fairness" doctrine. For instance, parents ordinarily give each child the same allowance unless differences between the children, such as age or duties, warrant different amounts. In fact, children are sensitive to issues of fairness long before they grasp more abstract ideas of justice. No doubt every parent has heard the plaintive cry "It's not fair—Johnny got more than I did" or "It's not fair—she always gets to sit in the front seat!" What children are sensing is unequal and, therefore, unfair treatment. The concept of fairness is inextricably tied to equality and impartiality.

Another theme of justice is the concept of *equality*. There is a predisposition to demand equity or equal shares for all. In contrast to the concept of equal shares is the idea of needs or deserts; in other words, we should get what we need or, alternatively, what we deserve by status, merit, or other reasons. The concept of equality is also present in retributive justice in the belief that similar cases should be treated equally—for instance, that all individuals who commit a similar crime should be similarly punished. Again, the alternative argument is that sometimes it serves the purpose of justice to treat similar crimes differently because of mediating or aggravating circumstances. Are there ever any situations where people are truly equal? If we want to distribute opportunities equally to equals, how would we measure equality? Do we assume that everyone starts off with the same skills, backgrounds, and family circumstances, or must we not take into account individual differences, societal goals, and a host of other factors in decisions such as whether to employ affirmative action plans, individualized sentences, and social services?

The concept of *impartiality* is at the core of our system of criminal justice. Our symbol of justice represents, with her blindfold, impartiality toward special groups and, with her scales, proportionally just punishments. Impartiality implies fair and equal treatment of all without discrimination and bias. It is hard to reconcile the ideal of "blind justice" with the individualized justice of the "treatment ethic" since one can hardly look at individual circumstance if one is blind toward the particulars of the case. Indeed, most would argue, individual differences and culpabilities should be taken into consideration—if not during a finding of guilty or innocence, then at least when sentencing occurs. The blindfold may signify no special treatment for the rich or the powerful, but then it must also signify no special consideration for the young, the misled, or those operating under extraordinary circumstances.

Distributive Justice

The concept of the appropriate and just allocation of society's goods and interests is one of the central themes in all discussions of justice. According to one writer, justice always involves "rightful possession" (Galston, 1980: 117–119). The goods that one might possess include economic goods (income or property), opportunities for development (education or citizenship), and recognition (honor or status). Obviously, if these items are in plentiful supply and everyone has enough of them, the concept of justice is not relevant. It is only in a condition of scarcity that a problem arises with the allocation of goods. Two valid claims to possession are *need* and *desert*. The principles of justice involve the application of these claims to specific entitlements.

Different writers have presented various proposals for deciding issues of entitlement. Lucas (1980: 164–165) lists several different distribution theories. One proposed by Ross would distribute goods to everyone according to merit, to everyone according to performance, to everyone according to need, to everyone according to ability, and to everyone according to rank and station. Vlastos proposes the following distribution: to each according to his need, to each according to his worth, to each according to his merit, to each according to his work, and to each according to agreements he has made. Rescher's theory would distribute goods to each as equals, to each according to her needs, to each according to her efforts and sacrifices, to each according to her actual productive contributions, to each according to the requirements of the common good, and to each according to a valuation of her socially useful services in terms of their scarcity in the essentially economic terms of supply and demand. Chaim Perelman's principles of distributive justice dictate the following: to each the same thing, to each according to his merits, to each according to his needs, to each according to his rank, and to each according to his legal entitlement (Raphael, 1980: 90).

The difficulty lies in determining the weight of each of the factors in a just allocation of benefits. The various theories can be categorized as egalitarian, Marxist, libertarian, or utilitarian, depending on which factors are emphasized (Beauchamp, 1982). Egalitarian theories start with the basic premise of equality or equal shares for all. Marxist theories focus on need over desert or entitlement. Libertarian theories promote freedom from interference by government in social and economic spheres; therefore, merit, entitlement, and productive contributions are given weight over need or equal shares. Utilitar-

---

After Cash Rains Down in Miami, Finders Remain Quiet Keepers

MIAMI—Police went from door to door through one of Miami's poorest neighborhoods Thursday, asking people to admit they scooped up some of the half million dollars that spilled from a Brinks truck and, if they did, to give it back.

Residents generally responded with a good laugh.

"Nobody's going to tell them," said Debbie, a resident of Overtown who, like most, would only give her first name.

"This is a once-in-a-lifetime thing," added another resident named George. "This couldn't happen to a more *deserving* neighborhood."

Thousands of dollars in coins, bills and food stamps rained down on the street Wednesday morning after an armored Brinks truck carrying $3.7 million overturned on an Interstate 95 overpass.

People swarmed over the area, digging money out of the dirt and scooping it off the street, stuffing bags, boxes and pockets before police took charge. An estimated $500,000 vanished.

Thursday, police knocked on 75 doors urging people to turn in the money, no questions asked, before a two-day grace period ends at noon Saturday. Nobody did.

After the grace period expires, police plan to seek television news videotape to aid them in identifying money grabbers. Those caught with more than $1,000 could face grand theft charges.

SOURCE: Associated Press. Reported in *Austin American-Statesman,* 10 Jan. 1997: A7. Emphasis added. Reprinted with permission of the Associated Press.

Which, if any, system supports the individual's justification that he or she "deserved" the stolen money?

---

ian theories attempt to maximize benefits for individuals and society in a mixed emphasis on entitlements and needs.

How do the theories apply to the wide disparities in salaries found in this country? For instance, a professional athlete's salary is sometimes one hundred times greater than a police officer's salary. Which principle might justify this discrepancy? Libertarian theories would shrug at such disparity; Marxist theories would not. Of the few distribution systems mentioned above, only the one proposed by Ross might support such a wide salary differential. Obviously, few would agree that workers in all jobs and all professions should be paid the same amount of money. First, not many people would be willing to put up with the long hours and many years of schooling needed in some professions if there were no incentives. Second, some types of jobs demand a greater degree of responsibility and involve greater stress than others. On the other hand, we can readily see that some remuneration is entirely out of proportion to an analysis of worth—for instance, it is hard to see how any corporate executive could deserve $10 million for one year's work. The same argument applies to athletes, rock musicians, and actors.

If we are primarily concerned with performance and ability, why do we not pay individual workers in the same job category differently if one works

---

QUERY

Determine what is a fair salary for these professions and occupations. Propose an average salary, balancing such factors as seniority and education.

Nurse: Electrician:

Elementary schoolteacher: Sanitation worker:

Police officer: Prison guard:

College professor: Software engineer:

City council member: Lawyer:

Secretary: Judge:

Now compare your responses to those of others. Is there general consensus on salaries for these positions? Compare your responses to published figures (you can find this information in a library or the career center of your university).

---

harder than the other? Although some production jobs pay according to how much is produced (the piecework payment method), most of us are paid according to a step-grade position, earning roughly what others in the same position earn. Which is the fairer system of payment? What about people who produce less on the piecework system because they are helping their coworkers or taking more time to produce higher quality products? Is it fair for them to earn less? If all work were paid according to production, how would one pay secretaries, teachers, or customer service workers, whose production is more difficult to measure?

Should we pay people according to need, as Marxist distribution systems propose? This sounds fair in one sense because people would get only what they needed to survive at some predetermined level. In that case, a person with two children would earn more than a person with no children. In the past, this was the argument used by employers to explain why they would favor men over women in hiring, promotions, and pay increases—because men had families to support and women did not. Two arguments were used against this type of discriminatory treatment; the first was that women deserve as much as men if they are of equal ability and performance; the second was that women also, more often than not, have to support families. These two arguments emphasize different principles of justice. The first is based on an equal-deserts argument; the second rests on an equal-needs argument.

Although race- and gender-based discrepancies in wages and hiring patterns are becoming a thing of the past, there are still continuing issues of fairness in employment rights. One such issue is family or pregnancy leave. The principle of justice that is being used to support the right to take leave (whether it be the unpaid leave mandated by Congress or paid leave) is not worth, merit, ability, or performance; rather, it is need. Does justice dictate an employee's right to family leave? This is not equal treatment (since we're discriminating against people who do not fit any category of the family leave bill, but desire leave for other reasons). In fact, this may be a question of *good-*

QUERY

You are on a promotion committee to recommend to the chief of police a candidate for a captain's position. All are lieutenants and have received similar scores in the objective tests available for the position. The candidates:

■ A thirty-nine-year-old woman who has served in this police department for nine years and has obtained a college degree and a master's degree by going to school at night. She has spent relatively little time in her career on the street (moving quickly to juvenile, community service, and DARE positions).

■ A forty-six-year-old white male who has also had experience in command positions in the army before joining the police force. He has fifteen years of experience—all in patrol positions—and has a college degree.

■ A forty-year-old Hispanic male with ten years of experience. He has been very active with the community; several community groups have endorsed him and demand that there be Hispanic representation on the command staff. He also has strong support among Hispanic officers, serving as their association president. He has a two-year college degree.

Who would you endorse? Why? If you need more information, what type of information would you want?

---

ness rather than *justice*. That is, it is a social good (good for society, good for the individual), but it is not a right. On the other hand, some people insist that there is a *natural right* to productive employment and also the ability to have a family; therefore, there is a state duty to provide adequate, affordable child care for workers and leave for pregnancy and sickness.

Just distribution of other goods in society is also problematic. Welfare is one example of this difficulty. Recently, the federal government has considerably scaled back federal programs with the expectation that state governments and private philanthropic organizations would assume more responsibility. What may occur is poor people in some states will receive drastically fewer benefits. The principle of need is the rationale we use to take from the financially solvent, through taxes, and give to those who have little or nothing. But what about those who have nothing because they choose not to work? There is a widespread perception that many on welfare rolls take advantage of the system. If there are such people, justice may dictate that they be dropped from welfare rolls. Few would argue that single mothers with children need assistance, but if a young woman has had several children with no visible means of support, depending on welfare to pay for the birth and continued support of each child, when does need end and abuse begin? Does justice dictate that we continue to give aid, or does it justify punishing her for taking advantage of the system? And if we decide that she does not deserve our help, how do we view her innocent children? Needs and rights are both part of this discussion. There is a belief that every individual has a *right* to bear children and that the state should never interfere with childbearing decisions. In this country we condemn those governments that coerce people to have more or fewer children than they desire. Courts take great care to protect our "privacy rights" concerning childbearing and child rearing. If we have a natural, inherent right to bear children, do we also have a right to state assistance in feeding and clothing them? When does this *right* turn into a *need* that can be denied?

Another "good" that society distributes to its members is opportunity. Many people would argue that education (at least at the university level) is a privilege that should be reserved for those few who have the ability and the drive to succeed. However, the educational system of this country is fundamentally democratic. Not only do we have guaranteed, in fact compulsory, education at elementary and secondary levels; we also have open admission to some universities. Moreover, remedial courses are available to help those without the skills to meet college standards. In fact, massive amounts of time and money are devoted to helping some students improve their skills and ultimately graduate from college. Recently, Texas state legislators have proposed that there be different fee structures at state universities and colleges for those with more than 180 college credit hours. The reason for this legislation is that tuition and fees only cover a portion of the cost of providing university education, and the rest is made up by taxpayers. The higher tuition costs for those with credit hours over what is necessary for a degree are designed to make these students pay more for their education after a certain level of education at state expense has been exceeded. Is this fair? What about reduced or waived tuition costs for the elderly? What distribution scheme supports such state initiatives?

There is also a compelling argument that although the *ideal* of education is democratic, the *reality* is that because of unequal tax bases, school districts are incredibly unequal and distribute the opportunity of education unequally. Although some school districts have swimming pools, computers in every classroom, and teachers with specialized education, other school districts make do with donated textbooks and buildings that are poorly heated and ventilated. State legislation to equalize school districts' funding by "taking away" from well-off school districts raises the ire of parents who move to expensive areas for the express purpose of providing an excellent education for their children. Then there are those parents who pay school taxes and then pay tuition to send their children to a private school to provide a better education for them. Should they receive some reimbursement of their taxes, or should they be expected to pay twice for the privilege of private schools?

It is difficult to reconcile the concepts of opportunity and ability. Affirmative action attempts to provide opportunities to groups that historically have been discriminated against—blacks, women, Hispanics. Now those groups that have been favored in the past—white males—feel that they are the new victims of discrimination. Some feel that taking affirmative steps to increase opportunities for minority groups has simply transferred unfair treatment to another group. What is acceptable to overcome previous discrimination? Unfortunately, a promise to hire "the best person for the job" is not enough, because historical and institutionalized discrimination will take many years to overcome. For instance, underfunded schools produce students who are less qualified, and then these individuals are denied jobs based on their lack of abilities. To assume that one is eliminating discrimination by hiring on the basis of individual abilities does not solve the problem of blocked access; it merely perpetuates it in a more subtle way. Recent Supreme Court decisions are ruling against affirmative action attempts, such as race-based criteria in law school and university admissions. States are also passing legislation to bar hiring decisions, promotions, and admission to state schools based on race. The same "equal protection" rights used to pass civil rights legislation in the 1960s are now being used to dismantle these programs. What effect such decisions will have on access to the opportunity of education remains to be seen. Some predict that the progress we have seen in educational and economic success for historically blocked minority groups will be negated.

This controversy only points out the extreme difficulty of determining a just distribution of goods. The fact that everyone is not equal, in terms of ability, performance, motivation, need, or any other measure, is easy enough to agree on. Very few people would argue that everyone in every position should receive the same salary, get the same education, and achieve the same status in society. On the other hand, to acknowledge inequality puts us in the position of distributing goods and other interests on the basis of other criteria, and it is here that problems arise. When injustice occurs, we sense it on the basis of fairness. We feel somehow that it is not fair that there are starving children and conspicuous wealth in the same country or the same world. We sense unfairness when people work hard yet still struggle to get along on poverty wages, while star actors or athletes make millions of dollars largely through luck or for contributions to societal welfare that seem trivial.

Another good to be distributed is status or recognition. Should a person who struggles to achieve a certain skill be rewarded more than a person who achieves the same skill with little effort? Should a person who struggled through a terrible childhood and achieved a modest measure of success be more highly regarded than a person who was born to status and privilege? Should we expect more from certain people than from others?

The various distributional theories outlined earlier include everything from status to societal need as bases for distributional equations. Some are obviously contradictory—for instance, how would one reconcile distribution according to equality and legal entitlement? Obviously, some people have much more than others and are entitled to these goods through inheritance or contract, but do they have a moral right to the goods as well? Does a corporate executive have a moral right to a multi-million-dollar salary while thousands of workers in the same company have been laid off or fired due to "downsizing"? Supply and demand might explain some extreme differences in economic rewards (such as athletes, musicians, and actors), but should they outweigh other factors such as merit or common good? Although rank and status certainly were part of Aristotle's and Plato's distributional equation, should we continue to include them as legitimate and fair criteria for distribution? On the other hand, even in the most egalitarian and democratic societies, individual differences in status and rank are accepted.

John Rawls's theory of justice proposes a basically equal distribution unless a different distribution would benefit the disadvantaged. Rawls believes that any inequalities of society should be to the benefit of those who are least advantaged (Rawls, 1971: 15). He proposes the following (cited in Kaplan, 1976: 114):

1. Each person is to have an equal right to the most extensive total system of basic liberties compatible with a similar system of liberty for all.

2. Social and economic inequalities are to be arranged so that they are both reasonably expected to be to everyone's advantage; and attached to positions and offices open to all (except when inequality is to the advantage of those least well-off).

Of course, Rawls has his critics. First, Rawls uses a heuristic device that he calls the *veil of ignorance* to explain the idea that people will develop fair principles of distribution only if they are ignorant of their position in society, since they may just as easily be "have-nots" as "haves" (Rawls, 1971: 12). Thus, justice and fairness are in everyone's rational self-interest since, under the veil of ignorance, one's own situation is unknown, and the best and most rational distribution is the one most equal to all. However, critics argue that the veil of ignorance is not sufficient to counteract humanity's basic selfishness: given the chance, people would still seek to maximize their own gain even if doing so involved a risk (Kaplan, 1976: 199). Second, critics argue that Rawls's preference toward those least well-off is contrary to the good of society. Rawls states that "all social values—liberty and opportunity, income and wealth and the bases of self-respect—are to be distributed equally unless an unequal distribution of any, or all, of these values is to the advantage of the least favored" (quoted in Sterba, 1980: 32). Critics believe that this preference is ultimately dysfunctional for society since if those least well-off have the advantages of society preferentially, there will be no incentive for others to excel. Some also argue that Rawls is wrong to ignore desert in his distribution of goods (Galston, 1980: 3).

In contrast to Rawls, Sterba (1980: 55) offers these principles to follow in distributive justice:

1. **Principle of Need.** Each person is guaranteed the primary social goods that are necessary to meet the normal costs of satisfying his basic needs in the society in which he or she lives.

2. **Principle of Appropriation and Exchange.** Additional primary goods are to be distributed on the basis of private appropriation and voluntary agreement and exchange.

3. **Principle of Minimal Contribution.** A minimal contribution to society is required of those who are capable of contributing when social and economic resources are insufficient to provide the guaranteed minimum to everyone in society without requiring that contribution or when the

---

QUERY

Do you believe we should have a national system of health care for everyone in this country? Why do you think that the concept has met with so much resistance by Congress and voters?

---

incentive to contribute to society would otherwise be adversely affected, so that persons would not maximize their contribution to society.

4. **Principle of Saving.** The rate of saving for each generation should represent its fair contribution toward realizing and maintaining a society in which all the members can fully enjoy the benefit of its just institution.

If we apply Sterba's distribution principles to health care in this country, we must agree that every citizen deserves a basic standard of health care necessary for survival (principle of need). Further, if an individual has enough resources to purchase additional care over this basic level, then that should be allowed to benefit both the purchaser, who would receive superior care, and the supplier, who would earn profit (principle of appropriation and exchange). Basic health care should be paid for by everyone according to ability to pay— that is, citizens should pay taxes and medical professionals should be required to provide some level of basic services at cost (principle of minimal contribution). Finally, there should be an upper limit on how much can be charged above cost by surgeons, hospitals, and other medical care providers. The expense of such services has increased so astronomically that it cannot be justified by fair profit principles and it endangers all citizens' ability to apportion their income in a way that ensures financial solvency (principle of saving).

An Aristotelian conception of distributive justice would encompass differential status and opportunity. Libertarian systems emphasize entitlements and merit. Marxist theories emphasize need. Current theories of justice, such as Rawls's theory, try to compromise between need and merit by balancing fairness with a preference toward those who have less. Relating these theories of justice to the ethical systems discussed in Chapter 2, we see that some are consistent only with certain theories of justice. For instance, the ethics of care is consistent with a Marxist theory of justice, since both emphasize need. Utilitarian theories try to maximize societal good, so some balance of need and merit would be necessary to provide the incentive to produce. Ethical formalism is solely concerned with rights; thus, issues of societal good or others' needs may not be as important as the individual's rights (however those might be defined). Rawls's theory is both utilitarian and Kantian since it demands a basic level of individual rights but also attempts to establish a preference toward those who have less, for the good of all society. Interestingly, how one resolves these questions concerning distributive justice has some relevance to the discussion of corrective or punitive justice, which will be discussed in the next section.

Corrective Justice

As mentioned before, corrective justice is concerned with dispensing punishment. As with distributive justice, the concepts of equality and desert, fairness and impartiality are important. Two components of corrective justice should be differentiated. *Substantive justice* involves the concept of just deserts, or how one determines a fair punishment for a particular offense; *procedural justice* concerns the steps we must take before administering punishment.

Substantive Justice   What is a fair punishment for the crime of murder? Many believe the only just punishment is death, since that is the only punishment of a degree equal to the harm caused by the offender. Others might say life imprisonment is equitable and fair. One's beliefs about what is fair punishment are usually related to one's perception of the seriousness of the crime. More-serious crimes deserve more-serious punishments.

Since the beginning of codified law, just punishment has always been perceived as punishment set in relation to the degree of harm incurred. This was a natural outcome of the early, remedial forms of justice, which provided remedies for wrongs. For instance, the response to a theft of a slave or the killing of a horse involved compensation. The only just solution was the return or replacement of the slave or horse. This remedial or compensatory system of justice contrasts with a punishment system: the first system forces the offender to provide compensation to the victim or the victim's family, and the second apportions punishment based on the degree of seriousness of the crime suffered by the victim. They both involve a measurement of the harm, but in the first case measurement is taken to adequately compensate the victim, and in the second it is to punish the offender. In a punishment-based system, the victim is a peripheral figure. The state, rather than the victim, becomes the central figure—serving both as victim and as punisher (Karmen, 1984).

Exercise

Rank the following crimes in order of seriousness, with 1 being the most serious and 14 being the least serious. Compare your rank orderings with those of others.

sexual assault (with force)	death caused by drunken driving
embezzlement of $15,000	tax evasion—$15,000
shoplifting of $15,000 of merchandise	assault (broken bones)
robbery of $15,000	sexual molestation (no penetration)
toxic waste dumping—damage unknown	murder (during barroom brawl)
perjury	drug possession (marijuana)
solicitation	murder (by one who solicited a contract killer)

Retributive Justice The concept of retributive justice is one of balance. The criminal must suffer pain or loss proportional to what the victim was forced to suffer. In an extreme form, this retribution takes the form of *lex talionis,* a vengeance-oriented justice concerned with equal retaliation ("an eye for an eye; tooth for a tooth"). A milder form is *lex salica,* which allows compensation; the harm can be repaired by payment or atonement (Allen and Simonsen, 1986: 4). A punishment equal to a harm is sometimes hard to determine. A life for a life might be easy to measure, but most cases involve other forms of harm. In other types of victimizations, how does one determine the amount of physical or mental pain suffered by the victim, or financial loss such as lost income or future loss? And if the offender cannot pay back financial losses, how does one equate imprisonment with fines or restitution?

Historically, corporal and capital punishment were used for both property crime and violent crime. With the development of the penitentiary system in the early 1800s, punishment became equated with terms of imprisonment rather than amounts of physical pain. In fact, the greater ease of measuring out prison sentences probably contributed to these sentences' success and rapid acceptance. One may sentence an offender to one, two, or five years, depending on the seriousness of the crime. Imprisonment not only was considered more humane than corporal punishment; it was also incapacitating, allowing the offender to reflect on his crime and repent. Further, it did not elicit sympathy for the offender from the populace.

On the other hand, a term of imprisonment is much harder to equate to a particular crime. While one can intuitively understand the natural balance of a life for a life, $10 for $10, or even a beating for an assault, it is much harder to argue that a burglary of $100 is equal to a year in prison or that an assault is equal to a term of two years. A year in prison is hard to define. Research on prison adjustment indicates that a year means different things to different people. For some, it may be no more than mildly inconvenient; for others, it may lead to suicide or mental illness (Toch, 1977).

In addition to retribution, imprisonment was tied to reform of the criminal offender. Reform or rehabilitation may be a laudable goal, but it has no place in a retributive scheme of justice. Retributive punishment is based on balancing the victim's harm with the offender's pain or suffering. Treatment involves no such balance; therefore, there is no retributive rationale for its existence. Philosophical support for treatment of criminal offenders is found in utilitarianism.

Retributive justice is not a simple equation, since other factors are taken into account in addition to the seriousness of the crime. For instance, *mens rea* (intent) has long been considered a necessary element in determining culpability. Those who are incapable of rational thought—the insane, the very young—are said to be incapable of committing wrong morally or legally; therefore, to punish them would be an injustice under a retributive framework. Other situations might prove to involve partial responsibility—for example, the presence of compulsion, coercion, or irresistible impulse. In these cases, most people feel that justice is not compromised by a lesser amount of punishment, even though the harm to the victim is obviously the same as if the offender had acted deliberately and intentionally. In this sense, we see that the amount of punishment is not solely measured by the amount of harm to the victim but involves characteristics of the offender as well.

Just punishment may also involve considering the participation of the victim. *Victim precipitation* refers to the victim's role in the criminal event. Some people fear that this examination has the potential to "blame the victim" for the crime rather than the offender. Nevertheless, some research indicates that the victim plays a significant part in some types of crime (Karmen, 1984: 78). Retributive justice would consider instances where the victim "caused" victimization by enraging or threatening the offender, or precipitated victimization by engaging in careless or dangerous behavior. This does not mean that individuals who go out late at night deserve to be robbed or that women who are out alone drinking deserve to be raped. Victim precipitation refers to those situations where, for instance, batterers taunt their victims to shoot them and they do. In this case, the batterer is ostensibly the victim because he has been shot, but an examination of his conduct would reveal that the so-called offender is also a victim and that the batterer's own behavior largely contributed to his victimization. In barroom brawls, pure luck often determines who becomes the injured and who becomes the offender. In these situations, the victim actually participates in the criminal event. We might allow for partial culpability, since the responsibility for the crime must be shared by both the offender and the victim. We see, then, that in a retributive justice system we must look not only at the seriousness of the crime to determine punishment, but also at the actions and mental states of both the offender and the victim.

Other factors also play a part in determining punishment, some of which would not be consistent with retributive justice. In earlier systems of justice, the status of the victim was important in determining the level of harm and thus the punishment. Nobles were more important than freemen, who were more important than slaves. Men were more important than women. Punishment for offenders was weighted according to these designations of the worth of the victim. Although we have no formal system for weighting punishment in this way and have rejected the worth of the victim as a rationale for punishment (except in a few cases, such as assaulting a police officer), many feel that our justice system still follows this practice informally. People argue that harsher sentences are given when the victim is white than when the victim is black and when the victim is rich as opposed to poor. In a similar manner, many argue that the justice system discriminates unfairly and unjustly against characteristics of the offender. Many believe that offenders receive harsher sentences because of their race, background, or income.

Whether or not these charges are true, it is important to recognize that earlier systems of justice, including the Greek and Roman, approved of and rationalized such discriminations as perfectly fair and just. Our system of justice has rejected these discriminations even while holding on to others—specifically, intent, partial responsibility, and, to some extent, victim precipitation. It is difficult, if not impossible, for everyone to agree upon a fair and equitable measurement of punishment when one allows for exceptions, mediating factors, and partial responsibility. That is why there is so little agreement on what is fair punishment. Even when two defendants are involved in a single crime, our system of justice can support different punishments under a retributive rationale.

In Rawls's theory of justice, retributive punishment is limited in the following way (quoted in Hickey and Scharf, 1980: 168):

> . . . the liberties of a person . . . may only be reduced, compared with the liberties of other people, when it is for the good of the least advantaged, considered from the "veil of ignorance" assumption of not knowing what role one will occupy.

This statement means that only when punishment can be shown to benefit the least advantaged (the victim) can it be justified; when the advantage changes (when the victim has been repaid), then punishment must cease. Hickey and Scharf (1980: 169) point out that this limitation is similar to that proposed by Norval Morris:

1. We must punish only to the extent that the loss of liberty would be agreeable were one not to know whether one were to be the criminal, the victim, or a member of the general public, and

2. The loss of liberty must be justified as the minimal loss consistent with the maintenance of the same liberty among others.

In both these propositions, the moral limit of punishment is reached when what is done to the criminal equals the extent of his or her forfeiture, as determined by the crime.

One other issue that must be addressed here is the concept of *mercy*. Seemingly inconsistent with any definition of retributive justice, mercy is, nevertheless, always associated with the concept. From the very beginnings of law, there has also been the element of forgiveness. Even tribal societies had special allowances and clemencies for offenders, usually granted by the king or chief. For instance, the concept of *sanctuary* allowed a person respite from punishment as long as she or he was within the confines of church grounds. Benefit of clergy, dispensation, and even probation are examples of mercy by the court. However, it must be made clear that mercy is different from just deserts. If, because of circumstances of the crime, of the criminal, or of the victim, the offender deserves little or no punishment, then that is what he or she deserves, and it is not mercy to give a suspended sentence or probation. On the other hand, if an offender truly deserves a period of imprisonment and the court forgives the offense and releases the offender with only a warning, then the individual has been granted mercy.

Murphie (1988) proposes that retributive emotions derive from self-respect, that it is a healthy response to an injury to feel angry, resentful, and, yes, even vengeful. However, it is also acceptable to forgive and extend mercy to one's assailant, if the forgiveness extends not from a lack of self-respect, but

---

Shakespeare, *The Merchant of Venice*

Portia (Act IV, Scene i)

> The quality of mercy is not strained;
> It droppeth as the gentle rain from heaven
> Upon the place beneath. It is twice blest;
> It blesseth him that gives and him that takes.
> 'Tis mightiest in the mightiest; it becomes
> The throned monarch better than his crown.
> His scepter shows the force of temporal power,
> The attribute to awe and majesty,
> Wherein doth sit the dread and fear of kings;
> But mercy is above this scept'red sway;
> It is enthroned in the hearts of kings;
> It is an attribute to God himself,
> And earthly power doth then show likest God's
> When mercy seasons justice. Therefore, Jew,
> Though justice be thy plea, consider this,
> That, in the course of justice, none of us
> Should see salvation. We do pray for mercy,
> And that same prayer doth teach us all to render
> The deeds of mercy. I have spoke thus much
> To mitigate the justice of thy plea,
> Which if thou follow, this strict court of Venice
> Must needs give sentence 'gainst the merchant there.

SOURCE: *William Shakespeare: The Complete Works* (Baltimore: Penguin Books, 1969).

Note: *The Merchant of Venice* employs many of the issues we discuss in this chapter. Here the plea for mercy emphasizes the relationship between justice and mercy. Shylock's demand for law (his pound of flesh) and the unwillingness of the court to deny it illustrate how law sometimes has little to do with justice. Then Portia's surprise argument—that because Shylock's contract mentioned only flesh and not blood, no blood could be spilled—is a perfect illustration of the law's slavish devotion to rule over substance. As a legal trick, this interpretation of a contract has not been bested yet in fiction or reality.

---

rather from a moral system. For instance, he points out that many religions include the concept of "turning the other cheek" and extending mercy to enemies. Mercy is appropriate when the offender is divorced in some way from her or his offense. One way to a separation is true repentance. Murphie (1988: 10) summarizes the points of mercy as follows:

1. It is an autonomous moral virtue (separate from justice).

2. It is a virtue that tempers or "seasons" justice—something that one adds to justice in order to dilute it and to make it stronger.

3. It is never owed to anyone as a right or a matter of desert or justice.

4. As a moral virtue, it derives its value at least in part from the fact that it flows from love or compassion while not losing sight of the importance of justice.

5. It requires a generally retributive outlook on punishment and responsibility.

Therefore, mercy is related to justice but is not necessarily a part of it. It is connected with a change in the offender—typically, there must be repentance—and it is connected with a quality of the victim—some form of compassion, charity, or benevolence. Other questions of mercy remain, however. Who has the right to extend mercy? At times, victims or the families of victims are upset with a sentencing judge because of the lenient sentence administered to the offender. Should victims be the only ones who have the right to give the gift of mercy?

Utilitarian Justice We have been discussing retributive justice as a rationale for and means to determine punishment. However, other rationales also support punishment. The alternative to retribution is utilitarianism. Whereas the goal of a retributive framework of justice is to restore a natural balance by righting a wrong or neutralizing criminal gain with an equal amount of loss or pain, the goal of a utilitarian framework is to benefit society by administering punishment to deter offenders from future crime. Beccaria (1738–1794) and Bentham (1748–1832) provide a utilitarian rationale for proportionality in punishment. Punishment should be based on the seriousness of the crime: the more serious the crime (or the greater the reward the crime offered the criminal), the more serious and severe the punishment should be.

A utilitarian framework of justice would determine punishment on the basis of deterrence. Bentham's *hedonistic calculus,* for instance, is concerned with measuring the gain of the crime so that the amount of threatened pain could be set to deter people from committing that crime; the goal is deterrence, not balance. Measurement is important in both retributive and utilitarian rationales of justice. In a retributive system, we measure to determine the proportional amount of punishment to right the wrong; in a utilitarian system, we measure to determine the amount of punishment needed to deter. We see that under the utilitarian framework, there is no necessity for perfect balance. In fact, one must threaten a slightly higher degree of pain or punishment than the gain or pleasure that comes from the criminal act; otherwise, there would be no deterrent value in the punishment.

When one argues for capital punishment on the basis of the protection of society, one is arguing from a utilitarian framework. When one argues for longer punishments for repeat offenders, one is also arguing the utilitarian philosophy. In some cases, retributive notions of justice and utilitarian notions of justice may conflict. If a criminal is sure to commit more crime, the utilitarian could justify holding him in prison as a means of incapacitation, but to hold him past the time "equal" to his crime would be seen as an injustice under a retributive system. Treatment, as mentioned before, is acceptable under a utilitarian justice system and irrelevant and unsupported by a retributive one. Deterrence is the primary determinant of justice under a utilitarian system, but desert is the only determinant of a retributive system of justice.

Procedural Justice We turn now to the procedure of administering punishment—our legal system. *Justice* and *law* are not synonymous; most writers describe law as objective and justice as subjective. Law includes the procedures and rules used to determine punishment or resolve disputes. It is a system of rules for human relations—the "whole field of the principles laid down, the decisions reached in accordance with them, and the procedures whereby the principles are applied to individual cases" (Raphael, 1980: 74). There is, then, a differentiation between justice and law. Justice is a concept of fairness; law is a system of rules.

The law is an imperfect system. Fuller (1969: 39) explores the weaknesses of law and describes ways that the procedure of law may fail to achieve justice. Possible failures include a failure to achieve rules at all so that every decision must be made on its own; a failure to publicize rules; retroactive application of law, which abuses the concept of justice; the existence of contradictory rules; too-frequent changes in rules; and a lack of consistency between the rules and their actual administration. These failures weaken the law's ability to resolve disputes or control conflict in an objective and fair manner.

Some argue that because of the legal system's inability to determine what is just, justice derives not from the application of legal rules but rather from deciding each case on its merits without regard to rule or precedent. Early equity courts in England were developed because of a dissatisfaction with courts of "law." The dissatisfaction came about because of the King's (legal) courts' emphasis on rules and precedent that, in some cases, frustrated the ends of justice.

Wasserman argues that legal precedent is an unsatisfactory way of determining justice since the particularity of each case is important; however, individual, intuitive decisions are no better since justice then becomes "unsteady" and "wavering" (cited in Feinberg and Gross, 1977: 28–34). Some have argued that property and interest cases can be decided by legal rule but that cases involving conflicts of human conduct cannot. Even this bifurcation is criti-

---

QUERY

- Let's assume that in a civil dispute, one side has a very strong claim and would almost surely win in court, yet because the attorney missed a filing deadline, the judge throws out the case. Do you believe this is fair?

- Consider the case of an individual who befriends an elderly person, takes of him, and provides him comfort in his old age even at the sacrifice of personal time and expense. When the elderly person dies, however, a distant relative who expressed the view that it wasn't her duty to take care of her relative inherits substantial assets. Is this fair? Is this just? If the law (which would typically uphold the inheritance absent any special elements such as contract or payment for personal services) does not support any recognition of the friend's nonlegal "rights" to any portion of the inheritance, what theory of justice might support it?

- In a death penalty case, new evidence emerged that supported the defendant's allegations of innocence, but the evidence was uncovered after the deadline for filing an appeal. Should the execution go forward?

cized, however, since the most straightforward contract disagreements may involve human action, misinterpretation, and interest (Wasserman, in Feinberg and Gross, 1977: 34).

We are left to assume that although a system of law is necessary for the ordered existence of society, it is not necessarily helpful in determining what is just. In fact, "moral rights" may differ from "legal rights," and "legal interests" may not be moral. On the other hand, legal rules very often specify the procedures and steps necessary in judicial decision making; if these rules and procedures are broken, we believe that an injustice has occurred.

In our system of justice, *due process* exemplifies procedural justice. Our constitutional rights of due process require careful inquiry and investigation before punishment or forfeiture of any protected right can be carried out by the state. One has the right to due process whenever the state seeks to deprive an individual of protected rights of life, liberty, or property. Due process is the sequence of steps taken by the state that is designed to eliminate or at least minimize error. Procedural protections such as a neutral hearing body, trial by a jury of peers, cross-examination, presentation of evidence, and representation by counsel do not eliminate deprivation or punishment, but they do result in more accurate and just deprivations and punishments. Thus, if due process has been violated—by use of a coerced confession, "tainted evidence," or improper police procedure—an injustice has occurred. The injustice does not arise because the offender does not deserve to be punished but because the state does not deserve to do the punishing, having relied on unfair procedures.

Some point out that procedural justice is recognized only for certain groups—specifically, "all persons born or naturalized in the United States. . . ." Illegal aliens and others seemingly have no rights recognized by the Constitution, which allows practices such as the incarceration of the Cuban "Marielitos" without any form of due process at all. Some of these refugees were imprisoned for over a decade in federal prisons without any finding of guilt, harm, or reason. Jimmy Carter, in 1993, discussed their imprisonment (quoted in Hamm, 1995: 39):

> Every nation that grossly violates human rights justifies it by claiming they are acting within their laws. The way we are doing it now is the same kind of human rights violation that we'd vehemently condemn if it was perpetrated in another country.

United States Constitution, Fourteenth Amendment

§1. All persons born or naturalized in the United States, and subject to the jurisdiction thereof, are citizens of the United States and of the state wherein they reside. No state shall make or enforce any law which shall abridge the privileges or immunities of citizens of the United States; nor shall any state deprive any person of life, liberty, or property, without due process of law; nor deny to any person within its jurisdiction the equal protection of the laws.

Is the right to be free from governmental deprivation of liberty without some finding of guilt or reason a *natural* right that every country must recognize, or a *legal* right that can be written into existence, written out of existence, and defined in whatever way and distributed to whatever groups selected by a governmental body?

The *exclusionary rule* is supposed to ensure that the state follows the correct procedural steps before exacting punishment by excluding illegal evidence from the trial. There is debate as to whether the exclusionary rule is a mere legal protective device created by the court or a natural inherent right embedded in the Constitution. The exclusionary rule has been subject to a great deal of criticism because it is perceived as a rule that lets criminals go free. A utilitarian framework might support punishment even if the procedural rules were broken, since the net utility of punishment may outweigh the violation of due process. Under utilitarianism, the justice of the punishment comes from its utility to society, primarily through its deterrence value. On the other hand, even a utilitarian may argue against punishment when the procedural protections have been broken if the damage to general respect for the law is greater than the deterrent utility of punishment. In fact, one of the rationales for the exclusionary rule is that it serves as a judicial "slap" to police departments and a deterrent against improper investigation procedures. This is clearly a utilitarian argument.

Would a retributive system of punishment accept a violation of due process if the offender was clearly guilty? It would seem that in this case, justice is violated whether one is punished or not. If we allow the offender to go free, then the crime has not been balanced by punishment. If we punish the offender, we violate our system of procedural justice and protection of individual rights.

Supreme Court decisions have shown reduced support for the exclusionary rule. Exceptions have been created that some say threaten to undermine the rule itself. For instance, the "inevitable discovery exception" allows the tainted evidence if it would have been discovered without the improper procedure (*Nix v. Williams,* 104 S.Ct. 250 [1984]). The "good will exception" was recognized by the Court in a case where the law enforcement officers thought they had a legal warrant even though the warrant and therefore their search was actually unlawful (*United States v. Leon,* 104 S.Ct. 3405 [1984]). Another exception to the exclusionary rule was recognized in *New York v. Quarles* (104 S.Ct. 2626 [1984]). In this case, since the officer's goal was public safety and not collection of evidence, his failure to give Miranda warnings did not result in excluding the evidence he obtained by questioning a suspect without Miranda warnings. The majority displayed distinctly utilitarian reasoning in their cost/benefit arguments to support the holdings of the previously mentioned cases. It may be that the Supreme Court will become reluctant to uphold sanctions against any but the most extreme misconduct by police and use a "shocking to the conscience" test rather than a test that measures the violation to procedural rights. In the "shocking to the conscience" test, police behavior is evaluated subjectively, against substantive rights to be free from outrageous governmental action, such as torture, forced blood sam-

---

QUERY

- An eighty-seven-year-old man living in Chicago is exposed as a soldier who took part in killing hundreds of Jewish concentration camp victims. U.S. extradition procedures are followed to the letter, and he is extradited to Israel to stand trial. Israeli law determines that courts in Israel have jurisdiction over Nazi war crimes. Israeli legal procedure is followed without error, and he is convicted of war crimes and sentenced to death. Analyze the case under procedural justice and substantive justice.

- Federal law enforcement agents determine that a citizen of another country participated in a drug cartel that sold drugs in the United States. A small group of agents goes to the foreign country, kidnaps the offender, drugs him, and brings him back to the United States to stand trial. Upon challenge, the government agents explain that, although these actions would have been unconstitutional and illegal against a citizen of the United States in this country, since they were conducted on foreign soil against a non-U.S. citizen, they were not illegal. What do you think?

---

ples or surgery, or, in the case most closely associated with the test, forced regurgitation (*Rochin v. California*, 343 U.S. 165 [1952]).

Due process and procedural justice applies not only to police behavior, but also to prosecutorial actions such as plea bargaining, improper trial tactics, illegal admission of evidence, and so on. These issues are discussed more fully in later chapters.

We have been discussing legal procedures for determining punishment, but in some cases legal procedures may be followed completely and injustice still occur. For instance, it is unlikely that anyone would argue that Nelson Mandela, when he was imprisoned in South Africa, or Andre Sakharov, a Soviet dissident, received just punishment even though the legal procedures of their respective countries might have been followed scrupulously. One can see that a legal system can contribute to injustice if procedures belong to unjust laws.

Justice for Victims Most of the preceding discussion regarding substantive and procedural justice has concerned the offender. In substantive justice, we are concerned with fair punishments; in procedural justice, we are concerned with fair procedures that lead to the decision to punish. What of the victim? In ancient codes of law, the focus was on compensating the victim. This focus changed to the state and punishment in English common law around the time of the Magna Carta (1215). Eventually two systems of law developed, one to deal with private wrongs (civil law) and one to deal with so-called public wrongs (criminal law). The two may overlap—a rape victim may sue her attacker in civil court concomitantly with a state prosecution; for example, the family of Nicole Simpson sues O. J. Simpson for wrongful death after he has been acquitted in a criminal trial of the murder. This does not create double jeopardy, and because rules of evidence and standards of proof are different, one may be acquitted in a criminal trial and still be held responsible civilly.

The legal theory of the state as opponent is that the harm done in any crime is only incidentally to an individual. The more important harm is the crime against the state. Victims may or may not agree with this proposition; after all, it is they who bleed, lose property, or die. The recent spate of legislation concerning "hate crimes" treats these actions differently from simple assaults. Although the victim of a beating defined as a "hate crime" may have similar injuries to an assault victim without the designation, the crime is considered more serious, and the offenders will probably receive longer sentences. The reason is that "hate crimes" are considered more injurious to the public peace than personal assaults.

Victimology has emerged as a separate discipline in criminology, and the new focus may help to provide a better balance between state harm and individual harm. For instance, victims' rights bills provide various protections and rights to victims of crime. Although it is popular for politicians to campaign with a pro-victim, crime-control agenda, their message panders to the voting public's fears rather than sheds light on a complex social problem where there are often no distinct lines between victims and offenders. The media also contribute to general fears and to the stereotype of the white middle-class victim and the lower-class minority criminal. Actually, minority groups and the poor are much more likely to be victimized. Most victims and offenders come from the same neighborhood. Criminals are often victims themselves of past or current crimes. Moreover, there are many more victims than those defined as such by the system. Customers of inner-city supermarkets that charge higher prices for items because they know their customers do not have transportation to shop competitively are victims of economic exploitation. There are victims of retail credit schemes in which furniture rental stores rent and repossess a single piece of furniture several times for multiple profit. There are victims of employers who pay less than minimum wage or suddenly do not pay at all because they know the employees will not protest—either because they are illegal aliens or because they desperately need the job. Finally, there are victims of slum landlords who must pay rent or be evicted even though the apartment has a multitude of health and safety hazards. These victims are rarely considered part of the "crime problem."

The media may be most responsible for creating a false perception of crime. Whereas violence occupies up to three-quarters of all television news time, it is a small percentage of actual crime (Elias, 1986: 43). The constant barrage of murders, rapes, and robberies in television drama contributes to the public's general fear of crime, as does the local news media's sensationalistic treatment of such crimes even while ignoring more pervasive social problems. In fact, an individual is more likely to die of pneumonia, cancer, heart disease, household fires, auto crashes, or suicide than of homicide (Elias, 1986: 43). This is not to say that violent crime is not a problem, but there is disproportionate emphasis on violence relative to other types of victimization.

In the real world, most victims suffer relatively small losses but receive virtually no help at all from the system. Police do not respond at all to many bur-

---

In the News . . .

In 1997, news stories raise questions of media ethics:

- In one case, the terrible sexual abuse and murder of a child in a prominent family in Colorado have created a media frenzy before police have been able to identify any suspects. One tabloid published crime scene photos of the body, shocking even some hardened newspaper professionals by the insensitivity and gratuitousness of the graphic nature of the photos, not to mention the issue of how the photos were obtained. Should crime scene photos of murders be published? Should those who provided them be prosecuted?

- In another case, in Dallas two prominent athletes were accused of raping a young woman at gunpoint. The police department immediately held a news conference, and papers across the country and world reported the allegations, along with the past legal troubles of one of the athletes. The woman then recanted, and police and prosecutors have charged her with providing a false report. Now some members of the media propose that they were "victims" of her false allegations, also claiming that the police department was at fault for having a news conference that they were bound to report. The athletes and their lawyers are demanding that the media report the recantation with the same enthusiasm the initial allegations were reported. Should the police department hold news conferences when their only evidence is a victim's allegation? Should the media withhold the accused party's name in a rape charge as they do the rape victim's, at least until they have probable cause?

---

glary calls because there are so many calls and so little the police can do about them. Assault calls may be handled informally and cavalierly when the combatants are acquaintances or relatives. Victims rarely have much to do with the system unless a suspect is arrested, a rare occurrence in many categories of crime. When there is a prosecution, the victim may feel used by the system since the goal is to get a conviction, not to provide aid or compensation. The prosecutor is more interested in how the jury will perceive the victim than how much the victim lost or suffered from the crime.

Recently, there has been a "rediscovery" of victims. Many states have enacted victims' rights bills that enumerate various rights that victims have under the law. These rights may include being present at trial (circumventing procedural rules that exclude victim witnesses from the courtroom during other testimony), being notified of any hearing dates and plea-bargain arrangements, submitting a victim-impact statement to be considered during the sentencing decision, and being treated courteously and compassionately by all law enforcement and justice system personnel. Some of these bills have created victim-witness programs in police departments or prosecutors' offices that attend to the needs of victim witnesses. Duties of program personnel may include keeping victims informed of their case, providing information, accompanying victims in court, and helping them fill out victim-compensation forms.

Texas Crime Victims Bill of Rights

A victim of a violent crime is (1) someone who has suffered bodily injury or death or who is the victim of sexual assault, kidnapping or aggravated robbery, (2) the close relative (spouse, parent, or adult brother, sister or child) of a deceased victim, or (3) the guardian of a victim. As a victim of violent crime, close relative of a deceased victim or guardian of a victim, you have the following rights:

1. The right to receive from law enforcement agencies adequate protection from harm and threats of harm arising from cooperation with prosecution efforts.
2. The right to have the magistrate take the safety of the victim or his family into consideration as an element in fixing the amount of bail for the accused.
3. The right, if requested, to be informed of relevant court proceedings and to be informed if those court proceedings have been canceled or rescheduled prior to the event.
4. The right to be informed, when requested by a peace officer concerning the defendant's right to bail and the procedures in criminal investigations and by the district attorney's office concerning the general procedures in the criminal justice system, including general procedures in guilty plea negotiations and arrangements, restitution, and the appeals and parole process.
5. The right to provide pertinent information to a probation department conducting a presentencing investigation concerning the impact of the offense on the victim and his family by testimony, written statement, or any other manner prior to any sentencing of the offender.
6. The right to receive information regarding compensation to victims of crime as provided by Subchapter B, Chapter 56, including information related to the costs that may be compensated under the Act and the amounts of compensation, eligibility for compensation, and procedures for application for compensation under that Act, the payment for a medical examination under Article 56.06 of this code for a victim of a sexual assault, and when requested, to referral to available social service agencies that may offer additional assistance.
7. The right to be informed, upon request, of parole procedures, to participate in the parole process, to be notified, if requested, of parole proceedings concerning the defendant in the victim's case, to provide to the Board of Pardons and Paroles for inclusion in the defendant's file information to be considered by the Board prior to the parole of any defendant convicted of any crime subject to this Act, and to be notified, if requested, of the defendant's release.

Victim-compensation programs are also being created in many states. These programs provide compensation for certain types of crime when the victim is without insurance or other means of reimbursement. Funding comes either through court costs paid into a general fund by all criminal offenders or through the state's general funds. Usually only violent crimes and not property crimes are targeted by such programs. However, they can provide help with such expenses as lost wages, hospital and doctor bills, and even burial ex-

Texas Crime Victims Bill of Rights *(continued)*

8. The right to be provided with a waiting area, separate or secure from other witnesses, including the offender and relatives of the offender, before testifying in any proceeding concerning the offender, if a separate waiting area is not available, other safeguards should be taken to minimize the victim's contact with the offender and the offender's relatives and witnesses, before and during court proceedings.

9. The right to prompt return of any property of the victim that is held by a law enforcement agency or the attorney for the state as evidence when the property is no longer required for that purpose, and

10. The right to have the attorney for the state notify the employer of the victim, if requested, of the necessity of the victim's cooperation and testimony in a proceeding that may necessitate the absence of the victim from work for good cause, and

11. (a) The right to counseling, on request, regarding acquired immune deficiency syndrome (AIDS) and human immunodeficiency virus (HIV) infection and testing for acquired immune deficiency syndrome, human immunodeficiency virus (HIV) infection, antibodies to HIV, or infection with any other probably causative agent of AIDS, if the offense is an offense under Section 21.11(a)(1), 22.011, or 22.021, Penal Code.

    (b) A victim is entitled to the right to be present at all public court proceedings related to the offense, subject to the approval of the judge in the case.

    (c) The office of the attorney representing the state, and the sheriff, police, and other law enforcement agencies shall ensure to the extent practicable that a victim, guardian of a victim, or close relative of a deceased victim is afforded the rights granted by Subsection (a) of this article and, on request, an explanation of those rights.

    (d) A judge, attorney for the state, peace officer, or law enforcement agency is not liable for a failure or inability to provide a right enumerated in this article. The failure or inability of any person to provide a right or service enumerated in this article may not be used by a defendant in a criminal case as a ground for appeal, a ground to set aside the conviction or sentence, or a ground in a habeas corpus petition. A victim, guardian or a victim, or close relative of a deceased victim does not have standing to participate as a party in a criminal proceeding or to contest the disposition of any charge.

SOURCE: Texas Code of Criminal Procedure, Art. 56.02.

penses, whether or not the offender is arrested. Restitution programs are much more common today than they have been, and these programs do target property victims as well as victims of violent crime. However, restitution programs help only victims of criminals who are caught, and that, unfortunately, is not very likely for crimes such as burglary or larceny.

Victims have a right to be treated fairly by the system. All people should be accorded the same level of service and treatment regardless of who they are. The "bag lady" should receive the same care as the mayor if both are mugged. Victims should also receive the same consideration in any punishment decision. The amount of punishment inflicted on an offender should not be based on the economic or social status of the victim, any more than it should be based on the economic or social status of the offender.

Other issues are not so simple. For instance, should the victim have equal say in the amount of punishment? What if the prosecutor believes that a plea bargain of probation is sufficient punishment considering the crime and the costs of a trial, but the victim demands imprisonment? Should a burglary victim have the right to veto a plea bargain? What about an assault victim? We spoke of mercy before; would not some argue that the state does not have the power to grant mercy, only the victim? These questions also relate to the decision to parole. Many states now have procedures whereby the victim or the victim's family has the right to address the parole board when the criminal's parole date comes up. Should these victims have the right to veto parole when the board would have otherwise paroled the criminal? We characterize the victim's feelings of vengeance as personal revenge and the state's as retribution or justice, with the implication that one is bad and the other is good. In fact, victims who "take the law into their own hands" become criminals themselves. But why is the state's determination of sufficient punishment any better than the victim's? Supposedly it is because the state has the power to objectively and rationally determine the correct measurement, but if there are other variables at work, such as goals of efficiency and convenience, then where is the objective measurement of punishment? Favoritism, bribery, and incompetence may also affect outcomes. Obviously, in these cases neither the victim nor the offender receives justice.

Some mistrust the current interest in victims' rights and believe that this recent concern is really a cynical manipulation of victim witnesses to advance the goal of making them better witnesses for the state. Also, because the definition of the victim continues to be narrow and limited to stereotypes, obfuscation about who are victims continues. This serves to blind those most at risk to the realities of their own victimization and protects those who victimize in ways other than street crimes, such as white-collar and social crimes (Elias, 1986).

We have a system of punishment and retribution that is oriented completely to the offender. What would a system be like if the emphasis was on the victim's rights, needs, and compensation? In a system with a primary emphasis on the victim rather than the offender, money would be spent on victim services rather than prisons. It would be victims who received job skills training, not offenders. Some of the money that now goes to law enforcement and corrections would be channeled to compensation programs for victims of personal and property crimes. Victims would be helped even if their offenders were not caught. The major goal would not be punishment, but service. Offenders would be peripheral figures; they would be required to pay restitution to victims, and punishment would occur only if they did not fulfill their obligation to their victims. Could such a system work? Would such a system provide better justice?

PARADIGMS OF LAW

The law serves as a written embodiment of society's ethics and morals. It is said to be declarative as well as active—it declares correct behavior and serves as a tool for enforcement. Law is both a prohibition and a promise. It cautions against certain types of behavior and warns of the consequences for ignoring the warning. *Natural law* refers to the belief that some law is inherently valid and can be discovered by reason. A corollary of this thought is that some behavior is intrinsically wrong *(mala in se)*. In contrast, positive law refers to those laws written and enforced by society. This type of law is of human construction and therefore fallible (Mackie, 1977: 232).

We can trace the history of law back to very early codes, such as the Code of Hammurabi (c. 2000 B.C.), which mixed secular and religious proscriptions of behavior. These codes also standardized punishments and atonements for wrongdoing. Early codes of law did not differentiate between what we might call public wrongs and private wrongs. As mentioned before, two different areas of law can be distinguished today: criminal law is said to be punitive, whereas civil law is reparative. The first punishes while the second seeks to redress wrong or loss. Of the two, criminal law is more closely associated with the moral standards of society, yet it is by no means comprehensive in its coverage of behavior. Nor is there unanimous agreement about what it should or does cover.

There are two basic paradigms that aid our understanding of the function of law in society. According to Rich (1978: 1), a paradigm is a "fundamental image of the subject matter within a science. . . . It subsumes, defines, and interrelates the exemplars, theories, and methods/tools that exist within it." The *consensus paradigm* views society as a community consisting of like-minded individuals who agree on goals important for ultimate survival. This view is functionalist since it sees law as an aid to the growth and/or survival of society. Under the *conflict paradigm,* society is perceived as being made up of competing and conflicting interests. According to this view, governance is based on power; if some win, others lose, and those who hold power in society promote self-interest, not a "greater good." A less extreme view than the conflict paradigm is *pluralism*. Although sharing the perception that society is made up of competing interests, pluralism describes more than two basic interest groups and also recognizes that the power balance may shift when interest groups form or coalitions emerge. These power shifts occur as part of the dynamics of societal change.

The Consensus Paradigm

According to the consensus paradigm, law serves as a tool of unification. Durkheim wrote that there are two types of law: the repressive, criminal law that enforces universal norms, and the restitutive, civil law that developed because of the division of labor in society and resulting social interests. In Durkheim's view, criminal law exists as a manifestation of consensual norms: "We must not say that an action shocks the common conscience because it is criminal, but rather that it is criminal because it shocks the common con-science" (Durkheim, 1969: 21). What this statement means is that we define an action as criminal because the majority of the populace holds the opinion that it is wrong. This "common" or "collective" conscience is referred to as *mechanical solidarity*. Each individual's moral beliefs are indistinguishable from the whole. The type of law that reflects this conscience is *repressive law*. The function of punishment, then, is the maintenance of social cohesion. Law contributes to the collective conscience by providing an example of deviance.

Although Durkheim recognized individual differences, he believed these differences, resulting from the division of labor in society, only made the indi-vidual more dependent on society as a part of a whole. His concept of *organic solidarity* draws the analogy of individuals in society as parts of an organism: all doing different things, but as parts of a whole. Individuals exist, but they are tied inextricably to society and its common conscience. *Restitutive law* is said to mediate those differences that may come about because of the division of labor. Even here the law serves an integrative function.

The consensus view would point to evidence that we all agree for the most part on what behaviors are wrong and the relative seriousness of different types of wrongful behavior. In criminology, the consensus view is represented by classical thinkers such as Bentham and Beccaria, who relied on the accepted definitions of crime in their day, without questioning the validity of these def-initions, only their implementation. Although the Positivists virtually ignored societal definitions of crime, Garofalo (1852–1932), a legal anthropologist, had an idea of natural law that might be considered a consensus concept. As defined earlier, natural law is the view that certain behaviors are so inherently heinous that they go against nature; therefore, there are natural proscriptions against such behavior that transcend individual societies or time periods (Kramer, 1982: 36). We have recent evidence that there is at least some con-sensus in people's definitions of what constitutes criminal behavior; studies have shown that not only do individuals in this culture tend to agree on the relative seriousness of different kinds of crime, but there is also substantial agreement cross-culturally as well (Nettler, 1978: 215). In the consensus para-digm, law is representative. It is a compilation of the do's and don'ts that we all agree on. Furthermore, law reinforces social cohesion. It emphasizes our "we-ness" by illustrating deviance. Finally, law is value-neutral—that is, it resolves conflicts in an objective and neutral manner.

The Conflict Paradigm

A second paradigm of law and society is the conflict paradigm. Rather than perceiving law as representative, this perspective sees law as a tool of power holders that they use for their own purposes, which are to maintain and con-trol the status quo. In the conflict paradigm, law is perceived as restrictive or repressive, rather than representative, and as an instrument of special interests. Basically, there are three points to the conflict paradigm: first, criminal definitions are relative; second, those who control major social institutions determine how crime is defined; third, the definition of crime is fundamentally a tool of power (Sheley, 1985: 1). Quinney (1969: 17) describes the conflict paradigm as follows:

> By formulating criminal law (including legislative statutes, administrative rulings, and judicial decisions), some segments of society protect and perpetuate their own interests. Criminal definitions exist, therefore, because some segments of society are in conflict with others. By formulating criminal definitions these segments are able to control the behavior of persons in other segments. It follows that the greater the conflict in interests between segments of a society, the greater the probability that the power segments will formulate criminal definitions.

Quinney's description of conflict theory draws heavily on Marxist definitions of power and power holders in capitalism. Quinney (1974: 15–16) outlines the following points as making up the conflict paradigm:

1. American society is based on an advanced capitalistic society.
2. The state is organized to serve the interests of the dominant economic class. . . .
3. Criminal law is an instrument of the state and ruling class to maintain and perpetuate the existing social and economic order.
4. Crime control in capitalist society is accomplished through a variety of institutions and agencies established and administered by a governmental elite. . . .
5. The contradictions of advanced capitalism . . . require that the subordinate classes remain oppressed by whatever means necessary. . . .
6. Only with the collapse of capitalist society and the creation of a new society . . . will there be a solution to the crime problem.

Advocates of the conflict paradigm would point to laws against only certain types of gambling or against the use of only certain types of drugs as evidence that the ruling class punishes only those activities that are engaged in by other classes. In other words, cultural differences in behavior exist, but only the activities of certain groups (the powerless) are labeled deviant. For instance, only some types of gambling are illegal: numbers running is always illegal, yet some states have legalized horseracing, dog racing, and/or casinos. Only some drugs are illicit: heroin and cocaine are illegal while Valium and alcohol are not. An even better example of differential definitions and enforcement is that federal drug laws impose more severe sanctions on crack cocaine than on powder cocaine. Many believe it is not merely a coincidence that crack cocaine is more likely to be the drug of choice for minorities (being cheaper), whereas powder cocaine is associated with Caucasians and social elites. Conflict theorists believe that laws are written to protect and benefit the powerful groups in society and their interests.

Recall Jeffrey Reiman's description of the difference between reporting a mining accident and a multiple murder. Despite the same result (dead victims), the mining company would probably go unprosecuted or receive very minor punishments for its role in the death of the miners. For the conflict theorist, this would be an example of how law has been written differentially to serve the interests of the power holders. The definition of what is criminal often excludes corporate behavior, such as price fixing, toxic waste dumping, and monopolistic trade practices, because these behaviors, although just as harmful to the public good as street crime, are engaged in by those who have the power to define criminality. The regulation of business, instead of the criminalization of harmful business practices, is seen as arising from the ability of those in power positions to redefine their activities to their own advantage. Even though the Occupational Safety Board, the Food and Drug Administration, the Federal Aeronautics Administration, and other similar governmental agencies are charged with the task of enforcing regulations governing business activities in their respective areas, no one seriously believes that the level of enforcement or labeling that results is as serious as in criminal law. Relationships between the watched and the watchdog agencies are frequently incestuous: heads of business are often named to governmental agencies, and employees of these agencies may move to the business sector they previously regulated.

Some draw parallels between corporate crimes and organized crime, or at least describe them as occurring in the same spectrum of behavior (Krisberg, 1975: 35). Certainly it is fairly well documented that large and small corporations engage in dishonest and even criminal practices. One study reported that from a sample of businesses, 60 percent reported enforcement activity in response to one of the following violations: restraint of trade, financial manipulation, misrepresentation in advertising, income tax evasion, unsafe working conditions, unsafe food or drug distribution, illegal rebates, foreign payoffs, unfair labor practices, illegal political contributions, and environmental pollution (Clinard et al., 1985: 205).

In criminology, the conflict view was represented by early theorists such as Bonger (1876–1940), a Marxist sociologist who explained crime causation as a result of economic power differential and the ability of power holders to label some behavior as criminal. During the 1960s, a small number of criminologists attempted to redefine criminals as political prisoners, based on their views that the state used criminal definitions to control minority groups (Reasons, 1973). Labeling theorists also questioned the criminal justice system's definitions by pointing out that only some offenders are formally labeled and treated as deviant. The conflict theory is represented by theorists such as Platt, the Schwendingers, Krisberg, Quinney, Taylor, Walton, and Young and Chambliss (Kramer, 1982: 41). The conflict theorists explain that the myth of justice and equality under the law serves to protect the interests of the ruling class, because as long as there is a perception of fairness, fundamental questions about the distribution of goods will not be raised: "The combination of formal legal equality and extreme economic inequality is the hallmark of the

---

Exercise

Discuss how the conflict and consensus paradigms would interpret the following:

- decriminalization of marijuana for medical purposes
- the passage of "hate crimes" legislation
- so-called state "ethics laws" that criminalize some practices of state legislators
- recent Supreme Court decisions invalidating the use of race in admissions procedures in universities and in competitions for state scholarships

---

liberal state" (Krisberg, 1975: 49). Law functions to depoliticize even the most obviously political actions of the oppressed by defining these actions as crime, but its greatest power is to hide the basic injustice of society itself.

Definitions are shaped by our paradigms of law. The Los Angeles riots of 1992 were sparked by the acquittal of four police officers who were video-taped beating Rodney King, a motorist who had outstanding arrest warrants for traffic violations. The riots were described by some as political action. According to this view, minorities who were frustrated by economic hopeless-ness and angered by the criminal justice system's oppressive and brutal treatment retaliated in like form. In this view, the riots were political state-ments against oppression. Alternatively, others described the same actions as blatant and simple criminality. In this perspective, violent individuals merely took advantage of the incident to exhibit their individual deviance. Conflict theorists would support the first definition, and consensus theorists would support the second.

Distinct from the conflict paradigm is the *pluralist paradigm*. In this view, law is seen as arising from interest groups, but power is more complicated than the bifurcated system described by the Marxist tradition. Roscoe Pound de-fines the following as interests protected by power holders: security against ac-tions that threaten the social group, security of social institutions, security of morals, conservation of national resources, general progress, and individual life. Power is exercised in the political order, the economic order, the religious order, the kinship order, the educational order, and the public order. Law and social control constitute the public order, and powerful interests affect the law by influencing the writing of laws and the enforcement of written laws (Quin-ney, 1974).

Pluralism views law as influenced by interest groups that are in flux. Some interests may be at odds with other interests, or certainly the interpretation of them may be. For instance, conservation of natural resources is a basic interest necessary to the survival of society, but it may be interpreted by lumber com-panies as allowing them to harvest trees in national forests as long as they re-plant or, alternatively, by conservation groups as mandating more wilderness areas. According to the pluralist paradigm, laws are written by the group whose voice is more powerful at any particular time.

Interest groups hold power, but their power may shrink or grow depending on various factors. Coalitions and shared interests may shift the balance of power. The definition of crime may change depending on which interest groups have the power to define criminal behavior and what is currently perceived to be in the best interests of the most powerful groups.

We might consider the *social contract* as combining some of the concepts of the conflict and consensus paradigms. According to the social contract theory, members of society originally were engaged in a "war of all against all"—a conflict perspective of human nature. In a rational response to the dysfunctional nature of such conflict, individuals freely gave up some of their liberties in return for protection—in essence, a consensus perspective of the legal system. According to Hobbes, each individual has chosen to "lay down this right to all things; and be contented with so much liberty against other men, as he would allow other men against himself" (from Hobbes, *Leviathan,* 1651, quoted in Beauchamp, 1982: 264). Law is viewed as a mutual contract and voluntary transfer of rights for the benefit of all.

LAW AND SOCIAL CONTROL

One can view law as a tool of behavior change (Hornum and Stavish, 1978: 148). In this theory, law is seen as a tool of "social engineering" and a way of changing behavior to a desired state (Aubert, 1969: 11). Law may influence behavior directly by prohibiting or mandating certain behavior, or indirectly by influencing social institutions such as family or education that, in turn, influence behavior (Dror, 1969: 93). Thus, law controls behavior by providing sanctions but also, perhaps even more importantly, by teaching people what behaviors are acceptable and what behaviors are intolerable.

There is no question that law restricts certain behaviors. The social contract theory explains that law is a contract—each individual gives up some liberties and in return is protected from others who have their liberties restricted as well. But how much liberty should be restricted, and what behaviors should be sanctioned? Rough formulas or guidelines indicate that the law should interfere as little as possible in natural liberties and should step in only when the liberty in question injures or impinges on the interests of another.

One author offers "mediating maxims" to govern the application of restrictive laws. First, risk assessment: Does the behavior involve risk to others? The second maxim is the minimum restriction rule: Is the restriction the minimum necessary to accomplish the end desired? Finally, interest balancing is applied: the individual interest in the activity is measured against society's interest in prevention.

How far should the law go in managing citizens' behavior? Obviously, we agree on laws that restrict behavior blatantly harmful to innocent victim—for instance, homicide—but there is no agreement on, for instance, the right of the government to regulate the means by which a property owner chooses to

---

Justifications for Law

1. The Harm Principle: to prevent harm to persons other than the actor when probably no other means are equally effective.
2. The Offense Principle: to prevent serious offense to persons other than the actor.
3. Legal Paternalism: to prevent harm—physical, psychological, or economic—to the actor.
4. Legal Moralism: to prohibit conduct that is inherently immoral.
5. Benefit to Others: when the prohibition of the action provides some benefit to other than the actor.

SOURCE: Feinberg, cited in Feibleman, 1985: xiii.

---

protect himself or herself. Should a lethal trap set for a burglar be defined as murder or self-protection? Family-violence legislation has only recently been written and even more recently enforced. Historically, the law allowed the household head to be the supreme power, even allowing physical violence to be used as long as it remained within the family. The *rule of thumb* was the common-law rule that allowed a husband to beat his wife if he used a stick no greater in diameter than his thumb. Most of us are repelled by family violence and believe that children and spouses have the right to be protected, but even today some people believe that family discipline is a private matter.

Recently, fear of AIDS has engendered debate over the limits of government intervention. Some people want AIDS victims to be registered and to be prohibited from many jobs and types of participation in the public sector. Some want mandatory testing in certain occupational groups. Others believe that these proposed laws are discriminatory and serve only to further stigmatize the sufferers. The balance between individual freedom and government control is reached with difficulty when fear and misunderstanding about the potential for danger fuel emotions.

There is no unanimity regarding certain behaviors, and some behaviors have been seen as more or less evil according to historical period. For instance, abortion has been ignored, outlawed, and then decriminalized. It is entirely possible that it may be redefined once again as criminal, as different groups' definitions of the relative rights of mothers and their unborn children become more powerful and the law shifts to reflect the changes in society. There may also be a continuous cycle of defining certain drugs as more or less evil, depending on which interest groups can influence the general definitions of society. In the following sections, we discuss in more detail two rationales for laws—legal paternalism and legal moralism.

Legal Paternalism

Many of our laws are *paternalistic*—they try to protect people from their own behavior. Examples include seat belt laws, motorcycle helmet laws, speed limits, drug laws, licensing laws, alcohol consumption and sale laws, smoking prohibitions, and laws limiting certain types of sexual behavior. The strict libertarian view would hold that the government has no business interfering in a person's decisions about these behaviors as long as they don't negatively affect others. The opposing view is that as long as a person is a member of society (and everyone is), he or she has a value to that society, and society is therefore compelled to protect the person with or without his or her cooperation.

It may also be true that there are no harmful or potentially harmful behaviors to oneself that do not also hurt others, however indirectly, so society is protecting others when it controls the individual. Speeding drivers may crash into someone else, drug addicts may commit crimes to support their habit, gamblers may neglect their families and cause expense to the state, and so on. You may remember that in Chapter 1 we limited moral judgments to behavior that influences another. The justification of paternalistic laws depends on the view that very little of what we do does not affect others, however indirectly.

Some believe that government can justify paternalism only with certain restrictions (Thompson, 1980). First, a paternalistic law is appropriate only if the decision-making ability of the person is somehow impaired, by lack of knowledge or something else. An example would be child labor laws or laws that restrict the sale and consumption of alcohol by children. In both cases, there is a presumption that children do not understand the dangers of such behavior and therefore need protection. The second rule of paternalism is that the restriction should be as limited as possible. For example, drunken driving laws define the point of legal intoxication as when one's ability to drive safely is impaired, not simply after any alcohol consumption at all. When mountain passes close, they are reopened as soon as it is relatively safe to cross them. Laws exist that ban the sale of cigarettes to minors, but cigarettes are still available to adults—who supposedly have reached a level of maturity to understand the dangers associated with smoking. Finally, the third rule regarding paternalism states that the laws should seek only to prevent a serious and irreversible error: a death from DWI, an accident on an icy road, and so on. These rules try to create a balance between an individual's liberty and government control (Thompson, 1980).

Paternalistic laws can be supported by an ethics of care. Remember that in this framework, morality is viewed as integral to a system of relationships. The individual is seen as having ties to society and to every other member of society. Relationships involve responsibilities as well as rights. We can expect the minimum level of care necessary for survival from society under the ethics of care. However, the corollary is that society also can care for us by restricting harmful behaviors. Rights are less important in this framework; therefore, to ask whether society has a right to intervene or an individual has a right to a liberty is not relevant to the discussion. Utilitarianism would also support paternalistic laws because of the net utility to society that results from protecting each of its members.

Other ethical systems may not so clearly support paternalistic laws. Individual rights are perhaps more important under ethical formalism than the

QUERY

Do you agree with laws that prohibit gambling? Drinking while driving? Underage drinking? Prostitution? Liquor violations? Drugs? Helmet laws for bicycles or motorcycles? Leash laws? Seat belts? Smoking in public places? Underage drinking or smoking laws? Can you think of any paternalistic laws not mentioned above?

other ethical systems; individuals must be treated with respect and as ends in themselves. This view results in recognizing the rights of individuals to engage in careless or even harmful behavior as long as it is consistent with the universalism principle of the categorical imperative. In other words, people may have the moral right to engage in self-destructive or careless behavior as long as they do not hurt others. Of course, the opposing argument would be that all behaviors prohibited by paternalistic laws have the potential to affect others indirectly.

Legal Moralism

The law also acts as the moral agent of society, some say in areas where there is no moral agreement. Sexual behavior, gambling, drinking and drug use, pornography, and even suicide and euthanasia are some areas in which the law defines morality and immorality. The laws against behavior in these areas may involve principles of harm or paternalism, but they also exist to reinforce society's definitions of moral behavior.

For example, consensual sexual behavior between adults arguably harms no one, yet the Georgia state law prohibiting sodomy was upheld by the Supreme Court in *Bowers v. Hardwick* (106 S.Ct. 2841 [1986]). What harm is the state preventing by prohibiting this consensual behavior? The answer may be harm to community standards of morality. Pornography is defined as obscene, and it is prohibited arguably because of moral standards, not harmful effect. One governmental commission concluded that pornography contributes to sex crimes (Attorney General's Commission on Pornography, 1986), but this commission's findings can be contrasted with those of an earlier Johnson Commission, which found that pornography does not contribute substantially to sex crimes (Report of the Commission on Obscenity and Pornography, 1970). Hence, we have a factual issue: Does it or does it not promote harm? This issue is associated with the harm principle. Yet even if pornography does not prove to be harmful to others, the legal morality principle endorses the government's right to prohibit the sale and purchase of pornographic materials to consenting adults. Under legal moralism, it is prohibited simply because it is wrong. Recently, the issue became even more complicated with the increasing use of the Internet and the ease with which individuals may obtain pornographic materials from anywhere in the world. If one concludes that pornography does not cause sex crimes, then should the government be concerned?

QUERY

Should the government set up a "sting" operation allowing individuals to download obscene pornography (e.g., sex acts involving children) from a web site and then prosecute those who do so?

If we accept the fact that laws are the embodiment of society's morals, then legal moralism as a justification for laws would be less controversial, but in our society there is by no means agreement that the government represents the people's view. Personal actions such as homosexuality and the use of pornography can be judged using the ethical systems discussed in Chapter 2, but it should also be recognized that whether an action is moral or immoral is a different question from whether there should be laws and governmental sanctions regarding the behavior.

In some cases, individuals may agree that a particular action is immoral but at the same time may not believe that the government should have any power to restrict an individual's choice. Some proponents of choice regarding abortion take great care to distinguish the difference between pro-choice and pro-abortion. To them, one does not have to approve of abortion to believe that it is wrong for government to interfere in the private decision of the individual to use the procedure. Similarly, some who advocate decriminalization of drugs do so because of cost effectiveness or libertarian reasons, not because they approve of drug use. We do not have a system in which the law completely overlaps with the moral code, and some would argue that it would be impossible in a society as heterogeneous as ours for this to occur.

Galvin (1988) proposes that only those actions that violate some universal standard of morality, as opposed to a merely conventional standard, should be criminalized. This "limited legal moralism" is similar to Durkheim's view of crime, specifically that certain actions are defined as criminal because everyone in society views the behavior as wrong. In Galvin's argument, only those behaviors that *everyone* viewed as wrong would be subject to criminal definitions; this would prevent the situation of some groups forcing their moral code on others.

In conclusion, we must allow for the possibility that some laws that are justified under legal moralism may not necessarily conform to our personal views of good and bad. Many criminal justice practitioners also feel that some of the so-called gray areas of crime are not very serious, so it is not surprising that one sees discretion operating in enforcement patterns. Police will routinely ignore prostitution, for instance, until the public complains; they will

---

Exercise

Analyze pornography, gambling, homosexuality, and drug use under the ethical systems discussed in Chapter 2.

routinely let petty drug offenders go, rather than take the trouble to book them; and they may let gamblers go with a warning if no publicity is attached to the arrest. Police use discretion in this way partly because these behaviors are not universally condemned.

IMMORAL LAWS
AND THE MORAL PERSON

In the previous section, we discussed laws prohibiting behaviors that are judged as immoral, at least by some part of the populace. In this section, we will look at laws and governmental edicts that are themselves immoral. Examples might include the laws of the Spanish Inquisition permitting large numbers of people to be tortured and killed for having different religious beliefs from the crown, or the laws of Nazi Germany demanding that Jews give themselves up to be transported to concentration camps and often death. Examples in this country might include the internment laws during World War II that forced American citizens of Japanese descent to give up land and property and be confined in internment camps until the end of the war, or the segregationist laws that once forced blacks to use different building entries and water fountains. These laws are now thought of as immoral, but they were not at the time. The most common example of "immoral" laws are those that deprive certain groups of liberty or treat some groups differently, either giving them more or fewer rights and privileges than other groups. Most ethical systems would condemn such laws, and an objective ethical analysis would probably prevent the passage of such laws in the first place.

The example of Japanese American internment can be used to illustrate how one might use the ethical systems to judge a specific law. The religious ethical framework would probably not provide moral support for the action because it runs contrary to some basic Christian principles, such as "Do unto others as you would have them do unto you." Ethical formalism could not be used to support this particular law since it runs counter to the categorical imperative that each person must be treated as an end rather than as a means, and to the universalism principle. The principle of forfeiture could not justify the action since these were innocent individuals, many of whom were fiercely loyal to the United States. The only ethical framework that might be used to support the morality of this law is utilitarianism. We must be able to show that the total utility derived from internment outweighed the negative effect it had

---

QUERY

What other laws have limited Americans' (or certain groups') freedoms? Can they be justified under any ethical rationale? If you believed a law to be immoral, would you violate the law?

on the Japanese Americans who lost their land and liberty. Did it save the country from a Japanese invasion? Did it allow other Americans to sleep better at night? Did the benefits outweigh the harm to Japanese Americans?

Are there any laws today that might be considered immoral? In other countries the legal climate has allowed torture and death squads to be used against political dissidents. If you lived in a South American country and knew of assassinations by government police and nighttime kidnappings and disappearances, would you follow a law that required you to turn in political subversives? If you lived in a troubled country in Europe, such as Bosnia, would you support a law that dispossessed a rival faction of their property? These issues are at the heart of our next discussion.

Can one be a moral person while enforcing or obeying an immoral law? Martin Luther King, Jr., Gandhi, and Thoreau agreed with St. Augustine that "an unjust law is no law at all." There is a well-known story about Henry David Thoreau, jailed for nonpayment of what he considered unfair taxes. When asked by a friend "What are you doing in jail?" Thoreau responded: "What are you doing out of jail?" The point of the story is that if a law is wrong, a moral person is honor-bound to disobey that law.

If moral people disobeyed laws, what would happen to the stability of society? Another story concerns Socrates. About to be punished for the crime of teaching youth radical ideas, he had the opportunity to escape and in fact was begged by his friends to leave the country, yet he accepted the drink of hemlock willingly because of a fundamental respect for the laws of his country.

Although to follow all laws regardless of their intrinsic morality may set up a situation like Nazi Germany, if we agree with the proposition that an unjust

---

QUOTATION

What there was, from the start, was the great silence, which appears in every civilized country that passively accepts the inevitability of violence, and then the fear that suddenly befalls it. That silence which can transform any nation into an accomplice.

The silence which existed in Germany, when even many well-intentioned individuals assumed that everything would return to normal once Hitler finished with the Communists and Jews. Or when the Russians assumed that everything would return to normal once Stalin eliminated the Trotskyites.

Initially, this was the conviction in Argentina. Then came fear. And after the fear, indifference. "Nothing happens to someone who stays out of politics."

Such silence begins in the channels of communication. Certain political leaders, institutions, and priests attempt to denounce what is happening, but are unable to establish contact with the population. The silence begins with a strong odor. People sniff the suicides, but it eludes them. The silence finds another ally: solitude. People fear suicides as they fear madmen. And the person who wants to fight senses his solitude and is frightened.

SOURCE: Timerman, Jacobo. *Prisoner Without a Name, Cell Without a Number,* trans. Toby Talbot (New York: Knopf, 1981): 51. Reprinted with permission of Alfred A. Knopf, Inc.

QUOTATIONS

Under a government which imprisons any unjustly, the true place for a just man is also a prison. . . . (Thoreau, quoted in Fink, 1977: 109)

[T]here are two types of laws[:] just and unjust. I would be the first to advocate obeying just laws. One has not only a legal but a moral responsibility to obey just laws. Conversely, one has a moral responsibility to disobey unjust laws. (Martin Luther King, Jr., quoted in Barry, 1985: ii)

---

law is no law at all, we may set up a situation in which all citizens follow or disobey laws at will, depending on their own conscience. If one held a relativist view of morality, specifically the belief that one can intuit morals or decide morality on an individual basis, then two people holding different moral positions could both be right even though one position might be inconsistent with the law. An absolutist view holds that there is only one universal truth, which would mean that if one knew a law to be wrong based on this universal truth, then that person would be morally obliged to disobey the law. Evidently, either position could support civil disobedience.

Civil disobedience is the voluntary disobedience of established laws based on one's moral beliefs. Rawls (1971) defines it as a public, nonviolent, conscientious, yet political act contrary to law and usually done with the aim of bringing about a change in the law or policies of the government. Many great social thinkers and leaders have advocated breaking certain laws thought to be wrong.

Many philosophers believe that the moral person follows a higher law of behavior that usually, but not necessarily, conforms to human law. However, it is an exceptional person who willfully and publicly disobeys laws he or she believes to be wrong. Psychological experiments show us that it is difficult for individuals to resist authority, even when they know that they are being asked to do something wrong. The Milgram experiments are often used to show how easily one can command blind obedience to authority. In these experiments, subjects were told to administer shocks to individuals hooked up to electrical equipment as part of a learning experiment. Unbeknownst to the subjects, the "victims" were really associates of the experimenter and only faked painful reactions when the subjects thought they were administering shocks. In one instance, the subject and "victim" were separated, and the subject heard only cries of pain and exclamations of distress, then silence, indicating that the "victim" was unconscious. Even when the subjects thought they were harming the "victims," they continued to administer shocks because the experimenter directed them to do so and reminded them of their duty (Milgram, 1963).

Although it is always with caution that one applies laboratory results to the real world, history shows that individual submission to authority, even immoral authority, is not uncommon. Those who turned in Jewish neighbors to

---

Civil Disobedience

1. It must be non-violent in form and actuality.
2. No other means of remedying the evil should be available.
3. Those who resort to civil disobedience must accept the legal sanctions and punishments imposed by law.
4. A major moral issue must be at stake.
5. When intelligent men [sic] of good will differ on complex moral issues, discussion is more appropriate than action.
6. There must be some reason for the time, place and target selected.
7. One should adhere to "historical time."

SOURCE: Hook, quoted in Fink, 1977: 126–127.

Nazis or those who participated in massacres of Native Americans in this country were only following the law or instructions from a superior authority.

To determine what laws are unjust, King used the following guidelines: "A just law is one that is consistent with morality. An unjust law is any that degrades human personality or compels a minority to obey something the majority does not adhere to or is a law that the minority had no part in making" (quoted in Barry, 1985: 3).

To explore this issue further, one could refer to the two paradigms of conflict and consensus. The consensus view of society would probably provide a stronger argument for the position of following laws whether one agrees with them or not. However, the conflict and pluralist perspectives hold that laws may be tools of power and are not necessarily the embodiment of the will of the people; therefore, individuals may legitimately disagree with immoral laws and have a duty to disobey them. From another perspective, Kohlberg might propose that only individuals who have reached higher stages of morality would think to challenge conventional definitions of right and wrong. Most of us struggle to achieve goodness using the definitions of the society we live in; very few reach beyond accepted definitions to meet a higher standard of morality, or perhaps have need to.

Remember that civil disobedience occurs when the individual truly believes the law to be wrong and therefore believes the enforcement of or obedience to it would also be wrong. We are not referring to chronic lawbreaking because of immediate rewards. Indeed, most criminals have a fairly conventional sense of morality. They agree with the laws, even though they break them. Even those gray-area laws that involve disagreement over the "wrongness" of the behavior are not proper grounds for disobedience unless one believes that the government is restricting an individual's liberty or immorally oppressing certain people.

One other issue needs to be addressed here, the widespread belief that law is synonymous with morality and that as long as one remains inside the law, one can be considered a moral person. Callahan (1982: 64) points out the following:

> We live in a society where the borderline between law and ethics often becomes blurred. For many, morality is simply doing that which the law requires; a fear of punishment is the only motivation for behavior in some minimally acceptable way.

Obviously, Callahan is concerned with the false perception of law as a total representation of morals. Many of us can feel satisfied that we live up to legal standards of behavior; fewer of us would be able to say that we live up to ideal moral standards.

The Criminal Justice Professional

For the criminal justice professional who must uphold the law, this discussion of law and morality is not just academic. Line staff often face questions of individual morality versus obedience and loyalty. The My Lai incident has almost passed out of this nation's consciousness, but at the time controversy existed over whether soldiers should follow their superiors' orders blindly or make an independent assessment of the morality of the action. In this case, several officers were prosecuted by a military court for killing women and children in a village during the war in Vietnam without any evidence that they were a threat to the unit's safety. The officers' defense was that their superiors gave the orders to take the village without regard to whether the inhabitants were civilians or guerrillas. The rationale was that often there wasn't time to establish whether a civilian was friendly or not and that, in any event, civilians often carried grenades and otherwise harmed American troops. There was vociferous discussion in support of and against the soldiers' actions. Movies such as *Platoon* provide dramatic fictional accounts of other actions carried out by officers and the dilemmas of soldiers who knew such actions were unethical and illegal. One can either excuse the individual from personal moral decisions when he or she follows orders, or one can condemn the behavior, allowing and supporting disobedience of established laws or orders that don't conform to a personal ethical standard. The Nuremburg war trials upheld the standard of personal accountability when war crimes were committed that were defined as actions that violated the Geneva Convention—whether in response to orders or not.

A soldier's dilemma is not all that different from a police officer's. At times police officers may receive orders that they know to be illegal and/or unethical. The hierarchical nature of police work is very similar to the military, which makes the analogy even more striking. Does the police officer (or any other criminal justice professional) have the duty to make moral decisions and use personal moral judgment, or is obedience to superiors mandatory?

Each individual is faced with moral choices in the course of her or his career. Some of these choices are easy to make. However, some of the hardest decisions involve going against superiors or colleagues. Even if the behavior is

---

QUERY

- If a police officer received orders to storm a hostage situation and there was certainty that many would be killed and there were other alternatives available, should he follow superiors' orders or refuse on the basis of his moral judgment?
- If a police officer was told to pick up an individual on minor charges repeatedly as a form of harassment to get the individual to serve as an informant, should she agree to do so or refuse?
- If an undercover officer was told to get the evidence "at any cost" even if it meant using drugs or sex to gain the trust of dealers, what should the officer do?
- If a prosecutor was trying a case and the judge was obviously biased against the accused and allowed many errors to occur that resulted in a violation of due process, should the prosecutor be thankful for good luck and accept an easy conviction or make a stand against the judge's actions?
- Should a correctional officer ignore the beating of an inmate who injured another officer when ordered to do so by his superior?

---

obviously illegal, it is difficult to challenge authority; when the accepted pattern of behavior has the law on its side, very few of us take an individual stand against the law or practice.

The passage of a law by legislators is only one step in the law's function as a social control. In order for the law to be effective, it must be enforced by law enforcement and violators must be prosecuted and punished. We know that the discretion present in each step of the criminal justice system creates a situation in which written laws do not necessarily represent the reality of en-

---

Literary Perspective

I didn't believe it. I couldn't. Three years later and here came the feds. I was trying, at long last, to go back to school. I didn't smoke dope, I barely drank beer. The first time in my life that I'd started to get any kind of grip on things and here came the feds. Investigating the investigation. But Gaines hadn't gone down for cocaine, he'd gone for trying to murder us.

They're saying the shooting case was wrong? I took one of his cigarettes and punched the lighter. "Is that what they're saying?"

He let his hands slide around to the bottom of the steering wheel and rolled his head sideways and back, until he was looking straight at me, slowly shaking his head no.

"Dodd admitted that you tried to stop the investigation, told them I was strung out, that [Chief] Nettle stonewalled you. That's all I know."

"And now Nettle's providing us with a lawyer."

"Technically it's the city. But you can bet he's behind it. Hell, he's got no choice but to tell the truth or cover his ass. What do you think it'll be?"

"So what's the drill?"

"Like always, baby. Deny, deny, deny."

SOURCE: Wozencraft, Kim. *Rush* (New York: Random House, 1990): 230. Reprinted with permission of Random House, Inc.

forcement. Police departments create prostitution crackdowns, traffic ticket "blizzards," drug sweeps, and pornography raids with more or less cyclical patterns, sometimes in response to political pressure, sometimes not. The enforcement is, for the most part, independent of legislative intent. In this sense, police are *de facto* definers of the law.

If we see laws as an "ought" in societal definitions of misbehavior, then enforcement policies must be viewed as the "is" of what is tolerated and what is not. Many laws on the books are routinely ignored and forgotten, especially in the area of private behavior. One might ask why such laws are not thrown out as irrelevant to the times in which we live. The reason they continue to exist is that no politician is going to champion removal of "ought" laws because it would seem that he or she was in favor of the behavior that the law defines as immoral. Therefore, in some states there are still laws against private sexual behavior, "blue" laws restricting business activity or the sale of liquor, and so on. On the other hand, some argue that to have laws that are ignored endangers the credibility of the entire legal system.

Studies indicate that most corruption and graft come from those gray areas of crimes such as prostitution, gambling, and drugs. It is easy to explain the emergence of unethical behavior by criminal justice professionals in these areas since such crimes do not have the same moral sentiments behind them as do "serious crimes," such as murder and child molestation. Many police officers who would have no problem letting a prostitute go free will risk their lives to catch a child killer. Part of this discretionary enforcement comes from a personal perception of the immorality of the behavior and also a perception of society's tolerance or intolerance of such behavior.

One might consider that the discretionary nature of law enforcement may, in some ways, bring some of the concepts of justice to law. Individual officers discuss "street justice." For instance, when a store owner has a legal right to prosecute a shoplifter, but the shoplifter is eighty-seven years old, poor, and shoplifting food so she can eat, the police officer may try to convince the store owner not to prosecute in an attempt to "soften" the harshness of the law. Prosecutors may "lose" evidence in a subjective judgment that a criminal defendant doesn't need to be prosecuted. Alternatively, police may differentially enforce the law against those whom they consider "assholes," and prosecutors may ask for continuances to keep a defendant in jail, knowing that the case will ultimately be dismissed. The trouble with "street justice" and "de facto justice" is that once law is ignored in favor of individual application of subjective justice, individual definitions on what is "fair" and "just" may be arbitrary and capricious.

Spader (1984) discusses discretion and the rule of law as "a golden zigzag" between fundamental values. In this discussion, discretion has positive and negative elements, as does the rule of law. Of course, the ideal is to use discretion wisely in pursuit of ethical goals.

Spader's Rule of Law Versus Rule of Man (Discretion)

Rule of Law	*Rule of Man*
(Positives)	(Positives)
equal protection, evenhandedness, due process, fairness, rationality, notice, visibility, predictability, centralized limits on power, universality	individualization, flexibility, mercy, compassion, equity, creativity, adaptability, informality, efficiency
(Negatives)	(Negatives)
inflexibility, harshness, rigidity, mandatory legalism, technicalities, red tape, blind formalism, inefficiency	disparity, inconsistency, arbitrary and capricious abuse, uncertainty, invisibility, uncontrolled provincialism

SOURCE: Adapted from Spader, D. "Rule of Law v. Rule of Man: The Search for the Golden Zigzag Between Conflicting Fundamental Values." *Journal of Criminal Justice* 12 (1984): 379–394.

CONCLUSION

In this chapter, we discussed the parameters of justice and then described law as the administration of justice. Whereas justice is a philosophical concept concerned with rights and needs, law is a series of rules that is often blind to individual circumstance and larger issues of fairness. There are restrictions on society's power to restrict behavior in the form of laws. Regarding the principles traditionally used to justify laws—harm, paternalism, and morality—each has individual controversies and questions that must be addressed.

Criminal justice professionals can be seen as mediating the harshness and inflexibility of law in the application of "street justice"; however, it is also recognized that the same discretion that allows them to perform benevolent acts allows them to act in arbitrary and oppressive ways as well. The moral commitment that professionals have toward the laws they are supposed to uphold influences their actions. Soldiers are more loyal when they believe in the morality of the war. Police are more determined when they believe in the laws they are enforcing. Prosecutors and defense attorneys are more committed to due process when they believe in it. Correctional officials are less likely to allow prisoners to corrupt them when they have a strong sense of their goals. And all criminal justice professionals are more likely to operate in an ethical manner when they believe in the validity and justness of the system that employs them. In the following chapters we will look more closely at some of the ethical decisions that criminal justice practitioners are forced to make and the moral dilemmas that confront them.

REVIEW QUESTIONS

1. Explain how Aristotle and Plato associated status with justice. What is the case today?
2. Discuss the differences among the various theories of distributive justice.
3. Define rectificatory justice, commutative justice, and corrective justice.
4. Discuss the differences between substantive justice and procedural justice.
5. What is the retributive argument for punishment? What is the utilitarian argument for punishment?
6. Discuss some issues in the area of victims' rights.
7. Discuss the conflict paradigm and the consensus paradigm. How is pluralism distinguished from conflict theory?
8. Discuss the three major justifications for law—harm, paternalism, and moralism. Give examples of each.
9. Explain how people distinguish between law and justice.
10. Explain Spader's "golden zigzag."

ETHICAL DILEMMAS

Situation 1

Two individuals are being sentenced for the crime of burglary. You are the judge. One of the individuals is a twenty-year-old who has not been in trouble before and participated only because the other individual was his friend. The second person has a history of juvenile delinquency and is now twenty-five. Would you sentence them differently? How do you justify your decision?

Situation 2

You ride a motorcycle, and you think it is much more enjoyable to ride without a helmet. You also believe your vision and hearing are better without one. Your state has just passed a helmet law, and you have already received two warnings. What will you do? What if your child was riding on the motorcycle? Do you think your position would be any different if you had any previous accidents and had been hurt?

Situation 3

You are asked to enforce a law that you believe to be wrong. For instance, you are supposed to protect a member of the Ku Klux Klan during a speech when your feelings are directly contrary to the views expressed by this individual, and you don't believe he should have the right to speak. What would you do?

What would you do if you were told to deliberately perform your job in such a way as to ensure that the speaker be injured by a hostile crowd?

Situation 4

You are a D.A. and are prosecuting a burglary case. The defendant is willing to plead guilty in return for a sentence of probation, and you feel that this is a fair punishment because your evidence may not support a conviction. However, the victims are upset and want to see the offender receive prison time. They insist that you try the case. What should you do?

SUGGESTED READINGS

Galvin, R. 1988. "Limited Legal Moralism." *Criminal Justice Ethics* (Summer/Fall): 23–34.

Hamm, M. 1995. *The Abandoned Ones*. Boston: Northeastern University Press.

Murphie, J. 1988. "Forgiveness, Mercy, and the Retributive Emotions." *Criminal Justice Ethics* 7(2): 3–15.

Rawls, J. 1971. *A Theory of Justice*. Cambridge, MA: Belknap Press.

Spader, D. 1984. "Rule of Law v. Rule of Man: The Search for the Golden Zigzag Between Conflicting Fundamental Values." *Journal of Criminal Justice* 12: 379–394.

5

Ethics and Law Enforcement

Chapter Objectives

Understand the role of law enforcement in a democracy, including the use of authority, power, force, and persuasion.

Compare the formal ethics of law enforcement with the values of the subculture.

Explore the limits of discretion and corresponding duties for law enforcement officers.

"I haven't beaten anyone this bad in a long time."

"Oh not again . . . why for you do that . . . I thought you agreed to chill out for a while. What did do [sic]?"

"I think he was dusted . . . many broken bones later after the pursuit."

(COMPUTER TRANSMISSION, OFFICERS POWELL AND WIND AFTER THE RODNEY KING INCIDENT [CHRISTOPHER COMMISSION, 1991A: 15])

The images of the Rodney King beating are indelibly imprinted on the psyche of the American public and will forever shade the image of law enforcement. In this one violent encounter, many of the elements discussed in this chapter are reflected: the "signification" of some citizens as criminal and deserving of greater police scrutiny; the P.O.P.O. ("pissing off a police officer") doctrine that describes how affronts to police authority often end in unethical uses of force; the quick resort to violence in a department that encouraged aggressive "crime control" police performance; the subcultural and organizational support and/or tolerance for such violence (evidenced by the computer messages that joked about it afterward); the initial easy acceptance of police and media definitions that justified such violence against some types of citizens (specifically, early reports indicating that Rodney King was a criminal, that he was a drug user, with the implication, therefore, that he deserved what happened to him); finally, the presence of societal divisions based on race and socioeconomic circumstance that shaped the perception of the justice. Arguably, the Simi Valley jury acquitted the officers because white, middle-class citizens must (and do) see their police force as good; therefore, they couldn't believe that institutionalized violence of this kind could exist in the "good guys." The guilty verdict in Los Angeles County was also predictable because in this world, doubt permeates public attitudes toward police—doubt that they tell the truth, doubt that they don't beat people, even doubt that they don't manufacture evidence to make a case. The O. J. Simpson trial was as much a trial of police credibility as it was the guilt or innocence of the defendant. It indicates in a dramatic way what happens when doubt replaces trust in police performance, and when police testimony is received with suspicion rather than credence.

Only because of the fateful intercession of an video camera did the King incident take on the national and international dimensions and spark the controversy and public condemnation that it did. The fact that an African American male motorist was beaten by police in Los Angeles is, unfortunately, not news; only the fact that it was taped made it an event. Ironically, the other tapes that came afterward—of California Highway Patrol officers, of Georgia officers, and others engaging in similar activities—quickly surfaced and disappeared as the media sensed the public's loss of interest in the issue.

THE POLICE ROLE IN SOCIETY

In this chapter, we take a critical look at law enforcement. To scrutinize and analyze police misconduct and the police role in society is not to disparage the thousands of officers who perform their job in an exemplary manner and epitomize the best of law enforcement. It is important to keep in mind as we discuss issues of law enforcement ethics that the majority of officers are honest and ethical and spend their careers simply trying to do a good job. These men and women usually don't appear on the front page of newspapers or on the evening news, but they pay the price for the few who do through decreased pubic confidence and even public scorn. We are concerned with individual deviance in this chapter, but even more so with institutionalized tolerance of such deviance, and the perceptions, world views, and values that shape and influence such tolerance. Honest and ethical officers shirk their responsibility when they treat fellow police as above the law. Even more troubling is the widespread sanctioning of those officers who do expose wrongdoing through social isolation and ridicule, or worse forms of punishment. Why do police—who supposedly are the law's agents—flaunt the law when fellow officers are involved?

Harsh scrutiny is often directed at police actions; officers feel that they are treated unfairly by the public and the media. There is a very important reason for such scrutiny—the police represent the "thin blue line" between disorder and order, between the "war of all against all" and law. Authority, force, discretion—these elements are inherent in the role of a law enforcement officer. No other criminal justice professional wields so much discretion over so many situations as part of everyday duties. No other criminal justice professional comes under so much constant and public scrutiny. However, this scrutiny is

---

QUOTATION

[N]o other public figure, or indeed any other human being, possesses greater authority over personal destiny. A jury, after a lengthy court trial and painful deliberation, may find a defendant guilty of murder and recommend the death penalty; the judge may respond by invoking the death penalty after more painful deliberation within his own conscience; and, finally, then the state may actually carry out that execution—perhaps after a dozen or so years of experiencing one appeal after another exhausted. But the police officer, in one split second, without the benefit of law school or judicial roles or legal appeals, acting as judge, jury and executioner may accomplish the same final result.

SOURCE: Murphy and Moran, 1981: 291.

---

understandable when one realizes that police are power personified. They often have the choice to arrest or not to arrest, to mediate or to charge, and in decisions to use deadly force, they even hold the power of life and death.

In this chapter, we will approach law enforcement with an underlying premise: that what drives individual decisions on the part of law enforcement officers and society's reactions to them derives from a perception of the mission of police in society. If one views police as a *crime control force,* certain presumptions follow: first, that criminals are the "enemy" and fundamentally different from "good" people; second, that police are the "army" that fights the enemy, using any means necessary to control, capture, and punish them; finally, that "good" people accept and understand that police are in a "war" and must be allowed deference in their decision making because they—not us—are the experts and only they "know the enemy." If one views police as *public servants,* other presumptions follow: first, that criminals are not a distinct group, that they shop, pay taxes, have kids and parents, and often are one's next-door neighbor; second, that police have limited ability to affect crime rates one way or the other since crime is a complex social phenomenon and, in fact, the history of law enforcement originates in order maintenance, not crime control; finally, that police as "public servants" serve *all* people and the laws that protect us. In effect, there is no "enemy" or, if there is, then "the enemy is us."

Police perception of their role as "crime fighters" will lead to certain decisions in their use of force, their definition of duty, their use of deception, and other decisions. Public perception of the police role as crime fighters leads to a willingness to accept certain definitions and justifications of behavior: that drug addicts are crazed, that individuals beaten must have deserved it, that all defendants must be guilty, and so on. Typically, only when it is impossible to fit reality into preconceived views of the "good" guys and the "bad" guys is there scrutiny. When a white person is the target of police brutality, when the victim of deadly force turns out to be a middle-class insurance agent, or when the public views police misconduct on the evening news, then the easy rationalization that good people don't get mistreated by law enforcement comes into question. Alternatively, a perception of the police role as public servant implies a much more restrictive view of police use of force and the rejection of a utilitarian—"the ends (of crime control) justify the means"—decision-making approach in favor of an approach more protective of due process and equal protection.

Crime Fighter or Public Servant?

Kappeler, Sluder, and Alpert (1994: 41) discuss the origins of law enforcement as including social service activities: police ran soup kitchens, provided lodging for indigents, and spurred moral reform movements against cigarettes and alcohol. Of course, early law enforcement was also involved in a utilitarian use of violence—e.g., they acted as the force for power holders in society and were union busters and political-machine enforcers. There was also frequent graft and other forms of corruption in early police departments. Much of the most extreme use of force was used against immigrants and the poor. The move toward police "professionalism" was spurred by several factors, one of which was to improve the image of police as objective enforcers of the law rather than political pawns. In effect, there was a real or perceived shift of police loyalty from political bosses to the law itself (Kappeler, 1994: 49). Part of this transformation involved the idea that police were crime fighters, professional soldiers in the war on crime—a concept that implies objectivity, professional expertise, and specialized training. This role deemphasized the social service role and ultimately led to policing characterized by detachment from the community being policed instead of integration in that community. A return to the roots of early law enforcement can be seen in the neighborhood policing movement, which involves having officers develop closer relationships with community leaders to help them solve some of the community problems that are believed to be associated with the development of disorder and lead to crime. Therefore, police officers may be involved in cleaning up parks, getting the city to raze abandoned houses, cleaning up graffiti, and so on. The elements of community policing include the following:

- a move away from a position of anonymity to direct engagement with the community which will give officers greater information about neighborhood problems
- freeing the officer from emergency response to engage in pro-active crime prevention
- more visible operations that increase police accountability
- decentralized operations that lead to greater familiarity with specific neighborhoods
- encouraging officers to see citizens as partners
- moving decisionmaking and discretion downward to patrol officers who know the neighborhood best
- encouraging citizens to take more initiative in preventing and solving crimes. (National Institute of Justice, 1992: 3)

With the recent trend toward neighborhood policing, we can describe a historical cycle that has moved police from public servants to professional crime fighters and back to public servants again. Although these descriptions are simplistic, they are valuable in understanding some issues. For example, patrol officers' resistance to neighborhood policing models may make sense if one views neighborhood policing as trading in the "crime fighter" role for a much less esteemed "social worker" role.

Neighborhood policing, or any other model, is obviously not a panacea. It is important to understand that both the crime fighter and public servant role have the potential and capacity for wrongdoing. The professional crime fighter may violate citizens' rights, and neighborhood police officers may exploit their position. Obviously, police in either model aren't all perfect; many examples of corruption and graft have been uncovered by various committees and investigative bodies (Barker and Carter, 1986; Murphy and Moran, 1981: 87). One study reported that by officers' own accounts, 39 percent of their number engaged in brutality, 22 percent perjured themselves, 31 percent had sex on duty, 8 percent drank on duty, and 39 percent slept on duty (Barker and Carter, 1986). Souryal also chronicles the extent of police deviance (1992: 300). Why do some police officers abuse their position? Unethical behavior is largely a matter of abuse of authority, force, or discretionary power.

AUTHORITY AND POWER

Klockars (1984) describes police control as comprising the following elements: authority, power, persuasion, and force. *Authority* is the unquestionable entitlement to be obeyed. Neither persuasion nor force is needed to achieve domination when one possesses authority. *Power* is similar to authority in that it is held by the organization, and the individual merely draws upon it as a representative of that organization, but it is different from authority in that power implies that there might be resistance to overcome. It also implies that if there is resistance then it will be crushed—power is the means to achieve domination. *Persuasion* may also be used in response to resistance but seeks to overcome it "by mobilizing signs, symbols, words, and arguments that induce in the mind of the person persuaded the belief that he or she ought to comply." Finally, *force* is different from the previous three means of control in that it is physical, whereas the other three are exercised through mental domination and control. When force is used, "the will of the person coerced is irrelevant" (Klockars, 1984: 532).

Police control and coercion, then, involve four different types of domination, from unquestioned authority to physical force. Why does law enforcement have the right to employ these types of control? "We give it to them" is the easy answer. "Police power" is a governmental right invested in federal, state, and local law enforcement agencies. It means that these organizations, unlike almost any other except perhaps the military, have the right to control citizens' movements to the point of using physical and even deadly force to do so. Cohen and Feldberg (1991) develop a careful analysis of and justification for police power and propose that it stems from the social contract. As discussed in an earlier chapter, Thomas Hobbes (1588–1679) and John Locke (1632–1704) created the concept of the social contract to explain why people have given up liberties in civilized societies. According to this theory, each citizen gives up complete liberty in return for societal protection against others. Complete freedom is given up in return for guaranteed protection. Police power is part of this *quid pro quo*—we give the police power to protect us, but we also recognize that this power can be used against us.

There are corollary principles to this general idea. First, each of us should be able to feel protected. If not, then we are not gaining anything from the social contract and may decide to renegotiate the contract by regaining some of the liberties given up, such as use of guns and first-strike options. Second, since the deprivations of freedoms are limited to those necessary to ensure protection against others, police power is circumscribed to what is necessary to meet the agreed-upon purpose. If police exceed this threshold, then the public rightly objects. Third, police ethics are inextricably linked to their purpose. If the social contract is the root of their power, it is also the root of their ethics. Cohen and Feldberg (1991) propose five ethical standards that can be derived from the social contract: fair access, public trust, safety and security, teamwork, and objectivity.

Delattre (1989) approaches police authority and power from a slightly different point of view. Delattre asserts that police, as public servants, need those qualities one desires in any public servant. He quotes James Madison, who stated that wisdom, good character, balanced perception, and integrity are essential to any public servant. Only if the person entrusted with public power has these qualities can we be assured that there will be no abuse of such authority and power: "granting authority without expecting public servants to live up to it would be unfair to everyone they are expected to serve" (Delattre, 1989: 79). In this proposition, the right to authority lies in the character of the person—if one has those virtues necessary to be a public servant, one has the right to use the authority invested in the role; if one does not have those virtues, then one should not be in that position to begin with.

All the unethical practices discussed in this chapter are abuses of one of the types of control and domination that Klockars identified. Abuses of discretion are abuses of authority, unlawful use of force is obviously an abuse of force, intrusive and deceptive investigative practices are abuses of power and persuasion, and so on. If we cannot be sure that we have Madison's public servants—people of wisdom, good character, balanced perception, and integrity—who need no guidance in how to perform in an ethical manner, how can the organization maximize the possibility of ethical action and minimize the abuses of the four types of control? The formal code of ethics of an organization attempts to provide such guidance.

FORMAL ETHICS FOR POLICE OFFICERS

Many organizations have either a value system or a code of ethics to educate and guide the behavior of those who work within the organization; some have both. An organizational value system identifies the mission and the important objectives of the organization. Just as individual values influence one's ethics, an organizational value system influences the ethics of the organization's members. For example, if a person's highest value is wealth, integrity may be sacrificed to achieve it; in a similar way, if the value system of an organization promotes profits over all else, customer satisfaction and quality may be sacrificed. A police department with a value system emphasizing crime control may allocate resources differently from one with a value system promoting community-oriented policing. Officers in these two departments may be rewarded differently, and the formal culture of the agency will encourage different behavior patterns.

A code of ethics is more specific to the behavior of the individual officer. A professional code of ethics addresses the unique issues and discretionary practices of that profession. Davis (1991) explains that there are three distinct kinds of codes: the first is an aspiration or ideal describing the perfect professional, the second provides principles or guidelines that relate to the value system of the organization, and the third provides mandatory rules of conduct that can serve as the basis of discipline. The code of ethics promulgated by the International Association of Chiefs of Police, which will be discussed shortly, is the first kind of code. It is an aspiration or ideal that describes the perfect police officer.

All police departments also have an oath of office that is a shorthand version of the value system or code of ethics. For instance, in a typical oath of office, duties are described that relate to service to the community and the sacred trust it entails for the officer.

The Law Enforcement Code of Ethics

The International Association of Chiefs of Police promulgated the Law Enforcement Code of Ethics, and many departments have used this code or adapted it to their own situations. Even though this code has been widely adopted, there is some question as to its relevance to individual police officers (Felkenes, 1984; Swift and Houston, 1993; Johnson and Copus, 1981: 59–65). One argument is that the code specifies such perfect behavior that it is irrelevant to the realities of most officers. The wide disparity between the code and actual behavior is detrimental to the validity and credibility of the code. For instance, Davis, referring to the code provision "I will never act officiously or permit personal feelings, prejudices, animosities or friendships to influence my decisions," writes that "any officer who takes this mandatory language seriously will quickly learn that he cannot do what the code seems to require. He will then either have to quit the force or consign its mandates to Code Heaven" (Davis, 1991: 18). Others argue that the code is vague, confusing, and impractical (Felkenes, 1984: 212).

Oath of a Police Officer

I, _____, a police officer for _____, USA, do solemnly swear (or affirm) that during my continuance in said office, I will to the best of my skill and ability, faithfully uphold the constitution of the United States, the constitution of the State of _____ and in all cases conform to and enforce the laws of the United States, the State of_____, and the Charter and Ordinances of the Consolidated Government of _____, USA.

I will execute the orders of my Superiors and in all cases comply with the rules and regulations governing the _____ Police Department and will report any violation thereof to my Superiors. I will not persecute the innocent, nor shield the guilty from prosecution or punishment, nor will I be influenced in the discharge of my duty by fear, favor or affection, reward or the hope thereof; and in all my acts and doings, I will be governed by the rules and ordinances applicable to the _____ Police Department.

So help me God.

SOURCE: Columbus Police Department, Columbus, Georgia. Reprinted with permission.

The opposing argument is that the code is valuable specifically because it provides an ideal for officers to aspire to. The code is a goal to work toward, not an average of all behaviors. It would be hard to be proud of a professional code that instructed an officer to be unbiased and objective unless there were personal reasons to favor one party or another, to be courageous unless personal danger were involved, or to be honest in thought and deed only when it served egoistic purposes. Since the code describes the highest standard of policing, all officers can improve because no officer is perfect. However, Davis (1991) contends that an aspirational code cannot be used to judge or discipline behavior that falls short of it. This comment is no doubt true; that purpose is served by departmental policies and rule books, which are more objective and enforceable. A code is far more valuable as a motivator than as a discipline device, a symbol rather than a stick.

The principle of justice or fairness is the single most dominant theme in the law enforcement code. Police officers must uphold the law regardless of the offender's identity. They must not single out special groups for different treatment. Police officers must not use their authority and power to take advantage of people. They must avoid gratuities because these give the appearance of special treatment. A second theme is that of service: police officers exist to serve the community. Another theme is the importance of the law: police are protectors of the Constitution and must not go beyond it or substitute rules of their own. Because the law is so important, police not only must be concerned with lawbreakers, but also their own behavior must be totally within the bounds set for them by the law. In investigation, capture, and collection of evidence, their conduct must conform to the dictates of law. The final theme is one of behavior: police, at all times, must uphold a standard of

---

Law Enforcement Code of Ethics

As a Law Enforcement Officer my fundamental duty is to serve mankind; to safeguard lives and property; to protect the innocent against deception, the weak against oppression or intimidation, and the peaceful against violence or disorder; and to respect the Constitutional Rights of all men to liberty, equality and justice.

I will keep my private life unsullied as an example to all; maintain courageous calm in the face of danger, scorn, or ridicule; develop self-restraint; and be constantly mindful of the welfare of others. Honest in thought and deed in both my personal and official life, I will be exemplary in obeying the laws of the land and the regulations of my department. Whatever I see or hear of a confidential nature or that is confided to me in my official capacity will be kept ever secret unless revelation is necessary in the performance of my duty.

I will never act officiously or permit personal feelings, prejudices, animosities or friendships to influence my decisions. With no compromise for crime and with relentless prosecution of criminals, I will enforce the law courteously and appropriately without fear or favor, malice or ill will, never employing unnecessary force or violence and never accepting gratuities.

I recognize the badge of my office as a symbol of public faith, and I accept it as a public trust to be held so long as I am true to the ethics of the police service. I will constantly strive to achieve these objectives and ideals, dedicating myself before God to my chosen profession . . . law enforcement.

SOURCE: Copyright the International Association of Chiefs of Police. Reprinted by permission.

---

behavior consistent with their public position. This involves a higher standard of behavior in their professional and personal lives than that expected from the general public (Bossard, 1981: 31). These elements are consistent with the "public servant" paradigm more so than the "crime fighter" paradigm, with the emphasis on service, justice for all groups, and higher standards for police behavior. In fact, this may be where the charges of vagueness and confusion stem from, since the code promotes a public servant ideal but everything that police are taught, believe from socialization, and are reinforced for from the public relates to their crime fighter stance.

Why is professional ethics important to law enforcement? First of all, ethics contributes to the image of law enforcement as a profession. There is continuing discussion on whether law enforcement is a profession; arguably, it is a matter of semantics and how one defines a profession. Sykes (1989) writes that a profession includes a body of specialized, internationally recognized knowledge, a pre-professional education and continuing education, legal autonomy to exercise discretionary judgment, lateral movement, and authorized self-regulation. According to some authors, since law enforcement is missing certain of these elements, it cannot be defined as a profession.

Whether or not officers have "legal autonomy to exercise discretionary judgment" is perhaps the most important debate in this discussion. One argument is that officers have much less discretion to make decisions than is thought since they must abide by the law; others point out that officers are allowed the latitude to decide whether or not to write tickets and whether to handle neighbor disputes with formal arrest or informal threat. Discretion grows or shrinks depending on which type of police–citizen interaction one looks at. Sykes (1989) argues that because law enforcement is an example of a classic bureaucratic organization, with rules, supervisors, and many lines of authority, these reduce discretion and the elements necessary to meet a definition of a profession. An alternative argument is that the nature of law enforcement involves problem solving; every situation is unique and must be handled differently, and "cookbook" approaches to law enforcement rarely work. These characteristics support the concept of the field as a profession. One might also suspect that the discussion holds more interest for academics than for the officer on the street. Whatever one calls the job, it requires a certain set of skills, and some people are better at it than others. One of the biggest differences between officers, in fact, is how they make decisions regarding the calls they respond to.

Ideally, a set of ethics will help the officer make these decisions in a lawful, humane, and fair manner. A code of ethics also helps engender self-respect in individual officers; self-pride comes from knowing that one has conducted oneself in a proper and appropriate manner. Further, a code of ethics contributes to mutual respect among police officers and helps in the development of an *esprit de corps,* or group sense of a common goal. Agreement on methods, means, and aims is important to these feelings. As with any profession, an agreed-upon code of ethics is a unifying element and one that can help define law enforcement as a profession, since it indicates a willingness to uphold certain standards of behavior and promotes the goal of public service, an essential element of any profession.

The Police Subculture and Formal Ethics

One of the forces most resistant to the adoption of an allegiance to a formal code of ethics is the police subculture. One characteristic of any profession or occupation is a special set of standards: certain behaviors may be considered acceptable for a member of that profession, even though the behaviors would be wrong if performed by anyone else. For instance, only doctors can ethically and morally cut open a person's chest, only lawyers should withhold information regarding lawbreaking by their clients, and only the military or other prescribed governmental agencies should be involved in obtaining the secrets of other countries. Police, too, have professional justifications for certain actions that would be wrong if engaged in by anyone else, such as speeding, using a weapon, and wiretapping. Professional ethics should guide these special privileges, but often the occupational subculture instead endorses standards of performance that take advantage of professional privileges and promote double standards.

Several writers have described the police and the police subculture; through these sources an image of the police and the police value system emerges that is very different from the value system described by formal ethics.

International Chiefs of Police Canons of Police Ethics

Article 1. Primary Responsibility of Job

The primary responsibility of the police service, and of the individual officer, is the protection of the people of the United States through the upholding of their laws; chief among these is the Constitution of the United States and its amendments. The law enforcement officer always respects the whole of the community and its legally expressed will and is never the arm of any political party and clique.

Article 2. Limitations of Authority

The first duty of a law enforcement officer, as upholder of the law, is to know its bounds upon him in enforcing it. Because he represents the legal will of the community, be it local, state, or federal, he must be aware of the limitations and proscriptions which the people, through law, have placed upon him. He must recognize the genius of the American system of government which gives no man, groups of men or institution absolute power, and he must insure that he, as a prime defender of the system, does not pervert its character.

Article 3. Duty to Be Familiar with the Law and with Responsibilities of Self and Other Public Officials

The law enforcement officer shall assiduously apply himself to the study of the principles of the laws which he is sworn to uphold. He will make certain of his responsibilities in the particulars of their enforcement, seeking aid from his superiors in matters of technicality or principles when these are not clear to him; he will make special effort to fully understand his relationship to other public officials, including other law enforcement agencies, particularly on matters of jurisdiction, both geographically and substantively.

Article 4. Utilization of Proper Means to Gain Proper Ends

The law enforcement officer shall be mindful of his responsibility to pay strict heed to the selection of means in discharging the duties of his office. Violations of laws or disregard for public safety and property on the part of the officer are intrinsically wrong; they are self-defeating in that they instill in the public mind a like disposition. The employment of illegal means, no matter how worthy the end, is certain to encourage disrespect for the law and its officer. If the law is to be honored, it must first be honored by those who enforce it.

Article 5. Cooperation with Public Officials in the Discharge of Their Authorized Duties

The law enforcement officer shall cooperate fully with other public officials in the discharge of authorized duties, regardless of party affiliation or personal prejudice. He shall be meticulous in assuring himself of the propriety, under the law, of such actions and shall guard against the use of his office or person, whether knowingly, or unknowingly, in any improper or illegal action. In any situation open to question, he shall seek authority from his superior officer, giving him a full report of the proposed service or action.

Article 6. Private Conduct

The law enforcement officer shall be mindful of his special identification by the public as an upholder of the law. Laxity of conduct or manner in private life, expressing either disrespect for the law or seeking to gain special privilege, cannot but reflect upon the police officer and the police service. The community and the service require that the law enforcement officer lead the life of a decent and honorable man. Following the career of a policeman gives no man special perquisites. It does give the satisfaction of safeguarding the American republic. The officer who reflects upon this tradition will not degrade it. Rather, he will so conduct his private life that the public will regard him as an example of stability, fidelity, and morality.

Article 7. Conduct Toward the Public
The law enforcement officer, mindful of his responsibility to the whole community, shall deal with individuals of the community in a manner such as will inspire confidence and trust. Thus, he will be neither overbearing nor subservient, as the individual citizen has neither an obligation to stand in awe of him nor a right to command him. The officer will give service where he can, and require compliance with the law. He will do neither from personal preference or prejudice but only as a duly appointed officer of the law discharging his sworn obligation.

Article 8. Conduct in Arresting and Dealing with Violators
The law enforcement officer shall use his powers of arrest in accordance with the law and with due regard to the right of the citizen concerned. His office gives him no right to prosecute the violator nor to mete out punishment for the offense. He shall, at all times, have a clear appreciation of his responsibilities and limitations regarding detention of the violator; he shall conduct himself in such a manner as will minimize the possibility of having to use force. To this end he shall cultivate a dedication to the service of the people and the equitable upholding of their laws whether in the handling of law violators or in dealing with the law abiding.

Article 9. Gifts and Favors
The law enforcement officer, representing government, bears the heavy responsibility of maintaining, in his own conduct, the honor and integrity of all governmental institutions. He shall, therefore, guard against placing himself in a position which any person can reasonably assume that special consideration is being given. Thus, he should be firm in refusing gifts, favors, or gratuities, large or small, which can, in the public mind, be interpreted as capable of influencing his judgment in the discharge of his duties.

Article 10. Presentation of Evidence
The law enforcement officer shall be concerned equally in the prosecution of the wrong doer and the defense of the innocent. He shall ascertain what constitutes evidence and shall present such evidence impartially and without malice. In so doing, he will ignore social, political, and other distinctions among the persons involved, strengthening the tradition of the reliability and integrity of an officer's word.

Article 11. Attitude Toward Profession
The law enforcement officer shall regard the discharge of his duties as a public trust and recognize his responsibility as a public servant. By diligent study and sincere attention to self-improvement he shall strive to make the best possible application of science to the solution of crime and, in the field of human relationships, strive for effective leadership and public influence in matters affecting public safety. He shall appreciate the importance and responsibility of his office, hold police work to be an honorable profession rendering valuable service to his community and the country.

Certain research has found police officers to be generally cynical, isolated, alienated, defensive, distrustful, dogmatic, authoritarian, and having a poor self-image (Johnson and Copus, 1981: 52). Some elements of the police value system are inconsistent with the high ideals of the code of ethics. For instance, Sherman (1982: 10–19) describes some common themes running through police attitudes. First, loyalty to colleagues is essential; second, the public, or most of it, is the enemy. Further, he explains that the values of police officers include the use of force, discretion, and a protective use of the truth.

Other writers have also discussed the theme of loyalty. Brown describes police loyalty as arising from a fundamental distrust of superiors and bureaucratic administration (Brown, 1981: 82). Muir explains loyalty by reference to the complicity that develops when police engage in individual rule breaking; once a police officer has violated a standard or rule, he or she is bound to re-

---

Police Values

1. Discretion A: Decisions about whether to enforce the law, in any but the most serious cases, should be guided by both what the law says and who the suspect is. Attitude, demeanor, cooperativeness, and even race, age and social class are all important considerations in deciding how to treat people generally, and whether or not to arrest suspects in particular.
2. Discretion B: Disrespect for police authority is a serious offense that should always be punished with an arrest or the use of force. The "offense" known as "contempt of cop" or P.O.P.O. (pissing off a police officer) cannot be ignored. Even when the party has committed no violation of the law, a police officer should find a safe way to impose punishment, including an arrest on fake charges.
3. Force: Police officers should never hesitate to use physical or deadly force against people who "deserve it," or where it can be an effective way of solving a crime. Only the potential punishments by superior officers, civil litigation, citizen complaints, and so forth should limit the use of force when the situation calls for it. When you can get away with it, use all the force that society should use on people like that—force and punishment which bleeding-heart judges are too soft to impose.
4. Due Process: Due process is only a means of protecting criminals at the expense of the law abiding and should be ignored whenever it is safe to do so. Illegal searches and wiretaps, interrogation without advising suspects of their Miranda rights, and if need be (as in the much admired movie, *Dirty Harry*), even physical pain to coerce a confession are all acceptable methods for accomplishing the goal the public wants the police to accomplish: fighting crime. The rules against doing those things merely handcuff the police, making it more difficult for them to do their job.
5. Truth: Lying and deception are an essential part of the police job, and even perjury should be used if it is necessary to protect yourself or get a conviction on a "bad guy." Violations of due process cannot be admitted to prosecutors or in court, so perjury (in the serious five per cent of cases that ever go to trial) is necessary and therefore proper. Lying to drug pushers about wanting to buy drugs, to prostitutes about wanting to buy sex, or to congressmen about wanting to buy influence is the only way, and therefore a proper way, to investigate these crimes without victims. Deceiving muggers

main silent regarding others' violations, even if they are more serious (Muir, 1977: 67, 72).

Scheingold (1984) has emphasized three dominant characteristics of the police subculture. First is the idea of cynicism. Police view all citizens with suspicion. Everyone is a possible problem, but especially those who fit a type. Regional differences exist in the language used to describe these types (*goofs, assholes, turds,* and so on), but the meaning is the same—these individuals are to be dealt with as if they have already committed a crime, because they probably have! Recruits learn this way of looking at others from older officers. Cynicism spills over to their relations with everyone, since they have found that friends expect favors and special treatment, and since police routinely witness negative behavior from almost all citizens. Their work life leads them to the conclusion that all people are weak, corrupt, and/or dangerous.

Police Values *(continued)*

into thinking you are an easy mark and deceiving burglars into thinking you are a fence are proper because there are not many other ways of catching predatory criminals in the act.

6. Time: You cannot go fast enough to chase a car thief or traffic violator, nor slow enough to get to a "garbage" call; and when there are no calls for service, your time is your own. Hot pursuits are necessary because anyone who tries to escape from the police is challenging police authority, no matter how trivial the initial offense. But calls to nonserious or social-work problems like domestic disputes or kids making noise are unimportant, so you can stop to get coffee on the way or even stop at the cleaner's if you like. And when there are no calls, you can sleep, visit friends, study, or do anything else you can get away with, especially on the midnight shift, when you can get away with a lot.

7. Rewards: Police do very dangerous work for low wages, so it is proper to take any extra rewards the public want to give them, like free meals, Christmas gifts, or even regular monthly payments (in some cities) for special treatment. The general rule is: take any reward that doesn't change what you would do anyway, such as eating a meal, but don't take money that would affect your job, like not giving traffic tickets. In many cities, however, especially in the recent past, the rule has been to take even those rewards that do affect your decisions, as long as they are related only to minor offenses—traffic, gambling, prostitution, but not murder.

8. Loyalty: The paramount duty is to protect your fellow officers at all costs, as they would protect you, even though you may have to risk your own career or your own life to do it. If your colleagues make a mistake, take a bribe, seriously hurt somebody illegally, or get into other kinds of trouble, you should do everything you can to protect them in the ensuing investigation. If your colleagues are routinely breaking rules, you should never tell supervisors, reporters, or outside investigators about it. If you don't like it, quit—or get transferred to the police academy. But never, ever, blow the whistle.

SOURCE: Reprinted by permission from Sherman, L. "Learning Police Ethics." *Criminal Justice Ethics* 1(1) (1982): 10–19. Copyright 1982 by the John Jay College of Criminal Justice.

The second value is related to the use of force. The police subculture embraces force for all situations wherein a threat is perceived. Threats may be interpreted as threats against the officer's authority rather than the physical person, so anyone with an "attitude problem" is thought to deserve a lesson in humility. Force is both expressive and instrumental. It is a clear symbol of the police officer's authority and legitimate dominance in any interaction with the public, and it is also believed to be the most effective method of control. It cuts across all social and economic barriers and is the most effective tool for keeping people in line and getting them to do what is required without argument.

Finally, there is the idea that police are victims themselves. They are victims of public misunderstanding and scorn, of low wages and vindictive administrators. This feeling of victimization sets police apart from others and rationalizes a different set of rules for them (Scheingold, 1984: 100–104). Scheingold (1984: 97) describes the police subculture as no more than an extreme of the dominant American culture; it closely resembles a conservative political perspective:

> If the police subculture is ultimately shaped by American cultural values, does it really make sense to talk about a separate subculture among American police officers? My answer is that the police subculture is not so much separate as an *in extremis* version of the underlying American culture. When Americans in general become preoccupied with crime, we also move in punitive directions, but our preoccupation with crime tends to be abstract and episodic. . . . The real difference between police officers and the rest of us is that coping with crime is their full-time job. There is, in short, reason to believe that they and we share the same values but that the police are distanced from us primarily by the nature of their work.

In other words, we all agree with certain elements of the police value system; if the general public is less extreme in its views, it is only because we have not had a steady diet of dealing with crime and criminal behavior as have the police. Furthermore, citizens are not too upset when the civil rights of "criminal types" are violated, only when police misbehavior is directed at "good" people.

Scheingold goes on to describe the factors that lead to the extreme nature of the police subculture. They include the fact that police typically form a homogenous social group, they have a uniquely stressful work environment, and they participate in a basically closed social system. Historically, police in the United States have come from the white middle and lower classes; they are similar racially, culturally, and economically. Because of these similarities, police feel themselves to be more similar to one another than to the public they encounter as a part of their job. Homogenous social groups lead to *group think;* everyone agrees with the group value or belief because to do otherwise would ostracize the individual. Police are further set apart by their work life. The job of a police officer entails a great deal of stress caused by danger and unpleasant experiences. Again, this results in the feeling that police are special and different from everyone else. Finally, because of strange working hours and social stigmatism, their social life tends to be totally involved with other police officers. This leads to closed viewpoints and legitimization of subcultural values (Scheingold, 1984: 97–100).

The subculture and the values described above may be breaking down among police departments today. Several factors contribute to the possible weakening of the subculture. The increasing diversity of police recruits has eliminated the social homogeneity of the work force. Many diverse groups are now represented in police departments, including African Americans, Hispanics, women, and the college-educated, even if only in token numbers. These different groups bring elements of their own cultural backgrounds and value systems into the police environment. Also, police unions with their increasing power formalize relationships between the line staff and the administration, and subculture methods for coping with perceived administrative unfairness are becoming more formal than informal. Increasingly, individual officers, especially those who come from other backgrounds not tied in as strongly to police tradition, may challenge the informal system rather than ignore or go along with obvious misconduct or corruption. Finally, civil litigation has increased the risk of covering for another officer. Although police officers may lie to Internal Affairs or even on a witness stand to save a fellow officer from sanctions, they are less likely to do so when large monetary damages may be leveled against them because of negligence and perjury. Yet it is still safe to say that the police, like any occupational group, maintain an informal subterranean value system that guides and provides a rationale for decision making. This value system is more influential than the police rule book or code of ethics.

It is apparent that the formal code of ethics or the organizational value system is quite different from subculture values. Violations of formal ethical standards such as the use of force, acceptance of preferential or discriminatory treatment, use of illegal investigation tactics, and differential enforcement of laws are all supported by the subculture. The police subculture has an ethical code of its own. Muir describes some elements of the informal police code: "You cover your men: don't let any officer take a job alone," "Keep a cool head," and "Don't backdoor it," a prohibition against certain gratuities (Muir, 1977: 191).

Another reason that subcultural values are not consistent with the code of ethics is related to social isolation and the feeling of victimization characteristic of the police subculture. When a group feels it is special for any reason, this perception may justify different rules or may be used to justify excusing the group from rules that apply to the rest of us. This is true for other professions as well; for instance, representatives and senators in Congress may feel it is appropriate to take trips and receive services at public expense because they could earn more money in the private sector than from their government salary. In similar ways, some police officers are able to justify behavior that would be wrong if engaged in by others because of their unique position. For instance, police may feel that use of force in some situations results in quick justice that the courts are unable to deliver. Police may feel justified in accepting gratuities because their pay is less than they feel they deserve.

Police also hear mixed messages from the public regarding certain types of crime. They are asked to enforce laws against gambling, pornography, and prostitution, but not too stringently. They are expected to enforce laws against drunk driving but also to be tolerant of individuals who aren't really "criminal." They are expected to uphold laws regarding assault, unless it is a family or interpersonal dispute that the disputants want to settle privately. In other words, we want the police to enforce the law unless they enforce it against us.

We also ask the police to take care of social problems such as the homeless without a great deal of concern about whether or not they step outside the law to do so. Extralegal means are acceptable as long as they are used when implementing desirable social goals. Citizens who want police to move the transients away from a street corner or get the crack dealers out of the neighborhood aren't concerned with the fact that the police have the power to control individuals' behavior only when a law has been broken. If a little "informal" justice is needed to accomplish the task, then that is fine. Yet when we accept power that exceeds the bounds of legality in those situations, then we must also be responsible for police use of power exceeding legality in other situations.

The police role as enforcer in a pluralistic society is problematic. The justification for police power is that police represent the public: "The police officer can only validly use coercive force when he or she in fact represents the body politic" (Malloy, 1982: 12). But if the police do not represent all groups, then their authority is defined as oppressive. It should be no surprise that police were seen as an invading army in the ghettos of the 1960s. They were not seen as representing the interests of the people who were the target of their force. More recently, the Los Angeles riots illustrate the tension between minority communities and police departments that are perceived as brutal and racist. Police encounter resistance from those groups that feel alienated and thus resent and do not accept police authority; on an individual level, some police officers may themselves have personal difficulties enforcing laws against the interests of certain groups: "The conflicting moral choices patrolmen are called on to make derive from deeply rooted conflicts over the use of police power within American society" (Brown, 1981: 78).

Whereas the formal code of ethics emphasizes the public servant role of law enforcement, the informal subcultural ethics emphasizes the crime fighter role. The public, too, probably expects the police to live up to the crime fighter role, hence Scheingold's observation of the overlap between public and police values and attitudes toward crime and criminals.

Interestingly, there is increasing evidence and belief that police are largely ineffectual in crime control. Crime rates ebb and flow for a variety of societal reasons, but police don't seem to have much of an impact, except in perhaps extremely localized and targeted instances—e.g., sweeps or campaigns of saturated patrol. Unless we are committed as a society to having a police officer on every corner, it is unlikely that they play much of a role in crime control.

On the other hand, neighborhood policing, if it leads to more integrated neighborhoods, reductions in social disorder and disorganization, and more citizen participation in controlling deviant members, may be more effective than traditional patrols; however, results thus far do not seem to show measurable changes in crime rates. Note that this measurement may be attempting to enforce crime-control measures on a public service mission. If neighborhood policing results in more respect, trust, and satisfaction on the part of the citizens, *even if it does not show crime-control results,* it would be a success—if one accepted the fact that police cannot be held responsible for crime rates and are, above all else, public servants.

DISCRETION AND DUTY

Discretion can be defined as the ability to choose between two or more courses of behavior. Law enforcement professionals have a great deal of discretion regarding when to enforce a law, how to enforce it, how to handle disputes, when to use force, and so on. Every day is filled with decisions—some minor, some major. An inherent element of all professions is discretion. Discretion is a necessary element in law enforcement; there is no one who would advocate full enforcement of all laws, but the need for discretion also leads to a greater dependence on individual ethical codes in place of rules and laws. Most ethical dilemmas that police officers face derive from their powers of discretion. These ethical dilemmas are part and parcel of the job. Muir describes moral dilemmas of the police officer as frequent and unavoidable, not academic, always unpopular with some groups, usually resolved quickly, dealt with alone, and involving complex criteria (Muir, 1977: 211).

Ethical dilemmas may differ depending on police function. Patrol officers are the most visible members of the police force and have a duty to patrol, monitor, and intervene in matters of crime, conflict, accident, and welfare. Investigating officers are primarily concerned with collecting evidence to be used in court. The ethical decisions that these two groups encounter are sometimes different. Patrol officers may have to make ethical decisions relevant to their decision-making power in defining crime and initiating the formal legal process, and they are subject to the temptations of gratuities. Undercover officers must make decisions regarding informants, deception, and target selection. Managers and administrators have ethical dilemmas of their own unique to the role of being responsible for others (Bossard, 1981: 25). We should also note that since most police departments in this country are small, many officers fulfill two or more functions, so their ethical dilemmas cross the boundaries designated above. Officers also face many common ethical dilemmas regarding the way they perform their job and interactions with fellow police officers and the public. Many of these dilemmas involve values of honesty, loyalty, and duty. In the following sections, we will discuss two categories of ethical dilemmas that officers may encounter. The first deals with those situations in which the officer has the discretion to choose between alternatives. The officer's ethics often determine how that decision is made. The second section addresses those situations involving the definition of the officer's duty.

Use of Discretion

Police possess a great deal of discretion in defining criminal behavior and their reaction to it. When police stop people for minor traffic violations, they can write tickets or give warnings. When they pick up teenagers for drinking or other delinquent acts, they can bring them in for formal processing or take them home. After stopping a fight on the street, they can arrest both parties or allow the combatants to work out their problems. In many day-to-day decisions, police hold a great deal of decision-making power over people's lives, because of their power to decide when to enforce the law.

One study found that police do not make arrests in 43 percent of all felony cases and 52 percent of all misdemeanor cases (Williams, 1984: 4). The amount of discretion and how it is used depend on the style of policing characteristic of a certain area. For instance, the "legalistic" style of policing is described as the least amenable to discretionary enforcement. In the "watchman" style, police define situations as threatening or serious depending on the groups or individuals involved, and act accordingly. The "caretaker" style treats citizens differently depending on their relative power and position in society (Wilson, 1976).

Brown describes four types of police officers, each with a different application of discretion: the "old style crime fighter," who is concerned only with action that might be considered crime control; the "clean beat officer," who seeks to control all behavior in his jurisdiction; the "service style," which emphasizes public order and peace officer tasks; and the "professional style," which is the epitome of bureaucratic, by-the-book policing (Brown, 1981: 224). Muir describes the following types: the "professional," who balances coercion with compassion; the "reciprocating officer," who allows citizens to solve problems and may engage in deals to keep the peace; the "enforcer," who uses coercion exclusively; and the "avoider," who either cannot handle the power he or she must use or fears it and so avoids situations where he or she may be challenged (Muir, 1977: 145). Each of these descriptions is obviously more detailed than our binary description of the crime control versus public servant model. However, all of these descriptions illustrate that officers approach their decision making with different beliefs about their mission and their role in society.

The very nature of policing necessarily involves some amount of discretion. Cohen (1985) describes discretion as balancing justice for the individual against justice for the group and points out that full enforcement would be unfair at times to individuals. Even courts have seemed to support police discretion over full enforcement (Williams, 1984: 26). However, this opens the door for unethical decisions. The power to make a decision regarding arrest creates the power to make that decision using unethical criteria, such as a bribe in return for not arresting. The power to decide how best to conduct an investigation also creates the power to entrap and select suspects in a biased or otherwise unfair manner. Selective enforcement may not necessarily be crime control but, rather, harassment to get an undesired person to leave an area (Brown, 1981: 160).

The Commission on Accreditation for Law Enforcement Agencies promulgates standards, and one of the standards states that law enforcement agencies should have "A written directive [that] defines the authority, guidelines, and circumstances where sworn personnel may exercise alternatives to arrest . . . " (CALEA, 1994). Besides standard directives, perhaps another effective way to encourage using discretion in an ethical manner is to delineate ethical versus unethical criteria for decision making. The decision to ticket a motorist stopped for speeding or to let him or her go with a warning can be made using ethical or unethical criteria. Those criteria that might be considered appropriate are miles over the speed limit, danger posed by the speeding (school zone or open road?), excuse used (emergency or late to work?), and probably others. Unethical criteria might be sexual attraction (or not), the identity of the motorist (fellow police officer, political figure, entertainment figure), the race of the motorist, the offer of a bribe, and so on. Other factors are less clear: Is the fact of a quota an ethical or unethical criterion? What about attitude? Many officers explain that a person may get a ticket, even for a minor violation, if she or he displays a hostile or unrepentant attitude. Is this merely an egoistic use of power on the part of an officer or a utilitarian use of the ticket as a tool for social learning? After all, if the individual does not display any remorse, there is little guarantee that the person won't commit the same violation as soon as the officer is out of sight.

Discretion and Discrimination

Officers' views of the world affect the way they do their job. If this view includes disparaging attitudes toward groups, it is clear that those groups may not receive the same protections as "good" citizens. The point is not that police officers are more prejudiced than the rest of us; it is that their special position creates the possibility that their prejudices could cause a citizen to receive less protection from the law than other citizens would:

> Essentially, when police act on personal prejudices while performing their jobs, they discriminate in the allocation of either services or enforcement of the law. Discrimination often takes the form of either to enforce the law differentially or to withhold the protections and benefits of the law. (Kappeler, Sluder, and Alpert, 1994: 175)

The treatment of two groups illustrates how discrimination may affect the rights of citizens. The changes we have seen in relation to police response to domestic violence were largely the result of public activism and legislative reaction to perceived unfairness. Until recently, police response to domestic violence calls was basically noninterference, with the perception that domestic violence was not a crime-control matter unless it involved injury amounting to felony assault, so women who were battered received different treatment depending upon whether their batterer was their intimate partner or a stranger and whether the crime was determined to be a felony or a misdemeanor. This situation is personified most dramatically by *Thurman v. City of Torrington*, 595

Dimensions of Police Discrimination

Administrators/Managers

Internal
- Refusing to place female officers in "dangerous" assignments.
- Placing minority employees in undesirable assignments.
- Promotion decisions made on the basis of race/ethnicity or other factors not related to the ability to perform the job.
- Refusing to commend officers for exceptional performance on the basis of such factors as race/ethnicity, gender, age.
- Segregation in assignment by assigning only African American officers to work together as partners or Caucasian officers to work together as partners.
- Failing to take corrective action when subordinates discriminate against co-workers.

External
- Making selection decisions on the basis of such factors as race/ethnicity, gender, political or religious affiliation.
- Refusing to respond to complaints by minority citizens or neighborhoods predominantly populated by minorities.
- Using police resources and personnel to harass certain segments of the community (e.g., businesses, community groups).
- By practice or custom, failing to provide police services to minority segments of the community (e.g., homosexuals, ethnic groups, religious groups).
- Failing to take corrective action when officers discriminate against citizens.

Officers

Internal
- Intimidating minority officers by threatening not to back them up on calls.
- Making racist or sexist comments in the presence of minority officers.
- Writing graffiti or posting offensive pictures on lockers belonging to minority officers.
- Sexual harassment.

External
- Not trying to solve crimes where minorities are victims.
- Harassing youths, college students, or other groups.
- Hassling businesses frequented by minorities.
- Not responding to, or purposefully delaying responding to, calls in minority neighborhoods.
- Use of racial slurs or derogatory language when dealing with Hispanic citizens.

SOURCE: Kappeler, V., Sluder, R., and Alpert, G. *Forces of Deviance: Understanding the Dark Side of Policing* (Prospect Heights, IL: Waveland Press, 1994): 173. Adapted by permission of Waveland Press, Inc. All rights reserved.

> **QUOTATION**
>
> *[T]o have public support and respect for the police, the police must first support and respect the community served.*
>
> ---
>
> SOURCE: Kappeler, Sluder, and Alpert, 1994: 184.

F. Supp. 1521 (D. Conn. 1984), which involved a woman who was beaten, stomped, and stabbed by her ex-husband on the front steps of her mother's house while a police officer sat in a car and watched. Obviously, there are few cases that are as dramatic as *Thurman*. Also, there are many other complicating factors to domestic violence, so how to intervene is not always a simple matter. Nevertheless, it must be recognized that part of the problem was a perception on the part of police that domestic violence was somehow different from stranger violence, and deserving of less intervention. A crime-control approach supports such discrimination; a public service model probably would not.

Homosexuals also receive different treatment. Kappeler, Sluder, and Alpert (1994: 176–184) discuss the case of Konerak Sinthasomphone—one of Jeffrey Dahmer's victims—as an example of police bias and discriminatory treatment of homosexuals and racial minorities. Sinthasomphone was the Laotian boy who was found wandering the street, incoherent, naked, and bleeding from the rectum. He had escaped from Dahmer's apartment after he had been drugged, tortured, and sexually abused. Two African American women called the police; when the police arrived, the women tried to tell them that Sinthasomphone was a minor, that he was hurt, and that Dahmer was the one who hurt him. Despite the women's attempts, police officers on the scene helped Dahmer take Sinthasomphone back to his apartment and waved away emergency medical technicians who were starting to examine him. If they had, they would have discovered the holes that Dahmer had already drilled into his skull and the acid that he had poured into the holes. Dismissing the incident as a "homosexual thing," the officers left Sinthasomphone with Dahmer, who strangled him shortly after they left.

This case is not about a mistake in judgment on the part of police officers. Their conduct represents a pattern of enforcement that allots police protection based on membership in certain categorical groups. If the Laotian boy had been white, if he had been a she, if Dahmer had been a minority member instead of a Caucasian, if the two women who requested assistance had not been African American, we might have seen a different response. Even more telling was the fact that even though the police chief suspended the officers involved, they were supported by the police union and ultimately reinstated with back pay. No further sanctions were taken against them.

These are merely examples of a pattern of discriminatory law enforcement, and there are other treatments of the subject elsewhere that provide more comprehensive treatment. It should also be noted that many changes in academy training and police policies have improved police response to certain groups such as battered victims and rape victims. Suffice to say here that if discretion is to be used widely, the individual prejudices and perceptions of groups such as women, minorities, and homosexuals must be recognized and decisions must be examined with an eye toward uncovering those decisions influenced by personal prejudices.

Above the Law? Many officers defend the use of professional courtesy to other officers stopped for speeding. Justifications for different treatment are diverse and creative. For instance, some honest justifications are purely egoistic: "If I do it for him, he will do it for me one day." Other justifications are under the guise of utilitarianism: "It's best for all of us not to get tickets, and the public isn't hurt because we are trained to drive faster." If the officer would let another person go with a warning in the same situation, it is not an unethical use of discretion. However, if every other person would have received a ticket (because of the danger involved, or mandatory law, or for whatever other reason) but the officer did not issue one because the motorist was a fellow officer, then that is a violation of the code of ethics (" . . . enforce the law . . . without fear or favor"). It is a violation of deontological universalism as well as utilitarianism: under deontological ethics, it is the officer's duty to enforce the law; under utilitarianism, the fact that the speeding officer can cause an accident just as easily as a civilian motorist means that the utility for society is greater if the ticket is issued, because it might make the officer slow down.

Officers as Peacekeepers Discretion also comes into play when the officer is faced with situations with no good solutions. Many officers agonize over family disturbance calls where there are allegations of abuse, or when one family member wants the police to remove another family member; other calls involve elderly persons who want police to do something about the "hoodlums" in the neighborhood, homeless people with small children who are turned away from full shelters, and victims of crime who are left without sufficient resources to survive. In response to all of these calls, officers must decide what course of action to take and can decide to do nothing at all. We will deal with these issues again in the next section.

Discretion is by no means limited to law enforcement. In each of the subsequent chapters, we will see that discretion is an important element in the criminal justice practitioner's role and plays a part in the creation of ethical dilemmas. Discretion in criminal justice has been attacked as contributing to injustice. McAnany (1981) chronicles disillusionment with discretion, citing such works as Davis's *Discretionary Justice* (1973) and the American Friends Service Committee's *Struggle for Justice* (1971). An argument might be made that solutions that attempt to establish guidelines for discretion are unsatisfactory since the suggested rules and standards either limit decision making to mechanistic applications of given rules or provide only rhetorical ideals with little or no enforcement capability. Dissatisfaction with discretion is caused by

---

Sorry, No Breaks!

According to the *New York Times* (December 8, 1995), Game Warden Joseph Dedrick of Caroline County, Virginia, is not the type of person to let someone go with a simple warning. Dedrick, on his day off (November 21), apparently went quail hunting and was lucky enough to bag one bird. Upon telling a friend about it, though, he was informed that quail season did not open until November 27, and the friend produced a game department brochure as proof. Mr. Dedrick, who has been a Game Warden for 27 years, immediately called his lieutenant and said: "We're going to have to get a warrant on me." Dedrick charged himself with a misdemeanor (hunting out of season), for which a judge could fine him $25.00 to $1,000.00.

SOURCE: "Sorry, No Breaks!" *The Ethics Roll Call* 3(1) (1996): 2. Reprinted with permission.

---

the misuse of discretion. However, when it is used wisely, objectively, and ethically, discretion is a necessary element in tempering law with humanity.

The Limits of Duty

Another ethical concern in general police practice involves the use of discretion in the performance of *duty*. It is now clearly established that most of police work is *order maintenance*. Police are called into situations that do not involve crime control and are often termed "social work" calls. Many police officers do not feel that these are legitimate calls for their time and either give them superficial attention or do not respond at all. Brown calls the skill police develop in avoiding these calls "engineering" (Brown, 1981: 142).

Police may respond to a domestic dispute and find a wife bruised but not seriously injured, upset, and without money or resources to help herself or her children. The officer may ascertain that departmental policy or law does not dictate any action and the woman is afraid to press charges, so the officer can leave with a clear conscience that official duties have been completed. However, the officer might take the woman to a shelter or otherwise help her get out of a bad situation. What is the ethical choice? It is difficult to determine the extent of the officer's responsibility in cases where there is not an offender to arrest or a law to enforce.

The formal code of ethics gives no clear guidelines on how much consideration police should give a citizen in distress. The caretaker style of policing found in small cities and suburbs, where police departments are community oriented, emphasizes service and encourages police assistance to victims or citizens who need it. Matthews and Marshall (1981) discuss the lack of departmental support for any action beyond the minimal obligations of duty. Those officers who become personally involved or commit the resources of the department beyond the necessary requirements are not rewarded, but viewed as troublemakers. Structural support for this ethical action does not exist. Officers who attempt to do what they believe is right often do so on their own, risking formal or informal censure. Referring again to our two paradigms of police as crime fighters or public servants, it is apparent that the deemphasis on service and, indeed, sanctions for performing some service functions are due to the police and public's view of police as crime fighters first and foremost. The approach of neighborhood policing changes these parameters considerably and renews the historical emphasis on peacekeeping and community integration functions, yet community policing holds favor with at least at this time a minority of officers, even while enjoying support and promotion from national organizations such as the Department of Justice.

In situations involving questions of duty, there are three questions to ask. First, what must police do under the law? Second, what does departmental policy dictate? Third, what do individual ethics dictate? A very altruistic, involved style of interaction where the police officer would be compelled to help the victims in any way possible is supported by the ethics of care, the ethics of virtue, utilitarianism, religious ethics, and ethical formalism. But a more self-protective standard, where the actions mandated would be only those necessary to maintain a self-image consistent with the police role as crime fighter, might also be justified using utilitarianism or ethical formalism. If police became personally involved in every case and went out of their way to help all victims, they would probably exhaust their emotional reserves in a very short time. As a matter of survival, police develop an emotional barrier between themselves and the victims they encounter. It is virtually impossible to observe suffering on a consistent basis if one does not protect oneself in such a way. Unfortunately, the result is often perceived as callousness, and because of the extreme personal resources needed to remain sensitive to individual pain, emotional deadening may result in unethical behavior toward individual victims.

QUERY

If a young boy, upset over a lost bicycle, approaches two police officers during their dinner, what do the strict guidelines of their job dictate? What is the ethical thing to do? Should they immediately interrupt their dinner and go search for the missing bicycle? Should they take a report to make the boy feel better, knowing they won't or can't do anything about it? Should they tell the boy to go away because they've had a hard night and are looking forward to a hot meal? Does it make a difference if police officers are not paid for their dinner hour?

If police encounter travelers who have been robbed during their passage through the city, should they leave such victims on the street to fend for themselves? Should they take them to a mission? Should they take up a collection to help them on their way?

If police respond to a burglary and find that the victim is desperately poor and the theft has left them without the resources to pay their rent, buy food, or keep the electricity on, what is their ethical duty? Once they have taken the report, can they leave with a clear conscience that their job has been done?

What Would You Do?

- It is ten minutes to OD time. You on-view an accident. Do you work the accident even though you want to go home, or do you avoid the accident by sneaking around it?
- You have received the same 911 call at the same location at least twenty times. Each time, it has been unfounded. You have just been dispatched to that 911 again. Should you check it or just clear it as unfounded without driving by?

When asked to share ethical dilemmas, police officers often raise the concept of duty. Officers are faced with the choice of responding to certain situations or not, leading to tempting opportunities to ignore duty.

Neither of the dilemmas in the box is a dilemma in the true sense of the word, which implies a difficult decision where both choices are equally valid and supported by ethical theory. In both cases, the officer's clear duty is to serve the public. On the other hand, these mundane, some might say trivial, decisions are faced by all officers, and their repeated decisions in such situations form the fabric of their moral character. How officers use their discretion—to file a report or not, to answer a call or not, to stop and investigate or not—is just as relevant to an evaluation of ethics as the decision to accept a gratuity or report the use of excessive force.

In the types of instances previously mentioned, officers must decide how much to get involved in any particular incident. Another issue of duty is raised by the nature of police work and how easy it is for officers to abuse their freedoms. Officers may report they are on a call, when in reality they are doing nothing or performing personal tasks such as shopping or standing in line at the post office. Some officers have been known to attend college classes during duty hours by informing the dispatcher that they are out on a call. Officers may turn in overtime slips for surveillance when in fact they were at home. They may misrepresent the times they started and finished the day. Finally, the way court appearances can be used to increase one's monthly salary is part of the socialization of every rookie. That these actions are wrong is not in question, and it is also true that they are not qualitatively different than the minor and not so minor egoistic actions of those in other occupations and professions: office workers leave early or call in sick to go to a ball game; salespeople call in to say that they are out making sales calls when, in fact, they are heading home for a quiet afternoon nap; businesspeople declare imaginary expenses on travel vouchers. Police officers, like all employees, rationalize these behaviors in a variety of ways, such as by pointing out their low pay or the fact that they sometimes do "police work" when off duty. The general acceptance of such behavior leads to an environment where each individual sets personal limits on the extent to which he or she will deviate from formal ethics. Even those who stop at minor transgressions must cover their actions by lying, which is another layer of deception added to the first.

CONCLUSION

In this chapter we have explored ethics and law enforcement. The issues discussed in this chapter—discretion, authority, and power—will be applied in the next chapter to the actions of police officers. In the chapters to come, we will see that these same themes apply to other criminal justice professionals as well.

We looked at the influence of the police subculture on ethical behavior and the subculture's opposition to formal ethical standards. We explored reasons for the lack of consistency between the two. The controversy regarding the police role in society as crime-control fighters or as public servants was also discussed. In the next chapter, it will become clear that one's view of the fundamental mission of police affects how one perceives the ethics of the various police practices that we will discuss.

REVIEW QUESTIONS

1. Discuss the elements of the formal code of ethics and contrast them with the subcultural values.
2. Define *discretion,* give examples of discretion, and discuss unethical and ethical criteria employed by police in their use of their discretion.
3. Analyze the extent of police duty according to the ethical systems discussed in Chapter 2.
4. Discuss the two perceptions of the police officer—crime fighter or public servant. Point to various police practices and innovations as supporting one or the other role.
5. Present the criticisms leveled against the use of any code of ethics for police officers.

ETHICAL DILEMMAS

Situation 1

As a patrol officer, you are only doing your job when you stop a car for running a red light. Unfortunately, the driver of the car happens to be the mayor. You give her a ticket anyway but the next morning get called into the captain's office and told in no uncertain terms that you screwed up, for there is an informal policy extending "courtesy" to city politicians. Several nights later you observe the mayor's car weaving erratically across lanes and speeding. What would you do? What if the driver were a fellow police officer? What if it were a high school friend?

Situation 2

You stop at a traffic accident and observe that a late-model Mercedes is blocking traffic. The driver of the car is an older, very well-dressed woman. She insists on waiting for the AAA wrecker driver she has summoned despite the fact that AAA told her it would be over an hour and the car is blocking traffic. There is a wrecker on the scene, and as the driver prepares to position his vehicle to tow the car, she blocks his way by standing by her vehicle and insisting that it not be towed. You have the legal authority to have her car towed, but it also appears that you may end up in a physical altercation with this woman. What would you do?

Situation 3

There is a well-known minor criminal in your district. Everyone is aware that he is engaged in a variety of crimes, including burglary, fencing, and drug dealing. On the other hand, you have been unable to make a case against him. Now he is the victim of a crime—he has reported that he has been assaulted and robbed at gunpoint. How would you treat his case?

SUGGESTED READINGS

Barker, T., and Carter, D. 1991. *Police Deviance.* Cincinnati: Anderson Press.

Dunham, R., and Alpert, G. 1989. *Critical Issues in Policing,* 2d ed. Prospect Heights, IL: Waveland Press.

Heffernan, W., and Stroup, T. 1985. *Police Ethics: Hard Choices in Law Enforcement.* New York: John Jay Press.

Kappeler, V., Sluder, R., and Alpert, G. 1994. *Forces of Deviance: Understanding the Dark Side of Policing.* Prospect Heights, IL: Waveland Press.

6

Law Enforcement Practices

Graft and Gratuities

The Incidence of Graft

The Ethics of Gratuities

Deception in Investigation and Interrogation

The Use of Undercover Officers

The Use of Informants

Justifications for Undercover Operations

Deception in Interrogation

Coercion and the Use of Force

Loyalty and Whistleblowing

Training and Management Issues

Change Efforts

Ethical Leadership

Conclusion

Review Questions

Ethical Dilemmas

Suggested Readings

Chapter Objectives

Become aware of the issues involved in
graft, gratuities, deception, excessive force, and loyalty.

Explore the role of management in police deviance.

Understand the public's participation in
and responsibility for police deviance.

GRAFT AND GRATUITIES

Corruption, graft, theft, and accepting bribes and gratuities are all examples of unethical law enforcement practices. We are concerned with how police rationalize their behavior but also why other officers tolerate and cover up such wrongdoing. Cohen refers to these behaviors as exploitation and describes exploitation as "acting on opportunities, created by virtue of one's authority, for personal gain at the expense of the public one is authorized to serve" (1986: 23). Taking bribes, participating in shakedowns, and "shopping" at a burglary scene are wrong and illegal. Some police are tempted by the opportunities for "fringe benefits," and then they develop the rationalizations necessary to live with themselves. Such rationalizations are made easier by the public's less-than-firm stance toward certain areas of vice—e.g., to accept protection money from a prostitute may be rationalized by the relative lack of concern the public shows for this type of lawbreaking. The same argument could be made about gambling or even drugs. We often formally expect the police to enforce laws while we informally encourage them to ignore the same laws. Signification occurs here as well. Although gambling carries connotations of the mob and organized crime, or numbers runners in the ghettos of our big cities, we typically don't think of church bingo or the friendly football pool down at Joe's Bar. If police were to enforce gambling laws against the stereotypical criminal, the public would support the action, but if the enforcement took place against upstanding citizens, there would be an outraged response. "Police Arrest Grandma Bingo Players!" would read the headlines. The solution is a choice: either accept police discretion to enforce, which in most cases will be used against the poor, minorities, and stereotypically criminal among us, or change the law and make it perfectly clear by statute that some gambling is OK and other types of gambling are not. Since the political feasibility of the latter solution is fairly limited—most politicians would not be eager to champion decriminalization of prostitution, drugs, or other types of vice—police are expected to make the distinction between "good" people and "bad." Good people should be excused, ignored, or, at worst, scolded for their involvement, and "bad" people should be investigated, caught, and punished—for example, the practice until recently of arresting prostitutes and letting "johns" go home, or ignoring campus crime while enforcement efforts target inner-city neighborhoods. The other possibility, of course, is that some police decide that a hypocritical public won't mind a few gambling operations, or a certain number of prostitutes plying their trade, or even a few drug dealers, so they might as well accept protection money. As long as the public supports certain types of illegal activities by patronage, it is no surprise that some police officers are able to rationalize nonenforcement.

Police routinely deal with the seamier side of society—not only drug addicts and muggers, but middle-class people who are involved in dishonesty and corruption. The constant displays of lying, hiding, cheating, and theft create cynicism. The following are some rationales that might easily be used by police to justify unethical behavior (Murphy and Moran, 1981: 93):

- The public thinks every cop is a crook—so why try to be honest?

- The money is out there—if I don't take it, someone else will.

- I'm only taking what's rightfully mine; if the city paid me a decent wage, I wouldn't have to get it on my own.

- I can use it—it's for a good cause—my son needs an operation, or dental work, or tuition for medical school, or a new bicycle. . . .

Sherman believes in the importance of a signification factor, or labeling an individual action acceptable under a personal rationale (Sherman, 1985a: 253). Many police develop along what Sherman (1982) called a "moral career," as they pass through various stages of rationalization to more serious misdeeds in a graduated and systematic way. Once an individual is able to get past the first "moral crisis," it becomes less difficult to rationalize new and more unethical behaviors. The previous behaviors serve as an underpinning to a different ethical standard, since one must explain and justify one's own behaviors to preserve psychological well-being (Sherman, 1982). Given constant exposure to others' misdeeds, peer pressure, and vague ideas of right and wrong in these situations, the question is not why some officers engage in corrupt practices but rather why more don't. Although research indicates the lack of evidence for an affinity argument to explain police corruption—that is, if deviant individuals are attracted to police work—an affiliation theory is persuasive, arguing that police learn from one another.

Murphy and Caplan (1989) argue that there are situational elements that "breed corruption," including lax community standards over certain types of behavior (gambling, prostitution), hesitation of the chief to enforce rules and discipline officers, tolerance by fellow officers, unguided police discretion and incompetence, and a lack of support from prosecutors and the courts (or corruption at that stage of the system as well).

Explanations of corruption can be described as systemic, institutional, or individual. The discussion above illustrates a systemic explanation of police deviance, focusing, as it does, on the relationship between the police and the public. Institutional explanations point to organizational problems (low managerial visibility, low public visibility, and peer group secrecy, among others). Institutional explanations also include looking at the police role in the crimi-

---

Suburb's Cops Charged with Taking Bribes

CHICAGO—The impoverished suburb of Ford Heights paid its officers as little as $6 an hour. To supplement their income, federal prosecutors say, six current and former officers took bribes from drug dealers, sometimes tipping them to the movements of other police agencies.

"You get what you pay for," said U.S. Attorney Jim Burns, who announced the bribery, extortion and racketeering charges Thursday against most of the town's police force, including a former chief.

Ford Heights is one of the nation's poorest areas, with an average household income of about $14,000 in 1990. Police pay starts at about $6 an hour and tops out at $20,000 annually.

Burns said former chief Jack Davis, who was arrested in July, helped distribute drugs and that about 20 dealers regularly paid bribes to officers so they could sell crack cocaine, powdered cocaine and heroin in a wide-open market.

The indictments leave the crime-plagued southeast Chicago suburb of 4,200 with three full-time police officers, a third of its usual strength.

"I'm not going to stand here and tell you the whole force was corrupt," Burns said. "It was not."

SOURCE: *Austin American-Statesman,* 11 Oct. 1996: A16. Reprinted with permission of the Associated Press.

Do you believe that "you get what you pay for . . . " is a good explanation of police deviance?

---

nal justice system (as the front-line interface with criminals), the tension between the use of discretion and bureaucraticism, and the role of commanders in spreading corruption. Individual explanations, such as the "rotten apple" idea, assume that the individual officer has deviant inclinations before he or she even enters the police department and merely exploits the position. Sloppy recruiting and the development of a police personality are also individual explanations (Johnston, 1995).

The Incidence of Graft

Muir described a small-town police department as relatively free from corruption, but even in this department, widespread patronage and petty bribery occurred because of the functional and beneficial aspects of this type of graft. For instance, a "security" firm was more or less given carte blanche to operate in legal and illegal ways to control burglaries in particular areas of the city. The police also overlooked gambling, after-hours liquor violations, and other minor infractions in exchange for information and cooperation. This behavior was seen as useful; in fact, it would be very difficult to convince the involved police officers that the behavior was at all wrong or unethical (Muir, 1977: 76):

> The point is that any police department, even one as free from graft as Laconia's, had a great deal of potential illegal patronage to dispense, giving it the power to purchase cooperation and social repression. Such a patronage system required complicity because it was outside the law. . . . Its

utility was so obvious and its initial cost so modest that even the most scrupulous of policemen found it difficult to speak out against it.

In larger cities, the prevalence of corruption is more extreme. The "Buddy Boys" in New York were able to operate almost openly in a precinct rife with lesser forms of corruption. Ultimately, thirty-eight officers in a precinct of only a little over two hundred were indicted for crimes ranging from drug use to drug sales and armed robbery. The Buddy Boys graduated from stealing cash and drugs from drug dealers during official arrests to planned thefts where they would, sometimes on duty, target crack houses or apartments and break in and steal drugs, cash, and other valuables. In at least one such instance, customers came to buy drugs, and the officers obliged by selling drugs through the door. They had relatively nothing to fear from their victims since the individuals targeted were minority drug dealers. Their victims could hardly report a robbery, and if other police in the precinct had any idea about what was going on, they evidently did little to investigate. The situation finally was exposed when IAD investigators caught two of the individual officers accepting protection money and forced them to wear "wires" to help gather evidence on the others. Ultimately, the police commissioner transferred all officers in the precinct to other divisions (Kappeler, Sluder, and Alpert, 1994).

Michael Dowd, another New York City police officer, testified to the Mollen Commission in 1993 that he and other officers accepted money for protecting illegal drug operations, used drugs and alcohol while on duty, robbed crime victims and drug dealers of money and drugs, and even robbed corpses of their valuables (Kappeler, Sluder, and Alpert, 1994: 201–202). An NBC *Turning Point* special titled "The Tarnished Badge" described how the IAD officer who attempted to investigate Dowd was, first, given no assistance or encouragement and then was sanctioned by his superiors for his dogged persistence in exposing Dowd's criminal behavior. Dowd was exposed and, ultimately, indicted and prosecuted only after police officers in a suburban city videotaped Dowd buying drugs (in uniform and in a police car).

The "Miami River Cops" also targeted drug dealers, and in their activities, they committed armed robberies of drug deals, collecting the cash and the drugs. These robberies eventually led to at least one homicide during the course of a robbery. Explanations of the River Cops' criminality include the rapid hiring of minorities during affirmative action drives without proper background checks; disaffection by white, mid-level supervisors who basically did not do their job of supervision, instead merely counting the days to retirement; ethnic divisions in the department; and the pervasive influence of politics in the department, which disrupted internal discipline mechanisms (Dorschner, 1989).

Exposés and police scandals focus public attention on these issues. New York City is an example, with scandals erupting in 1894, 1913, 1932, 1949, 1972, and 1993, but most large cities also have a history of corruption and exposure (Kappeler, Sluder, and Alpert, 1994: 197). Just as important as the individual decisions to break the law and commit illegal and unethical behavior are the tolerance and acceptance of such behavior on the part of honest officers and the subsequent cover-ups and mishandlings of investigations.

Several books, such as *Serpico* (Maas, 1973) and *Prince of the City* (Daley, 1984), detail the pervasiveness of this type of behavior in some departments and the relative ease with which individual officers may develop rationales to justify greater and greater infractions. For instance, the main character in *Prince of the City* progresses from relatively minor rule breaking to fairly serious infractions and unethical conduct, such as supplying drugs to an addicted informant, without having to make major decisions regarding his morality. It is only when the totality of his actions becomes apparent that he realizes the extent of his deviance. Taking bribes from prostitutes may lead to taking bribes from drug pushers and organized crime figures. Justifying stealing a few things from a store that has been burglarized and adding them to the list of stolen goods may lead to greater and more blatant thefts.

When one accepts gradations of behavior, the line between right and wrong can more easily be moved further and further away from an absolute standard of morality. Many believe that gratuities are only the first step in a spiral downward: "For police, the passage from free coffee at the all-night diner and Christmas gifts to participation in drug-dealing and organized burglary is normally a slow if steady one" (Malloy, 1982: 33). Malloy describes a passage from "perks" to "shopping" to premeditated theft (1982: 36).

Others dispute the view that after the first cup of coffee, every police officer inevitably ends up performing more serious ethical violations. Many police officers have clear personal guidelines on what is acceptable and not acceptable. Whereas many, perhaps even the majority, of police see nothing wrong with accepting minor gratuities, fewer police would accept outright cash, and fewer still would not actively condemn the thefts and bribes described earlier. The problematic element is that the gradations between what is acceptable or not can vary from officer to officer and department to department. If two officers differ on what is an acceptable gratuity, who is right?

Most misdeeds of police officers are only marginally different from the unethical behaviors of other professions—for instance, doctors may prescribe unneeded surgery or experiment with unknown drugs, businesspeople may cheat on their expense accounts, lawyers sometimes overcharge clients, and contract bidders and purchase agents might offer and accept bribes. It is an unfortunate fact of life that people in any profession or occupation will find ways to exploit their position for personal gain. This is not to excuse these actions but rather to show that police are no more deviant than other professional groups. In all of these occupational areas, there are some who exploit their position blatantly and perform extremely unethical behaviors, some who violate the ethical code in medium to minor ways, and many who attempt to uphold the profession's code of ethics and their own personal moral code.

The Ethics of Gratuities

There is no question that bribery and "shopping" are unethical and even illegal behaviors, but there is more controversy over the practice of giving and receiving gratuities. Although the formal code of ethics prohibits accepting gratuities, many officers feel there is nothing wrong with businesses giving "freebies" to a police officer, such as free admission or gifts. Many officers believe that these are small rewards indeed for the difficulties they endure in police work. Frequently, businesspeople offer gratuities, such as half-price meals, as a token of sincere appreciation for the police officers' work. So what could possibly be wrong with them? One author writes that gratuities "erode public confidence in law enforcement and undermine our quest for professionalism" (Stefanic, 1981: 63). How do gratuities undermine public confidence? Cohen believes that gratuities are dangerous because what might start without intent on the part of the officer may become a patterned expectation. It is the taking in an official capacity that is wrong, since the social contract is violated when citizens give up their liberty to exploit only to be exploited, in turn, by the enforcement agency that prevents them from engaging in similar behavior (Cohen, 1986: 26). To push this argument to the extreme, there doesn't seem to be much difference between someone coming into an inner-city store and demanding "protection money" (to avoid torching and vandalism) and a police officer coming in expecting liquor or other goods "for cost." How does the store owner know that his silent alarm will receive the same response speed if he is not grateful and generous to police officers?

Kania, on the other hand, writes that police "should be encouraged to accept freely offered minor gratuities and . . . such gratuities should be perceived as the building blocks of positive social relationships between our police and the public" (1988: 37). He rejects the slippery slope argument (that it leads to future deviance) and the unjust enrichment argument (that the only honest remuneration for police officers is the paycheck), proposing that gratuities actually help cement relations between the police department and the public. Officers who stay and drink coffee with store owners and businesspeople are better informed than those officers who don't, according to Kania. A gift freely given ties the giver and receiver together in a bond of social reciprocity. This should not be viewed negatively but rather as part of the neighborhood-oriented policing concept currently popular. He also points out that those who offer gratuities tend to be more frequent users of police services, justifying more payment than the average citizen. The only problem, according to Kania, is when the intent of the giver is to give in exchange for something in return and not as reward for past services rendered, or the intent of the taker is not to receive unsolicited but appreciated gifts, but rather to use the position of police officer to extort goods from business owners or, alternatively, if in response to an unethical giver who expects special favors, the officer has the intent to perform them.

Another issue that Kania alludes to but doesn't clearly articulate is that a pattern of gratuities changes what would have been a formal relationship into a personal, informal one. This moves the storekeeper-giver into a role more similar to a friend, relative, or fellow officer, in which case there are personal loyalty issues involved when the law needs to be administered. In the same way that an officer encounters ethical dilemmas when a best friend is stopped for speeding, the officer now has a similar situation when he or she stops the store owner who has been providing him or her with free coffee for the past

Relationships of Giver and Police

NAME	GIVER'S PERCEPTION	POLICE PERCEPTION
Ethical		
True Reward	gratitude for contribution or heroic deed	accepted with acknowledgement of significance to giver
True Gift	expression of gratitude for pattern of police services	accepted without further obligation
True Gratuity	expression of wish that legitimate police services will be continued	accepted in spirit of continuing reciprocal obligation
Unethical Only for Police		
Uncalled Debt	expression of wish that legitimate police services will be continued	accepted in credit for future legal, quasilegal, or illegal favors
Ethical Only for Police		
Bad Investment	offered to receive future legal advantages, secure favors, gain special status	accepted in spirit of continuing reciprocal obligation
Unethical and Illegal		
An Understanding	offered to receive future legal advantages, secure favors, gain special status	accepted in credit for future legal, quasilegal, or illegal favors
A Bribe	offered to exempt present illegal actions or omissions from police action	accepted to overlook or ignore present illegal activities
An Arrangement	offered to exempt ongoing illegal actions or omissions from police action	accepted to overlook or ignore ongoing illegal activities
A Shakedown	paid unwillingly to secure protection from police enforcement action	demanded to overlook or ignore present or future illegal activities

SOURCE: Adapted from Kania, R. "Should We Tell the Police to Say 'Yes' to Gratuities?" *Criminal Justice Ethics* 7(2) (1988): 37–49. Used with permission of The Institute for Criminal Justice Ethics and the author.

year. They have become, if not friends, at least personally involved with each other to the extent that one's formal duty becomes complicated.

Where should one draw the line between harmless rewards and inappropriate gifts? Is a discount on a meal OK, but not a free meal? Is a meal OK, but not any other item, such as groceries or tires or car stereos? Do the store or restaurant owners expect anything for their money, such as more frequent patrols or overlooking sales of alcohol to underage juveniles? Should they expect different treatment from officers than the treatment given to those who do not offer gratuities? For instance, suppose an officer is told by a convenience store owner that he can help himself to anything in the store—free coffee, candy, cigarettes, chips, magazines, and such. In the same conversation,

Literary Perspective

The proprietor of a large cafe in the precinct was the recipient of a PBA card. Serpico went to his place several times before he decided to stop eating his meals for nothing. His decision was not based on ethical considerations, although he had felt more and more uncomfortable sitting at a table in uniform, knowing he wasn't going to pay. Imagining people at other tables eyeing him and knowing it too. But what galled him was that when he and the other cops went into the cafe, the owner tried to palm off leftovers from the previous day or an item on the menu that wasn't moving. The longer he brooded about it, the more demeaning he found it, and anyway he liked to eat well, so one day after finishing his meal, Serpico asked the waitress for the bill.

"Oh, no, it's OK," she said.

Serpico picked up a menu, checked the prices and left the amount he owed on the table along with a tip. He was halfway down the block when the owner caught up to him with the money. "Hey," he said, "take this back. We don't charge for cops."

"How come?" Serpico replied.

"Aw, you know, the boys. I don't charge the boys. They all eat here."

"What's the matter, don't you have to pay for the food you serve?"

"Sure I do."

"Well," Serpico said, "I get paid a salary. I got money to eat whatever I want. I don't need your handouts."

"Listen, come in and eat anything you want. I'll tell you what. I'll charge you what it costs me. I just don't want to make a profit off you. Agreed?"

Serpico finally went along with the compromise, making up for the difference by leaving a larger tip, and the transformation whenever he entered the cafe was magical. "Frank," the owner would say, "try the roast beef today, rare just like you like it. Taste it, believe me, you'll see." And the waitresses began hovering over him. "You need anything, Frank? More coffee? What can I get you?"

It was a small thing, perhaps, but in retrospect, Serpico would see it as another indication of the growing estrangement between the police and much of the public, a breakdown of respect—a feeling that too many cops were taking whatever they could, not caring what anyone thought, whether or not it denigrated them, so that even the cafe owner, ostensibly a booster of policemen, was in fact treating them with disdain.

SOURCE: Maas, Peter. *Serpico* (New York: Bantam Books, 1973): 61–62.

the store owner asks the officer for his personal pager number "in case something happens and I need to get in contact with you. . . . " Is this a gift or an exchange? Should the officer accept or not? Many merchants give free or discount food to officers because they like to have police around, especially late at night. The questions then become the one asked frequently by citizens: Why are two or three police cars always at a certain place? Police response to this complaint is that they deserve to take their breaks wherever they want within their patrol area. If it happens that they choose the same place, that shouldn't be a concern of the public. However, an impression of unequal protection occurs when officers make a habit of eating at certain restaurants or congregating at certain convenience stores.

Free meals or even coffee may influence the pattern of police patrol and thus may be wrong because some citizens are not receiving equal protection. What happens when all surrounding businesses give gratuities to officers and a new business moves in? Do officers come to expect special favors? Do merchants feel pressured to offer them? Many nightclubs allow off-duty officers to enter without paying cover charges. Does this lead to resentment and a feeling of discrimination by paying customers? Does it lead to the officers' thinking that they are special and different from everyone else? Other examples of gratuities are when police accept movie tickets, tickets to ball games and other events, free dry cleaning, and free or discounted merchandise.

The extent of gratuities varies from city to city. In cities where rules against gratuities are loosely enforced, "dragging the sack" may be developed to an art form by some police officers who go out of their way to collect free meals and other gifts. One story is told of a large midwestern city where officers from various divisions were upset because the merchants from some areas provided Christmas "gifts," such as liquor, food, cigarettes, and other merchandise, while merchants in other divisions either gave nothing or gave less attractive gifts. The commander, finally tired of the bickering, ordered that no individual officer could receive any gifts and instead sent a patrol car to all the merchants in every district. Laden with all the things the merchants would have given to individual officers, the patrol car returned; the commander then parceled out the gifts to the whole department based on rank and seniority.

Officers in other departments are known for their skill in soliciting free food and liquor for after-hours parties. In the same vein, officers solicit merchants for free food and beverages for charity events sponsored by police such as youth softball leagues. The first situation is similar to an individual officer's receiving a gratuity, but the second situation is harder to criticize. Repeatedly, when asked about gratuities, officers bring up the seeming hypocrisy of a departmental prohibition against individual officers accepting gratuities yet at the same time an administrative policy of actively soliciting and receiving donations from merchants, such as pastries, coffee, and even more expensive fare, for departmental events.

It might be instructive to look at other occupations. Do judges or teachers receive any types of gratuities? Obviously, any attempt to give these professionals gifts would be perceived as an attempt to influence their decisions in matters involving the gift giver. Professional ethics always discourages gratuities in these situations, where the profession involves discretionary judgments about a clientele. Certainly, teachers cannot receive gifts from students and expect to maintain the appearance of neutrality. Judges are usually very careful to distance themselves from the participants in any proceeding. If there is a conflict of interest, if the judge is compromised by a relationships with or knowledge of the participants, then he or she is supposed to pass the case on to a neutral colleague. A revelation that a gift from either side was accepted by the judge would probably result in a mistrial, successful appeal, and the judge being removed by the commission on judicial conduct. The system of electing judges, as in Texas, is heavily criticized with the use of such terms as "justice for sale," since judges typically rely on attorneys for campaign contributions and these same attorneys practice in the judges' courts. The receipt of gifts or campaign contributions by politicians is a frequent news item. When members of Congress receive large amounts of money from special interest groups, the public is concerned with the neutrality of their voting. Many companies routinely distribute complimentary gifts to members of Congress. Although they would argue that these gifts do no harm and are only tokens of esteem, the perception is that some special favor is expected and that such favors are against the public interest.

However, it does not seem unusual or particularly unethical for a doctor, a lawyer, a mechanic, or a mail carrier to receive gifts from grateful clients. Whether gifts are unethical relates to whether one's occupation or profession involves judgments that affect the gift givers. The police obviously have discretionary authority and make judgments that affect store owners and other gift givers. This may explain why some feel it is wrong for police to accept gifts or favors. It also explains the difference between gratuities as discussed and those "gifts" such as a citizen who pays for a police officer's meal as she leaves the restaurant. In this case, because the police officer did not know of the reward (because the gift giver did not make his gift known), no judgment can be affected.

The ethical systems from Chapter 2 can be used to examine the ethics of gratuities. Religious ethics is not much help; no clear guidelines can be gleaned from religious proscriptions of behavior. Ethical formalism is more useful since the categorical imperative when applied to gratuities would indicate that we must be comfortable with a universal law allowing all businesses to give all police officers certain favors or gratuities, such as free meals, free merchandise, or special consideration. However, such a blanket endorsement of this behavior would not be desirable. The second principle of ethical formalism indicates that each should treat every other with respect as an individual and not as a means to an end. In this regard we would have to condemn gratuities in those cases where the giver or receiver had improper motives according to Kania's typology. If the business owner was expecting anything in return, even only the goodwill of the officer involved, then he would be using the police officer as a means to his own end and thus violating the second principle of ethical formalism himself.

If utilitarian ethics were used, one would have to formulate the relative good or utility of the interaction. On one hand, harmless gratuities may create good feelings in the community toward the officers and among the officers toward the community (Kania's "cementing the bonds" argument). On the other hand, gratuities often lead to perceptions of unfairness by shopkeepers who feel discriminated against, by police who feel that they deserve rewards and don't get them, and so on. In fact, the overall negative results of gratuities, even "harmless" ones, might lead a utilitarian to conclude that gratuities are unethical. There would be some differences in the argument if one used act utilitarianism versus rule utilitarianism. Act utilitarianism would be more likely to allow some gratuities and not others. Each individual act would be judged on its own merits—a cup of coffee or a meal from a well-meaning citizen to a police officer who was unlikely to take advantage of the generosity would be acceptable, but gifts given with the intent to elicit special favors would not. Rule utilitarianism would look to the long-term utility of the rule created by the precedent of the action. In this perspective, even the most innocuous of gratuities may be deemed unethical because of the precedent set by the rule and the long-term disutility for society of that type of behavior.

An ethics of care would be concerned with the content of the relationship. If the relationship between the giver and the receiver was already established, a gift between the two would not be seen as harmful. If there was no relationship—that is, if the store owner gave the gratuity to anyone in a blue uniform—then there may be cause for concern. A preexisting relationship would create ties between the two parties so that one would want to help the other with or without the gift. Kania's theory of social networking is appropriate to apply here. If there is not an existing relationship, then the gratuity may indicate an exchange relationship that is based on rights and duties, not care. Does the gift or gratuity harm the relationship or turn it into an exchange relationship? Officers can usually recite stories of store owners who gave gifts with an expressed purpose of goodwill, only to remind the officers of their generosity at the point where a judgment was made against them, such as a traffic ticket or parking violation. In this situation, the type of relationship isn't clear until "the bill is due."

The ethics of virtue would be concerned with the individual qualities or virtues of the officer. A virtuous officer could take free coffee and not let it affect his or her judgment. According to this perspective, no gift or gratuity would bias the judgment of the virtuous officer (which may be arguable). On the other hand, if the officer does not possess those qualities of virtue, such as honesty, integrity, and fairness, then even free coffee may lead to special treatment. Further, these officers would seek out gifts and gratuities and abuse their authority by pursuing them.

QUERY

Indicate which of the following—if offered freely with no *apparent* exchange expected—are ethically acceptable.

free coffee	only on duty	on or off duty
free gum, candy, etc.	only on duty	on or off duty
half-price meal	only on duty	on or off duty
free meal	only on duty	on or off duty
free dry cleaning	only for uniform	unrestricted
free admission to clubs	n/a	off duty
free lottery tickets	only on duty	on or off duty
free television set or other expensive merchandise		

If you decided that free coffee, meals, and other items were acceptable because they didn't cost much, how do you explain the fact that, over time, the cost of the coffee or meals consumed by police officers would equal that of the more expensive items?

An egoistic framework provides easy justification for the taking or giving of gratuities. It obviously makes police officers feel good to receive such favors, especially if they feel that they deserve them or that the favors are a measure of esteem or appreciation. Even if the person giving the gift had ulterior motives, the police officer could accept and be ethically justified in doing so under the egoistic ethical framework if the officer gained more from the transaction than he or she lost. In other words, if one could keep a positive self-image intact and obtain the gratuity at the same time, then one would be justified in doing so, and it would be a moral action. This discussion parallels very closely the police subcultural value of accepting bribes for doing something the police officer might have done anyway.

DECEPTION IN INVESTIGATION
AND INTERROGATION

According to one author, "deception is considered by police—and courts as well—to be as natural to detecting as pouncing is to a cat" (Skolnick, 1982: 40). Offenses involving drugs, vice, and stolen property are covert activities that are not easily detected. Klockars (1984) discusses "blue lies and police placebos." In his description of the types of lies police routinely use he differentiates "placebos" as being in the best interest of those being lied to—e.g., lying to the mentally ill that police will take care of laser beams from Mars, lying to people that police will keep an eye out for them, or not telling a person how a loved one was killed. The motive is benign, the effect relatively harmless. "Blue lies" are those used to control the person or make the job easier in situations where force could be used—e.g., to make an arrest easier, an officer will lie about where the suspect is being taken, or to get someone out of a bar, the officer will say that she only wants to talk.

Barker and Carter (1991) also propose a typology of lies, including accepted lies, tolerated lies, and deviant lies. Accepted lies are those used during undercover investigations, sting operations, and so on. These lies must meet the following standards:

- They must be in furtherance of a legitimate organizational purpose.
- There must be a clear relationship between the need to deceive and the accomplishment of an organizational purpose.
- The nature of the deception must be one wherein officers and the management structure acknowledge that deception will better serve the public interest than the truth.
- The ethical standing of the deception and the issues of law appear to be collateral concerns.

Tolerated lies, according to Barker and Carter, are those that are "necessary evils," such as lying about selective enforcement. Police may routinely profess to enforce certain laws (such as prostitution) while, in reality, use a selective manner of enforcement. Lies during interrogation or threats to troublemakers that they will be arrested if they don't cease their troublemaking are also tolerated lies.

Deviant lies are those used in the courtroom to make a case or to cover up wrongdoing. (One might argue with Barker and Carter that there is some evidence to indicate that for some police organizations or certain isolated examples of "rogue divisions," lies to make a case are so prevalent that they must be categorized as tolerated lies rather than deviant lies.)

Investigations often involve the use of informants, decoys, "covers," and so on. One possible result of these procedures is entrapment. In legal terms, entrapment occurs when an otherwise innocent person commits an illegal act because of police encouragement or enticement. Two approaches have been used to determine whether entrapment has occurred. The subjective approach looks at the defendant's background, character, and predisposition toward crime. The other, more objective, approach examines the government's participation and whether it has exceeded accepted legal standards. For instance, if the state provided an "essential element" that made the crime possible, or if there was extensive and coercive pressure on the defendant to engage in the actions, then a court might rule that entrapment had occurred (Kamisar, LeFave, and Israel, 1980: 510).

Stitt and James (1985) criticize the subjective test: it allows the police to entrap people with criminal records who might not otherwise have been tempted; it allows hearsay and rumor to establish predisposition; it forces the individual charged to admit factual guilt, which may stigmatize him or her; it provides a free rein for police discretion in choice of targets; and it degrades the criminal justice system by allowing the police to use misrepresentation and deceit. On the other hand, supporters say that the subjective test allows police to go after those most likely to harm society. The objective test would punish

---

A Case of Entrapment?

When police raided an X-rated mail order house, they found Keith Jacobsen's name and address, as well as the information that he had ordered two magazines: *Bare Boys I* and *Bare Boys II*, neither of which had been determined to be obscene material by any court. They created a fictitious company called "The American Hedonist Society" and sent Jacobson a membership application and questionnaire. He joined and indicated an interest in preteen sexual material. In other mailings over the course of three years, the government represented itself as "Midlands Data Research," "Hartland Institute for a New Tomorrow," and Carl Long, an individual interested in erotic material. Finally, a mailing from the government posing as the "Far Eastern Trading Company, Ltd." resulted in an order from Jacobson for *Boys Who Love*. He was arrested by federal agents after he accepted receipt.

SOURCE: Adapted from Dix, G. "When Government Deception Goes Too Far." *Texas Lawyer* 7(31) (1991): 12–13.

the police and let the criminal go free, forcing police to perjure themselves to save a case (Stitt and James, 1985: 133–136).

Legal standards, as we have discussed earlier, are very often useful guidelines for determining ethical standards, but not always. For instance, one might disagree with legal standards as being too restrictive if one believed that police should be able to do anything necessary to trap criminals. Alternatively, legal guidelines may not be sufficient to eliminate unethical behavior. For example, does a situation where police acting as drug buyers encourage a targeted individual to get them connections raise any legal problems? Probably not, as long as the police didn't entice or coerce the individual. Does it raise any ethical problems? One might look at the methods police use for selecting an individual target. Earlier we discussed discretion in police work. Selection of targets on any other basis than reasonable suspicion is a questionable use of discretion. Members of Congress convicted in the Abscam operation alleged improper conduct in the FBI's selection of targets; Marian Barry alleged he was "set up" because of his race after he was videotaped using drugs with a girlfriend in a hotel room. How targets are selected is a serious question; arguably, the selection should be based on reasonable suspicion. Sherman (1985b) reports that "tips" are notoriously inaccurate as a reason to focus on a certain person. Fundamentally, police operations that provide opportunities for crime change the police role from discovering who has committed a crime to one of discovering who might commit a crime if given a chance (Elliston and Feldberg, 1985: 137). For instance, a fake deer placed by the side of the road is used to entice overeager hunters, who are then arrested for violating hunting laws. Are only "bad" people tempted? This role expansion is arguably dangerous, undesirable, and inconsistent with the social contract basis of policing.

Police also undertake various "stings" in which they set up fencing operations to buy stolen goods. This action has been criticized as contributing to burglary. The opposing argument is that burglaries would occur regardless and that the good of catching criminals outweighs the negative possibility that burglars steal because they know the fence (police) will take their goods. Both of these arguments exist under a utilitarian framework. So even when using the same ethical system, a particular action may be supported as ethical or unethical. Other stings are even more creative, such as sending party invitations to those with outstanding warrants, or staging a murder and then arresting those (with outstanding warrants) who come out to see what is happening. The utility of such stings is undeniable. The only argument against them is that the government deception appears unseemly; it is possible that such actions may undermine public confidence in the police when they are telling the truth.

Journalists who unwittingly assist police by believing and publishing a false story also criticize this type of deception. There are a number of ethical issues in the relationship between the police and the media. Should the police intentionally lie to the media for a valuable end? An example might be lying about the stage of an investigation or to lie about the travel path of a public figure for security reasons. Should the media have complete power to publish or report crime activities regardless of the negative effect on the level of public fear or the possibility of receiving an unbiased trial? Should the media become so involved in hostage situations that they become the news rather than just the reporters of it? The situation involving David Koresh and his cult of Branch Davidians in Waco, Texas, in the spring of 1993 raised a number of questions concerning the relationship between the police and the media. For instance, the media were banished to a distance far away from the cult compound. Is this an acceptable use of police power, or does it infringe on the public's right to know? Could police have ethically used the media to deceive Koresh into giving up by feeding the media false information in response to his stated wish for a sign? Should the media have been better informed during the course of the final assault? These questions can all be analyzed using the ethical systems already described. A more recent situation involving the media concerned the bombing at the 1996 Summer Olympics in Atlanta. Should the FBI have disclosed to the public that Richard Jewell was its prime suspect and given the press the background information on him that led to the massive publicity and exposure of his life? The FBI's statements indicated a level of certainty regarding his guilt that turned out to be unsubstantiated. Jewell's experience resulted in a public letter of apology from the FBI and a lawsuit against the FBI and the television networks and the newspapers that violated his privacy, illustrating one reason that law enforcement may not want to be so forthcoming on the progress of investigations (FBI, 1996).

The Use of Undercover Officers

Undercover officers may have to observe or even participate in illegal activities to protect their cover. Undercover work is said to be a difficult role for the individual officer, who may play the part so well that the officer loses his or her previous identity. If the cover involves illegal or immoral action, the individual may have to sacrifice personal integrity to get an arrest. Marx cites examples of officers who have become addicted to drugs or alcohol and destroyed their marriages or careers because of undercover assignments (1985a: 109). Kim Wozencraft (1990), an ex-undercover narcotics officer, has written a novel in which two undercover officers use drugs and become friends with some of the pushers they are collecting evidence against, and although officials in the federal Drug Enforcement Agency (DEA), as well as local law enforcement, know that undercover officers sometimes use and even become addicted to drugs during the course of an investigation, they ignore or cover up such behavior in order to get successful convictions. Although the work is fiction, one suspects that at least some of the experiences that Wozencraft portrays are taken from reality.

Policemen routinely pretend they are "johns," and policewomen dress up as prostitutes. Do we want our police officers to engage in this type of activity? However, those community members who live in neighborhoods plagued with street prostitution may applaud any police efforts to clean up their streets. One important element of this debate is the type of relationship involved in

Literary Perspective

[An officer is discussing the end of an undercover operation in which he had pretended to be friends and business partners with members of a crime organization.]

The big day arrives. We go to the National Guard Armory that day at 4:00 in the morning. We're going to lock up like 28 mob figures in the state, then it was going to expand from there, once the investigation went to the grand jury. There's one hundred FBI agents, two hundred uniform troopers there when I walk in. Law enforcement up the ass. I think this is going to be the greatest day of my life. After two and half years, I'm finally coming back. The prodigal son.

I'm one of the main figures in the investigation, so I'm standing there next to all these people. We're supposed to get ready for this big press conference on the big raid. I don't have anything in common with them. They're the people I say yes sir and no sir to, that I have a military-like relationship that goes on between us, but it's no more than that. They don't come from my world and I don't belong in theirs. I wasn't able to sit with the troopers either. Nobody that looked like me was with the troopers. Those guys are turning, looking at me, pointing, but nobody is waving.

They start bringing in the defendants. They've picked them up and arrested them at their house. The armory is going to be the processing site. I was supposed to interview some of them. It would be a real shock value with me interviewing them. Maybe they would turn over quicker.

. . . I'm coming in, wearing a three-piece suit. My hands were behind my back. One of the guys says, "What did they pinch you for?"

"I'm with them," I said.

"You cocksucker," he says, and then he spit. They were just looking at me. I couldn't even look these guys in the eyes. Here's guys I hung out with, guys I broke bread with. I really came to like some of them. And they liked me, trusted me.

One guy comes up to me and says, "How could you do this, Ben? You're my friend. How could you do this?" He was sixty some years old. He was like anybody's grandfather, a nice guy, but he dealt in stolen securities. That's what we locked him up for. He put a heavy guilt trip on me. I couldn't look at him. I had to put my head down.

. . . Undercover is a very strange way to do police work, because you identify with them, the bad guys. It's a strange feeling to be trusted by someone and then betray them.

the police deception. The two extremes of intimacy are, on one hand, a brief buy–bust incident where the officer pretends to be a drug pusher and buys from a street dealer, and moments later an arrest is effected. At the other extreme would be a situation in which an undercover officer has an affair with a target of an investigation to maintain his or her cover. The second situation violates our sense of privacy to a much greater degree, yet there have been instances of detectives engaging in such relationships to gain confessions or other information. In one particular case, a private detective (not a police detective) engaged in this type of relationship over a period of months and even agreed to an engagement of marriage with the suspect in order to get a confession on tape (Schoeman, 1986: 21). In another case, an officer acted as a friend to a target of an investigation, to the extent of looking after his child and living in his house for six months. The purpose of the investigation was to get any evidence on the man so that the topless bar he owned could be shut down. Eventually, the officer found some white powder on a desk in the home that tested positive for cocaine, and a conviction was secured. The Supreme Court denied a writ of certiorari in this case (*United States v. Baldwin,* 621 F.2d 251 [1980]).

One of the reasons that some disagree with deceptive practices involving personal relationships is that they betray trust, an essential element of social life. As Schoeman (1985: 144) explains, intimate relationships are different from public exchanges and should be protected:

> Intimacy involves bringing another person within one's soul or being, not for any independently personal or instrumental objective, but for the sake of the other person or for the sake of the bond and attachment between the persons. . . . There is an expression of vulnerability and unenforceable trust within intimate relationships not present in business or social relationships. . . . Exploitation of trust and intimacy is also degrading to all persons who have respect for intimate relationships. Intimate relationships involve potential transformations of moral duties. Morally, an intimate relationship may take precedence over a concern for social well-being generally.

Note that he is probably arguing from an ethics of care position. In this ethical system, the relationship of two people is more important than rights, duties, or laws. There is no forfeiture in the ethics of care positions; thus, one can't say the suspect deserves to be deceived. The harm to the relationship goes in both directions. In cases where a personal relationship has developed, if the target is hurt by the deception, so too is the deceiver. Schoeman goes on to suggest some guidelines to be used when police interact with others in a deceptive manner. First, he believes that no interaction should go on longer than twenty-four hours without a warrant with probable cause. During this twenty-four-hour period, the officer may not enter any private area, even if invited, unless it is specifically to undertake some illegal activity. Second, although an undercover officer may engage in business and social relationships deceptively during the course of an investigation, he or she may not engage in intimate relationships. Finally, any evidence obtained in violation of the first two principles should be excluded from criminal trials against the targets (1985: 140). Police may criticize these suggestions. First, if there is probable cause, an arrest is possible, so why engage in a dangerous undercover operation? Second, almost all undercover operations last more than twenty-four hours. Finally, requiring a warrant is often unworkable given how undercover operations develop. The question remains: How can police best minimize the harm yet still obtain some utility from the action? This balancing is characteristic of utilitarian ethics.

Police engage in investigative deception because it is the best (or easiest?) way to investigate drug sales, prostitution, organized crime, illegal alien smuggling, and so on. It is almost necessary in undercover work, especially in the area of vice, to employ deception and techniques that might be considered entrapment. If the goal of police is crime control, then there is a clear inclination to use utilitarian rationales to justify deception as a means to an end. If the goal of police is public service, such activities are arguably harder to justify.

Marx (1985a: 106–107) proposes that before engaging in undercover operations, police investigators should ask the following questions:

1. How serious is the crime being investigated?
2. How clear is the definition of the crime—that is, would the target know that what he or she is doing is clearly illegal?
3. Are there any alternatives to deceptive practices?
4. Is the undercover operation consistent with the spirit as well as the letter of the law?
5. Is it public knowledge that the police may engage in such practices, and is the decision to do so a result of democratic decision making?
6. Is the goal prosecution as opposed to general intelligence gathering or harassment?
7. Is there a likelihood that the crime would occur regardless of the government's involvement?
8. Are there reasonable grounds to suspect the target?
9. Will the practice prevent a serious crime from occurring?

The Use of Informants

Police also use informants who often continue to commit crime while helping police by providing information on other criminal activities. The following describes an informant who had police protection withdrawn (Scheingold, 1984: 122):

> The problem is that by the time Detective Tumulty decided to bury Carranza, the informant had already committed, by his own count, two hundred crimes, and he had confessed over one hundred of them to the police. It is not surprising that business persons victimized by Carranza were not particularly pleased when they learned the police had failed to prosecute him.

Protection is sometimes carried to extreme limits. The federal witness protection plan has provided new identities several times to witnesses after they have accumulated bad debts or otherwise victimized an unwary public. The rationale for informant protection, of course, is that greater benefit is derived from using them to catch other criminals than their punishment would bring. This also extends to overlooking any minor crime that they engage in during

Getting Away with Murder?

Excerpts from Two Related Articles

Mark Garrett, a 25-year-old from Charlotte, N.C., died in 1987 during a fight with a co-worker, who shot him in the back of the head and dumped his body on a back road.

Since the killer was apprehended in 1991 Garrett's family members have taken some comfort in the belief that he was doing hard time in federal prison.

They were wrong.

Javier Cruz, an admitted cocaine trafficker from Colombia, served about 16 months in the Salem-Roanoke County Jail and a few days in a North Carolina prison for killing Garrett. He is now running a Roanoke County nightclub and living in a $288,000 home in Clearbrook—with help from the federal government.

A fugitive once on North Carolina's most wanted list and sought by the FBI, Cruz parlayed his ties with the Cali cocaine cartel into a career in Roanoke as an undercover informant that has lasted more than five years.

He's helped the U.S. Drug Enforcement Administration in one of the biggest undercover investigations in the country, law enforcement sources say. In exchange, agents helped him get a plea bargain on a first-degree murder charge and have put drug trafficking charges against him on hold for five years. . . .

Cruz was trafficking in massive quantities of cocaine, using Roanoke as a base. . . . Cruz was in charge of distribution for a major Colombian trafficker, Leonardo Rivera-Ruiz of New York, according to the DEA's affidavit. When they arrested Cruz, DEA agents seized $37,000 in cash concealed in his Buick parked in the garage of his Salem home. Another $300,000 was found hidden behind the back seat of his Cadillac in Florida. . . .

The DEA arrested him on the outstanding murder warrant instead of on drug charges, apparently so his associates wouldn't know that police were aware of his drug trafficking, preserving his value as a potential informant.

An agent from the DEA flew to Charlotte to urge the prosecutor to drop the charge in Garrett's death, arguing that his help could lead to arrests of major international traffickers.

Although the prosecutor, Steve Ward, refused to drop Cruz's murder charge outright, he did agree to a plea bargain on the reduced charge of involuntary manslaughter. Ward defends that decision, saying the evidence could support the self defense theory [that Cruz would use].

"I'd have an impossible time disproving his story," Ward said. "This was a good disposition given the circumstances." . . .

The Garretts were told that after Cruz finished helping the DEA on its drug case, he would come back to be sentenced for involuntary manslaughter.

In August 1992—16 months after his arrest—Cruz was brought back to Charlotte. But neither Garrett's family nor the police were notified.

Court and prison records indicate that Cruz received a three-year sentence Aug. 21 and that he was taken to a North Carolina prison. But he was credited with almost 16 months for time already served, and he walked out of the prison Aug. 27, 1992, according to North Carolina Department of Corrections records. . . .

The jail time Cruz was credited with apparently was served in the Salem-Roanoke County Jail, where he and Rivera—who also agreed to cooperate [with

(continued)

Getting Away with Murder? *(continued)*

---

the DEA]—were locked up by themselves on the sixth floor. . . . Federal agents visited them almost daily, and they were released from jail and returned more than a dozen times each, for periods ranging from a few days to two months. . . .

[Cruz said] he has repaid his debt to society by his work as an informant, work that including putting his life in jeopardy during trips to Colombia to meet with cartel leaders. . . . "There are more than 200 or 300 people in jail."

SOURCE: Vertefeuille, J. "Did He Get Away with Murder?" *The Roanoke Times,* 8 Nov. 1996: A1, A14. "Is Debt to Society Paid?" *The Roanoke Times,* 9 Nov. 1996: A1, A4. Reprinted with permission.

---

the period of time they provide information, or afterward if that is part of the deal (Marx, 1985a: 109). However, the ethical soundness of this judgment may be seriously questioned. Police use informants partly to avoid problems that undercover police officers would encounter if they attempted to accomplish the task, but also because informants are under fewer restrictions. As Marx reports,

> Informers and, to an even greater extent, middlemen, are much less formally accountable than are sworn law officers and are not as constrained by legal or departmental restrictions. As an experienced undercover agent candidly put it, "unwitting informers are desirable precisely because they can do what we can't—legally entrap."

An incident in Houston where an informant was killed in a drug buy brought to light the many ethical issues raised by using informants. This individual came to the police to help them identify pushers. He was married and had small children. He engaged in drug deals, and after they occurred, the police would arrest the drug sellers. In one such incident, the informant was in a motel room with the pushers and was evidently identified as an informant and killed before police could enter the room. The informant was not wearing a wire, and he had no weapon or means of protecting himself. Unlike the families of undercover police officers killed in the line of duty, his family is without benefits of compensation for his death (*Houston Post,* 24 Jan. 1993: A20). Some observers question the use of civilians in such dangerous operations. One might point out the fact that this informant freely volunteered his services, unlike some informants, who are threatened with prosecution if they do not cooperate.

Some officers openly admit that they could not do their job without informants. Some develop close working relationships with informants, while others maintain that you can't trust them no matter how long you've known them. There are disturbing questions one might ask about the use of private citizens for police means. It may be true that narcotics investigations are difficult, if not impossible, without the use of informants. If so, then guidelines and standards are needed to govern the use of informants. (The Commission on Accreditation for Law Enforcement Agencies [CALEA] has developed such standards.) In the next section, some general justifications are discussed that relate to all undercover and deceptive investigative tactics.

Justifications for Undercover Operations

Undercover operations have been criticized for the following reasons (Marx, 1992: 117–118):

1. They may generate a market for the purchase or sale of illegal goods and services.
2. They may generate the idea for the crime.
3. They may generate the motive.
4. They may provide a missing resource.
5. They may entail coercion or intimidation of a person otherwise not predisposed to commit the offense.
6. They may generate a covert opportunity structure for illegal actions on the part of the undercover agent or informant.
7. They may lead to retaliatory violence against informers.
8. They may stimulate a variety of crimes on the part of those who are not targets of the undercover operation (for example, impersonation of a police officer, crimes committed against undercover officers).

Ethical systems may or may not support undercover operations. The *principle of double effect* holds that when one does an action to achieve a good end and an inevitable but unintended effect is negative, then the action might be justified. For instance, if a woman having an operation to save her life loses her fetus, this is not immoral because under the principle of double effect, the death of the fetus was an unintended consequence of the good effect of saving the life of the woman. Of course, abortion would not be an appropriate example of the principle because the death of the fetus is intended. We might justify police action in a similar way if the unethical consequence, such as the deception of an innocent, was not the intended consequence of the action and the goal was an ethical one. However, deceiving the suspect could not be justified under the principle of double effect because that is an intended effect, not an unintended effect.

Religious ethics would probably condemn many kinds of police actions because of the deceptions involved. Ethical formalism would condemn such actions because one could not justify them under the categorical imperative. Further, innocent family members being used as a means to a conviction of an offender would also violate the categorical imperative. Utilitarian ethics might justify police deception and deceptive techniques if one could make the argument that catching criminals provides greater benefit to society than allowing them to go free by refusing to engage in such practices. Act utilitarianism would probably support deceptive practices, but rule utilitarianism might not, because the actions, although beneficial under certain circumstances, might in the long run undermine and threaten our system of law. Finally, egoism might or might not justify such actions depending on the particular officer involved and what his or her maximum gain and loss was determined to be.

Under act utilitarianism, one would measure the harm of the criminal activity against the methods used to control it. Deceptive practices, then, might be justified in the case of drug offenses but not for business misdeeds or for finding a murderer but not for trapping a prostitute, and so on. The difficulty of this line of reasoning, of course, is agreeing on a standard of seriousness. I might decide that drugs are serious enough to justify otherwise unethical practices, but you may not. Pornography and prostitution may be serious enough to some to justify unethical practices, but to others only murder or violent crime would justify the practices.

Cohen (1991) proposes a test to determine the ethical justification for police practices. His focus is the use of coercive power to stop and search, but we might apply the same test to analyze undercover or other deceptive practices. First, the end must be justified as a good—for instance, conviction of a serious criminal rather than general intelligence gathering. Second, the means must be a plausible way to achieve the end—for example, choosing a target with no reasonable suspicion is not a plausible way to reduce any type of crime. Third, there must be no better alternative means to achieve the same end: no less-intrusive means or methods of collecting evidence exist. Finally, the means must not undermine some other equal or greater end; that is, if the method results in loss of trust or faith in the legal system, it fails the test.

Many people see nothing wrong—certainly nothing illegal—in using any methods necessary to catch criminals. But we are concerned with methods in use before individuals are proved to be criminal. Can an innocent person, such as you, be entrapped into crime? Perhaps not, but are we comfortable in a society where the person who offers you drugs or sex or a cheap way to hook into cable turns out to be an undercover police officer? Are we content to assume that our telephone may be tapped or our best friend could be reporting our conversations to someone else? When we encounter police behavior in these areas, very often the practices have been used to catch a person whom we realize, after the fact, had engaged in wrongdoing, so we feel that police are justified in performing in slightly unethical ways. What protectors of due process and critics of police investigation practices help us to remember is that those practices, if not curbed, may just as easily be used on the innocent as well as on the guilty.

It is clear that norms support police deception during the investigative phase. Police view evidentiary restrictions as a hindrance to their mission of crime control. If their norms support deception during investigation, it is not surprising that they may protect themselves with deception when their methods are legally questioned. In fact, one of the problems with deceptive practices is that they may lead to more deception to cover up illegal methods. For

Ethical Justifications for and Arguments Against Undercover Work

For:

1. Citizens grant to government the right to use means which they individually forsake.
2. Undercover work is ethical when its targets are persons who freely choose to commit crimes which they know may call forth deceptive police practices.
3. Undercover work is ethical when used for a good and important end.
4. Undercover work is ethical when there are reasonably specific grounds to suspect that a serious crime is planned or has been carried out.
5. Undercover work is ethical when it is directed against persons whom there are reasonable grounds to suspect.
6. When citizens use questionable means, government agents are justified in using equivalent means.
7. Special risks justify special precautions.
8. Undercover work is ethical when it is the best means.
9. Enforce the law equally.
10. Convict the guilty.
11. An investigation should be as non-intrusive and non-coercive as possible.
12. Undercover work is ethical when it is undertaken with the intention of eventually being made public and literally judged in court.
13. Undercover work is ethical when it is carried out by persons of upright character in accountable organizations.

Against:

1. Truth telling is moral; lying is immoral.
2. The government should not make deals with criminals.
3. The government should neither participate in, nor be a party to crime, nor break laws in order to enforce them.
4. The government through its actions should reduce, not increase crime.
5. The government should not create an intention to commit a crime which is impossible to carry out.
6. The government should neither tempt the weak, nor offer temptation indiscriminately, nor offer unrealistically attractive temptations.
7. Do no harm to the innocent.
8. Respect the sanctity of private places.
9. Respect the sanctity of intimate relations.
10. Respect the right to freedom of expression and action.
11. The government should not do by stealth what it is prohibited from doing openly.

SOURCE: Marx, G. "Police Undercover Work: Ethical Deception or Deceptive Ethics." In *Police Ethics: Hard Choices in Law Enforcement,* ed. W. Heffernan and T. Stroup (New York: John Jay Press, 1985). All rights reserved. Reprinted by permission.

instance, Skolnick (1982) argues that weak or nonexistent standards during the investigation phase of policing lead directly to lying on the witness stand because that is sometimes the only way an officer can save his or her case.

It is unlikely that these investigative techniques will ever be eliminated; perhaps they should not be, since they are effective in catching a number of people who should be punished. Even if one has doubts about the ethics of these practices, it is entirely possible that there is no other way to accomplish the goal of crime control. However one decides these difficult questions, there are no easy answers. Also, it is important to realize that although for us these questions are academic, for thousands of police officers they are very real.

Deception in Interrogation

Deception often takes a different form in the interrogation phase of a case. Several court cases document the use of mental coercion, either through threat or promise. The use of the "father confessor" approach (a sympathetic paternal figure for the defendant to confide to) or "Mutt and Jeff" partners (a "nice guy" and a seemingly brutal, threatening officer) are other ways to induce confessions and/or obtain information (Kamisar, LeFave, and Israel, 1980: 54).

Skolnick and Leo (1982) present a typology of deceptive interrogation techniques. The following is a brief summary of their descriptions of these practices:

- Calling the questioning an interview rather than an interrogation by questioning in a noncustodial setting and telling the suspect that he is free to leave, thus eliminating the need for Miranda warnings.
- Presenting Miranda warnings in a way designed to negate their effect, by mumbling or by using a tone suggesting that the offender better not exercise the rights delineated or that they are unnecessary.
- Misrepresenting the nature or seriousness of the offense by, for instance, not telling the suspect that the victim had died.
- Using manipulative appeals to conscience through role playing or other means.
- Misrepresenting the moral seriousness of the offense—for instance, by pretending that the rape victim "deserved" to be raped to get a confession.
- Using promises of lesser sentences or nonprosecution beyond the power of the police to offer.
- Misrepresenting identity by pretending to be lawyers or priests.
- Using fabricated evidence such as polygraph results or fingerprint findings that don't really exist.

Skolnick writes that because physical means of coercion are no longer used—the infamous third degree—mental deception is the only means left for police officers to gain information or confessions from suspects. How does one get a killer to admit to where she left the murder weapon? If police are imaginative, they may be able to get the defendant to confess by encouraging her to think about what would happen if children found the gun. Or police may discover the location of a body by convincing the killer after he had refused to talk to police that the victim deserves a Christian burial (see *Brewer v. Williams*, 430 U.S. 387, 97 S.Ct. 1232, 51 L.Ed.2d 424 [1977]). Courts have ruled that police who use these methods are unconstitutionally infringing on the defendant's right to counsel because the conversations, even if not direct questioning, constitute an interrogation. However, other cases where police impersonate religious figures, for instance, find courts more accepting of police deceptions. Other than whether police have a legal right to deceive a suspect, one might also ask whether it is ethical to use deception to gain a confession and, if so, what are the limits of such deception?

It is certainly much easier to justify deceptive interrogation than physical coercion and intimidation, but their justifications are the same—that is, one uses means that are effective and perhaps necessary to get needed information from a resisting subject. However, most countries have refused to accept this justification for physical coercion and formally condemn the practice. Unfortunately, some countries still endorse physical coercion as acceptable police practice. Reports from Amnesty International document abuses in Chile, Argentina, and many other countries around the world. It is important to note that very often in these situations police are used as the means of control by the dominant political power. Therefore, they operate not under the law, as the code of ethics dictates, but above the law. Codes of ethics, adopted by many police departments that have recognized the danger of police power being misused, are very clear in directing police to abide by the law and not allow themselves to be used by people or political parties (Bossard, 1981).

Many would argue that whatever information is gained from an individual who is physically coerced into confessing or giving information is not worth the sacrifice of moral standards. The court is primarily concerned with prohibiting methods that would bring the truth of the confession into question. The original legal proscriptions against torture, in fact, come not from an ethical rationale, but from a legal rationale that torture makes a confession unreliable. Tortured victims might confess to stop their suffering; thus, the court would not get truthful information. Our concern is with the ethical nature of the action itself. If we agree that it is wrong to use physical force or coercion to obtain a confession, do we also agree that deception is an acceptable alternative? If we agree that some deception is acceptable, what are the limits on its use? Again, there seems to be room for reasonable people to disagree on this issue.

COERCION AND THE USE OF FORCE

Klockars (1983) describes the inevitability of certain unethical or immoral police behaviors as the "Dirty Harry problem," after the movie character who did not let the law get in his way when pursuing criminals. In Klockars's view, using immoral means to reach a desired moral end is an unresolvable problem because there are situations where one knows the "dirty act" will result in a good end, there are no other means to achieve the good end, and the "dirty act" will not be in vain. Klockars's example of this type of problem, taken from a movie, is a situation where a captured criminal refuses to tell the location of a kidnapped victim. Because the victim is sure to die without help, the police officer (played by Clint Eastwood) tortures the criminal by stepping on his injured leg until he admits the location. Obviously, this is an immoral act, but Klockars's point is that there is no solution to the situation. If the police officer behaved in a professional manner, the victim was sure to die; if he behaved in an immoral manner, there was a chance he could save a life. Academic literature does not generally present this dilemma, but in detective and police fiction, it is a dominant theme. Klockars's conclusion is that by engaging in "dirty" means for good ends, the officer has tainted his innocence and must be punished, because there is always a danger that dirty means will be redefined by those who use them as neutral or even good. Police may lose their sense of moral proportion if the action is not punished, even though the individual police officer involved may have no other way out of the moral dilemma.

Delattre (1989) also discusses the use of coercive power. He disagrees with Klockars that the officer must inevitably be tainted in the Dirty Harry situation. Delattre points out that if one chooses physical coercion, regardless of temptation, this leads to perjury and lying about the activity and perhaps other tactics to ensure that the offender does not go free due to the illegal behavior of the police officer. However, he also excuses the actions of those who succumb to temptation in extreme situations and perform an illegal act (Delattre, 1986: 211):

> Police officials are not tainted by refusing to step onto the slope of illegal action, neither are officials of demonstrated probity necessarily tainted by a last-ditch illegal step. Such an act may be unjustifiable by an unconditional principle, but it also may be excusable. . . . Still less does it follow that those who commit such acts are bad, that their character is besmirched, or that their honor is tainted.

One might argue that if officers commit an illegal and unethical act, it is hard for their character not to be affected or their honor tainted. To understand an action (in this case an act that results from anger or frustration) is not to excuse it. Delattre presents a virtue-based ethical system and evidently believes that an officer can have all the virtues of a good officer and still commit a bad action—in this case, the illegal use of force. His point that one act of violence does not necessarily mean that the officer is unethical in other ways is well taken. In fact, we usually reserve the terms *ethical* and *unethical* for actions rather than persons. The reaction of the officer to his or her mistake is the true test of character. Does the officer cover up and/or ask his or her partner to cover up the action? Does the officer lie to protect himself or herself? Or does the officer admit wrongdoing and accept the consequences?

Klockars's underlying point is more subtle: we all are guilty in a sense by expecting certain ones among us to do the "dirty work" and then condemning them for their actions. In times of war, and when dealing with other threats, the populace often wants results without wanting to know tactics. What percentage of the population cared that the CIA attempted to assassinate Fidel Castro or that the Attorney General's office during the Kennedy years used questionable tactics and violated the due process rights of Cosa Nostra members targeted in the campaign against organized crime? How many of us truly want to know about the clandestine operations of Special Forces? Klockars points out the position of those who perform the despicable acts that benefit the rest of us; we are comfortable in our ignorance and comfortable in our judgments, as long as we don't have to look too closely at our own role in the events. Police (and other law enforcement), in effect, become our "sin eaters" of early folklore; they are the shady characters on the fringe of society who absorb evil so that the rest of us may remain pure—shunned and avoided, these persons and their value are taken for granted.

Muir also discusses this necessity for the use of coercion: a good police officer, he writes, "has to resolve the contradiction of achieving just ends with coercive means" (Muir, 1977: 3). According to Muir, the successful police officer is able to balance willingness to use coercion with an understanding of humankind, which includes such traits as empathy and sympathy toward the weaknesses of human nature. If officers overemphasize coercion, they become cynical and brutal; if they overemphasize understanding, they become ineffectual:

> Under certain conditions, a youthful policeman was likely to come upon solutions to the paradoxes of coercive power which enabled him to accept the use of coercion as legitimate. However, if his solution to his moral problems required him to blind himself to the tragedy of the human condition, then he became an enforcer. Under other circumstances, a young policeman's choice of responses to paradox left him in conflict about the morality of coercion. Then he would be transfixed by feelings of guilt, would tend to evade situations which aroused those feelings, and would develop a perspective to justify his evasions. This kind of officer became either a reciprocator or an avoider. Finally some young officers found ways to exercise coercion legitimately without having to deny their "common sense of the oneness of the human condition." These men became professionals. (Muir, 1977: 24)

Up to this point we have been discussing the use of instrumental force—force used to achieve an end. Probably more incidents involving the unlawful use of force incidents display expressive force—force used in anger, frustration, or fear. The use of force by Los Angeles police against Rodney King mentioned before is an example of force used for instrumental or expressive ends, depending on who you believe. This case represents a situation in which policy, law, and ethics present different answers to this question: "Did the officers do anything wrong?" The legal question of unlawful use of force is contingent on whether the Los Angeles Police Department's use-of-force policy was legal and whether the officers conformed to departmental policy. The policy stated that the officers could use escalating and proportional force to a suspect's "offensive" behavior. The reason that two use-of-force experts—one for the prosecution and one for the defense—disagreed was that the policy, like many other policies in policing, depends on the ethical use of discretion. The defense use-of-force expert analyzed the video and identified offensive movements in every attempt to rise and every arm movement. The prosecution expert, who wrote the policy, testified that a suspect lying on the ground is not in a position to present offensive movements to officers. If an officer perceives offensiveness in every movement of every suspect, the policy justifies his or her use of force.

In other applications of the policy, one can see that the policy leaves a great deal of room for choice and that, in most cases, an officer's perceptions of the ethical use of force will become as powerful, if not more so, than the policy itself. If an officer gets shot at, this obviously would justify use of force under the policy, but if the officer decides that he or she is safe enough behind his or her patrol car to talk the suspect out of shooting again and into giving up the weapon, then the use-of-force policy would support that nonviolent response as well. If an officer is hit in the face by a drunk, the policy would support use of force since the drunk obviously performed an offensive action; however, the officer who accepts the fact that the drunk is irrational, allows for it, and simply puts the person in the back of the patrol car (in effect, giving him a "free punch") is also supported by the policy. In other words, the policy can be used to justify all but the most blatant abuse of police power, or not, depending on the interpretation of the individual officer.

Thus, in the Rodney King incident, an initial act of passing a police vehicle and leading officers in a high-speed chase (although the actual speed of such chase was subject to dispute) led to the involvement of twelve police cars, one helicopter, and up to twenty-seven officers. The incident resulted in King being struck at least fifty-six times, with eleven skull fractures, a broken cheekbone, a fractured eye socket, a broken ankle, missing teeth, kidney damage, external burns, and permanent brain damage (Kappeler, Sluder, and Alpert, 1994: 146). After the incident, officers justified their actions by the explanation that King was on PCP (he was not, and in fact his alcohol level was .075), impervious to pain, and wild. These claims were repeated in the newspapers and can be interpreted as the attempt to fit the use of force into a pattern that the public could understand and accept. In fact, police use of force probably became an incident in this case only because of the videotape. In other circumstances, it would hardly have rated a small newspaper article. The media typically become interested in police use of force when the victim cannot be fit into the stereotype of the "dangerous criminal": when he is a middle-class insurance agent (in the Miami case that sparked riots), Andrew Young's son (in a incident involving the Washington, D.C., police), or a high school athlete who would have been on his way to Yale on an academic/athletic scholarship.

Literary Perspective

I saw one guy arrested once for speeding and the police officer lost his temper. Of course, this highway patrolman brought it on himself, because he was bad-mouthing the guy. Finally—he's a man, too—the guy lost his temper and spit on the highway patrolman.

Right on the side of a U.S. highway on a Sunday afternoon, the highway patrolman wrestled the guy down, took a handful of hair and held his head down in the dirt and started packing the guy's mouth full of sand. The guy was choking and spitting and this patrolman was shoving sand in his mouth. "I'll teach you to spit at a trooper, boy." Those were his exact words. I'm standing in the background, watching the cars go by, slowing down to stare at this event. It looked bad.

SOURCE: Baker, Mark. *Cops* (New York: Pocket Books, 1985): 139–140. Copyright © 1985 by Mark Baker. Reprinted with permission of Simon & Schuster.

How do these people come to the attention of police? Often it is by challenging police authority—passing a patrol car, asking questions, challenging the stop, intervening in the arrest of another (Kappeler, Sluder, and Alpert, 1994: 159). In Klockars's description of authority, power, persuasion, and force, one might describe violence as being force brought into play when authority is denied. Individuals who challenge police authority become vulnerable to the use of force. Obviously, one point that should be made is that police must behave in ways to deserve their authority; the difference between legal use of force and excessive force is whether or not police have exceeded the means necessary to achieve a legitimate governmental purpose. Gratuitous violence in response to insults does not meet this definition, nor does force used to subdue a suspect when the only wrong committed was an insult.

Law enforcement responses to perceived challenges to authority are the effect of police socialization and are highly resistant to new policies or public pressure. Even with the heavy scrutiny placed on law enforcement after the Rodney King episode and the extreme public reaction to the spectacle of police use of force, several incidents involving other officers' abusive behavior toward motorists occurred shortly afterwards. It may be that this pattern is so ingrained in some police departmental cultures that it remains relatively unaffected.

Some officers seem to get involved in use-of-force situations repeatedly, while others, even with similar patrol neighborhoods, rarely get involved in such altercations. Thus, even if every use of force meets the guidelines of the policy, there are lingering questions as to why some officers seem to need to enforce the policy more often than others and why some interpret actions more often as offensive. According to Souryal (1992: 242), the report by the Independent Commission of the Los Angeles Police Department (1991) reveals that the top 5 percent of officers ranked by number of reports of the use of force accounted for more than 20 percent of all reports, and that of approximately 1,800 officers who had been reported for excessive use of force from

---

Use of Force

- A police officer pointed a gun at a 9 year old's head and threatened to pull the trigger. The child was not a suspect trying to evade the officers or posing any other threat. *McDonald v. Haskins,* 966 F.2d 292 (7th Cir. 1992)
- Two men on a motorcycle accidentally brushed the bumper of a DEA car. One DEA agent got out and began a physical altercation with the driver of the motorcycle. When the passenger intervened, both agents beat him and yelled anti-homosexual epithets. When the driver asked why they were beating the other man, he was beaten as well. *Anderson v. Branen,* 17 F.3d 552, rehearing denied 27 F.3d 29 (2nd Dis. 1994)
- An individual was met by police officers in the hallway of his apartment building who were there looking for a person who was making fraudulent calls. They shoved him against the wall, threatened him, struck him, and dragged him down the stairs. *Goetz v. Cappelen,* 946 F.2d 511 (7th Cir. 1991)

1986 to 1990, most had only one or two allegations, but forty-four had six or more, sixteen had eight or more, and one had sixteen allegations.

All information regarding police use of force is controlled by police, including the number of incidents, the taking of reports, and the amount of information recorded. The ability to access this information is limited, even in cases dealing with a challenge to the officer's use of force. The official version of any event is that force was necessary because of dangerous offensive actions, this interpretation is often supported by other police, and there is usually little evidence (unless there is a videotape). The victim is often an unsavory character who would be a poor choice for sympathy, and supporting witnesses may have their credibility questioned. Kappeler, Sluder, and Alpert (1994: 222) report that in Washington, D.C., widely known for incidents of brutality, including the one against Andrew Young's eighteen-year-old son, of twenty-one cases in which the Civilian Complaint Review Board recommended adverse actions against officers for use of force, the police chief took action in only five of them.

The most common explanations for police officer use of force are similar to those used to explain correctional officer use of excessive force—that force is the only thing "these people" understand or that "officers are only human" and consequently get mad or frightened or angry, just like anyone else would in that situation. The weakness of such arguments is obvious. If other people get mad and use force, it is called assault and battery and they are arrested and prosecuted. Even if the only thing "these people" understand is force, it removes the differences that we like to think exist between us to use reactive force against them. As stated before, the use of excessive force is probably not as pervasive in this country today as it was even twenty years ago. However, the concern is that it is hard to know what occurs because the data are not readily available and individual victims often do not come forward or, if they do, are not taken seriously.

It seems that there are always a few officers in every department who are truly abusers of power, but the other officers and an organizational culture protect these officers from sanctions. The more common ethical issue concerning the use of force is that of the officer who observes an unlawful use of force by another officer. This issue is addressed in the next section.

LOYALTY AND WHISTLEBLOWING

Do officers owe their primary loyalty to the department, to the society, or to their fellow officers? One of the most frequent and difficult ethical choices that officers confront is what to do when faced with the wrongdoing of another officer. Informing on one's peers has always been negatively perceived by a large contingent of any group, whether that group be lawyers, doctors, students, prisoners, or police officers. The "code of silence" discussed in relation to police work is present in other occupations and groups as well. Why we look away or do not come forward when others do wrong may be egoistic: we don't want to get involved; we don't want to face the scorn of others; we feel it's not our job to come forward when there are others who are supposed to look out for and punish wrongdoing; we don't want to alienate the peer who committed the wrong by reporting him or her. Of course, coming forward may be egoistic as well: we are afraid we will be blamed if the perpetrator is not correctly identified, or we will tell the truth to avoid punishment ourselves. With police, this loyalty often involves covering up for police who use excessive force, drink on duty, or otherwise commit unethical and even illegal actions. Cover-ups often involve many officers and even supervisors.

Loyalty in police work is explained by the fact that police depend on one another, sometimes in life-or-death situations. Loyalty to one's fellows is part of the *esprit de corps* of policing and an absolutely essential element of a healthy department. Ewin (1990) writes that something is wrong if a police officer doesn't feel loyalty to fellow officers. Loyalty is a personal relationship, not a judgment. Therefore, loyalty is uncalculating—we do not extend loyalty in a rational way or based on contingencies. Loyalty to groups or persons is emotional, grounded in affection rather than reflection. Wren (1985) also writes of loyalty as an internal moral position, as opposed to external reasoning, such as utilitarianism and deontological arguments. He points out that utilitarianism may defend or condemn informing on other police officers. Arguments against informing are that some activities labeled corrupt actually may further the ends of justice and that complete adherence to regulations would undermine detection and enforcement. Also, the loss of a skilled police officer, even though that officer may be moderately corrupt, is a loss to society. Arguments for informing are that the harm from a scandal caused by the individual's coming forward would be less than the good of the public's believing that the department was finally free from corruption and that individual corruption would come to a halt.

Police Cover-Up?

At the station house Niehus became obstreperous, in part he says because he was afraid that an arrest for drunk driving would jeopardize his status with his employer and with the army reserves in which he is a sergeant. The police handcuffed one of his arms to the chair in which they had told him to sit. He demanded to be allowed to call his lawyer and to this end tried to slide his chair across the room to the telephone. The defendant officers tried to stop him. Niehus says that they started hitting him and that he fell on the floor and curled up with the left side of his face on the floor and his right arm over his head to protect him. He says they kicked him between five and fifteen times in the head while he was lying there and some of the kicks struck the left side of his head even though it was resting on the floor. . . . The defendants testified that right after the fight with Niehus in the station house they took mug shots of him, but that when later they looked for the photos in Niehus's file they couldn't find them. They speculate that the camera was broken in the fight. But there was testimony . . . that the same camera was working fine the next day. And right after the fight the officers had talked with their supervisor by phone and the phone conversation had been routinely taped, but the tape was never produced. One employee of the police department testified that the tape was erased routinely, but another testified that the tape recorder was malfunctioning on the day of the fight, and the jury may have thought that this was one excuse too many. A third employee, whose job it was to monitor conversations in the booking room where the fight occurred, gave contradictory testimony about what she heard. . . . Given the degree of cooperation evident among the employees of the Berkeley Police Department, it is nearly certain that the custodian of the evidence would have made it available to the defendants had it been helpful to them.

SOURCE: *Niehus v. Liberio,* 973 F.2d 526 (7th Cir. 1992).

Another factor that must be taken into account is the public's lack of faith in police credibility after recurring examples of cover-ups. Sykes (1996) describes a civil case wherein a jury awarded $15.9 million in damages after a case of police brutality. Jurors simply did not believe the police version of the events, and a videotape supported the plaintiff's allegations that excessive force was used. The "cost" of police cover-ups eventually becomes public distrust of police testimony. As mentioned previously, perhaps the O. J. Simpson trial will eventually become the classic example of what happens when a jury loses confidence in police testimony. Prosecutors can ordinarily rely on a jury to take police testimony as fact and even favor police testimony over nonpolice witnesses. When police testimony is given no greater weight than any other witness—indeed, when jury members believe that police are prone to lie on the stand—then the justice system itself is at risk.

Deontological arguments can also be used to support exposing or not exposing other officers. Arguments for informing include the fact that a police officer has a sworn duty to uphold the law. Also, one cannot remain silent in one situation unless one could approve of silence in all situations (Kant's categorical imperative), and one must do one's duty. Arguments against informing include the idea that discretion and secrecy are obligations one assumes by joining a police force and that it would be unjust to subject an otherwise good and heroic police officer to the punishment of exposure (Wren, 1985: 32–33).

These arguments are what Wren calls external moral arguments, which he contrasts with internal arguments, such as loyalty. When one considers whether to come forward about the wrongdoing of others, external moral philosophies are rarely very well articulated. What often is the prime motivator is personal integrity. Yet the individual often feels great anguish and self-doubt over turning in friends and colleagues, and that is understandable since "a person's character is defined by his commitments, the more basic of which reveal to a person what his life is all about and give him a reason for going on" (Wren, 1985: 35). Thus, the issue of whistleblowing comes down to loyalty to persons or groups versus loyalty to one's principles of integrity and honesty.

Ewin (1990: 13) also points out that loyalty always refers to a preference for one group over another:

> Loyalty always involves some exclusion: one is loyal to X rather than to Y, with Y thus being excluded. At times, the reverse can also be true: that a group of people is excluded (whether or not they are properly excluded) can make them feel a common cause in response to what they see as oppression and can result in the growth of loyalty amongst them. That loyalty, provoked by a dislike and perhaps distrust of the other group, is likely to be marked by behavior that ignores legitimate interests and concerns of the other group.

The application to policing is obvious. If police feel isolated from the community, their loyalty is to other police officers and not to the community at large. If they feel oppressed by and distrust the police administration, they would draw together against the "common enemy." To address abuses of loyalty, one would not want to attack the loyalty itself because it is necessary for the health of the organization. Rather, one would want to extend the loyalty beyond other officers to the department, and to the community. Permeability rather than isolation promotes community loyalty, just as the movement

---

QUOTATION

At the trial, it just really angered me that deputies could identify suspects from booking photos, people they never knew, and describe in detail what actions people did that night, people they hardly ever saw. And yet throughout the entire trial I don't think there was ever one deputy who was able to identify their fellow deputies or any of the actions that their fellow deputies did that night.

SOURCE: Reported in Sykes, G. "How Much Is Our Credibility Worth?" *The Ethics Roll Call* 3(1) (1996): 5.

toward professionalism promotes loyalty to the principles of ethical policing as opposed to individuals in a particular department.

Wren believes that police departments can resolve the dilemma of the individual officer who knows of wrongdoing by making the consequences more palatable—that is, by having a fair system of investigation and punishment, by instituting helping programs for those with alcohol and drug problems, and by using more moderate punishments than dismissal or public exposure for other sorts of misbehavior. This is consistent with the ethics of care, which is concerned with needs and relationships. If the relationship can be saved and the need for honesty and change met, then that is the best alternative to the dilemma of exposing wrongdoing or not.

Delattre (1989) handles the problem differently but comes to somewhat similar conclusions. He turns to Aristotle to support the idea that when a friend becomes a "scoundrel" the moral individual cannot stand by and do nothing. Rather, one has a moral duty to bring the wrongdoing to the friend's attention and urge her or him to change. If the friend will not, then she or he is more scoundrel than friend, and the individual's duty shifts to those who might be victimized by the officer's behavior. One sees here not the ethics of care, but a combination of virtue-based and deontological duty-based ethics.

The practice of sanctioning individuals who come forward is an especially distressing aspect of loyalty. For the individual who tears the blue curtain of secrecy, sanctions can be extreme.

A typical example of retaliation is reported in a San Antonio newspaper concerning an officer in the San Antonio police department who arrested a sergeant for driving while intoxicated. Even though the officer previously averaged fewer than two complaints a year during his eleven years at the police department, after he arrested the sergeant, he received nine complaints resulting in a total of eighty-six days of suspension. He also experienced the follow-

---

FBI Suspends Agent Whose Charges Led to Critical Report

WASHINGTON—The FBI has suspended a scientist agent whose charges led to a still secret Justice Department report critical of some FBI crime lab workers. A Republican senator said Monday the suspension "appears to be a reprisal."

The FBI also took action regarding other employees criticized in the secret report, said officials who spoke on condition of anonymity. Three or four employees were transferred out of the FBI lab, but not suspended, these officials said.

. . . The inspector general hired a panel of outside scientists to evaluate the work of the lab after Whitehurst alleged in late 1995 that a pro-prosecution bias and mishandling of evidence may have tainted crime lab work or testimony on several high profile federal cases. . . .

SOURCE: Sniffen, M. *Austin American-Statesman*, 28 Jan. 1997: A5.

ing: he encountered hang-up calls on his unlisted home telephone, his be-longings were stolen, his car was towed away from the police parking lot twice, officers refused to sit next to him, and officers did not respond to his requests for back-up. Witnesses also reported that they overheard officers discussing what other forms of retaliation to take against him. The sergeant who was ar-rested for drunken driving was released before being taken to a magistrate, contrary to departmental policy, and received no disciplinary sanctions (Casey, 1996).

In situations where officers violate the unwritten "code," they experience similar sanctions to those described above. Those who terrorize their fellow officers evidently believe that a violation of trust has occurred that justifies the harassment. There are no ethical justifications for such actions, however, ex-cept for perhaps egoism. Unfortunately, in many cases, such as the one de-scribed above, administrators participate in and thereby encourage a continuation of the practice. In the last section in this chapter, the role of su-pervisors is examined.

TRAINING AND MANAGEMENT ISSUES

Although Chapter 11 is partially devoted to issues of management, a few mat-ters unique to law enforcement will be discussed here. Malloy (1982: 37–40) discusses several explanations of police corruption, including the rotten apple theory, which ascribes deviance to the individual; the political context theory, which points to structural supports for deviance; the unenforceable law ratio-nale, which notes that certain crimes are more likely to be involved than oth-ers; the informal code theory, which blames the police subculture for individual deviance; and the moral career theory, which explains deviance as a gradual movement from lesser to more serious deviant acts. Malloy also offers some possible solutions to police corruption: increase the salary of police, eliminate unenforceable laws, establish civilian review boards, and improve training. One might add this solution: improve leadership. Metz (1990) sug-gests several ways that police administrators can encourage ethical conduct among officers. He suggests setting realistic goals and objectives for the de-partment and providing ethical leadership, a written code of ethics, a whistle-blowing procedure that ensures fair treatment of all parties, and training in law enforcement ethics.

Change Efforts

Because so much of police work is unpredictable and encounters such a wide range of situations, it is impossible to fashion rules for all possible occurrences. What should take the place of extensive rules are strong ethical standards. As discussed before, police departments have formal ethical codes that are no doubt presented in the academy. However, the internalization of these standards by individual police officers is at best tenuous; once out in the field, the police officer encounters challenges and threats to the formal ethical code. The informal police subculture is the most obvious threat to the internalization of ethical standards. The informal police subculture is much more powerful than a framed ethics code or any academic discussions of ethics that took place in the academy.

Some writers believe that ethical standards themselves are at fault. They are so far removed from reality that they are worse than ignored—they encourage officers to believe there are no relevant ethical guides to behavior (Johnson and Copus, 1981: 78). On the other hand, if ethical standards are the highest aspiration of law enforcement, it is necessary that they be set at a level that is higher than an average of real behavior. However, the fact remains that there is a vast difference between the formal code of ethics and actual police behavior.

Education has been promoted as necessary if police are to continue to be "professional." However, education itself is certainly not a panacea, and, in fact, some of the officers with the worst examples of unethical behavior either had college degrees or scored above average on the academic tests to qualify for hiring. Nevertheless, study results often show that educated officers have positive qualities. Miller (1992) reports, for instance, on a study of New York City cadets who went through a type of co-op program. In this study, it was found that the new officers with college backgrounds placed more emphasis on a community orientation and less on traditional policing strategies, were less likely to believe that laws should be rigidly enforced, were more likely to believe that good officers can depart from standard operating procedures in order to solve a problem, were more likely to consider a college education important to their work, and were less likely to think that citizen complaints are an inevitable part of the job and less likely to believe that the ideals of politeness and decency are unworkable on the street. Some of the differences may raise more questions; for instance, if educated officers are more likely to believe it is acceptable to ignore the law, does this mean that they are *more* likely than officers without college degrees to use arbitrary and discriminatory criteria in their enforcement? If educated officers believe that officers can depart from standard operating procedures, are they harder to supervise and more likely to substitute individualistic definitions of justice rather than perform a service function and let the process control the outcome?

One example of training, rather than education, illustrates how the subculture can be used as a positive force. Police use of unreasonable force is an individual problem, but it also involves a question of values, because the police subculture does not condemn but rather protects police officers with aggressive tendencies. One attempt to change this situation involved a small group of Oakland, California, police officers and social scientists who were asked to deal with the problem. In this experiment, the police officers, who were chosen partly because of their inappropriate use of violence, confronted the issues of aggression and police authority and arrived at methods of coping with them. Police officers were asked to participate in a group created to deal with the problem of citizen complaints against police violence (Toch, Grant, and Galvin, 1973: 13):

> We would start (in the tradition of "organization development" teams) with a small group of men who would (1) inform themselves about parameters of the problem and devise an initial set of problem-solving strategies; in this context (2) we would prepare the men to take on roles as leaders for a larger problem-solving group, who would extend the effort further. This second group (or its sub-groups) could then expand the first team's effort, while engaged in both objective and self-directed inquiry. Ultimately, the larger group was expected to set up institutional arrangements in the form of a permanent problem-solving body within the department. Our first group was to be composed of officers defined as "strong" problem solvers; only some of these men were to be derived from the violence-experienced pool. The second generation was to be composed exclusively of violence-prone officers.

The early sessions defined the problem and developed projects designed to help resolve the problem. One of the projects was a panel of peer officers that reviewed violent incidents. Later, individual change was observed to occur even in some of the officers who had many citizen complaints against them. The primary motivation for change seemed to be a change in role perceptions and a comparison of one's own activities to those of others (Toch, Grant, and Galvin, 1975: 248–257).

Very probably, these officers were also developing different values regarding violence and its use. Notice the similarity between these techniques and the indirect methods of teaching morals discussed in Chapter 3. In both situations there is an opportunity to explore moral issues and alternative moral positions. This may, in turn, lead to the development of different and perhaps more advanced ethical standards. However, an alternative explanation is more consistent with learning theory. The officers in the experimental group were rewarded for negative expressions about violence. They were further rewarded when they developed methods for dealing with violent police officers. Thus, their value system matured after their behavior, and their behavior was influenced by the reward system, which became one that rewarded nonviolent behavior. Whichever explanation one prefers for the mechanism of change, it seems clear that involving police officers in such change efforts is a valuable and productive way to address problems such as the use of excessive force. There is no reason why similar methods cannot be applied to other ethical problems (Toch and Grant, 1991). These methods may, in fact, be more valuable than more traditional types of training or discipline.

Ethics training in the academy as well as offering in-service courses is common and recommended for all police departments today. However, what these courses might be able to accomplish is questionable. Many ethics courses use a moral reasoning approach, much as this book does, where various scenarios are examined in light of ethical perspectives, such as utilitarianism, to determine the right course of behavior. Implicit in this approach is the assumption that once what is right is determined, most officers will conform their behavior and/or make the right decision. A different perspective is offered by Delattre (1989) and Delaney (1990) that emphasizes the importance of character. In Chapter 2 we discussed the ethics of virtue, which answers the question "How does one live a good life?" with "Developing and forming good habits of character." This is the approach that Delattre and Delaney apply to police ethics. If one has a bad character, ethical analysis is irrelevant since that individual will continue to behave in conformance to his or her traits of avarice, deceptiveness, cowardice, and so on. An individual who has good character possesses those virtues necessary for moral and ethical decision making. Training may help one by reinforcing appropriate values, but one's character is already formed. What are the virtues necessary for a good police officer? Delattre discusses justice, courage, temperance, and compassion. Delaney discusses sagacity, sincerity, and persistence.

This approach would seem to negate the relevance of any attempts to improve the ethics of officers, since character is fairly well formed by the time one is an adult. Yet we might say that ethics training at this point serves to delineate those situations that may not be recognized as questions of ethics. Also, discussions of such dilemmas point out egoistic rationalizations for unethical behavior, making them harder to use by those who would try.

Swift and Houston (1993) present one such training course based on rule utilitarianism, which they believe is the best and most accepted basis for law enforcement ethics. The course they outline discusses the scope of the problem, identifies different problems (brutality, corruption, theft, misuse of authority), discusses how to decide what to do about them (resolving ethical dilemmas, ethical systems), presents rule utilitarianism, and discusses how to apply it. Other training options may involve a more balanced treatment of other ethical systems. All must resolve the issues of relativism versus absolutism, duty versus personal needs, and minor transgressions versus major transgressions.

Ethical Leadership

Most people agree that employee behavior is influenced more directly by the behavior of superiors rather than by the stated directives or ethics of the organization. Executives engaged in price fixing and overcharging should not be surprised that their employees steal company supplies or time. One cannot espouse ethical ideals, act unethically, and then expect employees to act ethically. Thus, regardless of formal ethical codes, police are influenced by the standards of behavior they observe in their superiors. One may note that most large-scale police corruption that has been exposed has implicated very high level officials. Alternatively, police departments that have remained relatively free of corruption have administrators who practice ethical behavior on a day-to-day basis. Even if leaders are not involved in corruption directly, encouraging or participating in the harassment and ostracism that is directed to those who expose wrongdoers supports an organizational culture where officers may be afraid to come forward when they know of wrongdoing. Another situation may be where there is perceived favoritism and the presence of cliques who do not receive punishment for behaviors that others would receive punishment for; this climate destroys the trust in police leadership that is essential to ensure good communication from the rank and file.

Administrators have their own unique ethical dilemmas to face. Budget allocations, the use of drug testing, affirmative action, sexual harassment, and decisions about corrupt officers all present ethical dilemmas for administrators and supervisors. For instance, some supervisors face problems when they are promoted from the ranks and have friends who now become their subordinates. Such friends may expect special consideration, leaving the supervisor to decide how to respond to such expectations. Supervisors also report ethical dilemmas over how they should allocate resources, such as a new patrol car or overtime. Should seniority take precedence over competence? Friendship over seniority? What should be done with officers who have drug or alcohol problems is another issue. If the administrator decides to counsel or suggest treatment without any change in duty status and the officer endangers the life of someone or actually harms a citizen or other officer due to the problem, is the administrator to blame? In many situations where police leaders must make decisions, lives, property, or liberty can be at stake. It is extremely important for supervisors and administrators to understand the impact their decisions and their behavior have on everyone in the organization.

CONCLUSION

In this chapter we have explored law enforcement practices and training and management issues. A theme that permeated this chapter (and Chapter 5) was the fundamental perception of the police role in society as either crime fighters or public servants. One's view of the fundamental mission of police affects each of the issues discussed. If crime control is the mission, then more utilitarian reasoning is employed to analyze police tactics. For instance, Cohen (1987: 53) uses a utilitarian approach in the following justification for police action:

1. The end must itself be good.
2. The means must be a plausible way to achieve the end.
3. There must be no alternative, better means to achieve the same end.
4. The means must not undermine some other equal or greater end.

Kappeler, Sluder, and Alpert (1994: 243) present the United States Department of Justice recommendations for the values of a police department as the following:

- Preserve and advance the principles of democracy
- Place the highest value on preserving human life

- Preventing crime as the number one operational priority
- Involving the community in delivering police services
- Belief in accountability to the community served
- Commitment to professionalism in all aspects of operations
- Maintaining the highest standards of integrity.

One sees a greater emphasis on the public servant role in this presentation of police values. Regardless of whether a department adopts a crime-control or public service orientation, there is probably the same amount of deviance as there is in any occupation or in the general population. The unique factors contributing to police deviance include elements of mixed goals, rationalizations accepted by the public, situational elements that provide more opportunities, and a subculture that covers up for individual deviants.

We began these two chapters on law enforcement and will also close them with the images of the use of force by the Los Angeles police. Some of us remember earlier images from the 1960s, wherein law enforcement officers appeared on newscasts beating and using attack dogs against peaceful civil rights demonstrators. One might hope that in the same way those negative images of the 1960s led to a greater professionalization, better training, and racial and sexual integration of police departments in the 1970s, so too can the Rodney King incident and the scrutiny that resulted lead to positive results and a new era of more ethical and thoughtful policing in the 1990s and beyond.

REVIEW QUESTIONS

1. Support the presence of police gratuities, and then criticize the presence of them.
2. Discuss the justifications and criticisms of undercover operations.
3. Explain the "Dirty Harry" problem.
4. Explain the explanations for the "blue curtain of secrecy." Is loyalty a good thing or a negative element of policing?
5. Discuss possible change efforts to reduce or eliminate various forms of police misbehavior.

ETHICAL DILEMMAS

Situation 1

You are a rookie police officer on your first patrol. The older, experienced officer tells you that the restaurant on the corner likes to have you guys around, so they always give free meals. Your partner orders steak, potatoes, and all the trimmings. What are you going to do? What if it were just coffee at a convenience store? What if the owner refused to take your money at the cash register?

Situation 2

You are a rookie police officer who responds to a call for officer assistance. Arriving at the scene, you see a ring of officers surrounding a suspect who is down on his knees. You don't know what happened before you arrived, but you see a sergeant use a tazer on the suspect and you see two or three officers step in and take turns hitting the suspect with their nightsticks about the head and shoulders. This goes on for several minutes as you stand in the back of the circle. No one says anything that would indicate that this is not appropriate behavior. What would you do? What would you do later when asked to testify that you observed the suspect make "threatening" gestures to the officers involved?

Situation 3

While on the witness stand you answer all the prosecutor's and defense attorney's questions. You complete your testimony and exit the courtroom knowing that you have specific knowledge that may help the defense attorney's case. You have answered all questions truthfully, but the specific question needed to help the defense was not asked. What should you do?

SUGGESTED READINGS

Barker, T., and Carter, D. 1991. *Police Deviance.* Cincinnati: Anderson Press.

Dunham, R., and Alpert, G. 1989. *Critical Issues in Policing,* 2d ed. Prospect Heights, IL: Waveland Press.

Heffernan, W., and Stroup, T. 1985. *Police Ethics: Hard Choices in Law Enforcement.* New York: John Jay Press.

Kappeler, V., Sluder, R., and Alpert, G. 1994. *Forces of Deviance: Understanding the Dark Side of Policing.* Prospect Heights, IL: Waveland Press.

7

�֍

Ethics and
Legal Professionals

Chapter Objectives

Become familiar with the source of legal ethics.

Understand the various perceptions of judicial processing.

Understand the various positions
taken on the attorney as a moral agent.

Learn the variety of ethical
issues faced by defense attorneys.

Just as the Rodney King incident directed public scrutiny toward the ethics of law enforcement, the O. J. Simpson trial has acted as a catalyst for the same degree of scrutiny toward the court system in this country. And in the same way that the King incident has been used to illustrate how racial prejudice, distrust, and class conflict affect law enforcement procedures, the Simpson case illustrates how these same issues carry over to judicial processing and influence the administration of justice.

Many people refer to the criminal justice system as the "criminal injustice system" because of a perception that practices in this nation's courtrooms do not necessarily conform to the ideals of justice. As mentioned in previous chapters, justice is a goal that is not necessarily synonymous with law, and a legal system may not always be capable of achieving moral justice. The basic elements of a justice system are an impartial fact-finding process and a fair and equitable resolution. The ethical and moral duties of those who work within the system are typically consistent with the concept of justice. However, the day-to-day practices of those who work in the system are sometimes inconsistent with the pursuit of justice, and perhaps even violate principles of law. Dishonesty and unethical behavior are probably no more prevalent in the legal profession than in many others, but there is a glaring disparity between the sanctity of the legal system and popular views of lawyers. In fact, instead of guardians of justice, lawyers are often considered to be scurrilous charlatans.

FIRST, LET'S KILL ALL THE LAWYERS . . .

Public perceptions of lawyers indicate that the public has little confidence in their ability to live up to ideals of equity, fairness, and justice. In a Gallup survey reported by *U.S. News & World Report,* lawyers were rated as "less ethical" and "less honest" than police officers, doctors, TV reporters, and funeral directors, among others. Only building contractors, politicians, and car salespeople (among a few others) had lower ratings than did lawyers (Kelly, 1982:

29). The public's opinion of attorneys was said to have reached a new low when it was disclosed that almost all of the Watergate figures were lawyers (Davis and Elliston, 1986: 43, 115). In the 1980s, the law scandal *de jour* was the savings and loan fiasco, in which the greed and corruption of those in the banking industry were ably assisted by the industry's attorneys, and the taxpayers picked up the bill for the bankrupt institutions and outstanding loans.

Apparently, even lawyers don't think much of their profession. In a 1992 California bar poll, 70 percent of lawyers would choose another career if they could and 75 percent would not want their children to be lawyers (Glendon, 1994: 85). Evidently, the widespread antipathy and distrust of lawyers are starting to make a dent in the number of college students who plan to go to law school; after many years of rising enrollments, law school admissions have stabilized, and some schools are seeing a drop in numbers of applicants.

The perception of the lawyer as an amoral "hired gun" is in sharp contrast to the ideal of the lawyer as an officer of the court, sworn to uphold the ideals of justice declared sacrosanct under our system of law. Interestingly, or perhaps not surprisingly, our government is made up largely of lawyers: a large percentage of elected officials are lawyers, twenty-three out of forty-one presidents have been lawyers, and thirteen out of the eighteen members of President Clinton's cabinet are lawyers (Glendon, 1994: 12). Our nation's leaders and historical heroes have just as likely been lawyers (Abraham Lincoln, for example) as generals, and our nation's consciousness is permeated with the belief in law and legal vindication.

We continue to have mixed perceptions of lawyers. On the one hand, the public tends to agree with a stereotype of lawyers as amoral, motivated by money, and with no conscience or concern for morality; on the other hand, the first response to any perception of wrong is to find a legal advocate and sue, with the belief that a lawyer will right any wrong and solve any problem.

History indicates that the ethics of those associated with the legal process have always been suspect. Plato and Aristotle condemned the advocate because of his ability to make the truth appear false and the guilty appear innocent. This early distrust continued throughout history; early colonial lawyers were distrusted and even punished for practicing law. For many years, lawyers could not charge a fee for their services because the mercenary aspect of the

---

QUOTATION

According to a recent poll commissioned by the National Law Journal, *nine out of ten parents interviewed would not want their child to grow up to be a lawyer. . . . In another survey, only 19 percent credited lawyers with "high or very high" ethical standards, ranking them below druggists, dentists and funeral directors. In yet another, only 12 percent expressed a "great deal of confidence" in lawyers—last out of fifteen major institutions studied.*

SOURCE: Roth, A., and Roth, J. *Devil's Advocates: The Unnatural History of Lawyers* (Berkeley, CA: Nolo Press, 1989): 157. Footnotes omitted.

profession was condemned (Papke, 1986: 32). Gradually, lawyers and the profession itself were accepted, but suspicion and controversy continued in the area of fees and qualifications. Partly to counteract public antipathy, lawyers formed their own organization, the American Bar Association (ABA), in 1878. Shortly afterwards, this professional organization established the first ethical guidelines for lawyers.

Perhaps the best explanation for the long-standing distrust of lawyers is that they typically represent trouble; no one needs a lawyer unless he or she feels a wrong has been done to them or a person needs to be defended. The ability of lawyers to argue either side raises a level of distrust. We would prefer an advocate to passionately believe in our cause, not be motivated by how much we can pay. In the next section, we explore basic perceptions that influence a lawyer's advocacy in our criminal justice system.

PERCEPTIONS OF JUDICIAL PROCESSING

As mentioned before, the ideal of the justice system is that two advocates of equal ability will each engage in a pursuit of truth, guided by a neutral fact finder, with the truth emerging from the contest. Actual practices in our justice system are very different. Various descriptions profess to offer a more realistic picture of the system. One approach is to look at judicial processing as a game. Each player has a certain role to perform, with rules and responsibilities. "Hidden agendas" (covert motivations and goals) exist. The adversarial system pits the defense attorney against the prosecutor, and the judge may be considered the umpire in this contest. The judge sets down the rules and, unless there is a jury, decides who wins the contest. The rationale for the rules is that the best person wins—obviously an optimistic view. If a powerful and rich defendant is able to hire the best criminal lawyer in the country complete with several assistants and investigators, the prosecutor (who is typically overworked and understaffed) is overwhelmed. Of course, this is the exception, and more commonly a defendant must rely on an overworked and probably inexperienced public defender or an attorney who can make criminal law profitable only by high caseloads and quick turnover. In these instances, the defense is outmatched by a prosecutor in a public office with greater access to evidence and investigative assistance. In addition, if the judge abdicates his or her umpire roll and takes a more active part in the proceeding, deciding early who will win, then the game is "fixed" at the outset.

A variation of game theory is offered by Blumberg (1969), who refers to the practice of law as a confidence game because both prosecutor and defense attorney conspire to appear as something they are not—adversaries in a do-or-die situation. What is more commonly the case is that the prosecutor and the defense attorney will still be working together when the client is gone; thus, their primary allegiance is not to the client, but to themselves. For defense attorneys this may involve either making the case appear more difficult than it is in order to justify their fee or, if the client has no resources, arbitrarily concluding a case that has merit. Attorneys may use their power for reasons other than the client's interest; in the following example cited by Blumberg (1969: 329), all actors cooperate in the conspiracy against the client:

> [Judges] . . . will adjourn the case of an accused in jail awaiting plea or sentence if the attorney requests such action. While explicitly this may be done for some innocuous and seemingly valid reason, the tacit purpose is that pressure is being applied by the attorney for the collection of his fee, which he knows will probably not be forthcoming if the case is concluded.

The game here is to make the client believe that the advocacy system is working for him or her whereas, in reality, it is being used against his or her interest. Other examples include attorneys asking for continuances because of a missing witness—"Mr. Green"—which, in reality, means simply that the attorney hasn't been paid yet and wants the court to exert pressure by keeping the client in jail or continuing the pending criminal case until payment is rendered. For this charade to be successful, all players in the system must cooperate; evidently, in many situations they do.

Great shows of anger and emotion in the courtroom help clients believe they are getting something for their money, but such performances are belied by the jocular relationship sometimes apparent between the defense attorney and the prosecutor shortly after trial or between courtroom sessions. In fact, many defense attorneys are ex-prosecutors. This is, in some respects, helpful to their clients because they know the way the prosecutor's office works and what a reasonable plea offer would be. But one also must assume that the prosecutorial experience of these attorneys has shaped their perceptions of clients and what would be considered fair punishments. Moreover, their continuing relationships with prosecutors overlap into their social and personal lives, so it is not surprising that allegiances are more often all lawyers against civilians, rather than defense versus prosecution.

Other authors have also used the analogy of a confidence game to describe the interaction among prosecutors, defense attorneys, and clients. For example, Scheingold (1984: 155) writes the following:

[T]he practice of defense law is all too often a "confidence game" in which the lawyers are "double agents" who give the appearance of assiduous defense of their clients but whose real loyalty is to the criminal courts. The defendant, from this perspective, is only an episode in the attorney's enduring relationships with the prosecutors and judges whose goodwill is essential to a successful career in the defense bar.

Another perspective describes our courts as administering *bureaucratic justice*. Each case is seen as only one of many for the professionals who work in the system. The goal of the system—namely, bureaucratic efficiency—becomes more important than the original goal of justice. Also, because each case is part of a workload, decision making takes on more complications. For instance, a defense lawyer may be less inclined to fight very hard for a "loser" client if he or she wants a favor for another client later in the week. The prosecutor may decide not to charge a guilty person in order to get him or her to testify against someone else. In this sense, each case is not separately tried and judged, but is linked to others and processed as part of a workload. The bureaucratic system of justice is seen as developing procedures and policies that, although not intentionally discriminatory, may contribute to a perception of unfairness. For instance, a major element in bureaucratic justice is the presumption of guilt, whereas the ideal of our justice system is a presumption of innocence. District attorneys, judges, and even defense attorneys approach each case presuming guilt and place a priority on achieving the most expeditious resolution of the case. This is the basic rationale behind plea bargaining, whether it is recognized or not: the defendant is presumed to be guilty, and the negotiation is to achieve a guilty plea while bargaining for the best possible sentence—the lowest possible is the goal of the defense while the highest possible is the goal of the prosecutor. Plea bargaining is consistent with the bureaucratic value system because it is the most efficient way of getting maximum punishment for minimum work.

Descriptions of bureaucratic justice such as the following (Scheingold, 1984: 158) allow for the fact that efficiency is tempered with other values and priorities:

> The concept of bureaucratic justice . . . provides the most persuasive account of how the participants in criminal process reconcile legal and bureaucratic forces. "Bureaucratic justice unites the presumption of guilt with the operational morality of fairness." . . . All participants in the criminal process behave as if a person who is arrested is probably guilty. Nevertheless, the coercive thrust of the presumption of guilt is softened somewhat by the operational morality of fairness that leads the participants to make certain that defendants get neither more nor less than is coming to them—that defendants, in other words, get their due.

Scheingold is referring to the practices of judges, prosecutors, and defense attorneys who adapt the system to their personal standards of justice. This is exemplified by a judge who determines that an individual offender is a threat to society and so overlooks errors during trial to make sure that the individual ends up in prison. In the same way, a person who is legally guilty may get a break because it is determined that he is a decent guy who made a mistake rather than a "bad character." Moreover, in almost all cases there may be general consensus on both sides about what is fair punishment for any given offender. Defense attorneys who argue for unrealistically low sentences do so in a desultory and uncommitted fashion, knowing that the prosecutor would not and could not offer such a sentence. Prosecutors put up very little argument when defense attorneys ask for sentences that fit office guidelines. Instead of describing the justice system as one that practices the presumption of innocence and takes careful steps to determine guilt, what may be more realistic is to view it as a system wherein all participants assume guilt, take superficial steps to arrive at the punishment phase, and operate under a value system that allocates punishment and mercy to offenders according to an informal consensus of fairness.

One other perception of the criminal justice system is that of Samuel Walker's "wedding cake" illustration, based on a model proposed by Lawrence Friedman and Robert Percival. In this scheme, the largest portion of criminal cases form the bottom layers of the cake, and the few "serious" cases form the top layer.

The top layer is most dramatically represented by cases such as the murder trial of O. J. Simpson. In this highly publicized case, the defendant had an extremely skilled (and highly paid) team of attorneys as well as trial consultants, investigators, and public relations specialists. Los Angeles County paid millions to keep up with its own team of attorneys, experts, and investigators. The criminal processing and trial proceeded with admirable speed. Each side worked incredibly hard and used an arsenal of tactics (that were then critiqued by armchair experts each evening). The case itself was used in law school evidence classes because of the wealth of material present in pre-trial discovery, exclusionary motions, jury selection, and the like.

The bottom of the cake is represented by a case such as that of William Carter Brooks. He was arrested for possession and sale of cocaine in August 1988. The judge who eventually would hear his case came to his cell and told him that he would be "70 years old and liking men" before he was released. In August he asked for appointed counsel, but the court ignored the request. In October he was given a preliminary hearing (without counsel and in front of the same judge). In November a second preliminary hearing was held on a related charge. In February he was finally indicted and continued to wait in jail for legal counsel. Finally, in March the court appointed a counsel for his arraignment. This attorney told Brooks he wouldn't accept collect calls from the jail and never met with him at all until the April plea-bargain hearing. At this hearing and nine months after his initial arrest, he still had no idea what the state's evidence was against him, had not had a single meeting with his attorney, and was faced with the decision to plead guilty or not to serious charges (Curridan, 1991: 65).

With the vast differences in "justice" experienced by these two men, it is no wonder that many believe that "justice is for sale" in this country, with lawyers as the panderers. What Walker in his wedding cake analysis makes clear is that cases such as that of Mr. Brooks are the bulk of criminal processing and cases such as that of Mr. Simpson are rare. However, since the public is exposed only to the top of the wedding cake, it develops a highly distorted perception of the system. The majority of the American public were perhaps most disgusted with the multitude of evidentiary rules and the Byzantine process of the trial itself; these concerns may be valid, but only for a very small portion of criminal cases. The vast majority of criminal defendants plead guilty after one or two short conversations with an attorney.

According to Walker's wedding cake analysis, the courtroom work group is believed to share definitions of seriousness and operate as a unit to keep the dynamics of the courtroom static, despite changes that are forced upon it. Changes such as the exclusionary rule, determinate sentencing, and other recent legislation have had surprisingly little impact on court outcomes because of a shared perception of serious crime and appropriate punishment. The vast majority of crime is considered trivial, and the processing of these cases involves very little energy or attention from system actors (Walker, 1985).

One might argue that the courtroom work group has at least been influenced by legislative and public pressure toward drug crimes. Even though drug crimes have not been seen as extremely serious by those who work in the justice system, these cases are filling the nation's courtrooms, and drug defendants are filling the nation's prisons. People are receiving longer sentences and are subject to determinate or mandatory sentences in a clear response to the political "war on drugs."

Dershowitz's view of the criminal justice system (see the Literary Perspective box) is probably, as Dershowitz admits himself, a bit overstated, but it is a slightly different illustration of the courtroom work group or bureaucratic justice system in operation. The major ethical problem with this (if it does represent reality) is that innocence, truth, and due process are ignored and overlooked as inconvenient.

ETHICAL ISSUES FOR
LEGAL PROFESSIONALS

A profession, as defined in Chapter 5, involves a specialized body of knowledge, commitment to the social good, the ability to regulate itself, and high social status (Davis and Elliston, 1986: 13). The presence of ethical standards is essential to the definition of a profession. More importantly, membership in a profession implies a special set of rules, different from those applied to everyone else. Very often these rules may involve a higher standard of behavior, but they may also involve greater privileges or the right to act in a different way

Literary Perspective

I have discerned a series of "rules" that seem—in practice—to govern the justice game in America today. Most of the participants in the criminal justice system understand them. Although these rules never appear in print, they seem to control the realities of the process. Like all rules, they are necessarily stated in oversimplified terms. But they tell an important part of how the system operates in practice. Here are some of the key rules of the justice game:

Rule I: Almost all criminal defendants are, in fact, guilty.

Rule II: All criminal defense lawyers, prosecutors and judges understand and believe Rule I.

Rule III: It is easier to convict guilty defendants by violating the Constitution than by complying with it, and in some cases it is impossible to convict guilty defendants without violating the Constitution.

Rule IV: Almost all police lie about whether they violated the Constitution in order to convict guilty defendants.

Rule V: All prosecutors, judges, and defense attorneys are aware of Rule IV.

Rule VI: Many prosecutors implicitly encourage police to lie about whether they violated the Constitution in order to convict guilty defendants.

Rule VII: All judges are aware of Rule VI.

Rule VIII: Most trial judges pretend to believe police officers who they know are lying.

Rule IX: All appellate judges are aware of Rule VIII, yet many pretend to believe the trial judges who pretend to believe the lying police officers.

Rule X: Most judges disbelieve defendants about whether their constitutional rights have been violated, even if they are telling the truth.

Rule XI: Most judges and prosecutors would not knowingly convict a defendant who they believe to be innocent of the crime charged (or a closely related crime).

Rule XII: Rule XI does not apply to members of organized crime, drug dealers, career criminals, or potential informers.

Rule XIII: Nobody really wants justice.

SOURCE: Dershowitz, Alan. *The Best Defense* (New York: Vintage Books, 1983): xxi.

from everyone else by virtue of that membership. Formal ethical standards for lawyers and judges were originally promulgated by the American Bar Association in the Model Code of Professional Responsibility. The original canons, adapted from the Alabama Bar Association Code of 1887, were adopted by the ABA in 1908 and have been revised frequently since then. Several years ago, the ABA switched its endorsement of the Model Code as the general guide for ethical behavior to the Model Rules of Professional Responsibility.

Today's Model Rules cover many aspects of the lawyer's profession, including such areas as client–lawyer relationships, the lawyer as counselor, the lawyer as advocate, transactions with others, public service, and maintaining the integrity of the profession. Ethical issues in criminal law may involve courtroom behavior, suborning perjury, conflicts of interest, use of the media, investigation efforts, use of immunity, discovery and the sharing of evidence, relationships with opposing attorneys, and plea bargaining (Douglass, 1981).

To enforce these ethical rules, the ABA has a standing committee on ethical responsibility to offer formal and informal opinions when charges of impropriety have been made. Also, each state bar association has the power to sanction offending attorneys by private or public censure or recommend to the court suspension of their privilege to practice law. Thus, the rules promulgated by the state bar have essentially the power of law behind them. The bar associations also have the power to grant entry into the profession since one must ordinarily belong to the bar association of a particular state to practice law there. Bar associations judge competence by testing the applicant's knowledge, but they also judge moral worthiness by background checks of the individual. The purpose of these restrictive admission procedures is to protect the public image of the legal profession by rejecting unscrupulous or dishonest individuals or those unfit to practice for other reasons. However, many feel that if bar associations were serious about protecting the profession, they would also continue to monitor the behavior and moral standing of current members with the same care they seem to take in the initial decision regarding entry (Elliston, 1986: 53).

A practicing attorney is investigated only when complaints have been lodged against him or her. The investigative bodies have been described as decentralized, informal, and secret. They do little for dissatisfied clients since typical client complaints involve incompetence—a vague and ill-defined term (Mark and Cathcart, 1986: 72). One study of client satisfaction found that the biggest complaint against attorneys was that too little time was given the client by the lawyer or that the lawyer was inaccessible (Arafat and McCahery, 1978: 205). Neither of these complaints is likely to receive a disciplinary ruling by an ethics committee.

More serious complaints occur as well, however. An article on attorney misconduct described a lawyer who embezzled 2.5 million dollars from a client and then, when she doggedly pursued him through court action and the bar disciplinary committee, hired someone to have her killed. Another case involved an attorney who did kill his wife and received only a 2½ year suspension from the practice of law (Weber, 1987). Many bar disciplinary committees are hopelessly understaffed and overburdened with complaints. Complaints may take years to investigate, and, in the meantime, if prospective clients call, they will be told only that the attorney is in good standing and has no substantiated complaints. And whereas individuals with complaints against their lawyers in the civil arena receive little enough satisfaction, criminal defendants are arguably even less likely to have anyone care or rectify incompetence or unethical behavior on the part of their attorney. "You get what you pay for" may be true to an extent, but even that phrase does not truly represent the possibility of a family mortgaging their home, signing over their cars, and emptying their bank account to an attorney who promises to represent a family member against a criminal charge and then find that the attorney will not answer calls, doesn't appear in court, or is unprepared and forgets to file necessary motions. Furthermore, the "blue curtain of secrecy" described as operating to protect errant police officers appears here as well, and the "pinstripe curtain of secrecy" ensures that incompetent attorneys continue to practice even while their antics are well-known by the local bar.

Law schools have been criticized for being singularly uninterested in fostering any type of moral conscience in graduating students. Several writers have condemned the law school practice of reshaping law students so that when they emerge "thinking like a lawyer," they have mastered a type of thinking that is concerned with detail and logical analysis but gives little regard to morality and larger social issues.

Gerry Spence, a flamboyant defense attorney, boasts of receiving low grades in law school—an indication, he believes, that he did not "sell out" to the mindset of bottom-line winning and profit above all else that is representative of law school indoctrination (Spence, 1989). Stover (1989) writes how public interest values decline during law school. The reason for this decline seemingly has to do with the low value placed on public interest issues by the law school curriculum, which also treats ethical and normative concerns as irrelevant or trivial compared to the "bar courses" such as contract law and torts. Morality and ethics are often made light of, even in professional responsibility courses, where there are more stories (humorous and otherwise) of how to get around the ethical mandates than stories of how to resolve dilemmas and maintain a sense of personal integrity.

To be fair, students' emphasis on salaries over public welfare is understandable when one considers that a law school graduate may owe close to $100,000 (or over) in student loans upon graduation. One graduate's experience is illustrative—a police officer changes careers in his thirties, finishes college, and is accepted into an Ivy League law school. His goals—to represent police officers in civil rights (Section 1983) cases and then perhaps pursue a judicial position—are based on the injustices he experienced in the system. Upon graduation, he owes $65,000 in loans. He is offered a position with a top-tier law firm at $69,000 per year; a starting position with the district attorney's office would bring approximately $34,000, and if he went into private prac-

---

QUOTATION

It takes a sturdy, tough kind of beast to carry the load up the rocky trails in the backcountry of the American justice system. Fighting for the rights of the people is more a matter of caring, of passion, than of breeding. . . . The fact is, we are selecting too many of the wrong kind for our fighters. Those who are fit for fighting are sent away. Many of those who can hear the people and speak their language cannot speak the language of the computer that stands guard at the door of our law schools. . . . Many who do survive the entrance cut are soon disgusted and leave, for law school is no place for human beings who care about other human beings. . . .

SOURCE: Spence, G. *With Justice for None* (New York: Penguin, 1989): 45.

tice his salary would be, in all probability, lower than that. He takes the position with the firm and, four years later, is still there, handling the type of legal cases and caught up with legal minutiae he never dreamed of before he went to law school. The small amount of *pro bono* work his firm allows him is as close as he'll ever come to the ideals he had when he went to law school.

The Attorney–Client Relationship

Many of the Model Rules involve the special relationship the attorney has with the client. The separation of professional and personal responsibility poses difficult issues. Many lawyers feel that loyalty to the client is paramount to their duties as a professional. This loyalty surpasses and eclipses individual and private decision making, and the special relationship said to exist between lawyer and client justifies decisions when the client's interests are at stake that might otherwise be deemed unacceptable. An extreme position is that the attorney is no more than the legal agent of the client. The lawyer is neither immoral nor moral, but merely a legal tool. This position is represented by the statement "I am a lawyer, first and foremost." A more moderate position is that the loyalty to the client presents a special relationship between client and lawyer, similar to that between mother and child or with trusted friend. This protected relationship justifies fewer actions than the one described above. The lawyer is expected to dissuade the client from taking unethical or immoral actions. Utilitarianism supports the special relationship in that it benefits us all to have these special attorney–client relationships available (Fried, 1986: 136). The ethics of care may also be used to support this position since the focus on the special relationship with the client and the needs of the client is consistent with this ethical system.

Many people reject perspectives that discount the lawyer's responsibility as an individual to make his or her own moral decisions. Lawyers are perceived as the legal *and* moral agents of their clients, rather than merely legal agents. Their personal responsibility to avoid wrongdoing precludes involving themselves in their clients' wrongdoing (Postema, 1986: 168). This position is represented by the statement "I am a person first, lawyer second."

Elliott Cohen (1991), an advocate of the "moral agent" position, believes that to be purely a legal advocate is inconsistent with being a morally good person in several ways. For instance, the virtue of justice would be

---

QUOTATIONS

The client never wants to be told he can't do what he wants to do; he wants to be told how to do it, and it is the lawyer's business to tell him how.

About half the practice of a decent lawyer consists in telling would-be clients that they are damned fools and should stop.

SOURCE: Reported in Glendon, M. *A Nation Under Lawyers* (New York: Farrar, Straus and Giroux, 1994): 76, 75.

inconsistent with a zealous advocate who would maximize the chance of his or her client's winning, regardless of the fairness of the outcome. A pure legal agent would sacrifice values of truthfulness, moral courage, benevolence, trustworthiness, and moral autonomy. Only if the attorney is a moral agent, as well as a legal advocate, can there be any possibility of the attorney's maintaining individual morality. Cohen (1991: 135–136) suggests some principles that attorneys must follow to be consistent with both goals:

1. Treat others as ends in themselves and not as mere means to winning cases.

2. Treat clients and other professional relations who are relatively similar in a similar fashion.

3. Do not deliberately engage in behavior apt to deceive the court as to the truth.

4. Be willing, if necessary, to make reasonable personal sacrifices—of time, money, popularity, and so on—for what you justifiably believe to be a morally good cause.

5. Do not give money to, or accept money from, clients for wrongful purposes or in wrongful amounts.

6. Avoid harming others in the process of representing your client.

7. Be loyal to your client and do not betray his confidences.

8. Make your own moral decisions to the best of your ability and act consistently upon them.

The rationale for these principles seems to be an amalgamation of ethical formalism, utilitarianism, and other ethical frameworks. Some may seem impossible to uphold and subject to bitter criticism on the part of practicing attorneys—for instance, how does one avoid harming others when one is an advocate for one side in a contest? There are losers and winners in civil contests as well as in criminal law, and lawyers must take responsibility for the fact that sometimes the loser is harmed in financial or emotional ways. How does one not betray the confidences of a client if they involve perpetrating a fraud upon the court? None of these issues are easy or subject to a simple application of ethical rules.

A Higher Standard of Behavior?

In Chapter 5 we discussed the concept of police officers, as public servants, being held to a higher standard of conduct than those they serve. This same principle applies to attorneys. The Model Code of Professional Responsibility for attorneys dictates that they should be "temperate and dignified" and "refrain from all illegal and morally reprehensible conduct." The Model Rules expect that "a lawyer's conduct should conform to the requirements of the law, both in professional service to clients and in the lawyer's business and personal affairs." These are prescriptions similar to those found in the Law En-

> ### QUOTATION
>
> *You're an attorney. It's your duty to lie, conceal and distort everything, and slander everybody.*
>
> _____
>
> SOURCE: Giradeaux, J. *The Madwoman of Chaillot* (adapted by Maurice Valency) (New York: Random House, Inc., 1949): Act Two.

forcement Code of Ethics. Both groups of professionals are expected to uphold a higher standard of behavior than the general public. They provide protection and help enforce the rules of behavior for the rest of us. Since both professions have a special place in society's attempt to control individual behavior, it is not unreasonable to expect a higher standard of behavior to apply.

However, what is alleged by some is that instead of a *higher* standard, lawyers (like some police officers) allow themselves a *double* standard. Lying is lying unless it's done by a lawyer, and then it is just doing one's duty, or a "misstatement of fact." Glendon (1994), in a highly critical overview of the legal profession, proposes that the legal profession has changed in very dramatic ways, not all of which have been for the better. Although the practice of law was once governed by rules of ethics and etiquette and lawyers acted like gentleman (literally, since the profession was for the most part closed to women, minorities, and the lower class), it has become open to those excluded groups in the last twenty-five years, but it has also become a world of "no rules" or, more accurately, only one rule: "winning is everything."

The Use of Discretion

As mentioned before, discretion exists at each stage of the criminal justice system. Professionals at each stage have the opportunity to use their discretion wisely and ethically, or, alternatively, they may use their discretion in an unethical manner. In the courts, prosecutors have discretion to charge and pursue prosecution or not, defense attorneys have discretion to accept or refuse cases and choose trial tactics, and judges have discretion to make rulings on evidence and other trial procedures, as well as dispense convictions and sentences.

One view of law is that it is neutral and objective and that formal rules of law are used in decision making (Pinkele and Louthan, 1985: 9). The reality is that lawmakers, law enforcers, and lawgivers have a great deal of discretion in making and interpreting the law. Law is political in that it is responsive to power interests. Far from being absolute or objective, the law is a dynamic, ever-changing symbol of political will. Just as lawmaking and interpretation are influenced by political will and power groups, individual lawgivers and those who work in the system also have a great deal of discretion in interpreting and enforcing the law. For instance, the Supreme Court interprets the constitutional or legislative intent, and these interpretations are far from being neutral or inviolate. This is not to say that discretion exists unfettered or operates in unsystematic ways. Louthan (1985: 14) offers the following observation:

> For some, discretion is "law without order," "the authority to make decisions according to one's own judgment . . . ," the "departure from legal rules"; in short, "normlessness." Others, though, would contend that while discretion may refer to a procedural context of decisions reached informally, it does not necessarily imply that decisions are made on an ad hoc basis, without order, and without reference to some kind of directional norm. Indeed, it can be argued that discretionary behavior itself becomes routine, that the environment of decision is one in which the actor thinks as much (maybe simultaneously, maybe first) about the norms or folkways of discretion and its related currencies of informal exchange as he does about what may be required by the rule of law.

If we accept that discretion is an operating reality in the justice system, then we must ask in what ways legal professionals use this discretion. Individual value systems replace absolute rules or laws, and these value systems may be ethical or unethical. For instance, judges may base a decision on a concept of fairness, or they may base a decision on prejudicial beliefs—e.g., that blacks are more criminal so they deserve longer sentences, or that women are not dangerous so they should get probation. In these examples, discretion is used in an unethical manner because prejudice has replaced fairness in decision making. These examples are clear, but there may be many other situations where one's biases and prejudices are not so easily identified.

Judges' rulings on objections are supposed to be based on rules of evidence, but sometimes there is room for interpretation and individual discretion. Again, some judges use this discretion appropriately and make decisions in a best effort to conform to the evidentiary rules, but other judges use arbitrary or unfair criteria, such as personal dislike of an attorney, disagreement with the rule, a desire for one side or the other to win the case, or, as in the case of one particular judge, awarding favorable rulings to each attorney by turns with no regard to the merit of each objection.

How does one know whether one is using discretion ethically or unethically? The best approach is to follow the law or legal rule and go outside established law only if there is an egregious violation of some higher standard of justice. A judge does not have to agonize over every decision to disallow illegal evidence that will allow a criminal to go free. The rule has been evaluated and judged as more worthy than the alternative. A prosecutor does not have to decide each plea bargain if there are some guidelines developed for everyone. When the rule or the law appears, on its face, to result in some miscarriage of justice, then the ethical systems can be applied to judge alternative courses of action.

In our legal system, discretionary decisions at the trial level can be reexamined through the process of appeal. Appeals are part of due process in that they serve as a check on the decision making of trial judges. Any gross errors will be corrected; any extremely unethical actions will result in a new trial. However, appeals are not conducted in all cases, and even in cases that are appealed, many errors go unnoticed and uncorrected. For instance, courtroom behavior is seldom noticed or corrected unless it extremely and blatantly violates constitutional rights.

The remainder of this chapter and the next chapter will explore the use of discretion in the courts by looking at the role responsibilities of the major actors in the system—the defense attorney, the prosecutor, and the judge. Obviously, these actors work with a criminal code that is handed down to them by the legislature. The formation of laws and the factors and compromises that go into a law's creation or revision constitute a subject matter that will be left to others. We will address the ethical questions that arise in the *implementation,* rather than the *creation,* of law.

ETHICAL ISSUES
FOR DEFENSE ATTORNEYS

The role of the defense attorney is to protect the due-process rights of the defendant. Due process is supposed to minimize mistakes in judicial proceedings that might result in a deprivation of life, liberty, or property. Due-process rights, including notice, neutral fact finders, cross-examination, and presentation of evidence and witnesses, are supposed to minimize the risk of error. The defense attorney is there to ensure that these rights are protected—for instance, during interrogation to make sure no coercion is used, at lineup to make sure it is fair and unbiased, and during trial to ensure adequate defense and cross-examination. This pure role of advocate is contradictory to the reality that the defense attorney must, if he or she is to work with the other actors in the court system, accommodate their needs as well as those of clients.

Defense attorneys are always in the position of balancing the rights of individual clients against overall effectiveness. Extreme attempts to protect one client's rights will influence the defense attorney's effectiveness for all clients. Furthermore, defense attorneys must balance the needs and problems of the client against their ethical responsibilities to the system and profession. Individual rights are balanced by other considerations.

Defense attorneys have a fairly negative reputation in the legal community, as well as with the general public. They are seen as incompetent and/or unable to compete on the higher rungs of the status ladder of law, those higher rungs being corporate, tax, and international law. Alternatively or additionally, they are seen as "shady" or "money grubbers" who get the guilty off by sleazy tactics. In fiction, defense attorneys are presented as either fearless crusaders who always manage to defend innocent clients (usually against unethical prosecutors) or as sleazy dealmakers who are either too burned out or selfish to care about their clients. The reality, of course, fits neither of these portrayals. Kittel (1990) finds that the majority of defense attorneys would not change

---

QUOTATION

By and large . . . big-city criminal administration is a jungle, a snake pit, an aggregation of horrors. It is a dismal swamp of no-hope for the offenders who make the process necessary. It is a livable turf for mean, venal and small-time chiselers whose only qualification is a license to practice law.

SOURCE: Abe Fortas, Associate Justice of the U.S. Supreme Court, quoted in Roth, A., and Roth, J. *Devil's Advocates: The Unnatural History of Lawyers* (Berkeley, CA: Nolo Press, 1989): 146.

---

their career given an opportunity to do so and that most chose their career because they were interested in the trial work it offered or for public policy reasons, as opposed to the common myth that criminal defense attorneys enter that field because they couldn't make it anywhere else.

As mentioned earlier, the system tends to operate under a presumption of guilt. Indeed, defense attorneys are often in the position of defending clients they know are guilty. The rationale for defending a guilty person is that a person deserves due process before a finding of guilt and punishment. Before punishment can be morally imposed, a fair procedure must ensure that the punishment is appropriate. To ensure appropriate punishment, a set of fact-finding procedures is necessary, and the defense attorney's role is to make sure that the rules are followed. If defense attorneys are doing their job, then we can all be comfortable with a conviction. If they do not do their job, then we have no system of justice, and none of us is safe from wrongful prosecution. Due process protects us all by making the criminal justice system prove wrongdoing fairly; the person who makes sure no shortcuts are taken is the defense attorney.

In the early 1990s the ABA promulgated its Standards for Criminal Justice. "The Defense Function," Chapter 4, covers a multitude of issues, such as these:

- the function of defense counsel
- punctuality, public statements
- duty to the administration of justice
- access, the lawyer–client relationship
- duty to investigate
- control and direction of litigation
- plea bargaining
- trial conduct
- appeal

QUERY

Would you be able to defend someone you knew was guilty of a murder? Rape? Drug crime?

One sees that these standards are much more specific than the Law Enforcement Code of Ethics. Instead of being aspirational, these standards are specific guidelines for behavior. They are not typically used for disciplinary actions. In this section, we will explore only a few of the many different ethical issues that confront defense attorneys in their representation of clients.

Responsibility to the Client

The basic duty defense counsel owes to the administration of justice and as an officer of the court is to serve as the accused's counselor and advocate with courage and devotion and to render effective, quality representation. (Standard 4-1.2(b))

Defense attorneys are always in the position of balancing the rights of the individual client against overall effectiveness. Extreme attempts to protect these rights will reduce the defense attorney's effectiveness for other clients. Furthermore, defense attorneys must balance the needs and problems of the client against their ethical responsibilities to the system and profession.

A lawyer is supposed to provide legal assistance to clients without regard for personal preference or interest. A lawyer is not allowed to withdraw from a case simply because he or she no longer wishes to represent the client. Only if the legal action is for harassment or malicious purposes, if continued employment will result in a violation of a disciplinary rule, if discharged by a client, or if a mental or physical condition renders effective counsel impossible can a lawyer be mandatorily withdrawn. In other cases, a judge may grant permission to withdraw when the client insists upon illegal or unethical actions, is uncooperative and does not follow the attorney's advice, or otherwise makes effective counsel difficult. Legal ethics mandate that people with unpopular causes and individuals who are obviously guilty still deserve counsel, and it is the ethical duty of an attorney to provide such counsel. In fact, although many people condemn attorneys, and especially the American Civil Liberties Union's attorneys, for defending such groups as the American Nazi Party or the Ku Klux Klan or individuals such as Charles Manson or notorious drug dealers, clearly they could not do otherwise under the ethical principles of their profession.

Some lawyers have no problem at all with defending "unworthy" clients. Drug cases are becoming well-known as lawyers' porkbarrels. Many lawyers have made millions of dollars defending major drug smugglers and dealers. In effect, they share in the wealth generated by illegal drugs. Is it ethical to accept any client able to pay large and continuing bills? It is commonly believed that anytime a criminal defendant can and will pay, a lawyer can always be found to take the case to trial and conduct innumerable appeals, no matter what the likelihood of winning.

Recently, the government has started using provisions under the Racketeer Influenced and Corrupt Organizations Statute (18 U.S.C. Sections 1961-68), usually referred to as RICO, to confiscate drug money, including fees already paid to attorneys. Defense attorneys object to this practice, protesting that it endangers fair representation for drug defendants because attorneys may not be willing to defend these clients when there is a possibility that their fees will be confiscated. Some prosecutors, it should be noted, have gone a step further and are starting to prosecute attorneys themselves if there is evidence that an attorney is engaged in a continuing conspiracy to further a criminal enterprise by his or her association with the client. This use of the RICO statute is extremely controversial, as are other uses of it that will be discussed later.

Many people are firmly convinced that the quality of legal representation is directly related to how much money the defendant can pay. When people can make bail and hire private attorneys, do they receive better justice? Do defense attorneys exert more effort for clients who pay well than they do for court-appointed clients? Obviously, professional ethics would dictate equal consideration, but individual values also affect behavior. If an attorney felt confident that his or her court-appointed clients received at least adequate representation, then could one not justify a more zealous defense for a paying client? Where adequate representation is vaguely and poorly defined, this question is even more problematic.

Confidentiality

Defense counsel should not reveal information relating to representation of a client unless the client consents after consultation, except for disclosures that are impliedly authorized in order to carry out the representation and except that defense counsel may reveal such information to the extent he or she reasonably believes necessary to prevent the client from committing a criminal act that defense counsel believes is likely to result in imminent death or substantial bodily harm. (Standard 4-3.7(d))

Attorney–client privilege refers to the inability of authorities to compel an attorney (through subpoena or threat of contempt) to disclose confidential information regarding his or her client; the ethical duty of confidentiality prohibits an attorney from disclosing to any person, or using for one's own gain, information about one's client obtained through the attorney–client relationship. The confidentiality protection is said to be inherent in the fiduciary relationship between the client and the attorney, but more important is that the client must be able to expect and receive the full and complete assistance of his or her lawyer. If a client feels compelled to withhold negative and incriminatory information, he or she will not be able to receive such assistance; thus, the lawyer must be perceived as a completely confidential agent of the client. Parallels to the attorney–client relationship are relationships between spouses and the priest–penitent relationship. In these cases the relationship creates a legal entity that approximates a single interest rather than two, so a break in confidentiality would violate the Fifth Amendment protection against self-incrimination (Schoeman, 1982: 260).

The only situations wherein a lawyer can ethically reveal confidences of a client are when the client consents, when disclosure is required by law or court order, when the intention of the client is to commit a crime and the information is necessary to prevent the crime, or when one needs to defend oneself or employees against an accusation of wrongful conduct. As mentioned before, the Model Rules have supplanted the Code of Professional Responsibility as the national model for legal ethics. One of the most debated portions was the part of this rule that specifies that an attorney may violate a client's confidence only to prevent a future crime involving imminent death or grievous bodily harm. The older code allowed disclosure to prevent any crime. Many states have refused to adopt this rule, or have enlarged it to include any crime. Neither situation of future crime applied to the Garrow incident (described in the accompanying box), so the lawyers felt ethically bound to withhold the location of two bodies from the family of the victims.

Too Confidential?

In July 1973, Robert Garrow, a 38-year-old mechanic from Syracuse, New York, killed four persons, apparently at random. The four were camping in the Adirondack Mountains. In early August, following a vigorous manhunt, he was captured by state police and indicted for the murder of a student from Schenectady. At the time of the arrest, no evidence connected Garrow to the other deaths. . . . The court appointed two Syracuse lawyers, Francis R. Belge and Frank H. Armani, to defend Garrow.

Some weeks later, during discussions with his two lawyers, Garrow told them that he had raped and killed a woman in a mine shaft. Belge and Armani located the mine shaft and the body of the Illinois woman but did not take their discovery to the police. The body was finally discovered four months later by two children playing in the mine. In September, the lawyers found the second body by following Garrow's directions. This discovery, too, went unreported; the girl's body was uncovered by a student in December. . . . Belge and Armani maintained their silence until the following June. Then, to try to show that he was insane, Garrow made statements from the witness stand that implicated him in the other three murders. At a press conference the next day, Belge and Armani outlined for the first time the sequence of events.

The local community was outraged. The lawyers, however, believed they had honored the letter and spirit of their professional duty in a tough case. "We both, knowing how the parents feel, wanted to advise them where the bodies were," Belge said, "but since it was a privileged communication, we could not reveal any information that was given to us in confidence."

Their silence was based on the legal code that admonishes the lawyer to "preserve the confidence and secrets of a client." The lawyer–client "privilege" against disclosure of confidences is one of the oldest and most ironclad in the law. If the defendant has no duty to confess his guilt or complicity in a crime, it can make no sense to assert that his lawyer has such a duty. Otherwise, the argument goes, the accused will tell his lawyer at best a deficient version of the facts, and the lawyer cannot as effectively defend the client. This argument frequently seems unconvincing; it certainly did to the people of Syracuse.

SOURCE: Harris, 1986: 114–115. Reprinted with permission of Wadsworth Publishing Company.

Harris (1986) evaluates the actions of Garrow's two lawyers under the utilitarian ethical framework and decides that they did the right thing since it would be ethically acceptable for lawyers to break client confidentiality only in cases in which a death or crime could be prevented by disclosure. This formulation is, as always, based on the greatest utility for society, and it is believed that society benefits in the long run from the presence of the attorney–client confidence. Therefore, this confidence should be sacrificed only when it endangers a life.

Religious ethics might condemn the attorneys' actions since withholding the location of the bodies was a form of deception. On the other hand, in the Catholic religion, a similar ethical dilemma might arise if someone confessed to a priest. It would be impossible for the priest to betray that confession no matter what the circumstances. Ethical formalism is also difficult to reconcile with the lawyers' actions. First of all, under the categorical imperative, the lawyers' actions must be such that we would be willing for all others to engage in similar behavior under like circumstances. Could one will that it become universal law for attorneys to keep such information secret? What if you were the parents who did not know the whereabouts of their daughter or even if she was alive or dead? It is hard to imagine that they would be willing to agree with this universal law. On the other hand, if one was the criminal, or one's son or daughter was the criminal, one would not want a lawyer to betray confidences that would hurt his case. If one were a lawyer, it is imagined that he or she would want a rule that encouraged a client to be truthful in order to provide an adequate defense. Ethical formalism is also concerned with duty; it is obvious that the duty of an attorney is always to protect the interests of his or her client. As with the utilitarian formulation, we might differentiate between circumstances of future crimes and circumstances of past crimes.

The ethics of care would be concerned with the needs of both the client and the parents in the case described. It would perhaps resolve the issue in a less absolutist fashion than the other rationales. For instance, when discussing this case in a college classroom, many students immediately decide that they would call in the location of the bodies anonymously, thereby relieving the parents' anxiety and also protecting to some extent the confidential communication. Although this compromise is unsupported by an absolute view of confidentiality since it endangers the client (perhaps he would not even be charged with the crimes if the bodies were never found), it protects the relationship of the attorney and the client and still meets the needs of the parents.

It should be noted that the rule of confidentiality does not apply to physical evidence. Anything that is discoverable in the possession of a client is equally discoverable if in the possession of an attorney. Therefore, an attorney must hand over files or other incriminating evidence subject to a valid search warrant, motion, or subpoena. If the attorney is merely told where these items may be found, he or she is not obliged to tell the authorities where they are. For instance, if a client tells an attorney a murder weapon is in a certain location, the attorney cannot divulge that information to authorities. However, if the client drops a murder weapon in the attorney's lap, he or she must offer it to police. If the attorney is told where a murder weapon is and goes to check, that information is still protected; however, if the attorney takes the weapon back to his or her office, then the attorney may be subjected to felony charges of obstruction of justice, or evidence tampering.

A defense attorney's ethics may also be compromised when a client insists on taking the stand to commit perjury. Disciplinary rules specifically forbid the lawyer from allowing perjury to take place; if it happens before the attorney realizes the intent of the client, the defense must not use or refer to the perjured testimony (Freedman, 1986; Kleinig, 1986). But if the attorney appears to disbelieve or discredit his or her client, then this behavior violates the ethical mandate of a zealous defense, and to inform the court of the perjury violates the ethical rule of confidentiality.

Pellicoti (1990) explains that an attorney should first try to dissuade the client from committing perjury. If the client persists in plans to lie, the attorney then has an ethical duty to withdraw from the case, and there is some authority that the attorney should disclose to the court that the client plans to lie. Withdrawal is problematic since it will usually jeopardize a case, and disclosure is even more problematic since, arguably, it affects the judgment of the hearing judge. An attorney may refuse to call witnesses who plan to lie, but if the defendant's testimony will be perjured, it is, arguably, a violation of his or her rights for the attorney not to allow the defendant to take the stand. *Nix v. Whiteside* (475 U.S. 157, 89 L.Ed.2d 123 [1986]) held that it did not violate the defendant's Sixth Amendment right to counsel for the attorney to refuse to help the defendant commit perjury. In this murder case, the defendant told his lawyer that he had not seen a gun in the victim's hand. At a later point, he told his attorney that if he didn't testify that he saw a gun, he would be "dead" (lose the case). The attorney told him that if he testified falsely, he would have to impeach him and would seek to withdraw from the case. The defendant testified truthfully, was found guilty, and then appealed based on ineffective counsel. The court found that the right to counsel did not include the right to an attorney who would suborn perjury.

Pellicoti (1990) describes the "passive" role and the "active" role of an attorney with a client who commits perjury. In the passive role, the attorney asks no questions during direct examination that would elicit untruthful answers, and may make a statement that the client is taking the stand against the advice of an attorney. The attorney does not refer to perjured testimony during summation or any arguments. The active role allows for the attorney to disclose to the court the fact of the perjured testimony. There is no great weight of authority to commend either approach, leaving attorneys in a difficult ethical dilemma. For some attorneys, the best solution is not to know about the lie in the first place.

As long as the attorney only has doubts about the veracity of his client's testimony, there is no legal duty to disclose; in fact, the weight of authority indicates that the attorney with doubts should proceed with the doubtful testimony—any disclosure of such doubts is improper and unethical. Thus, some

---

Literary Perspective

But Sandy Stern, with whom I have done business for better than a decade, against whom I have tried half a dozen cases, and who on matters of gravity, or of little consequence, has always known that he could accept my word—Sandy Stern has never asked me if I did it.

SOURCE: Turow, Scott. *Presumed Innocent* (New York: Farrar, Straus and Giroux, 1987): 137–138. Copyright © 1987 by Scott Turow. Reprinted by permission of Farrar, Straus & Giroux, Inc.

---

attorneys tell their client "Before you say anything, I need to tell you that I cannot participate in perjury and if I know for a fact that you plan to lie, I cannot put you on the stand" or ask their client "What do I need to know that is damaging to this case?" rather than if the client is guilty of the crime. Of course, then there is the observation of many attorneys that all defendants lie about everything and you can't believe them anyway. If this is true, then some attorneys may conclude that there are always doubts and thus allow testimony to occur.

Conflicts of Interest

> Defense counsel should not permit his or her professional judgment or obligations to be affected by his or her own political, business, property, or personal interests. (Standard 4-3.5(a))

Attorneys are specifically prohibited from engaging in representations that would compromise their loyalty to their clients. Specifically, attorneys must not represent clients who may have interests that conflict with those of the attorney—for instance, an attorney may not represent a client who owns a company that is a rival to one in which the attorney has an interest. The attorney also must not represent two clients who may have opposing interests—for instance, co-defendants in a criminal case, since very often one will testify against the other. The attorney would find it impossible in such situation to represent each individual fairly. Disciplinary rules even prohibit two lawyers from a single firm from representing clients with conflicting interests. In some informal and formal decisions from ethics committees, this rule has even been used to prohibit legal aid or public defender offices from defending co-defendants, although this is a fairly routine practice (American Bar Association, 1986).

Although attorneys may not ethically accept clients with conflicting interests, there is no guidance on the more abstract problem that all criminal clients in a caseload have conflicting interests if their cases are looked upon as part of a workload rather than considered separately. Many defense attorneys make a living by taking cases from people with very modest means or taking court-appointed cases with the fee set by the court. The defense attorney then becomes a "fast-food lawyer," depending on volume and speed to make a profit. What happens here, of course, is that quality may get sacrificed along the way. When lawyers pick up clients in the hallways of courtrooms and from bail bondsmen's referrals, the goal is to arrange bail, get a plea bargain, and move on to the next case. Guilt or innocence has very little to do with this operation, and rarely does the case come to trial.

About 90 percent of the cases in the criminal justice system are settled by a plea bargain (Senna and Siegel, 1987). The defense attorney's goal in plea bargaining is to get the best possible deal for the client—probation or the shortest prison sentence that the prosecutor is willing to give for a guilty plea. The defense attorney is aware that he or she cannot aggressively push every case without endangering the ongoing relationship with the prosecutor. A courtroom appearance may be an isolated event for the client, but for the defense attorney and prosecutor, it is an ongoing, weekly ritual—only the names of the defendants change. Because of the nature of the continuing relationship, the defense attorney must weigh present needs against future gains. If the defense becomes known as unwilling to play ball, reduced effectiveness may hurt future clients.

Even if one approves of plea bargaining because of its benefits to the system, there are some practices that take place, such as trading cases or "train justice," that are much more problematic. When a defense attorney has several cases to bargain, he may trade off on some to get better deals for others. No ethical system would seem to justify this practice. Clearly, conflicts of interest may exist even when the clients are not related or associated in any way.

Another conflict of interest may occur if the attorney desires to represent the client's interests in selling literary or media rights. Standard 4-3.4 specifically forbids entering into such an agreement before the case is complete. The temptations are obvious—if the attorney hopes to acquire financial rewards from a share of profits, his or her professional judgment on how best to defend the client may be clouded. Whether putting off signing such an agreement until the case is complete removes the possibility of unethical decisions is debatable.

In the O. J. Simpson trial, it appears that every major player has or is planning to write a book about the trial. One wonders if trial tactics and speeches aren't evaluated, at least in passing, on how they will appear in a later first-person narrative or movie-of-the-week screenplay. The potential for biased judgments are obvious—for instance, if an attorney has a client who has committed a particularly spectacular crime, there is the potential for celebrity status only if the case comes to trial, so a plea bargain—even if attractive to the client—in this case may be less carefully considered by the attorney, even subconsciously. Since many litigators have a strong inclination for theatrics to begin with, the temptation of Hollywood cannot be overestimated.

Zealous Defense

Defense counsel, in common with all members of the bar, is subject to standards of conduct stated in statutes, rules, decisions of courts, and codes, canons, or other standards of professional conduct. Defense counsel has no duty to execute any directive of the accused which does not comport with law or such standards. Defense counsel is the professional representative of the accused, not the accused's alter ego. (Standard 4-1.2(e))

Few would challenge the idea that all people deserve to have their due-process rights protected. However, what many people find unsettling is the zeal with which some defense attorneys approach the courtroom contest. How diligent should the defense be in protecting the defendant's rights? A conflict may arise between providing an effective defense and maintaining professional ethics and individual morality. Lawyers should represent clients zealously within the bounds of the law, but the law is sometimes vague and difficult to determine. Some actions are simply forbidden. The lawyer may not engage in motions or actions to intentionally and maliciously harm others, knowingly advance unwarranted claims or defenses, conceal or fail to disclose that which he or she is required by law to reveal, knowingly use perjured testimony or false evidence, knowingly make a false statement of law or fact, participate in the creation or preservation of evidence when he or she knows or it is obvious that the evidence is false, counsel the client in conduct that is illegal, or engage in other illegal conduct. The attorney is also expected to maintain a professional and courteous relationship with the opposing attorneys, litigants, and witnesses and to refrain from disparaging statements or badgering conduct. The defense attorney must not intimidate or otherwise influence the jury or trier of fact or use the media for these same purposes.

Despite these ethical rules, practices such as withholding evidence, manufacturing evidence, witness badgering, and defamation of victims' characters are sometimes used as tactics in the defense arsenal. For instance, the practice of bringing out the sexual history of rape victims is done purely to paint her as a victim who deserved or asked for her rape. Even though rape-shield laws exist that prohibit most exposés of sexual history, attorneys still attempt to bring in such evidence. Destroying the credibility of honest witnesses is considered good advocacy. For instance, if a witness accurately testifies to what he or she saw, a good attorney may still cast doubt in the jurors' minds by bringing out evidence of the use of glasses, mistakes of judgment, and other facts that tend to obfuscate and undercut the credibility of the witness. Attorneys will do this even when they know that the witness is telling the truth. To not question the credibility of a prosecution witness is to perform the defense attorney's function in a less than zealous manner.

In some cases defense attorneys go to extreme lengths to change the course of testimony, such as bribing witnesses, allowing their client to intimidate a

---

QUOTATION

[A]n advocate in the discharge of his duty, knows but one person in all the world, and that person is his client. To save that client by all means and expedients, and at all hazards and costs to other persons, and, among them, to himself, is his first and only duty, and in performing this duty he must not regard the alarm, the torments, the destruction which he may bring upon others.

SOURCE: Lord Brougham, 1820. Quoted in Glendon, M. *A Nation Under Lawyers* (New York: Farrar, Straus and Giroux, 1994): 40.

witness, instructing their client to destroy physical evidence or to manufacture an alibi and then commit perjury. In Chapter 5, criminal behavior on the part of law enforcement officers was discussed as abhorrent but rare, and this is also the case with blatantly criminal behavior on the part of attorneys. Most ethical conflicts occur over more subtle questions of how far one should go to provide a zealous defense.

It is sometimes difficult to determine when a defense attorney's treatment of a witness is badgering as opposed to energetic cross-examination, or when exploring a witness's background is a character assassination as opposed to a careful examination of credibility. To hide physical evidence is illegal, but to not go look for it is perhaps appropriate under legal ethics. Doubts about the veracity of a defendant's story must always be concluded by allowing the client the benefit of the doubt. Some attorneys focus attacks on opposing counsel—female attorneys report that opposing male attorneys attempt to infantilize, patronize, or sexualize them in front of the judge and jury as a trial tactic to destroy their credibility. Young attorneys encounter treatment by opposing counsel—with such comments as "what my young colleague here has evidently not learned yet . . . "—designed to provide the jury with the view that the older attorney is more wise, honest, or mature than the younger attorney. Personal attacks on credibility and more subtle attempts to influence juries' perceptions of opposing counsel may also occur—such as talking during opposing counsel's opening or closing; rolling one's eyes in response to a statement or question; and making other verbal or physical gestures indicating disbelief, amusement, or disdain. These tactics are obviously not in the same category as bribing witnesses or manufacturing evidence, but they can be questioned as appropriate or ethical.

Defense attorneys may sacrifice their integrity for the sake of a case. For instance, in one trial, a defense attorney and a prosecutor were getting ready to try a barroom murder case. The prosecutor was able to present only one eyewitness to the shooting—the bartender. No one else in the bar was willing to testify that they saw anything. The prosecutor had other circumstantial evidence of the defendant's guilt, but the eyewitness was crucial. Unfortunately, the bartender had a ten-year-old murder conviction—a fact that would reduce his credibility in the jury's eyes. This fact could be brought out by the defense under the rules of evidence; however, the prosecutor could petition the court to have the fact suppressed and have a good chance of succeeding since it bore no relevance to the case and would be prejudicial, but she did not file the appropriate motion. Just before the trial was about to start, the prosecutor asked the defense attorney if he was going to bring out this fact on his cross-examination of the bartender. If he planned to do so, the prosecutor would have asked for a continuance and filed a motion to have it suppressed, or at least brought it out herself on direct to reduce its impact. He told her specifically and clearly that he had no intention of using that information or questioning the witness about it since it was so long ago and irrelevant to the case. When the direct examination of this witness was over and the defense attorney started his cross-examination, his very first question was "Isn't it true that you were convicted of murder in 19--?" Although the prosecutor may have committed an error in judgment by trusting the defense attorney, the defense attorney deliberately misled the prosecutor as to his intentions—he lied. Zealous defense is a weak rationale for lying. When asked about his actions, the defense attorney explained that it "just slipped out" and complained that the prosecutor took these things "too seriously." This behavior is an example of a lie used for short-term gain, an egoistic rationalization, and a view of due process as a game since when an opponent is offended by the lie, she is taking things "too seriously." In this case, the defense attorney may have lost more than he gained by the trick; a conviction was achieved in spite of the witness's background, and the attorney found that previously helpful and cooperative prosecutors were suddenly unwilling to agree to continuances, closed their files to him even though it was generally an "open file" office, and in other ways treated him as untrustworthy, which indeed he was.

A recent innovation in trial tactics is the development of "scientific" jury selection. Attorneys often contend that a trial has already been won or lost once the jury has been selected. Whether or not this is true, attorneys are becoming increasingly sophisticated in their methods of choosing which members of a jury panel would make good jurors. A good juror is defined not as one who is unbiased and fair, but as someone who is predisposed to be sympathetic to that attorney's case. The ability to use these methods is limited only by a budget. Some lawyers, such as the famed "Racehorse" Haynes of Houston, have used methods such as surveying a large sample of the population in the community where the case is to be tried to discover how certain demographic groups feel about issues relevant to the case so that these findings can be used when the jury is selected. Other attorneys hire jury experts, psychologists who sit with the attorney and, through a combination of nonverbal and verbal clues, identify those jury panel members who are predisposed to believe the case presented by the attorney. Another method uses a "shadow jury"—a panel of people selected by the defense attorney to represent the actual jury that sits through the trial and provides feedback to the attorney on the evidence being presented during the trial. This allows the attorney to adjust his or her trial tactics in response. Some of these methods were used in the William Kennedy Smith rape trial in Florida, which resulted in an acquittal. More recently, they were used in the O. J. Simpson case. Attorneys have always used intuition and less sophisticated means to decide which jury members to exclude, but these tactics are questioned by some as too contrary to the basic idea that a trial is supposed to start with an unbiased jury (Smith and Meyer, 1987).

Can our ethical systems help to determine what actions are ethically justified in defending a client zealously? Utilitarianism and egoism would probably allow a greater range of actions depending on the particular interests or rewards represented by the case. Ethical formalism and religion might restrict the actions of a defense attorney to those allowed by a strict interpretation of the Model Rules.

Are Trial Consultants Good for Justice?

The O. J. Simpson murder trial introduced millions of Americans to a relatively new figure in the nation's courts: the trial consultant. These professionals—many of whom work in fields such as psychology, communications and marketing—help lawyers pick juries and develop trial strategies. Curiosity about them accelerated when a jury acquitted Simpson after deliberating less than four hours. But consultant-picked juries have produced other surprising results:

- William Kennedy Smith was acquitted of rape charges in 1991 in Florida.
- Lyle and Erik Menendez, who admitted killing their parents, were spared by separate hung juries in L.A. in 1994. (They were convicted in a second trial.)

With such high-profile verdicts, the public could reasonably ask how consultants are affecting our court system. What role do they play in the search for truth and justice? To lawyers, it is a matter of figuring out why jurors exposed to the same evidence reach different conclusions.

"Clearly, it must be due to pre-existing attitudes," says Shari Diamond of the American Bar Foundation. "In scientific jury selection, the consultant helps identify which backgrounds will be associated with favorable or unfavorable reactions."

What They Do

Consultants provide services ranging from witness preparation to mock trials, juror profiles and phone surveys on public attitudes about a case. They may use "shadow juries," people selected to mirror the real jury, who are asked their impressions about the trial. They also may offer advice on things like effective posture, clothing choice and tone of voice.

One powerful tactic is to use "focus groups," informal talk sessions, to find out opinions about a case. Jo-Ellan Dimitrius, the Simpson team's consultant, says the defense thought of using the video-taped testimony of a neighbor's maid. "We changed that after we played the tape to focus groups and found she was off the charts of believability," Dimitrius says.

Consultants work on an estimated 6000 trials a year, mostly civil cases. The American Society of Trial Consultants, a professional organization, has more than 400 members. Most are independent, but some are employed by companies like DecisionQuest, FTI Corp. and National Jury Project.

Top consultants charge upwards of $150 an hour. Dimitrius customarily gets $300 an hour but lowered her rate for Simpson. "If we had charged the full rate for what we did, it would have been at least a $500,000 deal," she says.

Picking a Jury

Part of a consultant's job may be to help lawyers screen potential jurors. In the Simpson trial, candidates were asked to fill out a 78-page list of questions devised by Judge Ito, defense and prosecution attorneys and Jo-Ellan Dimitrius. (Don Vinson, the prosecution's consultant, was not involved.) Actual questions included: "What TV shows do you watch? Do you think police are trustworthy? Do you attend church?"

This information is then used to screen jurors. . . . The argument is that clever consultants can use the preemptory challenge to stack juries or "dumb them down," arriving at the least sophisticated or educated group.

(continued)

Are Trial Consultants Good for Justice? *(continued)*

Simpson's acquittal brought heated arguments that consultants know ways to stack juries. "Lawyers will argue that this is all part of an adversarial system," says Stephen J. Adler, author of *The Jury: Disorder in the Courts.* "But it doesn't have to work that way. It might serve the public better to remove preemptory challenges and take strategy out of jury selection. I think that would be a step toward getting truth and justice."

"Given the time, money and energy spent [on the Simpson trial]," Adler adds, "there might have been more confidence in the decision of a jury chosen not by consultants but by picking 12 names out of a hat."

SOURCE: Gavzer, B. *Parade* Magazine, 5 Jan. 1997: 20. Copyright © 1997. Reprinted with permission of the author and publisher.

Aronson discusses two methods for resolving ethical dilemmas. The first is called the "situational model," wherein lawyers weigh the priorities in each case and decide each case on the particular factors present. For instance, client confidentiality may be less of a priority when a new crime is threatened but be paramount in other considerations. The "systems model," on the other hand, would be a more absolute or legalistic model in that behavior would always be considered wrong or right depending on the ethical rule guiding the definition (Aronson, 1977: 59–63). Obviously, these two systems of decision making bear a great deal of resemblance to the situationalist and absolutist models discussed in Chapter 2.

CONCLUSION

In this chapter we have examined the source of legal ethics and the reasons that the public seems to have such a poor opinion of the ethics of legal professionals. One might expect that the public's respect and trust for legal professionals, as guardians of the justice system, would be high, but that is not the case. Part of the reason is the advocacy role that attorneys embrace and the ability to take "either side" in a controversy. Observers have made analogies that compare the practice of law to a game, with one side winning and the other side losing depending on the skill of the players. In the practice of criminal law, one side is represented by the defense attorney, and the other is rep-

---

QUERY

Should defense attorneys shop for lenient judges, prepare witnesses, attack the credibility of witnesses, and engage in other actions designed to get the defendant the best chance of acquittal?

---

resented by the prosecutor. There are similar duties for both parties, but there are also crucial differences in the duties and ethical responsibilities of these professionals. In the next chapter, we will continue our discussion by exploring the ethics of prosecutors and judges.

REVIEW QUESTIONS

1. What are the three models of judicial processing described in this chapter?
2. What are the advantages of and problems with plea bargaining?
3. Describe the moral agent, legal agent, and special relationship views of the attorney–client relationship.
4. What is the source of formal ethics for attorneys? Describe the history of the origin of these ethics.
5. Describe at least three issues related to the defense attorney's ethical obligations.

ETHICAL DILEMMAS

Situation 1

Your first big case is a multiple murder. As defense attorney for Sy Kopath you have come to the realization that he really did break into a couple's home and torture and kill them in the course of robbing them of jewelry and other valuables. He has even confessed to you that he did it. However, you are also aware that the police did not read him his Miranda warning and that he was coerced into giving a confession without your presence. What should you do? Would your answer be different if you believed that he was innocent or didn't know for sure either way?

Situation 2

You are completing an internship at a defense attorney's office during your senior year in college. You plan to enter law school after graduation and pursue a career as an attorney, although you have not yet decided what type of law to practice. Your duties as an intern are to assist the private practitioner you work for in a variety of tasks, including interviewing clients and witnesses, organizing case files, running errands, and photocopying. A case that you are helping with involves a defendant charged with armed robbery. One day while you are at the office, the defendant comes in and gives you a package for the attorney. In it you find a gun. You believe, but do not know for a fact, that the gun is the one used in the armed robbery. When the attorney returns, he instructs you to return the package to the defendant. What should you do? What should the attorney do?

Situation 3

Review the Garrow case discussed in this chapter. What would you have done as the defense attorney in this case? Is it substantially different from the situation above? If so, why?

Situation 4

You are aware of a colleague who could be considered grossly incompetent. He drinks and often appears in court intoxicated. He ignores his cases and does not file appropriate motions before deadlines expire. Any person who is unlucky enough to have him as a court-appointed attorney usually ends up with a conviction and a heavy sentence because he does not seem to care what happens to his clients and rarely advises going to trial. When he does take a case to trial, he is unprepared and unprofessional in the courtroom. You hear many complaints from defendants about his demeanor, competence, and ethics. Everyone—defense attorneys, prosecutors, and judges alike—knows this person and his failings, yet nothing is done. What should you do?

SUGGESTED READINGS

Gershman, B. 1990. *Prosecutorial Misconduct*. New York: Clark Boardman.

Glendon, M. 1994. *A Nation Under Lawyers*. New York: Farrar, Straus and Giroux.

Radelet, M., Bedau, H., and Putnam, C. 1992. *In Spite of Innocence*. Boston: Northeastern University Press.

Scheingold, S. 1984. *The Politics of Law and Order*. New York: Longman.

Spence, G. 1989. *With Justice for None*. New York: Penguin.

8

The Ethics
of Prosecution

Chapter Objectives

Review the role of discretion in the legal system.

Understand how the role of prosecutors is
qualitatively different from the role of defense attorneys.

Understand the ethics of judges in the criminal justice system.

In the last chapter we explored the ethics of the defense attorney. As a pure advocate, the defense attorney has an overriding goal and purpose of pursuing a client's interest. As long as he or she does not run afoul of the law or ethical mandates, the client's defense is the defense attorney's sole objective. Prosecutors and other court actors have a more abstract function. Prosecutors do not have an individual client; rather, the system and society itself are the clients. Pursuit of justice rather than pursuit of the best interest of the client characterizes the aims of prosecutors and judges.

ETHICAL ISSUES FOR PROSECUTORS

As the second line of decision makers in the system, prosecutors have extremely broad powers of discretion. The prosecutor acts like a strainer—he or she collects some cases for formal prosecution while eliminating a great many others. Because of limited resources, the difficulty of enforcing outdated or unsupported laws, and weak cases, prosecution of every case is impossible. It may be inappropriate in some situations to impose criminal sanctions, even when laws have been broken, because these particular laws are so trivial or so lacking in public support. Early diversion of such cases saves taxpayers money and saves individuals trouble and expense.

To guide discretion, there are ethical standards relating specifically to the role of the prosecutor. Chapter 3 of the ABA Standards for Criminal Justice covers the prosecution function. These standards cover topics similar to those for defense attorneys, but they also make special note of the unique role of the prosecutor as a representative of the court system and the state, rather than a pure advocate.

Use of Discretion

A prosecutor should not institute, or cause to be instituted, or permit the continued pendency of criminal charges when the prosecutor knows that the charges are not supported by probable cause. A prosecutor should not institute, cause to be instituted, or permit the continued pendency of criminal charges in the absence of sufficient admissible evidence to support a conviction. (Standard 3-3.9(a))

The prosecutor must seek justice, not merely a conviction. Toward this end, prosecutors must share evidence, exercise restraint in the use of their power, represent the public interest, and give the accused the benefit of reasonable doubt. Disciplinary rules are more specific: they forbid the prosecutor from pursuing charges when there is no probable cause and mandate timely disclosure to defense counsel of evidence, especially exculpatory evidence or evidence that might mitigate guilt or reduce the punishment.

One court has described the prosecutor's functions in the following way (*State v. Moynahan,* 164 Conn. 560, 325 A.2d 199, 206; cert. denied, 414 U.S. 976 [1973]):

> As a representative of the people of the state, [the prosecutor] is under a duty not solely to obtain convictions but, more importantly, (1) to determine that there is reasonable ground to proceed with a criminal charge [citation omitted]; (2) to see that impartial justice is done the guilty as well as the innocent; and (3) to ensure that all evidence tending to aid in the ascertaining of the truth be laid before the court, whether it be consistent with the contention of the prosecution that the accused is guilty.

Despite these ideals of prosecutorial duty, an unstated influence over prosecutorial discretion is that prosecutors want to and must (to be considered successful) win. Their choice of cases is influenced by this. Law enforcement considerations also influence prosecutorial action. If there is a bargain to be struck with an informant, if a lesser charge will result in testimony or information that could lead to further convictions, then this is considered in decision making. Finally, the pressure of public opinion is a factor to consider. Prosecutors may pursue cases they might otherwise have dropped if there is a great deal of public interest in the case.

Prosecutors can elect to charge or not. Their decision is influenced by political and public pressures, the chance for conviction, the severity of the crime, a "gut" feeling of guilt or innocence, prison overcrowding, and the weight of evidence. The prosecutorial role is to seek justice, but justice doesn't mean the same thing to everyone and certainly does not mean prosecuting everyone to the fullest extent of the law. Whether or not to charge is one of the most important decisions of the criminal justice process. The decision should be fair, neutral, and accomplished with due process, but this is an ideal that is sometimes lost. Prosecutors don't usually use their charging power for intimidation or harassment, but other factors may be involved in the decision to charge. For instance, a prosecutor may have a particular interest in a type of crime such as child abuse or drugs that results in the prosecutor pursuing these type of cases more intensely. Public pressure over a particular crime may impel the prosecutor to charge somebody quickly. Public perception may also influence a prosecutor not to charge. Prosecutors in state capitols often have "public integrity" units that prosecute wrongdoing on the part of public officials. Prosecutors may charge at election time for political purposes, or they may be falsely accused of such political considerations when they do charge politicians with public integrity violations.

The decision not to charge is also open to ethical scrutiny. To give one person who participated in a brutal crime immunity to gain testimony against others is efficient, but is it consistent with justice? To not charge businesspeople because they are good citizens is highly questionable, as is not charging because the individual is a relative of a powerful figure. In some situations, prosecutors do not charge because of an outpouring of public sympathy or support for the accused, perhaps because of the type of crime or identity of the victim. Prosecutors who do not charge in these cases may attribute the reason to lack of evidence or the unlikelihood of obtaining a conviction, but their political popularity probably also has something to do with their decision.

Various studies have attempted to describe prosecutors' decision making; one cites office policy as an important influence. *Legal sufficiency* is an office policy that weeds out those cases in which the evidence is not strong enough to support further action. *System efficiency* is an office policy with goals of efficiency and accountability; all decisions are made with these goals in mind, so many cases result in dismissals. Another policy is *defendant rehabilitation,* which emphasizes diversion and other rehabilitation tools rather than punitive goals. Finally, *trial sufficiency* is an office policy that encourages a permanent definition of the charge to stick with through trial (Jacoby, Mellon, and Smith, 1980).

Another study looks at the prosecutor as operating in an exchange system. The relationship between the prosecutor and the police is described as one of give-and-take. Prosecutors balance police need or wishes against their own vulnerability. The prosecutor makes personal judgments as to which police officers can be trusted. Exchange also takes place between the prosecutor's office and the courts. When the jails become overcrowded, more recommendations may be made for deferred adjudication and probation; when dockets become impossible, charges may be dropped. Finally, exchange takes place between defense attorneys and prosecutors, especially since many defense attorneys have previously served as prosecutors and may be personally familiar with the procedures and even personalities in the prosecutor's office (Cole, 1970).

Discretion is considered essential to the prosecutorial function of promoting individualized justice and softening the impersonal effects of the law. On the other hand, discretion is the key element in the general perception of the legal system as unfair and biased toward certain groups of people or individuals. Solutions to the problem of prosecutorial discretion may include regulation or internal guidelines. For instance, an office policy might include a procedure for providing written reasons for dropping charges, and this procedure would respond to charges of unbridled discretion.

Conflicts of Interest

A prosecutor should avoid a conflict of interest with respect to his or her official duties. (Standard 3.1-3(a))

Part-time prosecutors present a host of ethical issues. A Bureau of Justice Statistics bulletin (1992) reported that 47 percent of prosecutors held their jobs as a part-time occupation (Dawson, 1992: 1). Obviously, there is the possibility of a conflict of interest. It may happen that a part-time prosecutor has a private practice, and situations may occur where the duty to a private client runs counter to the duty of the prosecutor's duty to the public. In some cases, it may be that a client becomes a defendant, necessitating the prosecutor to hire a special prosecutor. Even when there are no direct conflicts of interest, the pressure of time always poses a conflict. The division of time between the private practice, where income is correlated with hard work, and prosecuting cases, where income is fixed no matter how many hours are spent, may result in a less energetic prosecutorial function than one might wish.

It is well-known that the prosecutor's job is a good stepping-stone to politics, and many use it as such. In these cases, one has to wonder whether cases are taken on the basis of merit or on their ability to place the prosecutor in the public eye and help his or her career. Winning also becomes more important.

The RICO statute has increasingly been used as a tool to confiscate property and money associated with organized criminal activity. Once this tactic was approved by the courts, a veritable flood of prosecutions began that were designed, it seems, primarily to obtain cash, boats, houses, and other property of drug dealers. Making decisions based on the potential for what can be confiscated rather than other factors is a very real and dangerous development in this type of prosecution.

The origin of civil forfeiture was in the Comprehensive Drug Abuse and Control Act of 1970 and the Organized Crime Control Act of 1970. Both of these laws allowed mechanisms for the government to seize assets gained through illegal means. Eventually, the types of assets vulnerable to seizure were expanded, including those assets *intended* to be used as well as those gained by or used in illegal activities. All states have passed similar asset-forfeiture laws. The "take" from asset forfeiture increased from $27.2 million in 1985 to $874 million in 1992. There are a number of problematic issues with asset forfeiture. First, a civil forfeiture hearing can take place without any criminal prosecution and without the presence of the alleged criminal; the government must only reach an evidentiary standard of probable cause, and then the burden of proof shifts to the individual to prove his or her innocence (unlike a criminal trial, which has a much higher burden of proof placed on the prosecutor throughout the trial). Despite a recognized acceptance of the purpose of forfeiture to be punitive, the individual is allowed much less due process than if it was a criminal prosecution. The exclusionary rule does not apply to civil forfeiture proceedings, so some allege that police are now "pursuing" assets instead of criminals, because in a civil proceeding the defendant does not receive legal aid (Jenson and Gerber, 1996).

Perhaps one of the most troubling aspects of civil forfeiture is that third parties are often the ones most hurt by the loss; spouses or parents of a suspected drug dealer may lose their home. In one of the most widely publicized forfeiture cases, a man solicited a prostitute; the state instituted proceedings and was successful in seizing the car he was driving when he solicited the prostitute—which was, in fact, his wife's car! This case received so much press because the Supreme Court ruled that no constitutional violation occurred with the forfeiture, even though his wife had nothing to do with the criminal activity.

In other cases the Supreme Court has ruled that the Eighth Amendment prohibiting excessive fines did apply to civil forfeiture; therefore, the government must regulate its forfeiture to some standard of proportionality with the crime. Another case indicated that the accused must be provided notice and some type of adversarial hearing before assets can be seized unless there are "exigent" circumstances (Jensen and Gerber, 1996). There are some indications that prosecutorial zeal in this area is starting to be looked upon with concern by courts. There have definitely been abuses, and the mercenary acquisitiveness of government officials seems contrary to their role as protectors of due process.

Plea Bargaining

> A prosecutor should not knowingly make false statements or representations as to fact or law in the course of plea discussions with defense counsel or the accused. (Standard 3-4.1(c))

As discussed earlier, there are serious ethical concerns over the practice of plea bargaining. Most conclude that plea bargaining, even if not exactly "right," is certainly efficient and probably inevitable. Even in those jurisdictions that have moved to determinate sentencing, what has happened is that plea bargaining has become charge bargaining instead of sentence bargaining. Should we measure the morality of an action by its efficiency? This efficiency argument is similar to that used to defend some deceptive investigative practices of police. If the goals of the system are crime control or bureaucratic efficiency, then plea bargaining makes sense. If the goals of the system are the protection of individual rights and the protection of due process, then plea bargaining is much harder to justify under a utilitarian argument, or any other. Obviously, plea bargaining would fail under the categorical imperative, since the individual is treated as a means in the argument that plea bargaining is good for the system.

Arguments given in defense of plea bargaining include the heavy caseloads, limited resources, legislative overcriminalization, individualized justice, and legal problems of cases (legal errors that would result in mistrials or dropped charges if the client didn't plead) (Knudten, 1978: 275). If we concede that plea bargaining can be justified, there are remaining ethical problems over specific practices relating to plea bargaining. Prosecutors may over-charge—that is, charge at a higher degree of severity or press more charges than could possibly be sustained by evidence—so that they can bargain down. Prosecutors may even mislead defense attorneys about the amount of evidence or the kind of evidence they have or about the sentence they can offer to obtain a guilty plea. Only 36 percent of chief prosecutors reported that explicit criteria for plea bargains were in place in 1990 (Bureau of Justice Statistics, 1992). Guidelines providing a range of years for certain types of charges would help the individual prosecutors maintain some level of consistency in a particular jurisdiction.

Gershman (1990) documents prosecutors engaged in false promises, fraud, misrepresentation of conditions, deals without benefit of counsel, package deals, and threats during plea bargaining. Critics contend that prosecutors hold all the cards in the dealmaking of plea bargaining. Defense attorneys can take what is offered (perhaps without knowing the nature of the evidence against the client) or argue, but most of the time arguing with a plea-bargain offer does not do the client much good and does the attorney even less.

Media Relations

The prosecutor has an important relationship with the press. The media can be enemy or friend depending on how charismatic or forthcoming the prosecutor is in interviews. Sometimes cases are said to be "tried in the papers," with the defense attorney and the prosecutor staging verbal sparring matches for public consumption. Prosecutors may react to cases and judges' decisions in the paper, criticizing the decision or the sentence and in the process

---

QUOTATION

The prosecuting attorney wields enormous power in the day-to-day life of a defense attorney and can exert considerable influence on the fate of his clients. Since plea bargaining is the dominant mode of resolving criminal cases, the defense lawyer must always look for a deal; and it is the prosecuting attorney who must agree to it. In some jurisdictions, the prosecuting attorney also makes sentencing recommendations that often carry considerable weight with the judge.

On a more personal level the prosecutor can make the defense attorney's life pleasant or miserable in countless small, but important, ways: by agreeing to or by opposing continuances; by opening or closing files for discovery; by waiving or insisting on technical requirements; by recommending or denigrating the attorney to prospective clients; by being generally agreeable or disagreeable. And many prosecutors are not reluctant to exercise their power in order to exact favors from defense attorneys. I am not suggesting that there is anything improper in all this, although it is often unseemly and sometimes borders on the unethical. I am only suggesting how important it is to remain on the good side of the prosecutor's office.

SOURCE: Dershowitz, A. *The Best Defense* (New York: Vintage Books, 1983): 355.

denigrating the dignity of the system. More often, the defense attempts to sway the press to a sympathetic view of the offense, which is easier to accomplish during prosecutorial silence.

ABA Model Rule 3.6(b) is a prohibition of out-of-court statements that a reasonable person should expect to have a substantial likelihood of materially prejudicing a proceeding. Prosecutors are probably not as guilty of using the media to try a case as are defense attorneys, but when they do make statements, it's possible there is more damage done, since defense attorneys are expected to make statements to exonerate their client and disparage the state's case. The rule specifies that no statements should be given involving any of the following topics:

- the character, credibility, reputation, or criminal record of a party, suspect, or witness
- the identity of a witness
- the expected testimony of a party or witness
- the performance or results of any test or examination
- the refusal of any party to submit to such tests or examinations
- the identity or nature of physical evidence
- inadmissible information
- the possibility of a guilty plea
- the existence or contents of a confession or admission
- the defendant's refusal to make a statement
- an opinion about the guilt or innocence of the defendant or suspect
- a statement that the defendant has been charged with a crime unless it is in the context that a charge does not mean the party is guilty

   The following facts may be disclosed:

- the general nature of the claim or charge
- any information in a public record
- the fact that the matter is being investigated and the scope of the investigation
- the schedule of litigation
- a request for assistance in obtaining information
- a warning of danger
- the identity, residence, occupation, and family status of accused
- information to enable the accused's capture (if at large)
- the fact, time, and place of arrest
- the identity of investigating and arresting officers

One wonders, when reading the papers and listening to television news reports, if prosecutors and defense attorneys have ever read these rules! Certainly in high-profile cases they seem to be ignored.

Zealous Prosecution

The duty of the prosecutor is to seek justice, not merely to convict. (Standard 3-1.2(c))

Just as the defense attorney is at times overly zealous in defense of clients, prosecutors may be overly ambitious in order to attain a conviction. The prosecutor, in preparing a case, is putting together a puzzle—each piece represented by a fact or some other type of evidence. Any piece of evidence that doesn't fit the puzzle is sometimes conveniently ignored. The problem is that this type of evidence may be exculpatory, and the prosecutor then has a duty to provide it to the defense.

The prosecutor is trying just as hard as the defense to put together a strong case. Tactics such as using witnesses with less than credible reasons for testifying, preparing witnesses (including both appearance and testimony), and "shopping" for experts are prosecutorial tools as well as defense tools. Witnesses are not supposed to be paid, but their expenses can be reimbursed, and this often is incentive enough for witnesses to say what they think the prosecutor wants to hear. Although these practices are not necessarily unethical, the result may influence the outcome of the trial.

There are very few controls on the behavior of prosecutors in the courtroom. Voters have some control over who becomes a prosecutor, but once in office most prosecutors stay in the good graces of a voting public unless there is a major scandal or an energetic competitor. In cities, most work is conducted by assistant prosecutors who are hired rather than elected. Misconduct in the courtroom is sometimes orally sanctioned by trial judges, and perhaps an appellate decision may overturn a conviction, but these events are rare. Gershman (1991) writes that prosecutors misbehave because it works and they can get away with it. Because misconduct is scrutinized only when the defense attorney makes an objection and then files an appeal, and even then the appellate court may rule that it was a harmless error, there is a great deal of incentive to use improper tactics in the courtroom. Although some misconduct may result in a case being overturned, very seldom does the individual prosecutor face any personal penalties.

Ordinarily, then, prosecutors' misbehavior is unchecked; it may take the form of persistent reference to illegal evidence, leading witnesses, nondisclosure of evidence to the defense, appeals to emotions, and so on. One prosecutor admitted that early in his career he sometimes made faces at the defendant while his back was to the jury and the defense attorney wasn't looking. The jury saw the defendant glowering and looking angry for no discernible reason, which led to a negative perception of his sanity, temper, or both. Of course, the defense attorney may be engaged in the same type of actions, so the contest between them becomes one of effectiveness of methods and "tricks" rather than an attempt to abide by the strictures of law or ethical considerations.

In some cases, prosecutors, along with police, deliberately ignore evidence, destroy exculpatory evidence, lie about evidence, or do not share exculpatory evidence with the defense. Radelet, Bedau, and Putnam (1992) gathered together dozens of capital cases where innocent defendants were convicted of crimes they did not commit. Some were sentenced to death. False convictions can occur because of incompetent defense counsel and unethical and illegal practices on the part of prosecutors and police.

One such case is illustrative. Clarence Brandley was a high school janitor in a small Texas town near Houston. In 1980 a young woman on a visiting girls' volleyball team disappeared while her team was practicing. The school was empty except for five janitors and the volleyball team. A search uncovered the girl's body in the school auditorium; it was later determined that she had been raped and strangled. Clarence Brandley and another janitor found the body and were the first to be interrogated by police. Brandley was black; the other janitor was white. The police officer who interrogated them reportedly said, "One of you two is going to hang for this." And then said to Brandley, "Since you're the nigger, you're elected." Police and prosecutors then evidently began a concerted effort to get Brandley convicted. Evidence that might have been helpful to the defense was "lost" (such as Caucasian hairs near the girl's vagina that were never tested and compared to those of the other janitors), witnesses were coerced into sticking to stories that inculpated Brandley (one of the janitors reported that he had been threatened with jail if he didn't promote the story supporting Brandley's guilt), witnesses who came forward with contrary evidence were ignored and sent away (the father-in-law of one of the janitors who later became a prime suspect told the prosecutor that this man had told him where the girl's clothes would be found two days before police actually found them), and defense attorneys were not told of witnesses (such as a woman who came to the prosecutor after the second trial and stated that her common-law husband had confessed a murder to her and ran away the same night the girl's body had been found). This woman's husband had worked as a janitor at the school, had been fired a month previous to the murder, but had also been seen at the school the day of the murder. What defense attorneys eventually discovered was that in all probability this man, and another janitor, had abducted and murdered the girl. The other janitors had seen the girl with these two men (not Brandley) but had lied during the two trials. Here are the words of an appellate judge who ruled on the motion for a new trial:

> In the thirty years that this court has presided over matters in the judicial system, no case has presented a more shocking scenario of the effects of racial prejudice . . . and public officials who for whatever motives lost sight of what is right and just. . . . The court unequivocally concludes that the color of Clarence Brandley's skin was a substantial factor which pervaded all aspects of the State's capital prosecution against him. (quoted in Radelet, Bedau, and Putnam, 1992: 134)

Yet, even after this finding, it took another *two years* for the Texas Court of Criminal Appeals to rule that Brandley deserved a new trial. Clarence Brandley served nine years on death row before his defense attorneys finally obtained his freedom. He was at one point six days away from execution. Others have been executed, and only afterward has evidence or perpetrators' confessions exonerated the accused and exposed the prosecution's misconduct that led to the miscarriage of justice (Radelet, Bedau, and Putnam, 1992).

Whereas some of the cases described by the authors above involved pure and extreme racial prejudice, probably a more common factor in misguided prosecution is a more subtle form of racism—one shared by many in the criminal justice system—a prejudgment of the guilt of the accused, especially if he is a black man. There is a pervasive stereotypical belief that all defendants are guilty, and most defendants are black. This thought pattern shapes and distorts decision making on the part of prosecutors who sift and use evidence in a way to support their predetermined beliefs. When Charles Stuart described a fictional assailant who robbed him and murdered his pregnant wife and Susan Smith described a fictional assailant who abducted and killed her children, they both selected black men. This information was immediately received as consistent with common realities of crime. Even though these cases did not result in a false finding of guilt for some innocent black man, they could have, and if Radelet, Bedau, and Putnam's facts are accurate, such miscarriages of justice have occurred and are probably continuing to occur.

The important point to consider is that when police or prosecutors allow their biases and prejudices to influence their decision making, evidence is lost or ignored, witnesses are discounted and disbelieved, tests aren't conducted, and true perpetrators literally "get away with murder" if there is a convenient suspect who looks guilty. This is an ever-present and pervasive reality in our justice system and probably accounts for why there is such a divergence in the perceptions of blacks and whites regarding the fairness of the system. For instance, in a recent Gallup poll, 71 percent of whites say murder charges against Simpson were probably or definitely true, but only 28 percent of blacks feel that way (reported in Mitchell and Banks, 1997: J7). Is this a reflection of a different way of measuring evidence or a different perception of trust in law enforcement and legal professionals' ability to collect and interpret evidence? Is a lack of trust warranted?

Expert Witnesses

A prosecutor who engages an expert for an opinion should respect the independence of the expert and should not seek to dictate the formation of the expert's opinion on the subject. (Standard 3-3.3(a))

Expert witnesses, who can receive a fee, are often accused of compromising their integrity for money or notoriety. The use of expert witnesses has risen in recent years. Psychiatrists often testify as to the mental competency or legal insanity of an accused. For many years, forensic experts have testified regarding factual issues of evidence. Today, criminologists and other social scientists may be asked to testify on such topics as victimization in prison, statistical evidence of sentencing discrimination, the effectiveness of predictive instruments for prison riots and other disturbances, risk assessment for individual offenders, mental health services in prison, patterns of criminality, the battered woman syndrome, and so on. When the expert is honest in his or her presentation as to the limitations and potential bias of the material, no ethical issues

---

QUOTATION

Kenneth Nimmich, chief of the FBI's Scientific Analysis Section, says that since the agency opened its DNA profiling laboratory last December, scientists there have established a protocol and methodology that is fit for use as a national standard. "The computerized equipment and procedures we use have the highest attainable levels of accuracy," Nimmich said. "We hope, and indeed encourage, private laboratories around the country to adopt our protocol so that when we talk among ourselves we'll all be speaking the same language."

SOURCE: Anderson, C. "DNA Evidence Questioned." *ABA Journal* (Oct. 1989): 18–19.

---

arise. However, expert witnesses may testify in a realm beyond fact or make testimony appear factual when some questions are not clearly answerable. Because of the *halo effect*—essentially, when a person with expertise or status in one area is given deference in all areas—an expert witness may endow a statement or conclusion with more legitimacy than it may warrant. When expert witnesses do take the stand, they run the risk of having their credibility attacked by the opposing side; credibility is obviously much easier to attack when a witness has attempted to present theory or supposition as fact or conclusion, either for ideological reasons or because of pressure from zealous attorneys. Those who always appear on either one side or the other may also lose their credibility. For instance, a doctor who is used often by prosecutors in one jurisdiction during capital sentencing hearings has become known as "Dr. Death" because he always determines that the defendant poses a future risk to society, which is one of the necessary elements for the death penalty. Although this doctor is well-known to both prosecutors and defense attorneys by reputation, juries would not be expected to know of his predilection for finding future dangerousness and would take his testimony at face value unless the defense attorney brings this information out during cross-examination.

Competing expert witnesses who present entirely different "facts" to the jury create an atmosphere of cynicism and distrust. There is a tendency to believe that expert witnesses are neutral, so there is more tendency to believe their testimony, but recent cases have brought to light that expert witnesses may be incompetent in their methodology or interpretation, they may testify to certain facts for political or other reasons, or they may simply enjoy the notoriety of testifying. Since much of expert testimony concerns scientific principles that are incomprehensible to laypeople, the potential for being misled by an expert witness is magnified.

The use of expert witnesses can present ethical problems when the witness is used in a dishonest fashion. Obviously, to pay an expert for his or her time is not unethical, but to shop for experts until one is found who benefits the case may be unethical since the credibility of the witness is suspect. Experts are used to prove facts in essentially the same manner as eyewitnesses are used. When eyewitnesses differ as to what they have seen, the explanation is that one or the other person is either wrong or is lying. It is no different with expert witnesses; however, since they profess to have extensive knowledge in the area, it is more difficult to conclude they are mistaken. Another difficulty is presented when either side obtains an expert who develops a conclusion or set of findings that would help the other side. Ethical rules do not prohibit an attorney in a civil matter from merely disregarding the information, without notice to the opponent that there is information that could benefit his or her case. However, prosecutors operate under a special set of ethics since their goal is justice, not pure advocacy. Any exculpatory information is supposed to be shared with the defense; this obviously includes test results and may also include expert witness findings.

The use of DNA evidence has risen dramatically in recent years. Based on the scientific principle that no two individuals possess the same DNA (deoxyribonucleic acid), a DNA "fingerprint" is analyzed from organic matter such as semen, blood, hair, or skin. Whereas a blood test can identify an individual only as being a member of a group (e.g., all those with blood type A positive), DNA testing can determine, with a small margin of error, whether two samples come from the same individual. It has been described as the greatest breakthrough in scientific evidence since fingerprinting, but there are problems with its use. Careless laboratory procedures render results useless, and there are no enforced guidelines or criteria for forensic laboratories conducting DNA tests. Without vigorous investigation and examination of lab results from the opposing counsel, incorrect DNA test results or poorly interpreted results may be entered as evidence and used to determine guilt or innocence.

Prosecutorial Misconduct

Examples of prosecutorial misconduct typically involve ignoring the procedural protections of due process. When prosecutors are too zealous in their attempts to obtain a conviction, their role as officer of the court is ignored and they become judge and jury. The following are some specific examples of actions that summarize the ethical concerns raised above.

FBI Lab Alters Findings

A series of articles in major newpapers brought to light an investigation and report concerning the FBI's vaunted crime laboratory. Evidently the investigation was initiated by a senior chemist—Frederic Whitehurst—who alleged that chemists were pressured to change their findings to support the prosecution's case in some cases and there were cases where supervisors even changed lab reports. One of the many cases implicated in allegations of altered lab findings is the Oklahoma City bombing. Whitehurst also alleges that he was punished for speaking out by a suspension and transfer. The Justice Department's Office of the Inspector General is investigating the allegations.

SOURCE: Serrano, R. "FBI Agents Allegedly Pushed Lab Workers to Alter Findings." *Austin American Statesman.* 30 Jan. 1997: A3.

Communications with Defendants When a criminal defendant is represented by an attorney, the prosecutor should not attempt any communication with the defendant outside the presence of the attorney. The attorney's presence is designed to eliminate the possibility of improper or intimidating behavior, illegal deals, and improper interrogation or plea-bargain offers.

Ex Parte Communications with the Judge Prosecutors and judges work together on a daily basis. There is a prohibition on attorneys and judges discussing a case outside the presence of the other attorney; because of working conditions, this is much more likely to apply to prosecutors than to defense attorneys. The reason for the rule is fairness. It is not fair for the judge to hear "one side" without the other side there to defend its point of view. This rule applies to casual conversations as well as more formal interchanges or offerings of information.

Failure to Disclose Evidence Perhaps the most common charge leveled against prosecutors, failure to disclose evidence stems from a duty to reveal exculpatory evidence to the defense (if the defense files a motion requesting such evidence). Prosecutors who give excuses such as "It wasn't important" or "I didn't believe it" provide weak rationalizations for ignoring a basic difference between their role and the role of the defense attorney. Whereas the defense attorney's only mission is the defense of his or her client, the prosecutor's role is to seek justice. This means that all evidence should be brought forward and shared so that "truth shall prevail."

Duty to Correct False Testimony Similar to a defense attorney's quandary when a witness commits perjury, a prosecutor must also take steps to avoid allowing false testimony to stand. In point of fact, the prosecutor's role is the easier one because there are no conflicting duties to protect a client; therefore, when a prosecution witness perjures himself or herself, the prosecutor has an affirmative duty to bring it to the attention of the court.

Conflict of Interest This area is more relevant to part-time prosecutors than full-time ones and exposes the problems that occur when a prosecutor is also engaged in a private practice of law. Prosecutors should not be engaged in criminal defense work, should not accept any civil case that relates to a criminal matter under their jurisdiction, and should not accept cases offered because of or through their official capacity.

Ethical issues of the prosecutor are similar to those of the defense attorney in that they are seen as opposing players; however, prosecutors have a qualitatively different role because of their discretionary power in the decision-making process. It is their discretion in charging that moves someone along or diverts the person from the system. Prosecutors' role as an officer of the court then puts them in a very powerful position and, as such, may result in different ethical questions.

ETHICAL ISSUES FOR JUDGES

Perhaps the most popular symbol of justice is the judge in his or her black robe. Judges are expected to be impartial, knowledgeable, and authoritative. They guide the prosecutor, defense attorney, and all the other actors in the trial process from beginning to end, helping to maintain the integrity of the proceeding. This is the ideal, but judges are human, with human failings.

Ethical Guidelines

To help guide judges in their duties, the Code of Judicial Conduct was developed by the American Bar Association. This code identifies the ethical considerations unique to judges. The primary theme of judicial ethics is impartiality. If we trust the judge to give objective rulings, then we must be confident that his or her objectivity isn't marred by any type of bias.

Judges may let their personal prejudices influence their decisions. To avoid this possibility, the ABA's ethical rules specify that each judge should try to avoid all appearance of bias as well as actual bias. Judges must be careful to avoid financial involvements or personal relationships that may threaten objectivity. We expect judges, like police officers and prosecutors, to conform to higher standards of behavior than the rest of us. Therefore, any hint of scandal in their private lives also calls into question their professional ethics. The obvious rationale is that judges who have less admirable personal values cannot judge others objectively, and those judges who are less than honest in their financial dealings do not have a right to sit in judgment of others.

There are a number of problematic issues in the perceived objectivity of judges. For instance, in those states where judges are elected, the judges must solicit campaign contributions. These monies are most often obtained from attorneys, and it is not at all unusual for judges to accept money from attorneys who practice before them. Does this not provide at least the appearance of impropriety? This situation is exacerbated in jurisdictions that use court appointments as the method for indigent representation. In these jurisdictions, judges hand out appointments to the same attorneys who give money back in the form of campaign contributions, or have other ties to the judge. In one jurisdiction, it was discovered that a female attorney, in her first year out of law school, received appointments totaling over $100,000 from a family court judge with whom she had a personal relationship (Harper, 1992: A9). Obviously, the appearance, if not the actuality, of bias is present in such a situation.

Use of Discretion

Judges' discretion occurs in two major areas. The first area is in the interpretation of the law in court cases. For instance, a judge may be called upon to assess the legality of evidence and make rulings on the various objections raised by both the prosecutors and the defense attorneys. A judge also writes instructions to the jury that are extremely important because they set up the legal questions and definitions of the case. The second area of judicial discretion is in sentencing decisions.

How Would You Rule?

Assume you are a judge with the appropriate jurisdiction to decide the following:

1. You must decide whether to sentence Timothy McVeigh to death or to a life term with no possibility of parole.

2. You are an appellate judge and must decide whether or not to set aside a conviction of a woman who murdered an infant. The defense alleges that the Sheriff violated attorney–client privilege by obtaining a warrant to seize a map drawn by the convicted woman showing where the baby was buried. She drew the map for her lawyer and, as such, legal experts contend it should be protected by attorney–client privilege. The trial judge granted the warrant because of testimony by the Sheriff and his deputies that they believed the baby might still be alive and they needed the map to find him, but evidence presented to you indicates that all law enforcement officials involved believed that the baby was dead and only wanted the map to help convict the offender. On the other hand, there is overwhelming evidence of guilt and a new trial would subject the parents to continued reminders of their loss.

3. You are a judge called upon to decide whether or not Paula Jones can bring a civil suit of sexual harassment against President Clinton. Your ruling will set a precedent for all future sitting presidents.

4. You must decide whether or not a particular artwork is obscene. The artist has painted a series of sex scenes, including bondage, sadomasochism, bestiality, and necrophilia interspersed with paintings of nude children at play. She states that her art has redeeming social qualities because it is a statement of the many faces of humanity. The series of paintings is being displayed in a public gallery supported by city and federal funds. The district attorney has filed for an injunction to close the show due to obscenity. How would you rule? How did you decide?

Judges must rule on the legality of evidence; they may make a decision to exclude a confession or a piece of evidence because of the way it was obtained and by so doing allow the guilty to go free. The exclusionary rule has generated a storm of controversy since it may result in a guilty party avoiding punishment because of an error committed by the police. The basis for the exclusionary rule is that one cannot accept a conviction based on tainted evidence. The ideals of justice reject such a conviction because accepting tainted evidence, even if obtained against a guilty party, is a short step away from accepting any type of evidence, no matter how illegal, and thus poses a threat to the whole concept of due process. The conviction is so violative of due process that it is ruled void. A more practical argument for the exclusionary rule is that if we want police officers to behavior in a legal manner, then we must have heavy sanctions against illegalities. Arguably, if convictions are lost due to illegal evidence collection, police will reform their behavior. Actual practice provides little support for this argument, though. Police have learned how to get around the exclusionary rule, and, in any event, cases lost on appeal are so

---

A Judicial "Raspberry"

A judge was removed from office for conduct ranging from "giving the finger" to a defendant who came to court late to making a sound commonly referred to as a "raspberry" in response to a defendant's testimony.

SOURCE: *Spruance v. Commission on Judicial Qualifications*, 13 Cal. 3d 778 (1975).

---

far removed from the day-to-day decision making of the police that they have little effect on police behavior. Recent court decisions have created several exceptions to the exclusionary rule. Judges who decide to exclude evidence and set aside convictions do so by disregarding short-term effects for more abstract principles—specifically, the protection of due process.

Ethical frameworks may or may not be of much help in deciding whether to apply the exclusionary rule. Religious ethics don't give us much help unless we decide that this ethical system would support vengeance and thus would permit the judge to ignore the exclusionary rule in order to punish a criminal. On the other hand, religious ethics might also support letting the criminal go free to answer to an ultimate higher authority, since human judgment was in this case imperfect. Egoism would support the decision to let a criminal go free or not depending on the effect it would have on the judge's well-being. The categorical imperative would support the exclusionary rule since one would not want a universal rule accepting tainted evidence. On the other hand, one would have to agree to retrying all criminals, regardless of the severity of the crime, whenever the evidence was tainted despite the possibility of further crime or harm to individuals. Act utilitarianism would support ignoring the exclusionary rule if the crime was especially serious or if there was a good chance the offender would not be retried successfully. The utility derived from ignoring the rule would outweigh the good. However, rule utilitarianism could be used to support the exclusionary rule, since the long-term effect of allowing illegal police behavior would be more serious than letting one criminal go free.

The judge is called upon to decide many and various questions throughout a trial. Of course, he or she has the law and legal precedent as guidance, but in most cases each decision involves a substantial element of subjectivity. Judges have the power to make it difficult for either the prosecutor or the defense attorney through their pattern of rulings on objections, evidence admitted, and even personal attitude toward an attorney, which is always noted by the jury and is influential in their decision.

The second area of judicial discretion is in sentencing. The following makes clear the small amount of training judges receive for this awesome responsibility (Johnson, 1982: 20):

Few judges have the benefit of judicial training sessions prior to embarking upon the often bewildering and frequently frustrating task of pursuing

that vague, if not indefinable, entity so commonly known as justice. . . .
Thus, it is not uncommon for the new judge, relying upon a philosophy
often formulated hastily, to be placed in the unenviable position of pro-
nouncing a sentence upon another human being without any special
preparation.

Judges' decisions are scrutinized by public watchdog groups and appellate-
level courts. In fact, one wonders if judges aren't overly influenced in their
sentencing by the current clamor for strict punishments. On the other hand,
if judges are supposed to enact community sentiment, perhaps it is proper for
them to reflect its influence. Is there one just punishment for a certain type of
offender, or does the definition of what is just depend on community opinion
of the crime, the criminal, and the time?

Evidence indicates that the decision making of judges is actually based on
personal standards, since no consistency seems to appear between the decisions of individual judges in the same community. One study found that two
judges in Louisiana had remarkably different records on numbers of convictions. The two also differed in their patterns of sentencing (Pinkele and
Louthan, 1985: 58). It must be noted that others believe there is a general
consistency among sentencing practices and that the system provides a basic, if
rough, consistent pattern of sentencing.

Judicial Misconduct

Examples of judicial misconduct are fairly rare, perhaps because judges' behavior is more shielded than other actors in the system. Operation Greylord
in Chicago is probably the most well-known recent exposé of widescale judicial corruption. This investigation resulted in convictions of thirty-one attorneys and eight judges for bribery. Judges accepted bribes to "fix" cases,
meaning to rule in favor of the attorney offering the bribe. Not unlike the
"blue curtain of secrecy" described in Chapters 5 and 6, not one attorney
came forward to expose this system of corruption, even though it was fairly
well-known what was occurring (Weber, 1987: 60).

Judges' neutrality is questioned when they voice strong opinions in issues
or cases. Talking to the media used to be rare, but now many judges find a
venue to express their views, take a stand, and act as advocate. Many question
this role for judges. Some question judges' motives in allowing cameras in the
courtroom—personal vanity rather than the interests of justice could be an
issue. There seems to be real concern that judges and lawyers play to the camera to perhaps the detriment of the swift resolution of the case.

Judges' relationships with other actors in the system are always suspect. For
instance, the fact that Judge Ito in the O. J. Simpson case was married to a
homicide detective caused many to question whether he could be objective
when the defense planned to attack the credibility of police procedure. On
the other hand, since many of those who work in the justice system develop

friendships, socialize, and sometimes marry others in the system, to recuse oneself from every case that involved some overlapping acquaintances or relations would be impossible for many judges.

Courtroom decorum is established by the judge, and if he or she displays an irreverent or self-aggrandizing attitude, or flaunts the law, his or her behavior degrades the entire judicial process. Some judges seem to be overly influenced by their power—as was the case of one district court judge who instructed courtroom workers to address him as "God." Most courtroom gossip includes the idiosyncrasies of some judges, like the judge who is reputed to keep a gun under his robes and points it at tardy attorneys, the judge who arrested citizens in the hall outside his courtroom for creating a public disturbance because they were talking during a court session, the judge who ordered a woman arrested for contempt when she wrote a scathing letter to a newspaper regarding his competence, the judge who sentenced a man to probation for killing his wife (excusing such behavior in open court with a statement indicating that the nagging victim deserved it), or the judge who signed an order of execution with a smiley face. These individuals illustrate that putting on a black robe doesn't necessarily give one the wisdom of Solomon.

Other forms of unethical behavior are less blatant. Judges have a duty to conclude judicial processing with reasonable punctuality. However, there are widespread delays in processing, and part of the reason is the lack of energy with which some judges pursue their dockets. In the same jurisdiction, and with a balanced assignment of cases, it is not unusual for one judge to have only a couple dozen pending cases and another judge to have literally hundreds. The reason is that judges routinely allow numerous continuances, set trial dates far into the future, start the docket call at 10:00 A.M. and conclude the day's work at 3:00 P.M., and in other ways take a desultory approach to swift justice.

Once again, we must be careful not to paint with too broad a brush. The most egregious examples of unethical behavior such as taking bribes or trampling the due-process rights of defendants are performed by only a few judges, in the same way that extreme behaviors are committed by only a small percentage of police officers, defense attorneys, and prosecutors.

Business as Usual?

A judge was removed from office for beginning proceedings in the absence of tardy counsel, questioning witnesses himself, excusing himself from the bench for periods of time and instructing the attorneys to carry on without him, and pressuring the District Attorney's office to drop charges pending against friends and relatives.

SOURCE: *Gonzalez v. Commission on Judicial Performance,* 188 Cal. Rptr. 880 (1983).

CONCLUSION

According to the basic tenets of our law, the accused is innocent up to the point of conviction. Prosecutors, judges, and defense attorneys are all "officers of the court" and as such are sworn to uphold the highest principles of our law, including this basic assumption of innocence. However, in the day-to-day operations of courthouse politics and bureaucracy, the rights of individuals may compete with the goal of efficient processing.

The presence and use of discretion in the criminal justice system are pervasive, and decision makers are often influenced by individual values and ethics that prompt them to stray from the parameters of structured laws and rules. Thus, it is crucial that these professionals remember and believe in the basic tenets of due process and be ever vigilant against the influence of prejudice or bias in the application of law toward the pursuit of justice.

REVIEW QUESTIONS

1. Describe at least three issues related to the prosecutor's ethical obligations.

2. Describe at least three issues related to the judge's ethical obligations.

3. What are the problems with expert witnesses?

4. Using moral and ethical criteria, analyze some recent innovations designed to improve crime prevention. Some possibilities to consider are such innovations as preventive detention, neighborhood justice centers that mediate rather than find guilt or innocence, the use of a waiver to adult court for violent juvenile offenders, increased sentences for gang-related or drug-related crimes, and criminalization of nonpayment of child support.

5. Using ethical and moral criteria, evaluate recent courtroom practices. Examples include the use of videotaped testimony, allowing television

---

QUOTATION

We lawyers may be dull, but the least among us lives on the moral edge. More than most other professionals, we are daily forced to face up to the plurality of human goods, the inevitability of conflict among them, and the necessity for tragic choices. That puts us only a hairline away from relativism, quietism, and moral compromise. What keeps the scholar true to the quest for knowledge, the judge striving for impartiality, and the practitioner faithful to client and court? Only a set of ingrained habits and attitudes that are shored up, sustained, nourished, and animated by a vital ongoing community—in other words, a tradition.

SOURCE: Glendon, M. *A Nation Under Lawyers* (New York: Farrar, Straus and Giroux, 1994): 243.

cameras into the courtroom, and victim statements during sentencing.

6. Watch a movie that presents a legal dilemma (for example, *Criminal Law, Penalty Phase, Presumed Innocent, The Witness*) and analyze the dilemmas using one of the ethical frameworks described in this book.

ETHICAL DILEMMAS

Situation 1

You are a deputy prosecutor and have to decide whether or not to charge Joe W. Crum with possession and sale of a controlled substance. You know you have a good case because the guy sold to the local junior high school and many of the kids are willing to testify. The police are pressuring you to make a deal because he has promised to inform on other dealers in the area if you don't prosecute. What should you do?

Situation 2

You are a judge who must sentence two defendants. One insisted on a jury trial and, through his defense attorney, dragged the case on for months with delays and motions. He was finally convicted by a jury. The other individual was his co-defendant and pleaded guilty. Apparently, they were equally responsible for the burglary. How will you sentence them?

Situation 3

You are a member of a jury. The case is a child molestation case in which the defendant is accused of a series of molestations in his neighborhood. You have been advised by the judge not to discuss the case with anyone outside the courtroom and especially not to anyone on either side of the case. Going down in the elevator after the fourth day of the trial, you overhear the prosecutor talking to one of the police officer witnesses. They are discussing the fact that the man has a previous arrest for child molestation but that it has not been allowed in by the judge as being too prejudicial to the jury. You were pretty sure the guy was guilty before, but now you definitely believe he is guilty. You also know that if you tell the judge what you have heard, it will probably result in a mistrial. What would you do?

Situation 4

You are a prosecutor in a jurisdiction that does not use the grand jury system. An elderly man has administered a lethal dose of sleeping tablets to his wife, who was suffering from Alzheimer's disease. He calmly turned himself in to the police department, and the case is on the front page of the paper. It is entirely up to you whether to charge him with murder or not. What would you do? What criteria did you use to arrive at your decision?

SUGGESTED READINGS

Gershman, B. 1990. *Prosecutorial Misconduct*. New York: Clark Boardman.

Glendon, M. 1994. *A Nation Under Lawyers*. New York: Farrar, Straus and Giroux.

Radelet, M., Bedau, H., and Putnam, C. 1992. *In Spite of Innocence*. Boston: Northeastern University Press.

Scheingold, S. 1984. *The Politics of Law and Order*. New York: Longman.

Spence, G. 1989. *With Justice for None*. New York: Penguin.

9

The Ethics
of Punishment
and Corrections

Chapter Objectives

Understand the definitions of punishment and
treatment and the basic rationales for punishment.

Learn how the ethical frameworks justify punishment.

Become familiar with the arguments
for and against capital punishment.

Understand the role that discretion,
authority, and power play in corrections.

Become familiar with the ethical
rationales for community corrections.

Explore the ethical issues involved
with privatization of corrections.

Throughout this text, we have followed the individual's progress through the criminal justice system. We have explored each phase of the process—the writing of laws, the targeting of individuals for investigation, the collection of evidence, the prosecution, and, finally, conviction and sentencing. We have now reached the punishment phase. After someone has been found guilty of a criminal offense, an array of possible sanctions and treatments are possible. A suspended sentence may be given, restitution or community service may be ordered, or probation with stringent or not-so-stringent conditions may be required. If the crime is serious, the offender dangerous, or both, incarceration for a period of time, ranging from one day to life, is a possibility. During incarceration the wrongdoer may be required to participate in treatment programs ranging from self-help groups such as Alcoholics Anonymous to psychosurgery. The ultimate sanction the state can impose, of course, is death.

According to one author (Leiser, 1986: 198), several elements are essential to the definition of *punishment:*

1. There are at least two persons—one who inflicts the punishment and one who is punished.
2. The person who inflicts the punishment causes a certain harm, or unwanted treatment, to occur to the person who is being punished.
3. The person who inflicts the punishment has been authorized, under a system of rules or laws, to harm the person who is punished in the particular way in which he or she does.

4. The person who is being punished has been judged by a representative of that authority to have done what he or she is forbidden to do or to have failed to do what he or she is required to do by some relevant rule or law.

5. The harm that is inflicted upon the person who is being punished is specifically for the act or omission mentioned in Condition 4.

We need also to define *treatment*. According to correctional terminology, *treatment* may be anything used to induce behavioral change. The goal is to eliminate dysfunctional or deviant behavior and to encourage productive and normal behavior patterns. In prison, treatment includes diagnosis, classification, therapy of all sorts, education, religious activity, vocational training, and self-help groups.

The infliction of punishment and even treatment is usually limited by some rationale or guideline. For instance, von Hirsch (1976: 5) presents the following restrictive guidelines:

1. The liberty of each individual is to be protected so long as it is consistent with the liberty of others.

2. The state is obligated to observe strict parsimony in intervening in criminals' lives.

3. The state must justify each intrusion.

4. The requirements of justice ought to constrain the pursuit of crime prevention (that is, deterrence and rehabilitation).

We will explore "just deserts" versus deterrence and treatment more fully in the following pages. In this chapter, we will first explore the various rationales for punishment, briefly discuss capital punishment in particular, and then revisit our continuing theme of discretion. In the next chapter, we will examine ethical issues related to correctional personnel, in both institutional and community corrections.

RATIONALES FOR
PUNISHMENT AND CORRECTIONS

Does society have the right to punish or correct miscreants? If it does, where does that right comes from? The rationale for punishment and corrections comes from the social contract. In the same way that the social contract forms the basis for police power, it also provides a rationale for further control in the form of punishment and corrections. To review this concept: we avoid social chaos by giving the state the power to control us. In this way we protect ourselves from being victimized by others by giving up our liberty to aggress against others. If we do step outside the bounds, the state has the right to control and punish us for our transgressions. Concurrently, the state is limited in the amount of control it can exert over individuals—to be consistent with the social contract, the state should exert its power only to accomplish the protection purpose; any further interventions in civil liberties are unwarranted.

As a subsystem of the criminal justice system, corrections might be characterized as having mixed goals to a greater extent than the other two subsystems. Crime prevention/public protection is the clear goal of law enforcement, even if there is some question as to whether crime control or due process should be emphasized, and the pursuit of justice is the clear mission of the court system. However, corrections pays homage to several masters, including the principles of retribution, reform, incapacitation, deterrence, and rehabilitation. The long-standing argument between proponents of punishment and proponents of treatment reveals a system without a clear mandate or rationale for action. Garland (1990) writes that even the state's goal of punishment is problematic since it is marked with inconsistencies between the intent and the implementation. The "moral contradictions" are that it seeks to uphold freedom by means of its deprivation and it condemns private violence by using state violence.

Can treatment and punishment occur at the same time? Or, as many critics argue, are some correctional officials paying lip service to a treatment ethic while continuing to do the same things they've always done? Public opinion toward criminals has become more punitive, resulting in the virtual abandonment of the treatment ethic and rehabilitation as a goal. Such shifts in public opinion and correctional cycles of reform raise the question of whether a punishment system in which sentencing and the definition of just punishment is relative and changes with time can ever be an ethical or moral one. We simply do not seem to agree on what an individual offender deserves; therefore, specific punishments for similar crimes vary according to time, place, persons involved, and other factors.

An important question to ask is "Who are we punishing?" Studies show that only a very small minority of individuals who commit crimes end up in prison. A larger percentage receive correctional sanctions of some other kind. Therefore, only a portion of individuals receive the sanctions deserved by all offenders; furthermore, we may assume that those numbers are not representative of the larger population. Those in our jails and prisons are there not only because they committed crimes, but also because they are poor, members of a minority group, or powerless.

Those selected for imprisonment tend to commit certain types of crimes, and those who commit other crimes avoid the more punitive sanctions of the corrections system. For instance, big business routinely bilks consumers out of billions of dollars annually and chalks up the punitive fines incurred to operating expenses, yet it would not be uncommon in some jurisdictions for a shoplifter to be sent to prison. Streams and land are routinely polluted by industrial waste, but again punitive fines are the typical sanctions, and these cannot begin to restore what has been taken away in the flagrant pursuit of financial profit. In fact, such costs are typically passed on to the consumers, so, in effect, taxpayers suffer the crime and then also pay the fine. Very seldom do we see executives responsible for company policy go to prison. White-collar criminals routinely receive fines, probation, or short stays in halfway houses whereas so-called street criminals receive prison sentences. Many people question the justification of punishment when only a very small, select group of offenders is being punished.

Our views of criminals have changed several times over the course of history. Long ago, criminals were viewed as sinners with no ability to change their behavior, so punishment and incapacitation were seen as the only logical ways to respond to crime. Bentham (1748–1833) and Beccaria (1738–1794) viewed the criminal as rational and as having free will, and therefore saw the threat of punishment as a deterrent. Neoclassicists such as Quetelet (1796–1894) and Querry (1802–1866) recognized that some groups of people could not be held entirely responsible for their actions and therefore believed that they should not be punished. The insane and the young were treated differently because they were considered moral infants, not possessing the sense to refrain from wrongdoing. Then the positivist school influenced thinking to the extent that all criminal acts were believed to be merely symptoms of an underlying pathology. The passage from the 1870 Prison Congress exemplifies this view.

The treatment programs created in the last one hundred years or so operate under the assumption that we can do something to offenders to reduce their criminal activity. That "something" may involve treating a psychological problem, such as a sociopathic or paranoid personality; addressing social problems, such as alcoholism or addiction; or resolving more pragmatic problems, such as chronic unemployment, with vocational training and job placement. Obviously, the perception of the criminal influences the rationale for correction and punishment. The two major justifications for punishment and treatment are *retribution* and *prevention*. The retributive rationale postulates that punishment is an end in itself whereas the preventive approach views punishment as a means rather than an end and embraces other responses to crime. The retributive rationale is probably more consistent with a view of the criminal as rational, and the prevention rationale, with certain exceptions, is more consistent with the view of the criminal as somehow less responsible for his or her behavior.

1870 Prison Congress

A criminal is a man who has suffered under a disease evinced by the perpetration of a crime, and who may reasonably be held to be under the dominion of such disease until his conduct has afforded very strong presumption not only that he is free from its immediate influence, but that the chances of its recurrence have become exceedingly remote.

SOURCE: Quoted in Mitford, 1971: 104.

Retribution

As mentioned before, the social contract provides the rationale for punishment. As long as one is a member of society, one has implicitly agreed to society's rules and right to punish. One criticism of the social contract theory is that it is completely contingent on a consensus perspective of society. That is, the members of society are assumed to share the same goals, beliefs, and power. The ideal state is one of agreement, which is seen as entirely possible. All people benefit from the social contract because they get to keep what they've got, with the assumption that what they've got is fairly equally distributed. The conflict perspective views society as made up of a number of conflicting groups; when one wins, the other loses, because their interests can never be the same. Obviously, the social contract theory is difficult to reconcile with a conflict perspective, since for some no advantages ensue from the sacrifice of liberties. If someone perceives himself or herself as disenfranchised from society, does the right to punish still exist? Can we still use the social contract as the rationale for punishment?

The retributive rationale for punishment is consistent with the social contract theory. Simply stated, the retributive rationale is that the individual offender must be punished because he or she deserves it. Mackie (1982: 4) describes three specific types of retribution. The first, *negative retribution,* dictates that one who is not guilty must not be punished for a crime; the second, *positive retribution,* demands that one who is guilty ought to be punished; and the third, *permissive retribution,* says that one who is guilty may be punished. This formulation states that retribution may support punishment but may also limit punishment. There are limits to who may be punished (only those who commit crimes) and restrictions on the amount of punishment (only that sufficient to balance the wrong). Further, this formulation implies that punishment need not be administered in all cases. The exceptions, although not discussed by Mackie, may involve the concepts of mercy or diminished responsibility.

Our system of justice was created to take the place of private vengeance. We do not allow victims to seek their own revenge but rather replace "hot vengeance" with "cool justice," dispassionate in its determination and distribution. The social contract supports the notion that it is intrinsically right for the state, rather than the victim's family, to execute a killer. The state has taken over the necessary task of punishment to ensure the survival of society by preventing private vengeance. Intentionally inflicting pain on another is perhaps an evil, but if it meets the definitional elements of punishment, it can be justified.

Another retributivist justification for punishment is that it is the only way the individual can achieve salvation. In fact, we owe the offender punishment because only through suffering can atonement occur, and only through atonement or *expiation* can the offender achieve a state of grace. Some would strongly object to this interpretation of religious ethics and argue that Christianity, while supportive of just punishment, does not necessarily support suffering as the only way to achieve a state of grace: there must be repentance, and there is also room for forgiveness.

One other view consistent with retribution is that punishment balances the advantage gained by a wrongdoer. The criminal act distorts the balance and parity of social relationships, and only a punishment or similar deprivation can restore the natural balance that existed before the criminal act.

The question of whether to punish the crime or the criminal is long-standing and important in any discussion of retributive punishment. Bentham believed that each criminal offense deserves a measure of punishment calculated to balance the potential pleasure or profit of the criminal offense. However, the neoclassicists allowed some characteristics of the offender to influence the punishment decision. This debate continues today with those who argue for determinate sentencing over indeterminate sentencing. Determinate sentencing punishes the offense, with the length of the sentence determined by the seriousness of the crime. Indeterminate sentencing, on the other hand, allows judges a great deal of discretion so that they can tailor the punishment to fit the individual offender. A young offender may get a second chance because he has the potential to change; a woman may receive probation instead of prison because she has an infant to take care of; a habitual criminal may be the unhappy recipient of an increased sentence because he is considered unsalvageable. This type of individualized justice is inconsistent with a retributive rationale since punishment is based on who the criminal is rather than on what the criminal did.

Habitual offender laws or the so-called "three strikes" laws punish according to the offense and the offender in a way because the offender receives a longer term (perhaps even a life sentence) for the crime of conviction, but also because of prior crimes (which arguably he or she has already been punished for). The Supreme Court has ruled that habitual felon laws are not unconstitutional, but the policy implications of the "three strikes" laws are still very much in debate.

What is an appropriate amount of punishment? This is a difficult question, even for the retributivist. The difference between a year in prison and two years in prison is unmeasurable in everything but the number of days on the calendar. Prison may be more of a deprivation for some than for others. Should this be considered during sentencing? Punishment of any kind affects individuals differently; for instance, a whipping may be worse than death for someone with a low tolerance for pain, better than prison for someone with a great need for freedom, and perhaps even pleasurable for someone who enjoys physical pain. Our present system of justice very seldom recognizes these individual vulnerabilities or sensitivities to various punishments.

Sentencing studies routinely show that little or no agreement exists regarding the type or amount of punishment appropriate for a wrongdoer. Disparity in sentencing is such a problem that many reforms are aimed at reducing or even eliminating judges' discretion. Yet when legislators take on the task themselves by setting determinate sentences, their decisions are arrived at by obscure methods, probably more influenced by political pressure and compromise

Violent Crime Down, No Thanks to Three Strikes

Remember the notorious Jerry Dewayne Williams? He was the five-time loser caught stealing a slice of pepperoni pizza in July of 1994. Under California's new three-strikes law, the then-27-year-old was sentenced to a mandatory 25 years to life.

Williams immediately became a symbol for the California law's rigidity. The 21 other states that enacted three-strikes laws confined their harshest penalties to a few repeat violent or serious offenders, as does federal law. California listed 400 crimes for which an offender could face life.

Well, guess what? Last month, with new discretion from the state Supreme Court, a judge reduced some of Williams' previous nonviolent felonies, such as joyriding and drug possession, to misdemeanors. So, Williams will be out in two years, not 23. . . .

The [National Institute of Justice] studies found that while [California's] expansive law rounded up lots of crooks, they were not the ones people feared.

Of 2,750 felons sent away for 25 to life through last December, 85% were for non-violent crimes. Marijuana possession was four times as likely to lead to a third strike as murder, rape and kidnapping combined.

And the price tag is huge. Three strikes will add 25,000 additional prisoners by 2001 at a cost of $1 billion a year. Three-strikes cases also are adding $300 million annually in court and other costs. . . .

And all three studies see worrisome racial patterns. African-Americans make up 7% of California's population and 20% of those arrested for felonies, but 40% of third-strike convictions—numbers that demand closer scrutiny.

And all this despite meager evidence that three strikes reduces crime.

The studies found crime rates in states without three strikes plummeting as much or more than in California. In 1994 and 1995, when California reported an 11% drop in violent crime, New York state saw its violent-crime rate drop 21%. New York City fared even better, with a 25% plunge. Nationally, the FBI's household survey [*sic*—author meant the National Crime Survey] found a 10% drop in violent crime in 1995 alone. . . .

SOURCE: *USA Today*, 24 Feb. 1997: 10A. Copyright 1997 by USA Today. Reprinted with permission.

Is the author arguing from a retributive or prevention rationale?

rather than coming from any fair and equitable standard. The basic premise of retribution is that the offender deserves punishment. However we arrive at the final decision of what punishment offenders should receive, if we are retributivists, we feel the balance is restored when they have suffered, as they have made their victims suffer.

Prevention

Three common justifications or rationales for punishment can all be subsumed under a general heading of prevention. Prevention assumes that something should be done to the offender to prevent future criminal activity. The three possible methods of prevention are deterrence, incapacitation, and treatment. Each of these goals is based on certain assumptions that must be considered in

---

Court Allows Judges to Consider Acquittals in Boosting Sentences

WASHINGTON—Judges may stiffen prison terms of convicted defendants by considering charges on which they were acquitted, the Supreme Court ruled 7–1 Monday.

The result can be that criminals found guilty of one charge and acquitted of another can face the same prison sentence as if they had been convicted on both.

Many judges and legal scholars consider such a result unjust. One Supreme Court dissenter, John Paul Stevens, called it "perverse." The other dissenter, Anthony Kennedy, said the decision "does raise concerns about undercutting the verdict of acquittal."

But the practice is widespread and is supported by the Clinton administration. And the tough-on-crime court majority found nothing legally wrong. . . .

SOURCE: Epstein, A. (Knight-Ridder Washington Bureau). *Austin American-Statesman,* 7 Jan. 1997: A4.

Is the court ruling consistent with retributivism or not? Remember that in retributivism, one is punished for the offense, rather than for individual characteristics of culpability.

---

addition to the relevant moral questions—for instance, it is a factual question as to whether people can be deterred from crime, but it is a moral question as to what we should do to an individual to ensure deterrence.

Deterrence Specific deterrence is what is done to offenders to prevent them from deciding to commit another offense. General deterrence is what is done to an offender to prevent others from deciding to engage in wrongful behavior. The first teaches through punishment; the second teaches by example.

Our right to deter an individual offender is rooted in the same rationale used to support retribution. By virtue of membership in society, individuals submit themselves to society's controls. If we feel that someone's actions are damaging, we will try various means to persuade him or her to cease that activity. The implicit assumption of a deterrence philosophy is that in the absence of controls, society would revert back to a junglelike, dangerous "war of all against all"; we need the police and official punishments to keep us all in line. Under this rationale, the true nature of humankind is perceived to be predatory and held in check only by external controls, or a blank slate that is formed by the messages received from society; thus, we must relay the message through punishment that offenses will not be tolerated. Several criminologists, such as Wilson, van den Haag, and Posner, are known as deterrence advocates and support deterrence as a justification of punishment. In recent years, general deterrence has given way to specific deterrence because empirical support for the efficacy of general deterrence is lacking (von Hirsch, 1985).

Von Hirsch (1976), a punishment advocate, proposes a utilitarian argument for deterrence in that he does not deny that punishment creates suffering, but he justifies such suffering by proposing that the offenders' suffering prevents a greater amount of suffering for innocent victims. Note that his justification here does not include the concept that offenders should suffer because they deserve it. The rationale hinges on the existence of averted suffering and victimization.

The rationale of specific deterrence depends on the effectiveness of punishment in deterring future behavior. Unfortunately, it is very difficult to find any studies that show that anything we do to the offender, whether under the heading of punishment or treatment, has any predictable effect on subsequent behavior. Arguments are made that this ineffectiveness is due to implementation problems; in other words, punishment doesn't deter because it is inconsistent, uncertain, and slow. If punishment was applied more consistently and with more swiftness, the argument goes, then we would see a deterrent effect. Treatment advocates ruefully point out that there are implementation problems with treatment as well, that it has never been financially supported, and that prison administrators lack commitment to the ideals of treatment.

The amount of punishment needed for deterrence is even more problematic if we seek to deter others. First, it becomes much harder to justify. If we know that a term of imprisonment either will not deter an offender or is much more than what would be needed to deter an individual but is the amount needed to deter others, it is questionable whether this further punishment can be justified. A clear example of this situation is the so-called passion murderer; the likelihood of this person's killing again is slim, but he or she is usually given a long sentence to make it clear that killing will not be tolerated. (There is, of course, also a good retributive rationale for the long sentence.) Under deterrence theory, the offender is only a tool to teach a lesson to the rest of us. Durkheim said that the value of criminals is in establishing the parameters of acceptable behavior. By their punishments, we can define ourselves as good and resolve to stay that way.

If one's goal is purely general deterrence, there does not necessarily need to be an original crime. Consider a futuristic society wherein the evening news routinely shows or describes the punishments received by a variety of criminals. The crime—or the punishment, for that matter—does not have to be real to be effective. If punishing innocent people for crimes they might do were just as effective as punishing criminal offenders, this action might satisfy

---

Rationale for Deterrence

1. Those who violate others' rights deserve punishment.
2. However, there is a countervailing moral obligation to not deliberately add to the amount of human suffering, and punishment creates suffering.
3. Deterrence results in preventing more misery than it creates, thus justifying punishment.

SOURCE: Adapted from von Hirsch, 1976: 54.

the ends of deterrence but would obviously not be acceptable under any system of ethics, except perhaps act utilitarianism. Actually, the reality of sentencing is not that much different from the situation just described, in that what the public hears about sentences bears little resemblance to what the individual offender actually serves, except perhaps in states that have determinate sentencing laws. Although the public is becoming more sophisticated in this regard, not many know that when the judge sentences an offender to fifteen years in prison, with good time, time served, and parole, the actual prison time may be much less. However, actual time served seems to be an inconsistent phenomenon having more to do with prison overcrowding, politics, and availability of prison cells rather than some standard of justice. For those states like Texas, which have finally built their way out of a prison overcrowding problem, prisoners are now likely to serve much longer portions of their sentences and parole is less common. Their crimes haven't changed, just the number of prison cells available.

Incapacitation Another purpose of punishment is to prevent further crime through incapacitation. Strictly speaking, incapacitation does not fit the classical definition of punishment, since the purpose is not to inflict pain but only to hold an offender until there is no risk of further crime. The major issue concerning incapacitation is prediction; unfortunately, our ability to predict is no better for incapacitative purposes than it is for deterrence purposes. Two possible mistakes may be made: releasing an offender who commits further crimes and not releasing an offender who would not. We are willing to tolerate more of the second error, but we must take some risks unless we choose to keep all offenders locked up indefinitely. However, there is no political incentive, other than the high cost of imprisonment, to take the risk. Anytime people advocate early release, they become easy targets for public censure.

Carrying the goal of incapacitation to its logical conclusion, one would not have to commit a crime at all to be declared potentially dangerous and subject to incapacitation. Our statistics can narrow street crime down to a fairly identifiable subgroup in our society—unemployed, young, black males. If we wanted to reduce a substantial portion of crime, we could incapacitate this whole group of people. We don't because of an abhorrence of punishing innocent parties, even for the purpose of protection. However, we now incarcerate career criminals, not for their last offense but for what they might do in the future. We justify habitual felon laws by the prediction that these criminals will continue to commit crime. Statistical studies have found that a small group of offenders commit a disproportionate share of crime, and those individuals can be identified by background characteristics such as how many crimes they have committed, how young they were when they committed their first crime, whether they are addicted to drugs, and so on (Greenwood, 1982). Selective incapacitation is a policy to incarcerate these individuals for longer periods of time than other criminals—the current model of selective incapacitation is the so-called three strikes laws, which make great newspaper copy but are really no different than the old habitual felon laws. The argument for selective incapacitation is that such a practice will reduce crime at a lower cost than imposing longer periods of incarceration for all offenders. The argument is obviously utilitarian since retributive punishment would not favor disparate punishments for similar crimes. The real question is whether we ought to hold someone for what he might do rather than what he has done.

Treatment If we can find justification for the right to punish, can we also find justification for treatment? Treatment can be considered as one type of specific deterrence since it is an attempt to prevent future crime by changing the criminal offender. Treatment is considered to be beneficial to the individual offender as well as to society. It is a very different approach from the moral rejection implicit in retributive punishment. Treatment implies acceptance rather than rejection, support rather than hatred. On the other hand, the control over the individual is just as great as with punishment; some people, in fact, would say it is greater.

What is treatment? We sometimes consider anything experienced after the point of sentencing to be treatment, including education, prison discipline, and religious services. Can treatment be experimental? Must it be effective to be considered treatment? A court was obliged to define treatment in *Knecht v. Gillman,* 488 F.2d 1136 (1973). Inmates challenged the state's right to use apomorphine, a drug that induces extreme nausea and a feeling of imminent death, as a form of aversive conditioning. In its holding, the court stated that calling something treatment did not remove it from Eighth Amendment scrutiny. In other words, merely labeling some infliction of pain as treatment would not necessarily justify it. *Treatment* was further defined as that which constitutes accepted and standard practice and which could reasonably result in "cure." More recently, the court had occasion to consider whether or not prison officials could administer antipsychotic drugs against the will of the prisoner. Despite arguments concerning an inherent right of all to be free from such intrusive control, the court held in *Washington v. Harper,* 494 US 210 (1990), that an inmate's right to refuse such medication did not outweigh the state's need to administer such drugs if there was a showing that the inmate posed a security risk.

What we think needs to be cured is another problem. Recall the discussion of whether our society could be characterized by consensus or conflict. Treating a deviant may be justifiable if one believes that society is basically homogeneous in its values and beliefs, but viewed from a conflict perspective, treatment may look more like brainwashing and a coercive use of power. Civil libertarians would point out that it is no accident that political dissidents in totalitarian states are often handled as if they have mental problems and are treated with mind-altering drugs and other brainwashing regimens. The greater intrusiveness inherent in treating the mind is sometimes considered worse than punishment.

According to some experts, treatment can be effective only if it is voluntary. Nevertheless, it is true that much of the treatment inmates and other correctional clients participate in is either implicitly or directly coerced. Providing

---

Literary Perspective

On Tuesday, February 27, the U.S. Supreme Court rekindled the convict's worst nightmare.

The court, by a vote of six to three, gave prison officials sweeping power to force convicts to take psychotropic drugs against their will. The ruling may have played well on the street, but it cast a dread pall over the feelings of many of us convicts.

To those of us who have watched convicts being plied with drugs that made them total zombies, the decision was maddening. It's true that some convicts need to be medicated, but we have seen others who don't need the drugs being forced to take them by incompetent and tyrannical bureaucrats.

Justice Anthony M. Kennedy, writing for the majority, said: "Given the requirements of a prison environment, the state may treat a prison inmate who has a serious mental illness with antipsychotic drugs against his will if the inmate is dangerous to himself or others and the treatment is in the inmate's best medical interest."

Justice John Paul Stevens said in dissent that a mock trial before a prison tribunal doesn't satisfy due process and that a competent individual has a constitutional right to refuse antipsychotic medication. . . .

It's no secret that federal and state prison officials have for years been forcing convicts to take these drugs. But knowing we had recourse to the courts, the officials used discretion about whom they forced them on. Now that we are stripped of access to outside courts, things look grim for our future. . . .

SOURCE: Martin, D. *Committing Journalism: The Prison Writings of Red Hog* (New York: Norton, 1993). Originally published in the *San Francisco Chronicle*, 18 Mar. 1990.

---

treatment for those who want it is one thing; requiring those who are resistant to participate in psychotherapy, group therapy, religious activities, or chemotherapy is quite another. It is not justifiable under a retributivist ethical system; is it consistent with a prevention perspective?

The Justice Model and the Just Deserts Model

Two current rationales for punishment have been termed the *justice model* and the *just deserts model*. Early advocates of the justice model describe the perspective as including concepts relating to the nature of humankind, the function of law, and the right of society to punish (see the box describing the justice model).

QUERY

- If you knew for certain that prison did not deter, would you still be in favor of its use? Why?
- If we could predict future criminals, would you be willing to incapacitate them before they commit a crime in order to protect society?
- Should we have guidelines for what we do in the name of treatment? What should they be?

The Justice Model

1. The criminal law is the "command of the sovereign."
2. The threat of punishment is necessary to implement the law.
3. The powerful manipulate the chief motivators of human behavior—fear and hope—through rewards and punishments to retain power.
4. Socialization of individuals, however imperfect, occurs in response to the commands and expectations of the ruling social–political power.
5. The criminal law protects the dominant prescribed morality (a system of rules said to be in the common and best interest of all), reflecting the enforcement aspect of the failure of socialization.
6. In an absence of any absolute system of justice or "Natural Law," no accurate etiologic theory of crime is possible, nor is the definition of crime itself historically stable.
7. Although free will may not exist perfectly, the criminal law is largely based upon its presumed vitality and forms the only foundation for penal sanctions.
8. A prison sentence represents a punishment sanctioned by a legislative body and meted out through the official legal system against a person adjudged responsible for his behavior. Although a purpose of such punishment may be deterrence or rehabilitation, more specifically, such punishment is the deprivation of liberty for a fixed period of time.
9. When corrections becomes mired in the dismal swamp of preaching, exhorting, and treating it becomes dysfunctional as an agency of justice. Correctional agencies should engage prisoners as the law otherwise dictates; as responsible, volitional, and aspiring human beings, and not conceive of them as patients.

SOURCE: Fogel, D., and Hudson, J. *Justice as Fairness* (Cincinnati: Anderson, 1981): vii. Reprinted with permission.

This model may be seen as part of a backlash against the abuse of discretion that characterized the rehabilitative era; it promotes a degree of predictability and equality in sentencing by reverting back to earlier retributive goals of punishment and restricting the state's right to use treatment as a criterion for release.

The just deserts model is also retributive and bases punishment on "commensurate deserts" (von Hirsch, 1975: xxvi). As the spokesman for this view, von Hirsch (1985: 138) disagrees with deterrence and punishment theorists who feel that retributive and deterrent or incapacitative goals can be combined:

[A] desert rationale utilizes the criminal record in a wholly different fashion than selective incapacitation would. (1) Desert calls for primary emphasis on the seriousness of the crime, with only a secondary role (if any) given to the criminal record. Selective incapacitation, by contrast, rests almost entirely on the prior criminal history and on status factors such as employment and drug use. (2) Desert relies on convictions, whereas selective incapacitation techniques need to utilize arrests or other non-adjudicative indicia of prior offending. (3) Desert requires the sentence, to the extent that prior crimes are considered, to take into account only those features that bear on those crimes' blameworthiness, such as their number and seriousness; a selective incapacitation approach tends toward the use of other features of previous crimes that have no relevance to their reprehensibleness.

However, von Hirsch does approve of a system of punishment that incorporates incapacitative features in judging the weight of a crime by its recidivism potential. Offenders who commit similar crimes are punished equally, but the rank ordering of crimes is determined by recidivistic potential. This system, "categorical incapacitation," combines deserts and prevention but in a way that, according to von Hirsch, is not unjust to the individual offender (von Hirsch, 1985: 150). Von Hirsch continues to disagree with the "new rehabilitationists," who he feels are trying to resurrect a rehabilitative ethic with the rationale that humane conditions during incapacitation require some treatment options. Von Hirsch believes that while treatment options may be offered within the same categories of punishments, they should never be substituted for punishment itself or be part of the equation (von Hirsch and Maher, 1992).

Garland (1990) offers a different view. He believes that if social control is what is desired, then the emphasis should be placed on ways of accomplishing that purpose other than punishment after the fact. If we had a system that was better at socializing and integrating its citizens—he calls this a system of social justice and moral education—then we would not have to worry so much about punishing them. The punishment that was still necessary would be viewed as morally expressive rather than instrumental, and would be retributive rather than attempt prevention goals.

Restorative Justice

A relatively recent philosophical approach to crime and punishment, distinct from the justice model or the just deserts model, has been called *restorative justice*. Reichel (1997) briefly describes the origins of the movement during the development of restitution and community service sentences in the 1970s. Although these innovative sentences were originally touted as rehabilitative, as rehabilitative goals lost favor with public sentiment, rationales and justifications were redefined, and, instead of rehabilitation, restoration or reparation (for the victim) became the philosophical rationale behind such programs (Bazemore and Maloney, 1994). Whether restitution was individual (with compensation paid directly to the victim) or symbolic (where the community benefited from the offender's labor or payments), the idea was to restore the victim to his or her condition before the victimization event, or if the victim was not easily identifiable, to produce a measurable positive effect for the community. For instance, Bazemore and Maloney (1994) discuss one program where community service offenders helped rebuild a town ravaged by a tornado. The goals of the approach are as follows:

1. The service meets a clearly defined and obvious need.
2. Service should symbolically link offender and victim, or offender and his or her community.
3. Offenders should be viewed as resources, and outcome measures are directed to the work itself (rather than the offender's behavior).
4. Offenders should be involved in planning and executing the projects.
5. Included should be a sense of accomplishment, closure, and community recognition. (adapted from Bazemore and Maloney, 1994: 27)

The historical origins of and analogies to restorative justice can be found throughout recorded history; early laws demanded victim compensation, and reparation has a much longer history than does penal servitude.

Individuals (cf. Umbreit, 1994; Umbreit and Carey, 1995; van Ness and Heetderks Strong, 1997) now believe that restorative justice quite appropriately places the emphasis back onto the victims, but can also be life affirming and positive for the offender as well. The key is in finding a method of restoration that is meaningful and somehow related to the offense instead of merely punitive labor—such as the infamous rock pile—which is meaningless and devoid of worth to the victim, the offender, or society.

The similarities and overlap between restorative justice and the peacekeeping model described in Chapter 4 are obvious. Both approaches are consistent with the ethics of care and might be considered a "feminine" model of justice because of the emphasis on needs rather than retribution. One wonders what meaning and impact a restorative justice program might have on the offender. If one can assume that a retributive, punitive orientation results in an offender's perception of unfairness (through denial of victim, denial of injury, or a belief that a more serious victimization was visited upon the offender), then it is interesting to speculate that perhaps the offender would not be able to generate the rationalizations and excuses for his or her behavior if involved in a restorative justice program that focuses attention on the injuries of the victim and does not involve stigma, banishment, or exclusion for the offender.

ETHICAL FRAMEWORKS
FOR CORRECTIONS

The various rationales for punishment just described are well established, and most can be found in many texts. The ethical systems that were introduced in Chapter 2 are less commonly discussed in corrections texts, but they form the underlying philosophical rationale for the goals or missions of retribution and prevention (including deterrence, incapacitation, and treatment). Ethical formalism and utilitarianism receive a disproportional amount of attention here, but the reader is urged to apply the other ethical systems as well.

Utilitarianism

Utilitarianism is often used to support the last three rationales of punishment: deterrence, incapacitation, and treatment. According to utilitarianism, punishing or treating the criminal offender benefits society, and this benefit outweighs the negative effect on the individual offender. This is a teleological argument because the morality of the punishment is determined by the consequences derived—reduced crime. The following describes the utilitarian argument for punishment (Borchert and Stewart, 1986: 316):

> [T]raditional utilitarian thinking has concluded that having laws forbidding certain kinds of behavior on pain of punishment, and having machinery for the fair enforcement of these laws, is justified by the fact that it maximizes expectable utility. Misconduct is not to be punished just for its own sake; malefactors must be punished for their past acts, according to law, as a way of maximizing expectable utility.
>
> The utilitarian principle, of course, has implications for decisions about the severity of punishment to be administered. Punishment is itself an evil, and hence should be avoided where this is consistent with the public good. Punishment should have precisely such a degree of severity (not more or less) that the probable disutility of greater severity just balances the probable gain in utility (less crime because of the more serious threat). The cost, in other words, should be counted along with the value of what is bought; and we should buy protection up to the point where the cost is greater than the protection is worth.

Bentham was the major proponent of the utilitarian theory of punishment and established basic guidelines for its use. Bentham believed that punishment works when it is applied rationally to rational people, but is not acceptable when the person did not make a rational decision to commit the crime, such as when the law forbidding the action was passed after the act occurred, the law was unknown, the person was acting under compulsion, or the person was an infant, insane, or intoxicated. The utility of the punishment would be lost in these cases; therefore, punishment could not be justified (Borchert and Stewart, 1986: 317).

All of Bentham's rules ensure that punishments are acceptable to the utilitarian framework. The basic formula provides that the utility of punishment to society outweighs the negative of the punishment itself. Utilitarian theory also supports treatment and incapacitation if they can be shown to benefit society. If, for instance, treatment and punishment had equal amounts of utility for society, treatment would be the more ethical choice because it has a less negative effect on the individual. Likewise, if incapacitation and punishment are equally effective in protecting and providing utility to society, then the choice with the least negative utility would be the ethical one.

Bentham's Rules of Punishment

1. That the value of the punishment must not be less, in any case, than what is sufficient to outweigh that of the profit of the offense.
2. The greater the mischief of the offense, the greater is the expense it may be worth while to be at, in the way of punishment.
3. When two offenses come in competition, the punishment for the greater offense must be sufficient to induce a man to prefer the less.
4. The punishment should be adjusted in such manner to each particular offense, that for every part of the mischief there may be a motive to restrain the offender from giving birth to it.
5. The punishment ought in no case to be more than what is necessary to bring it into conformity with the rules here given.
6. That the quantity of punishment actually inflicted on each individual offender may correspond to the quantity intended for similar offenders in general, the several circumstances influencing sensibility ought always to be taken into the account.
7. That the value of the punishment may outweigh the profit of the offense, it must be increased in point of magnitude, in proportion as it falls short in point of certainty.
8. Punishment must be further increased in point of magnitude, in proportion as it falls short of proximity.
9. When the act is conclusively indicative of a habit, such an increase must be given to the punishment as may enable it to outweigh the profit, not only of the individual offense, but of such other like offenses as are likely to have been committed with impunity by the same offender.
10. When a punishment, which in point of quality is particularly well calculated to answer its intention, cannot exist in less than a certain quantity, it may sometimes be of issue, for the sake of employing it, to stretch a little beyond that quantity which, on other accounts, would be strictly necessary.
11. In particular, this may be the case where the punishment proposed is of such a nature as to be particularly well calculated to answer the purpose of a moral lesson.
12. In adjusting the quantum of punishment, the circumstances by which all punishment may be rendered unprofitable ought to be attended to.
13. Among provisions designated to perfect the proportion between punishments and offenses, if any occur which by their own particular good effects would not make up for the harm they would do by adding to the intricacy of the code, they should be omitted.

SOURCE: Bentham, 1843/1970.

Ethical Formalism

Contrast the utilitarian views toward punishment discussed in the previous section with Kant's (see box). Ethical formalism clearly supports a retributive view of punishment. It is deontological because it is not concerned with the consequences of the punishment or treatment, only its inherent morality. It would support the idea that a criminal is owed punishment because to do otherwise would not be according him or her equal respect as a human. How-

---

QUOTATION

Juridical punishment . . . can be inflicted on a criminal, never just as instrumental to the achievement of some other good for the criminal himself or for the civil society, but only because he has committed a crime; for a man may never be used just as a means to the end of another person. . . . Penal law is a categorical imperative, and woe to him who crawls through the serpentine maze of utilitarian theory in order to find an excuse, in some advantage to someone, for releasing the criminal from punishment or any degree of it, in line with the pharasaical proverb "it is better that one man die than that a whole people perish"; for if justice perishes, there is no more value in man living on the earth. . . . What mode and degree of punishment, then, is the principle and standard of public justice? Nothing but the principle of equality. . . . Thus, whatever undeserved evil you inflict on another person, you inflict on yourself. . . .

SOURCE: Kant, quoted in Borchert and Stewart, 1986: 322.

---

ever, the punishment should not be used as a means to any other end but retribution. Treatment is not supported by ethical formalism because it uses the offender as a means to protect society.

Several arguments support this retributive rationale. First, Mackie (1982) discusses the universal aspects of punishment: the urge to react in a hostile manner to harm is an element inherent in human nature; therefore, one might say that punishment is a natural law. Another supporting argument is found in the principle of forfeiture, which postulates that when one intrudes on an innocent person's rights, one forfeits a proportional amount of one's own rights. By restraining or hurting a victim in some way, the aggressor forfeits his or her own liberty; in other words, he or she forfeits the right to be free from punishment (Bedau, 1982).

Ethics of Care

The ethics of care would support treatment over retributive punishment and would also support the concept of restorative justice because it is concerned with the needs of the victim. Several authors have discussed the ethics of care in relation to the justice and corrections system. For instance, Heidensohn (1986) and Daly (1989) discuss differences in the perception of justice from a care perspective versus a retributive perspective. They discuss these as female and male perceptions, respectively. The female care perspective emphasizes needs, motives, and relationships. The corrections system, ideally, should be supported by a caring ethic since it takes into account offender needs, and community corrections especially emphasizes the relationship of the offender to the community. In this perspective, one should help the offender to become a better person, because that is what a caring and committed relationship would entail. Retributive punishment and deterrence are not consistent with the ethics of care. However, some say that retribution and a care ethic are not, nor should they be considered, dichotomous. Restorative justice might be considered the merger of the two in that this approach views the offender as responsible for the wrong committed but the responsibility is satisfied by reparation to the victim rather than by punishment and pain.

Rawlsian Ethics

John Rawls presents an alternative to utilitarianism and retributivism. Rawls's defense of punishment starts with Kant's proposition that no one should be treated as a means and with the idea that each should have an "equal right to the most extensive basic liberty compatible with a similar liberty to others." According to Rawls, a loss of rights should take place only when it is consistent with the best interests of the least advantaged. Rules regarding punishment would be as follows (cited in Hickey and Scharf, 1980: 169):

1. We must punish only to the extent that the loss of liberty would be agreeable were one not to know whether one were to be the criminal, the victim, or a member of the general public [the veil of ignorance].

2. The loss of liberty must be justified as the minimum loss consistent with the maintenance of the same liberty among others.

Furthermore, when the advantage shifts—when the offender instead of the victim or society becomes the one with the least advantage—then punishment must cease. This theory leaves a lot of unanswered questions, since it seems that if victims were chosen carefully—for instance, if only those who would not suffer financially or emotionally from victimization were selected—then the criminal, especially if he or she comes from an impoverished background, would still be at a disadvantage and, thus, not morally accountable for his or her actions. On the other hand, Rawls's system does seem to be consistent with the idea that the criminal act creates an imbalance of some previous state of parity and that punishment should be concerned with regaining that balance. The utilitarian thread in this proposition is that by having this check-and-balance system in the determination of punishment, all of society is benefited.

PUNISHMENT AND
TREATMENT ALTERNATIVES

We have discarded many punishments that historically were found acceptable, such as flogging, hanging, banishment, branding, cutting off limbs, drawing and quartering, and pillories and stocks. Although we still believe society has the right to punish, what we do in the name of punishment has changed substantially. As a society, we became gradually uncomfortable with inflicting physically painful punishments on offenders, and as these punishments were discarded, imprisonment was used as the substitute. Inside prison, we have only relatively recently abandoned physical punishments as a method of control. No longer are the whip and strap used, although there are still those working in the system who remember the time when they were used with impunity.

Humane Punishment

The Supreme Court has given legal reasons for the abolition of most types of corporal punishment. The Eighth Amendment protects all Americans from cruel and unusual punishment. Although what is "cruel and unusual" is vague, several tests have been used to define the terms, such as the following, discussed in *Furman v. Georgia,* 408 U.S. 238, 92 S.Ct. 2726, 33 L.Ed.2d 346 (1972):

1. "Unusual" (by frequency): Those punishments that are rarely, if ever used thus become unusual if used against one individual or a group. They become arbitrary punishments because the decision to use them is so infrequent.

2. "Evolving standards of decency": Civilization is evolving and punishments considered acceptable in the nineteenth century are no longer acceptable in the twentieth century.

3. "Shock the conscience": A yardstick for all punishment is to test it against the public conscience. If people are naturally repelled by the punishment, then it must be cruel and unusual by definition.

4. "Excessive or disproportionate": Any punishment that is excessive to its purpose or disproportionately administered is considered wrong. For instance, if greater amounts of punishment are given to one group than to another or to one individual in comparison to like individuals.

5. "Unnecessary": Again, we are looking at the purpose of the punishment in relation to what is done. If the purpose of punishment to deter crime, then we should only administer an amount necessary to do so. If the purpose is to protect and the offender presents no danger, then prison should not be used.

These tests have eliminated the use of the whip and the branding iron, yet some say that we may have done nothing to move toward humane punishment and that, in fact, we may have moved away from it. Graeme Newman points out the possibility that corporal punishment, at least the less drastic kinds such as whipping, is actually less intrusive in a person's life than a prison sentence. In fact, physical punishment may be more of a deterrent and yet less damaging to a person's future. After all, a whipping takes perhaps days or weeks to get over, but a prison sentence may last years and affect all future earnings (Newman, 1978: 270).

A criminal offender may be sentenced to probation instead of prison. A fine or other conditions of probation may be attached. For instance, a probationer may be required to perform community service, pay court costs, pay

---

QUERY

What is more harmful to the individual, whipping or a prison sentence? Which is the more ethical? Which would you prefer?

restitution to the victim, find employment, submit to drug tests and complete drug counseling, or conform to any number of other conditions. Some recent examples of conditions include those convicted of Driving While Intoxicated being required to have an instrument that measures their blood alcohol level attached to their car, the use of electronic monitoring instruments, and, in one case, being forced to donate blood to a blood bank. So-called "shaming" conditions include DWI offenders having special license plates that indicate to other drivers that the driver has been convicted of DWI, probation officers putting signs up in the yard or nailing them to the door of convicted sex offenders warning people that a sex offender lives there, announcing to one's church congregation one's criminal conviction and asking for forgiveness, and taking out an advertisement in the town newspaper for the same purpose. These conditions are rarely challenged in court because the offender would usually prefer them to a prison sentence. However, there is some question as to the legal authority for such conditions, and we could also examine them in light of the ethical systems above. One real question concerning the "shaming" conditions is the effect such conditions have on family members of offenders and whether these conditions constitute a type of extralegal punishment for them completely outside the due-process procedures of trial and conviction.

Capital Punishment

What sets capital punishment apart from all other punishments is its quality of irrevocability. This type of punishment leaves no way to correct a mistake. For this reason, some believe that no mortal should have the power to inflict capital punishment, because there is no way to guarantee that mistakes won't be made. Certainly, Radelet, Bedau, and Putnam's (1992) collection of cases concerning innocent people who were executed in error supports this viewpoint.

The Bureau of Justice Statistics (1996) reports that the thirty-one prisoners executed in 1994 were seven fewer than those executed in 1993. Most had been under the sentence of death for ten years or more. At the end of 1994, about 2,890 prisoners had a death sentence; 1,645 were white, 1,197 were black, 23 were Native American, 17 were Asian American, and 8 were classified as Other. One-third had no prior felony convictions.

The major ethical positions that can support the death penalty are utilitarianism and retributivism. Because of controversy over the factual issues involved, utilitarian arguments are used both to defend and condemn capital punishment. If we believe, as do retentionists, that capital punishment is just because it deters people, then we must show proof that it does indeed deter. The abolitionists present evidence that it does not.

Arguments for the retention of the death penalty include considerations of justice and considerations of social utility. Considerations of justice involve the retributivist, deontological view that the moral order is upset by the commission of an offense, and the disorder can only be rectified by punishment equal in intensity to the seriousness of the offense. Utilitarians view the evil of capital punishment as far outweighed by the future benefits that will accrue to

Death Penalty Cases, 1994			
Executions During 1994		*Prisoners Under Sentence of Death*	
Texas	14	Texas	394
Arkansas	5	California	381
Virginia	2	Florida	342
Delaware	1	Pennsylvania	182
Florida	1	Illinois	155
Georgia	1	Ohio	140
Idaho	1	Alabama	135
Illinois	1	Oklahoma	129
Indiana	1	Arizona	121
Maryland	1	North Carolina	111
Nebraska	1	Tennessee	100
North Carolina	1	Georgia	96

SOURCE: Adapted from Bureau of Justice Statistics Bulletin, *Capital Punishments 1994* (Feb. 1996). U.S. Department of Justice.

society. For example, execution might lead to such socially desirable effects as protection from the violent criminal and deterrence of other potential criminals. Walker (1985: 79) summarizes the evidence marshaled on both sides of the deterrence question and finds very little support for the proposition that executions are useful deterrents. Further explorations of the issue also conclude that there is little reason to believe that capital punishment has any deterrent effect (Kronenwetter, 1993).

Abolitionists emphasize the "inherent worth and dignity of each individual." The taking of a human life is judged a morally unacceptable practice and is believed to be nothing more than vengeance (Mappes, 1982: 83–87). Utilitarianism may also support the idea that executions create a net negative effect on society, because although criminals may receive what they deserve, society is negatively affected by the brutalizing image of execution. This view would be one consistent with the idea that "violence begets violence," and, far from showing societal intolerance toward murder, capital punishment is seen as actually cheapening human life and encouraging blood lust.

Religious ethics have been used both to support and condemn capital punishment. The Old Testament law supporting the taking of "an eye for an eye" is used by retentionists whereas the commandment "Thou shalt not kill" is used by the abolitionists. The ethical justification of capital punishment presents serious and probably unresolvable problems. It is a telling commentary that for as long as society has used capital punishment to punish wrongdoing, critics have defined it as immoral (Johnson, 1991).

Questions also arise about the methods and procedures of capital punishment. Should all murderers be subject to capital punishment, or are some murders less serious than others? Should we allow defenses of age, mental state, or reason? If we do apply capital punishment differentially, doesn't this open the door to bias and misuse?

Evidence indicates that capital punishment has been used arbitrarily and discriminatorily in this country. Minorities are more likely to be executed, especially when their victims are white—yet the Supreme Court has stated that evidence of statistical disproportionality in administration (in Georgia, black offenders charged with killing a white were 4.3 times more likely to be sentenced to death than those charged with killing a black) is not enough to invalidate the death penalty (*McClesky v. Kemp,* 481 U.S. 279 [1987]).

Because our justice system is based on rationality, executions of the mentally ill and the mentally retarded have been vehemently criticized. The Supreme Court has ruled that executing the mentally ill is cruel and unusual (*Ford v. Wainwright,* 477 U.S. 399 [1986]). Miller and Radelet (1993) present a detailed account of the *Ford* case, describing the mental deterioration of Ford and the long ordeal of appeals before the Supreme Court finally ruled. They also point out the ethical issues involved when psychiatrists, other medical professionals, and psychologists participate in procedures that involve certifying someone as "death ready" and then assist in the administration of the chosen method of execution. There are deep and divisive views in these professions regarding the seeming inconsistency between identifying oneself as a helping professional and then helping someone be put to death.

There is no constitutional bar to executing the mentally retarded, although evidence of mental retardation can be presented to the jury to consider in mitigation of sentence (*Penry v. Lynaugh,* 107 S.Ct. 2934 [1989]). The *Penry* case involved a man who had committed a brutal rape and murder but who had an IQ that was just barely above the level that would ordinarily result in institutionalization. After the Supreme Court ruled that the state of Texas could execute someone who was mentally retarded but that the trial judge must allow evidence of mental retardation to be provided to the jury in consideration of mitigation, a retrial resulted in a second death sentence from the new jury.

Finally, although one would assume that the offender must have had to kill someone to receive a death sentence, that is not the case. In *Tison v. Arizona,* 481 U.S. 137 (1987), the Court ruled that crime partners in a felony that resulted in a death could be executed even if they did not kill the victim and they did not intend a death to occur. The Tison brothers had no criminal records, but they helped their father escape from an Arizona prison. During the escape, their father and a fellow escaped convict killed a family after kidnapping them for their car. The brothers were horrified, but by this point were felons themselves. A massive search ensued, and they were separated from their father, who eventually ended up dying of exposure in the desert. One wonders if the fact that he escaped his punishment was the reason that the brothers were then tried for capital murder. Responding to their appeal, the Supreme Court affirmed the state's right to execute for "felony murder"— where crime partners become responsible for any murder that occurs in the course of a felony they participate in, regardless of their actual commission of the killing.

Question: If we executed all the people who are currently on death row—2,890 in 1994, according to the Bureau of Justice Statistics—would public sentiment continue to support the death penalty? Would we become even more blasé about its occurrence, or would sentiment shift to disgust and dismay over the numbers of individuals killed? Is the very fact that capital punishment is used so sparingly part of the reason behind majority support for its existence?

Unless the Supreme Court revises its current position, which seems unlikely, the legality of executions is not in question even though the procedures used to arrive at the decision to execute may continue to be challenged. However, the morality of capital punishment is still very much a topic of debate, and it elicits strong feelings on the part of many people; we have only briefly introduced this topic in this section and urge the reader to pursue the excellent available literature on the subject.

COMMUNITY CORRECTIONS

Community corrections has a more positive and helpful image than does institutional corrections. Yet even in this subsystem of the criminal justice system, the ideals of justice and care become diluted by bureaucratic mismanagement and personal agendas. Professionals in community corrections do not have the same power to use physical force as police and correctional officers do, but they do have a great deal of nonphysical power over the clients they control. Their authority and power can be used wisely and ethically or become subverted to personal ends.

Community corrections is supported by the ethics of care. It promotes the needs of the offender and his or her relationship to the community. It is not banishment, as in a prison sentence, but rather control and care in the community or a reintegration back into the community. Another philosophical rationale for it comes from restorative justice—the idea that the offender must restore the victim to some previous state of wholeness and that community corrections is the vehicle for the offender to do this. Of course, other ethical frameworks may also be used to support the concept of community corrections. Because this correctional alternative costs much less than institutional corrections, a utilitarian rationale can be used. It is better for both society and the offender if the cheapest method of controlling and correcting behavior can be found. Even ethical formalism can be used to provide a rationale for community corrections if the offender's crime can be viewed as deserving only a sentence to community corrections as opposed to prison. Souryal writes that community corrections "signifies moral concern for the individual, one that is consistent with the natural law ethics of 'dignity of man,' the constitutional ethics of individualized treatment and *perhaps* the religious ethics of redemption" (1992: 356; italics in original).

Typically, community corrections is a term that encompasses jails, halfway houses, work release centers, probation, parole, and any other intermediate sanctions, such as electronic monitoring—either as a condition of probation or as a sentence in itself.

The use of electronic monitoring, usually through computer-generated monitoring employing ankle bracelets and a telephone, raises issues of privacy. Such sanctions are said to blur the line between the offender and his or her family. Some contend that the use of surveillance techniques against offender populations is spilling over into other contexts. For instance, drug testing started with probationers and now seems to be common in the workplace. Some workplaces use the polygraph, monitor employees' calls, use video cameras, and in other ways apply the surveillance practices created for lawbreakers to the rest of us (Staples, 1997).

The use of alcohol programs and threat of punitive sanctions raise issues of personal liberty and freedom—since alcohol is a legal substance, should we punish convicted felons for drinking while on probation? The argument is that convicted felons do not have to accept conditions of probation that prohibit alcohol—they could choose prison—but is that a legitimate choice? Further, while such conditions may make sense for those convicted of Driving While Intoxicated, do the technical conditions of "no alcohol" make sense for a burglar who did not attempt to explain or defend his actions by claiming to be drunk at the moment of the crime?

The danger of intermediate sanctions is that because they are typically so innocuous, they are used more frequently for offenders who may not have received any formal system response in years past. This problem of *net widening* is not only problematic from an ethical stand, but also for purely pragmatic reasons of cost. Can we foresee a time when a large portion of the population is on some type of governmental monitoring status? Some say it is already here. We may be happy to note that tax monies may not be burdened by such monitoring since the trend to charge offenders supervision fees is growing. Still, other than providing employment for the legions of criminal justice students who are graduating from colleges and universities, are there good reasons for the dramatic expansion of the net of corrections?

PRIVATE CORRECTIONS

A controversy currently exists over the issue of private corrections. Although punishment is a state function, some states are now entering into contracts with private companies. Private prisons are built and then leased to the state or, in some cases, actually run by the private corporation, which bills the state for the service. Many have objected to the profit motive being introduced into corrections and point to a number of ethical issues raised by private "profiteers." First, there are potential abuses of the bidding process, as in any situation where the government contracts with a company for services or products. Money may change hands to ensure that one organization receives the contract, companies may make informal agreements to "rig" the bids, and other

For Private Prisons, Crime Does Pay

Sorry to be late clueing you to this great new money-making opportunity, but there may still be time to get in on the seminar that will show you how to imprison people for fun and profit.

The brochure promises to tell you how to "Maximize Investment Returns in this Explosive Industry."

Forget all the trendy cyberstuff. If you're looking for something really reliable, what better to invest in than human misbehavior? It has been a sure thing since Cain and Abel.

Seventy-five folks had signed up by last week, and there was room for more at the conference Wednesday through Friday in Dallas.

Instead of a smiley face, the brochure grins with a big graph curve showing that something called the Private Prison Index is soaring above the Standard & Poor's 500 as a way to cash out the American dream.

"While arrests and convictions are steadily on the rise," we are told, "profits are to be made—profits from crime. Get in on the ground floor of this booming industry now!" Revenues in the U.S. prison industry, we learn, topped $30 billion last year.

The United States imprisons a larger part of its people than any other country. Imprisonment has set new records every year for the past 15 or so.

Balking at the cost—but ducking cheaper and more effective alternatives for fear of being called soft on crime—state legislatures are privatizing prisons in hopes of saving money.

Corporate America has caught the scent of new public money, and not only the bottom feeders. The Dallas conference boasts participants from AT&T, Merrill Lynch, Price Waterhouse and other golden-logo companies. Yes, crime is serious and must be punished; and, yes, prisons have to be part of the justice mix; and, no, criminals shouldn't be turned loose to prey on the innocent.

But we, the people, have few powers more awesome than to deprive our errant fellow citizens of their liberty through imprisonment. When we necessarily use that power, don't we have a moral obligation to take responsibility directly?

There is something faintly obscene about, in effect, leasing prisoners in job lots to corporations that figure to make big bucks from their incarceration.

The operators of some private prisons argue, though quietly, that because they run businesses, not government, they have no obligation, except contractual, to respect the constitutional rights of men and women put in their charge.

Some corporate prisons already bar journalists, almost guaranteeing abuses will grow in the resulting dark.

Privatization will create strong business lobbies against nonprison responses to crime, and in the unlikely event prison populations ever slump, well, the lobby can just push legislators, always suckers for such pressure, to make sentences longer and to make more of them mandatory.

In addition to detailing the allure of prison investment, the Dallas conference will hype the further money to be made hawking food, health care and juvenile services to Prisons 'R' Us.

Crime, of course, does pay, and this won't be the first time it pays better in the boardroom than in the street.

SOURCE: Teepen, Tom. (Cox Newspapers). Reprinted in *Austin American-Statesman,* 12 Dec. 1996: A15. Reprinted with permission of Cox Newspapers.

potentially corrupt practices may go on. In Texas, for instance, officials in a private corrections company were indicted for violating competitive bidding procedures (*Houston Post,* 31 Oct. 1991: 26A). The laws at issue were murky; however, in essence the question was whether by creating a nonprofit organization that contracted with the counties to build several prisons, the companies created a monopoly and eliminated the counties' ability to receive competitive bids for materials or services. Legal as well as ethical issues abound when private and public motives are mixed.

In the building phase, private corporations may cut corners and construct buildings without meeting proper standards for safety. Many examples exist in the private sector of inspectors having been bribed to ignore defects in materials or building. Managing the institution also raises the possibility that a private contractor will attempt to maximize profits by ignoring minimum standards of health and safety and will, if necessary, bribe inspectors or monitors to overlook the deficiencies. It has certainly happened in other areas, such as nursing homes, that those who contract with the state government and receive state monies reap large profits by subjecting clients to inhumane conditions (Merlo, 1992).

In a more general sense, some feel that punishment and profit are not compatible, and historically linking the two has led to a variety of abuses (such as the contract labor system in the South). Although the decision to use private corporations is made by legislators, correctional administrators are faced with a variety of ethical dilemmas because of it, such as whether to support the idea, whether to accept a part-time position as a consultant to a private corporation when one has decision-making authority over issues that concern the corporation, whether to take anything of value from the corporation (from a free lunch to a "grant" for personal study), and whether to allow one corporation to have insider information in order to prepare a more favorable bid. On the other hand, private corporations report that some state systems subject them to endless and picayune rules and continually audit them to the point that it appears that state prison officials are trying to find noncompliance in order to return the "action" to state actors. There is probably some truth that some corrections department officials are not happy to have legislators approve the use of private contractors and would like to see them fail. It will take some time to determine whether private corrections is an overall positive step in corrections or a negative one.

CONCLUSION

In this chapter we have looked at some of the ethical rationales for punishment. What we do to offenders has a substantial connection with our views on such things as free will and determinism, the capacity for individual change, and the basic nature of humankind. Punishment has always been used against those who hurt other members of society and thus might be considered consistent with natural law. However, the limits of punishment have been more changeable and have been subject to the laws and mores of each historical era. Today, our punishments primarily consist of imprisonment or some form of restricted liberty, such as probation or parole. In the next chapter, we concentrate on those correctional professionals who are responsible for imposing society's will on offenders.

REVIEW QUESTIONS

1. Discuss the major rationales of punishment.
2. Now defend the rationales of punishment through the use of the ethical systems.
3. Support "three-strike" laws through a retributive rationale and then through a utilitarian rationale.
4. State your belief on the use of capital punishment and the reasons for your position. Now take the opposite side and give the reasons for this view.
5. What are some ethical problems with treatment?
6. Discuss the "net widening" issue.
7. Support or criticize private corrections and give your reasons.

ETHICAL DILEMMAS

Situation 1

A legislator has proposed a sweeping new crime and punishment bill with the following provisions for punishment. Decide each issue as if you were being asked to vote on it:

- mandatory life term for any crime involving a weapon
- corporal punishment (using an electrical apparatus that inflicts a shock) for all personal violent crimes
- mandatory prison sentences for DWIs
- public executions
- abolition of probation, to be replaced with fines and prison sentences for those who are not able to pay or unwilling to do so

Situation 2

Another legislator has suggested an alternate plan with the following provisions. Vote on these.

- decriminalization of all drug crimes
- mandated treatment programs for all offenders who were intoxicated by alcohol or other drugs at the time of the crime

- restructuring the sentencing statutes to make no crime's sentence longer than five years, except for homicide and attempted homicide
- implementation of a restorative justice initiative that mandates restitution for all victims

Situation 3

Your state is one of the few that allows relatives of homicide victims to witness the execution of the perpetrator. Your brother was killed in a robbery, and the murderer is about to be executed. You receive a letter advising you of the execution date and your right to be present. Would you go?

SUGGESTED READINGS

Bedau, H. 1991. "How to Argue About the Death Penalty." *Israel Law Review* 25, 466–480.

Kronenwetter, M. 1993. *Capital Punishment: A Reference Handbook.* Santa Barbara, CA: ABC-CLIO.

Murphy, J. 1985/1995. *Punishment and Rehabilitation.* Belmont, CA: Wadsworth.

Radelet, M., Bedau, H., and Putnam, C. 1992. *In Spite of Innocence: Erroneous Convictions in Capital Cases.* Boston: Northeastern University Press.

10

�֎

Ethics for Correctional Professionals

Chapter Objectives

Become familiar with the ethical issues for correctional officers, treatment professionals, and probation and parole officers.

Understand some of the unique ethical issues for correctional managers and administrators.

I n this chapter we will examine some ethical issues for correctional professionals, much the same way we have done previously with other criminal justice professionals.

CORRECTIONAL PROFESSIONALS

Institutional correctional personnel can be divided into two groups: (1) correctional officers and their supervisors, and (2) treatment professionals, a group that would include educators, counselors, psychologists, and all others connected with programming. These groups have different jobs and also, not surprisingly, are presented with different ethical questions. There are also correctional professionals associated with community-based corrections, specifically probation and parole officers and their supervisors. Jail officers, halfway house personnel, and treatment counselors in community-based, residential drug and alcohol programs may also be considered correctional professionals. In this book we devote a disproportionate amount of attention to prison officers, primarily because most of the available information concerns prison personnel. A number of ethical issues that treatment personnel may be faced with are similar to those experienced in a more general way by all treatment professionals, so available sources dealing with ethics in the helping professions would also be applicable to those who work in the corrections field (see, for instance, Corey, Corey, and Callanan, 1988).

Use of Discretion and Authority

We have previously discussed how discretion plays a role in each phase of the criminal justice system. In corrections, discretion is involved when a correctional officer decides to write a disciplinary ticket or merely delivers a verbal reprimand; this is similar to police discretion in making the decision to arrest. Discretion is also involved when the disciplinary committee makes a decision to punish an inmate for an infraction: the punishment can be as serious as increasing sentence length through loss of good time, or as minor as a temporary loss of privileges. What punishment may be administered depends on state law and Supreme Court decisions related to prisoners' rights, but also largely on the discretion of disciplinary committees. A similar decision-making process would be that of a parole hearing officer in a revocation procedure. This type of discretion is similar to the discretion of the prosecutor and judge in a criminal trial.

Correctional psychiatrists, psychologists, and counselors have a responsibility to the correctional client. Like the defense attorney, they must use discretion to balance the client's needs against the larger needs of the system or institution. Their role may actually involve more ambiguity than the defense lawyer's since there is some question as to whether they owe their primary allegiance to the offender or to society.

Hence, we see that similarities exist between correctional personnel and the other practitioners discussed thus far. As always, when the power of discretion is present, the potential for abuse is also present. Professional ethics should guide individual decision makers in their use of discretion, but, as with law enforcement and legal professionals, adherence to a code of ethics is influenced by the occupational subculture and institutional values—at least for correctional officers. Formal ethics for correctional personnel will be discussed in more detail shortly.

Use of Authority and Power

Correctional officers (C.O.'s) are similar to police officers in that their uniform represents the authority of the institution quite apart from any personal power of the person wearing it. Some C.O.'s are uncomfortable with this authority and do not know how to handle it. Some C.O.'s revel in it and misperceive the bounds of authority given to them as a representative of the state. The following statement is a perceptive observation of how some C.O.'s misuse and misperceive the authority they have (Kauffman, 1988: 50):

> [Some officers] don't understand what authority is and what bounds you have within that authority. . . . I think everyone interprets it to meet their own image of themself. "I'm a corrections officer [slams table]! You sit here! [Slam!] You sit there!" Rather than "I'm a person who has limited authority. So, you know, I'm sorry gentlemen, but you can't sit there. You are going to have to sit over there. That's just the rules," and explaining or something like that the reason why.

This officer obviously recognized that the uniform bestows the authority of rational and reasonable control, not unbridled domination. It is also true that the power of the C.O. is limited. In actuality, it is impossible to depend on the authority of the uniform to get tasks accomplished, and one must find personal resources—respect and authority stemming from one's personal reputation—in order to gain cooperation from inmates.

Some officers who perceive themselves as powerless in relation to the administration, the courts, and society in general may react to this perceived powerlessness by misusing their little bit of power over inmates. They may abuse their position by humiliating or abusing those in their control.

Probation and parole officers have a different type of authority and power over offenders. They have the power to recommend release or revocation.

This power is also limited since probation and parole officers' recommendations can be ignored by the judge or hearing officer. Yet the implicit power an officer has over the individuals on his or her caseload must be recognized as an important element of the role, not to be taken lightly or misused.

Thus, in ways somewhat similar to those of police officers, correctional officers and probation and parole officers have power over offenders. They have the full range of coercive control, including loss of liberty through physical force if necessary. Their power may be misused; a blatant example would be an officer who beats an inmate, a psychologist ordering an antipsychotic drug for a troublesome inmate knowing full well he is not psychotic, or a probation officer who coerces sex from a probationer in return for not filing a violation report. All are abuses of power; these possibilities exist because of the powerlessness of the offender relative to the correctional professional. A sensitivity to ethical issues involves the recognition and respect that one has for this element of the profession.

CORRECTIONAL OFFICERS

During the rehabilitative era of the 1970s, professional security staff in corrections exchanged their old label of *guard* for a new one—*correctional officer.* However, the slang terms used to describe these individuals, such as *hack, screw,* and *turnkey,* have been more resistant to change. Although increasing professionalism and greater knowledge acquisition now characterize the individuals in this occupation, correctional officers, by any name, are still perceived as operating under punitive goals and doing little to improve the negative environment of the prison.

The American Correctional Association's Code of Ethics outlines formal ethics for correctional professionals. The original code was adopted in 1975 and was revised in 1990. The changes between the 1975 version and the 1990 version were largely minor, including changing male pronouns to gender-neutral language. The other consistent change was all references to the offender as *client* were deleted in favor of the use of the term *individual* or *person.* This change may be interpreted as moderating the influence of the treatment ethic and medical model in corrections. There exist many similarities between this code and the Law Enforcement Code presented in Chapter 5. For instance, integrity, respect for and protection of individual rights, and service to the public are emphasized in both codes, as are the importance and sanctity of the law. Also, the prohibition against exploiting professional authority for personal gain is stressed in both codes.

Another similarity between this code and the Law Enforcement Code is the disparity that sometimes exists between the ideal behavior it describes and what actually occurs. The ACA Code of Ethics describes the ideal behavior of correctional staff; however, as was discussed in Chapter 5, on law enforcement, subcultural values may be inconsistent with and subvert formal ethical

American Correctional Association Code of Ethics

The American Correctional Association expects of its members unfailing honesty, respect for the dignity and individuality of human beings, and a commitment to professional and compassionate service. To this end we subscribe to the following principles.

- Members will respect and protect the civil and legal rights of all individuals.
- Members will treat every professional situation with concern for the person's welfare and with no intent of personal gain.
- Relationships with colleagues will be such that they promote mutual respect within the profession and improve the quality of service.
- Public criticism of colleagues or their agencies will be made only when warranted, verifiable and constructive in purpose.
- Members will respect the importance of all disciplines within the criminal justice system and work to improve cooperation with each segment.
- Subject to the individual's right to privacy, members will honor the public's right to know and will share information with the public to the extent permitted by law.
- Members will respect and protect the right of the public to be safeguarded from criminal activity.
- Members will not use their positions to secure personal privileges or advantages.
- Members will not, while acting in an official capacity, allow personal interest to impair objectivity in the performance of duty.
- No member will enter into any activity or agreement, formal or informal, which presents a conflict of interest or is inconsistent with the conscientious performance of his or her duties.
- No member will accept any gift, service or favor that is or appears to be improper or implies an obligation inconsistent with the free and objective exercise of his or her professional duties.
- In any public statement, members will clearly distinguish between personal views and those statements or positions made on behalf of an agency or the Association.
- Each member will report to the appropriate authority any corrupt or unethical behavior where there is sufficient cause to initiate a review.
- Members will not discriminate against any individual because of the basis of race, gender, creed, national origin, religious affiliation, age or any other type of prohibited discrimination.
- Members will preserve the integrity of private information; they will neither seek data on individuals beyond that needed to perform their responsibilities, nor reveal nonpublic data unless expressly authorized to do so.
- Any member who is responsible for agency personnel actions will make all appointments, promotions or dismissals in accordance with established civil service rules, applicable contract agreements and individual merit, and not in the furtherance of partisan interests.

SOURCE: Adopted August 1975 at the 105th Congress of Correction; revised August 1990 at the 120th Congress of Correction. Reprinted with permission of the American Correctional Association, Lanham, MD.

codes. This is also the case with correctional personnel. Although the ethical code clearly calls for fair and objective treatment, integrity, and high standards of performance, the actual practices of correctional staff may be quite different.

The Correctional Officer Subculture

The subculture of the correctional officer has never been as extensively described as the police subculture, but some elements are similar. First of all, the inmate may be considered the enemy, along with superiors and society in general. Moreover, the acceptance of the use of force, the preference toward redefining job roles to meet minimum requirements, and the willingness to use deceit to cover up wrongdoing are evident in both subcultures (Johnson, 1987; Crouch, 1980). Kauffman (1988: 85–112), in an excellent study of the officers' world, notes the following norms of the correctional officer subculture:

1. Always go to the aid of another officer. Similar to law enforcement, the necessity of interdependence ensures that this is a strong and pervasive norm in the correctional officer subculture. Kauffman describes a "slam" in Walpole Prison as when the officer slams a heavy cell door, which reverberates throughout the prison building, bringing a dozen officers to his or her aid in minutes—an obvious parallel to the "officer down" call in law enforcement.

2. Don't lug drugs. This prohibition is to ensure the safety of other officers, as is the even stronger prohibition against bringing in weapons for inmates. The following norm against "ratting" on a fellow officer may except informing on an officer who is a known offender of this lugging norm.

3. Don't rat. In similar ways to the law enforcement subcultural code and, ironically, the inmate code, correctional officers also hate those who inform on their peers. Kauffman notes two subordinate norms: never rat out an officer to an inmate, and never cooperate in an investigation or, worse yet, testify against a fellow officer in regard to that officer's treatment of inmates.

4. Never make a fellow officer look bad in front of inmates. This applies regardless of what the officer did, since it jeopardizes the officer's effectiveness and undercuts the appearance of officer solidarity.

5. Always support an officer in a dispute with an inmate. Similar to the previous provision, this prescribes behavior—not only should one not criticize a fellow officer, but one should support him or her against any inmate.

6. Always support officer sanctions against inmates. This is a specific version of the previous provision. This includes the use of illegal physical force as well as legal sanctions.

7. Don't be a white hat. This prohibition is directed at any behavior, attitude, or expressed opinion that could be interpreted as sympathetic to-

ward inmates. Kauffman also notes that it is often violated and does not have the strong subcultural sanctions that accompany some of the other norms.

8. Maintain officer solidarity against all outside groups. Similar to police officers, correctional officers feel denigrated and despised by society at large. This norm reinforces officer solidarity and includes prohibitions against any other group, including the media, administration, or public.

9. Show positive concern for fellow officers. This norm promotes goodwill toward other officers. Two examples are never leave another officer a problem, which means don't leave unfinished business at the end of your shift for the next officer to handle; and help your fellow officers with problems outside the institution, meaning lending money to injured or sick officers or helping out in other ways.

Kauffman notes that this code may vary from institution to institution depending on such factors as permeability, the administration, the level of violence from inmates, architecture, and the demographic profile of officers. Distrust of outsiders, dissatisfaction, and alienation are elements of both the police and the correctional officer subcultures. In both professions, the individuals must work with sometimes unpleasant people who make it clear that the practitioner is not liked or appreciated. Further, there is public antipathy (either real or perceived) toward the profession, which increases the social distance between criminal justice professionals and all others outside the profession. In addition, the working hours, the nature of the job, and the unwillingness to talk about the job to others outside the profession intensify the isolation that workers feel. One additional point to be made about the occupational subculture is that both law enforcement and corrections have been changed by the entry of minorities, the college educated, and women into the ranks.

It should also be pointed out that some researchers feel that some of the values embedded in the correctional officer subculture may not be shared by

---

The Prisoners on the Other Side of the Bars

Some convicts hate all prison guards. They perceive them as the physical manifestation of their own misery and misfortune. The uniform becomes the man, and they no longer see an individual behind it.

Many guards react in kind. The hatred is returned with the full force of authority. These two factions become the real movers and shakers in the prison world. They aren't a majority in either camp, but the strength of their hatred makes its presence known to all.

. . . Amid all the hatred, insanity, and violence, large numbers of them quit before long. The ones with families who need the job find themselves trapped in a cage of their own. . . .

SOURCE: Martin, D. *Committing Journalism: The Prison Writings of Red Hog* (New York: Norton, 1993): 94–95. Originally published in the *San Francisco Chronicle*.

most officers—a concept referred to as *pluralistic ignorance.* This refers to the idea that a few outspoken and visible members shape the perception that all group members have toward the characteristics of the majority. In corrections, this may mean that a few officers endorse and publicize subcultural values, whereas the majority, who are silent, privately believe in different values (Johnson, 1987: 130). Kauffman found this to be true in attitudes toward the use of force and toward the value of treatment. Individually, officers expressed more positive attitudes than they believed to be typical of the subculture (1988: 179). This situation is probably true of the police subculture as well.

Relationships with Inmates

One would assume that the general relationship between officers and inmates is one of hatred. That is not necessarily the case. As Martin (1993), an ex-prisoner, points out, the posturing and vocalization from either side come from a small number, with the majority of inmates and officers living in an uneasy state of truce, hoping that no one goes over the line on either side. Those officers who engage in unethical activities can go in one direction or another—there are officers who become too friendly with inmates, and there are officers who conduct campaigns of harassment or terror against inmates.

One serious threat to an officer's ethics and professionalism occurs when relationships with inmates become personal. Gresham Sykes discussed the issue of reciprocity in supervision: officers become dependent on inmates for important task completion and the smooth management of the tier; in return, C.O.'s may overlook inmate infractions and allow a certain degree of favoritism to enter their supervision style (cited in Crouch, 1980: 239).

One example of a type of reciprocal relationship that may lead to unethical actions is that between an officer and an informant. Hassine (1996: 119), an ex-prisoner, relates that the widespread use of informants created several negative elements in the prison where he was housed, including pervasive tension and distrust within the inmate population, particularly between parole violators and long-termers, because parole violators were more likely to snitch

---

QUOTATIONS

I never shake hands with an inmate. . . . They neither are nor ought to be viewed as equals. (George Beto, administrator of Texas prison system, 1962–1972, quoted in Dilulio, 1987: 177)

. . . the Sergeant had succeeded in making me feel even more isolated from the world that existed outside the prison walls. I was no longer so proud to be an American. I was just a convict without rights. . . . (Victor Hassine, inmate, 1996: 52)

Because legitimate power is so unevenly distributed between the keepers and the kept, left to its own inertia abuses of that power will inevitably creep into any prison without diligent and sensitive oversight. (Patrick McManus, state correctional official, reported in Martin, D., 1993: 333)

to obtain favorable treatment in their short stay; the practice also resulted in more drugs in prison, according to Hassine, because informers would inform only on that activity that they didn't have a stake in, they did not inform on some drug smuggling schemes in order to create targets that they could then inform on, and officers elevated snitches to higher status positions through granting them favored jobs and privileges. Marquart and Roebuck (1986) also discuss the practice of giving special privileges in return for informing. According to these officers, prisons were, for the most part, managed on information supplied by snitches.

When C.O.'s become personally involved with inmates, their professional judgment is compromised. Involvement is possible because of proximity and close contact over a period of time, combined with shared feelings of victimization by the administration. Officers may start to feel they have more in common with inmates than with the administration, especially now that officers are more likely to come from urban areas and from minority groups and are more demographically similar to the inmates they supervise. Identification and friendship may lead to unethical conduct, such as ignoring infractions or doing illegal favors for an inmate. McCarthy (1991) writes of this exchange relationship as an incentive for further corruption. He also points out that lack of training, low visibility, and unfettered discretion also contribute to a variety of corrupt behaviors.

The subcultural norms against sympathizing with or becoming too friendly with inmates as described by Kauffman (1988) are indicative of the preventive steps taken to avoid this identification. An officer who identifies with inmates is not to be trusted. The subculture minimizes the possibility of co-optation by the prohibition against friendliness and the socialization process, which results in a (socialized) correctional officer's view of inmates as animalistic and not worth human sympathy. Kauffman also notes that inmates themselves make it difficult for C.O.'s to continue to hold sympathetic or friendly views. In her study, new officers were continually harassed by inmates until the neutral or positive views they held at entry were replaced with negative views. She described Walpole in the 1970s as overrun with rats and roaches, with excrement smeared on the walls and garbage ankle-deep on the floors—inmates wouldn't clean up, and officers could not. Extreme inmate-on-inmate violence, including mutilations and torture, was commonplace, and officers feared being thrown from the tiers, being knifed in the back, or being hit in the head by soup cans or other heavy objects thrown from the tiers above. This description obviously is not representative of most prisons, then or now, but the elements of inmate hostility, fear, and hopelessness are characteristic of all prisons.

Another type of problem occurs when the actions of female C.O.'s may be misinterpreted by male inmates. Even if the female C.O. is merely expressing a professional interest in the inmate, or when she performs her job in a manner that is more interactive than that of male C.O.'s, a male inmate may see the female C.O. as desiring a personal relationship. Female C.O.'s must learn to interact with male inmates in such ways as to make it clear that they do not desire personal involvement. Of course, there are also situations where romantic relationships do develop—between female C.O.'s and male inmates, between male C.O.'s and female inmates, and between C.O.'s and inmates of the same sex. These are always against institutional rules, unethical, and sometimes dangerous to prison security.

Just as officers may act in unethical ways when they like an inmate, officers have the power to make life difficult for the inmate they do not like. These extralegal harassments and punishments may include "forgetting" to send an inmate to an appointment, making an inmate stay in keeplock longer than necessary, or pretending not to hear someone locked in a cell asking for toilet paper or other necessary items. Lombardo (1981) notes the practice of putting an inmate in keeplock on a Friday even without a supportable charge because the disciplinary committee would not meet until the following Monday to release the inmate, the use of profanity toward inmates even in front of families, not notifying an inmate of a visitor, and losing passes. Kauffman (1988) notes that during the time period she studied, officers sometimes flushed cell toilets to aggravate inmates, dumped good food into the garbage, withheld toilet paper or matches, reported "tips" of contraband in a cell that resulted in a shakedown, scratched artwork, and in other innumerable informal ways made the targeted inmate's life miserable.

Because prisoners are in a position of need, having to ask for things as simple as permission to go to the bathroom, officers have the power to make inmates feel even more dependent than necessary and humiliated because of their dependency. The relative powerlessness of the officers in relation to their superiors, the administration, and society in general creates a situation where some take advantage of their only power—that over the inmate.

Even more so than police, C.O.'s work every day with large numbers of men or women who simply do not like—indeed, sometimes hate—the correctional officer for no other reason than the uniform he or she is wearing. There is always the potential of injury from an unprovoked attack, while subduing an inmate, while breaking up a fight, or from being taken hostage. Officers will say this last possibility is never far from their minds and may affect to a certain extent their supervision of inmates, since it is potentially dangerous to be personally disliked.

On the other hand, on a day-to-day basis inmates are not that much different from anyone else; some are friendly, some are funny, and some are good conversationalists. A comfortable alliance is sometimes formed between the guards and the guarded, especially in work settings, that is not unlike a foreman–employee relationship. This strange combination of familiarity and fear results in a pervasive feeling of distrust. Officers insist that "you can be friendly with inmates, but you can never trust them." Mature officers learn to live with this basic inconsistency and are able to differentiate situations in which rules must be followed from those in which rules can be relaxed. Younger and less perceptive officers either take on a defensive attitude of extreme distrust or are manipulated by inmates because they are not able to tell the difference between goodwill and gaming.

Use of Force

The use of force is a legal and sometimes necessary element of correctional supervision, and most observers say that severe beatings and the use of coercive force—such as the abuse that occurred in Arkansas and is described in the box—simply do not occur today. Nor does the array of physical coercion exist, such as the "tune ups" that occurred in the Texas prisons and involved "verbal humiliation, profanity, shoves, kicks, and head and body slaps"; "ass-whipping," using blackjacks and batons to inflict injury; and severe beatings reserved for those few inmates who attacked staff members (Crouch and Marquart, 1989: 78). However, there are still reports that force is used as an extralegal punishment against unruly or aggressive inmates. Part of the problem lies in the vagueness of the term *necessary force;* this may mean that the resort to violence is the absolute last alternative available, or it may mean that force is used when it is the most convenient way to get something accomplished (Morris and Morris, cited in Crouch, 1980: 253).

During the course of a fistfight or a struggle with an inmate, officers react to violence instinctively—that is, without much rational thought as to whether a blow is necessary or gratuitous. Premeditated beatings inflicted on inmates, usually for a previous attack on a fellow officer, are harder to understand or justify. C.O.'s may view such beatings as utilitarian in that they serve as warnings to all inmates that they will receive similar treatment if they attack C.O.'s; thus, the action protects all officers to some extent from inmate aggression. Officers might also defend the action on retributive grounds, since the inmate would probably not be punished for the attack through legal channels. However, these retaliations always represent the most brutal and inhumane aspects of incarceration and damage the integrity of all correctional professionals.

Evidence that such beatings still exist can be found in court cases. For instance, in *Hudson v. McMillian* (503 U.S. 1 [1992]) the Supreme Court dealt with a case involving an inmate who had been forced to sit in a chair while two officers hit him in the head and chest area, with a lieutenant looking on. The state argued that since there was no "serious injury," there was no constitutional violation, since cruel and unusual punishment had to involve serious injury. Although some justices agreed with this logic, the majority held that injuries need not be serious for a constitutional violation to occur if they stemmed from such abuse at the hands of correctional officers.

QUOTATION

[L]ashing an inmate ten times a day with the "hide," a five-foot leather strap capable of maiming. This official method of discipline was augmented by such illegal but customary techniques as inserting needles under the fingernails, crushing knuckles and testicles with pliers, hitting the inmate with a club, blackjack, or "anything you can lay your hands on," kicking inmates in the groin, mouth, or testicles—and, of course, use of the infamous "Tucker Telephone."

SOURCE: Murton, T. *The Dilemma of Prison Reform* (New York: Irvington Publications, 1976): 147.

QUOTATION

When prison officials maliciously and sadistically use force to cause harm, contemporary standards of decency always are violated.

SOURCE: Justice Sandra O'Connor, *Hudson v. McMillian,* 112 S.Ct. 995, 997 (1992).

Bowker (1980) and other authors describe correctional officer victimization of inmates that runs the gamut from psychological torture and racial discrimination to severe physical abuse. The explanations for why this type of behavior on the part of officers exists include the officers' pervasive sense of fear and the C.O. subculture that tolerates if not encourages such victimization. Crouch and Marquart (1989) and Crouch (1986) also discuss the use of violence as a rite of passage for the correctional officer, a way to prove oneself as a competent officer. Buro (1995) describes a more systemic brutality in the Hawaii prison system that eventually led to an investigation by the U.S. Attorney General's office.

The use in federal prisons of SORT teams—the prison version of SWAT teams—is a new wrinkle in the use of force in prison. These officers, who respond to incidents in full riot gear, which makes them look like a mixture of a professional football team, astronauts, and toxic waste disposal experts, epitomize depersonalized violence—they are so fully padded, helmeted, and hooded that they can hardly feel pain, and they come in such numbers that the individual inmate is immediately overwhelmed. This approach is touted as actually preventing official brutality and minimizing the injuries that can occur to inmates and officers alike when there is an altercation. The highly trained team members subdue an inmate before he can strike any blows; they are so swift that the inmate is stripped, handcuffed, and picked up and carried away in a matter of minutes. Of course, the very depersonalization of such teams leads to worries about abuse. In the same way an inmate can be subdued, stripped, and moved by the team, they can also take him down a flight of stairs, with his head hanging and hitting every step. Their masks give them the anonymity that was not available to officers in the "old days," when inmates were just called into the captain's office for a "tune up." In fact, in some prisons it is a practice not to let it be known which officers are on the team—because of the hatred that prisoners feel for team members.

Loyalty and Whistleblowing

There are many similarities between police and correctional staff in use-of-force abuses, the code of silence, and feelings of isolation. There are also differences. The most striking difference between the two jobs is that C.O.'s must deal with the same people daily in a closed, oppressive environment. Police officers have freedom of movement and can avoid peers or citizen troublemakers to a certain extent, but C.O.'s have no such luxury. If a C.O. fears an inmate, he or she must still face him or her every day. If a C.O. violates the correctional subcultural code, the sanctions are felt perhaps even more acutely because one must work closely with other C.O.'s all day long. Whereas police officers cite the importance of being able to trust other officers as backups in violent situations, one could make the argument that C.O.'s need to trust each other more completely, more implicitly, and more frequently, given that violence in some institutions is pervasive and unprovoked, and the C.O. carries no weapon. An officer described to Kauffman (1988: 207) the result of violating peer trust:

> If an incident went down, there was no one to cover my back. That's a very important lesson to learn. You need your back covered and my back wasn't covered there at all. And at one point I was in fear of being set up by guards. I was put in dangerous situations purposely. That really happened to me.

Fear of violating the code of silence is one reason that officers do not report wrongdoing. Loyalty is another. C.O.'s feel a strong *esprit de corps* that is similar to the previously discussed loyalty among police. This positive loyalty also results in covering for other officers and not testifying or reporting offenses. McCarthy (1991) discusses types of corrupt behaviors in a prison, including theft, trafficking in contraband, embezzlement, and misuse of authority. These offenses are known yet unreported by other correctional officers because of loyalty and subcultural prohibitions against "ratting."

A pattern of complicity also prevents reporting. New officers cannot possibly follow all the many rules and regulations that exist in a prison and still adequately deal with inmates on a day-to-day basis. Therefore, before too long, they find themselves involved in activity that could result in disciplinary action. Because others are usually aware of this activity and do not inform supervisors, an implicit conspiracy of silence develops so that no one is turned in for anything because each of the others who might witness this wrongdoing has engaged in behavior that could also be sanctioned (Lombardo, 1981: 79).

General Conduct and the "Good Officer"

Historically, correctional officers have been described as role models for inmates. In reference to an early and idealistic view of who should be hired and for what reasons, one author writes that this was a "pursuit of men with 'special gifts of personality and character' capable of achieving the moral transformation of their fellow men merely by the exercise of 'personal influence'" (Hawkins, cited in Crouch, 1980: 55). This was, by and large, probably a false dream, but it has always been true that no one else in corrections has more day-to-day contact with inmates than C.O.'s do. For this reason, it is important to look at the types of individuals hired to fill correctional officer positions and how they respond to the environment of the prison.

Officers, of course, are individuals, and the most interesting research in this area is that which describes the ways they respond to the demands and job pressures of corrections. Some researchers have found that officers fall into various adaptational types: some are violence-prone, using the role of correctional officer to act out an authoritarian role; another type serves time in prison much the same way as the inmates do, avoiding trouble and hoping that nothing goes wrong on their shift; and other officers seek to enlarge their job description and perceive their role as including counseling and helping the inmate rather than merely locking doors and signing passes. This type of officer has been called the human service officer and incorporates the tasks of providing goods and services, acting as a referral agent or advocate, and helping with institutional adjustment problems (Johnson, 1987: 142).

Not surprisingly, C.O.'s and inmates tend to agree on a description of a good officer. A good officer is described as one who treats all inmates fairly with no favoritism, but who does not always follow rules to the letter. Discretion is used judicially; when a good officer makes a decision to bypass rules, all involved tend to agree that it is the right decision. A good officer is not quick to use force, nor afraid of force if it becomes necessary. A good officer treats inmates in a professional manner and gives them the respect they deserve as human beings. A good officer will treat the inmate in the way anyone would like to be treated; if the inmate abuses the officer, then that inmate earns different treatment. In some cases such an officer will go far outside regular duties to aid an inmate who is sincerely in need; however, he or she can detect gameplaying and cannot be manipulated. These traits—consistency, fairness, and flexibility—are confirmed as valuable by research (Johnson, 1987: 139). Although many officers in prisons reach this ideal, the trend today seems to be a less honorable approach to the position because of the pressures described below.

Recent changes have taken away much of the service functions that C.O.'s used to perform. Lombardo (1997), in his update of an older study, found that in the ten years that ensued since his first study, much of the ability of C.O.'s to grant favors had been taken away. For instance, telephones in the yard eliminated the need for C.O.'s to run interference for inmates and get them a pass to make a phone call. This situation increased the autonomy of inmates, but it reduced the ability of the C.O.'s to develop helping relationships with inmates

---

QUOTATION

They've got problems. They get bad news letters, they stay in and brood about it. I call the service unit and get a "it's none of your business." . . . I had a guy working for me, a good worker, a Muslim. Everybody was down on him. They said he'd be a bum. I said let's see what he does. I asked what his problem was and he said that he got a bad letter. His little girl had an operation. He didn't know how serious it was, but he was worried. I tried to make arrangements for him to make a phone call. I had a couple of friends up there, you make them after a while. . . . He got his phone call and perked up.

SOURCE: Anonymous correctional officer quoted in Lombardo, 1997: 196.

or, to put a more negative interpretation on their loss, it reduced their ability to create debts from the inmate—favors owed in return for favors given. C.O.'s have much less discretion today, and practically every decision that, in the past, had been made by a C.O. is now made by sergeants and specialized officers. Consequently, C.O.'s feel less responsibility to help inmates or even take responsibility for security issues.

Like police, correctional officers feel that court decisions and administrative goals have not supported their needs and have sacrificed their safety to meet inmates' demands. One result of this feeling that superiors and society do not protect their interests is an individualistic response to the ethical issues that may come up in the course of the job. The following presents a fairly negative view of the correctional officer's ethical position (Carroll, cited in Crouch, 1980: 318):

> [T]he officers are not working for the inmates, they are working for themselves. Unable to secure compliance with their directives by the enforcement of a set of impersonal rules, they seek to secure compliance by means of friendships, overlooking infractions, and providing highly desired information to inmates. Their behavior is not so much a repudiation of the goal of custodial control as it is an attempt to maintain order, and at the same time to protect themselves, in the face of institutional changes that have made order more difficult to maintain and their position more vulnerable.

Correctional officers report much stress, and stress-related illnesses such as hypertension are common, as well as social problems such as alcoholism and divorce. Some reports indicate that these problems exist in higher numbers with correctional officers than with police officers. Correctional officers feel criticized and even scorned by many, and it is little wonder that they adapt to their role by such means, yet it is important to understand the consequences of such a position. Kauffman (1988: 222) talked to officers who reported that they had lost their morality in the prison. These officers experienced anguish at the change that was wrought in them by the prison environment:

> Initially, many attempted to avoid engaging in behavior injurious to inmates by refusing (openly or surreptitiously) to carry out certain duties and by displacing their aggressions onto others outside the prison or themselves. As their involvement in the prison world grew and their ability to abstain from morally questionable actions within the prison declined, they attempted to neutralize their own feelings of guilt by regarding prisons as separate moral realms with their own distinct set of moral standards or by viewing inmates as individuals outside the protection of moral laws. When such efforts failed, they shut their minds to what others were doing and to what they were doing themselves.

Without a strong moral and ethical code, correctional officers may find themselves drifting into relativistic egoism: what benefits the individual is considered acceptable, despite long-term effects or inconsistencies with their role and their personal value system. This results in feelings of disillusionment and anomie, and the side effects can be serious dissatisfaction and depression. To maintain a sense of morality in an inherently coercive environment is no easy task, yet a strong set of individual ethics is probably the best defense against being changed by the negative environment of the prison.

Corruption

McCarthy (1995) discusses the major types of corruption engaged in by correctional officers and other officials in institutional corrections. His categories include theft, trafficking, embezzlement, and misuse of authority. Under misuse of authority he details the following:

- accepting gratuities for special consideration for legitimate purposes
- accepting gratuities for protection of illicit activities
- mistreatment/harassment or extortion of inmates
- mismanagement (e.g., prison industries)
- miscellaneous abuses

Open corruption existed thirty years ago in many prisons, as described in the boxed quotation from Tom Murton, but scandals also continue today with predictable regularity.

An associate superintendent from a prison in Pennsylvania testified before an investigative committee of the state legislature after a four-day riot in which inmates and officers were savagely beaten (cited in Hassine, 1996: 149–152). His testimony detailed the widespread corrupt practices of many of the officers and supervisors in the prison, including the following:

- An officer was beaten up by other officers in the prison.
- An officer was caught smuggling in contraband (sneakers, coffee, chewing gum, letters, etc.) for inmates.
- An officer was caught attempting to deliver methamphetamine.
- An officer allowed an inmate into restricted housing, where he beat another inmate for two hours.

QUOTATION

Rackets abounded in Arkansas, and these rackets forced inmates to pay bribes in order to receive goods and services to which they were already entitled. For example, inmates who ran the kitchen charged other inmates for food. Inmates who could not pay the bribes did not get enough to eat. In the hospital, a prison doctor paid each inmate $5 for blood plasma, which he sold to a laboratory for $15, making an estimated $140,000 a year.

SOURCE: Murton and Hyams, 1969: 109.

- An officer raped an inmate.
- A female officer sent an inmate money and personal items, visited an inmate at another institution, and wrote letters to inmates.
- A staff member appeared at work under the influence of cocaine.
- An instructor was found with a box of ammunition and alcoholic beverages in his van at the rear gate of the prison.
- An activities director embezzled funds from the inmate Jaycees and Lifers association.
- An officer engaged an inmate in a fistfight in the dayroom over losing a bet with the inmate.
- An instructor smeared peanut butter into a black inmate's hair, put flour and jelly in other inmates' hair, rubbed an onion in the face of another, conducted a mock hanging off a steam pipe dressed as a Ku Klux Klan member, and abused others verbally—his actions were directed only to African American inmates.
- A labor foreman purposely slammed on his brakes and flipped an inmate over the hood of his truck.
- A food service supervisor allowed a food fight in the kitchen.
- An officer engaged in horseplay—punching and wrestling an inmate.
- An officer was investigated for shoplifting.

Questionable practices are engaged in by individuals in every level of the prison structure. In Texas, the director of the Department of Corrections was investigated for his business association with a Canadian company that made VitaPro—a vegetable-based protein substance that evidently tasted bad and created digestive problems for some people. It was discovered that (a) the state prison system had warehouses full of this product because inmates wouldn't eat it and the state was locked into a contract that mandated a certain number of pounds of it had to be bought every month; (b) the contract, which was

---

Graterford Prison—Pennsylvania

Inmates told a recent State Senate hearing that it was common practice among prisoners at Graterford to avoid punishment for infractions and to cover up evidence of drug use by paying officers to alter records.

At the hearing, an inmate who was a clerk at Graterford from 1992 to this January, Jonathan Brown, told the State Senate Judiciary Committee about officers' selling furloughs and other privileges, and about drug trafficking among officers. He said [an inmate] paid officers to cover up his disciplinary infractions, though the allegations have not been proved and are under investigation.

SOURCE: Purdy, M., 1995, reprinted in Hassine, 1996: 156.

Prison Audit Finds Questionable Expenses

Some agencies or firms doing business with the Texas prison system illegally used taxpayers' money for $1200 worth of Christmas presents for judges, for a $1600 fine for federal safety violations and for political campaign contributions, a new state audit revealed Thursday. . . .

SOURCE: Ward, 1996: B1.

---

worth millions, had not been approved by the Board of Criminal Justice, an overseer body, because of a loophole that allowed products for prison industry to avoid the bidding and approval process, yet the only relationship this product had to prison industry was that prisoners repackaged the stuff and sent it to other prisons; (c) the director, immediately upon leaving his job, started as a thousand-dollar-per-day consultant with the same company.

Corruption exists in prisons today, and it will probably continue to exist, but there are measures that can be used to address the existence of corruption. Correctional managers should generate a strong anti-corruption policy (obviously, managers should not be engaging in corrupt practices themselves). Such a policy would include proactive measures such as mechanisms to investigate and detect wrongdoing, reduce opportunities for corruption, screen employees using state-of-the-art psychological tools, improve working conditions, and provide good role models in the form of supervisors and administrators who follow the Code of Ethics presented earlier in this chapter (McCarthy, 1991).

Jail Officers

Very little has been written about jail officers. They are often considered a hybrid of police and correctional officers. Often, jail officers are deputies who must complete their assignment at the jail before they can "promote" to street patrol. Sometimes jail officers are those street deputies who are being punished for some misbehavior on the street. In other situations, jail officers are not deputies, have a separate title and pay scale (usually lower), and often aspire to pass peace officer certification and fill deputy slots. In all the above situations, the tasks and skills associated with managing jail inmates are discounted and ignored. There is a need for greater recognition of the profession of jail officer; the position should not merely be a dreaded rite-of-passage assignment, a punishment, or a stepping-stone to deputy status, since the body of knowledge required to do the job well is different from that which a street deputy needs. Recently, there has been an attempt to professionalize the image of jail officers, starting again with a code of ethics.

Arguably, the job of jail officer is even more difficult than that of correctional officer since jail officers must deal with a transitory population rather than a fairly stable one. Offenders come into jail intoxicated, suffer from undi-

---

American Jail Association Code of Ethics for Jail Officers

As an officer employed in a detention/correctional capacity, I swear (or affirm) to be a good citizen and a credit to my community, state, and nation at all times. I will abstain from all questionable behavior which might bring disrepute to the agency for which I work, my family, my community, and my associates. My lifestyle will be above and beyond reproach and I will constantly strive to set an example of a professional who performs his/her duties according to the laws of our country, state, and community and the policies, procedures, written and verbal orders, and regulations of the agency for which I work.

On the job I promise to:

Keep — The institution secure so as to safeguard my community and the lives of the staff, inmates, and visitors on the premises.

Work — With each individual firmly and fairly without regard to rank, status, or condition.

Maintain — A positive demeanor when confronted with stressful situations of scorn, ridicule, danger and/or chaos.

Report — Either in writing or by word of mouth to the proper authorities those things which should be reported, and keep silent about matters which are to remain confidential according to the laws and rules of the agency and government.

Manage — And supervise the inmates in an evenhanded and courteous manner.

Refrain — At all times from becoming personally involved in the lives of the inmates and their families.

Treat — All visitors to the jail with politeness and respect and do my utmost to ensure that they observe the jail regulations.

Take — Advantage of all education and training opportunities designed to assist me to become a more competent officer.

Communicate — With people in or outside of the jail, whether by phone, written word, or word of mouth, in such a way so as not to reflect in a negative manner upon my agency.

Contribute — To a jail environment which will keep the inmate involved in activities designed to improve his/her attitude and character.

Support — All activities of a professional nature through membership and participation that will continue to elevate the status of those who operate our nation's jails.

Do my best through word and deed to present an image to the public at large of a jail professional, committed to progress for an improved and enlightened criminal justice system.

SOURCE: American Jail Association. Reprinted with permission.

---

agnosed epilepsy or other diseases, may suffer overdoses (as in the chilling newspaper account of the overdose death), and may be suicidal. Visitation is more frequent, and family issues are more problematic in jails than prisons. The constant activity and chaotic environment of a jail often create unique

---

Jail Guards Taunt Prisoner Dying of Cocaine Overdose

FORT PIERCE, FLA.—A man who swallowed cocaine when he was arrested died after jailers ignored his pleas for help and taunted him in a three-hour ordeal captured on video by a jail surveillance camera.

Two sheriff's deputies were later fired, and five others disciplined.

Anderson Tate moaned, thrashed and chanted prayers for more than three hours while bound to a chair Dec. 3 at the St. Lucie County Jail. Jail employees and deputies walked past him, and one made fun of him.

"I don't want to die. I'm burning up," he said on the footage released Wednesday. "I'm 300 degrees. I've got too much cocaine in my system."

State prosecutors are investigating and will decide whether to bring criminal charges against the officers.

Ellis Rubin, an attorney for Tate's mother and sister, said he will seek a federal civil rights investigation. Tate is black; six of the officers are white, and the other is Hispanic.

"I can't see them tying a white woman to a chair and taunting her for 3½ hours," Rubin said. "We know the routine, especially where blacks are concerned. It's just a disgrace."

Tate had been pulled over for not having a license plate and driving without a valid license. He apparently swallowed some cocaine he was carrying when he was arrested but initially refused medical treatment, said St. Lucie County Undersheriff Dennis Williams.

One of the fired deputies taunted Tate, clapping and stomping his feet to the beat of Tate's chants and fanning him with a clipboard when he said he was burning up, Williams said.

Jail officials didn't become alarmed until the 22-year-old man went into convulsions and stopped breathing. Tate died about 11 hours later at a hospital.

Rubin said a jail nurse checked on Tate three times.

Williams called the officers' behavior unacceptable. Deputies told investigators that they knew something wasn't right but that everyone assumed someone else was taking charge, the undersheriff said.

SOURCE: Associated Press. *Austin American-Statesman,* 8 Feb. 1997: A16. Reprinted with permission.

---

ethical dilemmas. One can also find the same type of unethical behavior that one finds with police and correctional officers—jail officers can be uncaring and insensitive to human needs. Then, again, that description has sometimes been directed to those in the correctional environment who are supposed to help the inmate—the treatment staff.

TREATMENT STAFF

Treatment specialists have their own ethical dilemmas. Although hired by the state, many feel their loyalties lie with the offender. Prison psychologists may be privy to information or confessions that they feel bound to hold in confidence even though the security of the prison may be jeopardized. The professional goal of all treatment specialists is to help the client. This may be fundamentally inconsistent with the prison (or jail) environment, which emphasizes punishment.

Making the decision on whether the individual is cured or not also involves mixed loyalties. Any treatment necessarily involves risk. How much risk one is willing to take depends on whether the public should be protected at all costs, in which case few people would be released, or whether one feels that the public must risk possible victimization in order to give offenders a chance to prove themselves.

Another dilemma is the administration of treatment programs. If a program has potential, someone must make decisions on who gets into it. Ideally, one would want similar people in the treatment program and in a control group. However, it is sometimes hard to justify withholding the program from some people who may sincerely wish to participate. Laypersons have difficulty understanding the concepts of random sampling and control groups. Pressure sometimes exists to admit anyone who sincerely wants a chance to participate despite what this might do to experimental design.

Another, more basic issue is the ethics of providing treatment to people who do not want it. In particular, psychiatrists and psychologists have to reconcile their professional ethics in two fields, corrections and psychiatry, and at times this is hard to do. Psychiatrists in corrections, for instance, feel at times that they are being used for social control rather than treatment. Disruptive inmates, although needing treatment, pose security risks to prison officials, so intervention, especially chemotherapy, often takes the form of control rather than treatment.

The practice of using antipsychotic drugs is especially problematic for treatment professionals. Although the Supreme Court has determined that the administration of such drugs to unwilling inmates is not unconstitutional, the practice must be scrutinized and held to due-process protections in order to uphold professional ethical standards. Should a helping professional ever be

---

QUOTATION

[discussing an inmate who was not violent, but was extremely talkative, loud, and inclined to discuss his delusions]

As it was, John's illness needed to be controlled, not because he was unhappy with it, but because those around him found it objectionable. What can the psychiatrist do in cases like this? He has the uneasy task of respecting "his" patient's wishes, of listening to the demands of the prison guards to keep the patient from disturbing the peace, of obeying the orders from the prison bureaucracy to treat the patient, of heeding the request from the other inmates to do something to quiet "the crazy guy . . . or else," and last but not least, of paying attention to his own needs to do his best and to obtain a modicum of job satisfaction. Practically all of these demands are antithetical.

SOURCE: Arboleda-Florez, 1983: 52.

A Prescription for Torture (March 18, 1990)

Every federal prison has men shuffling around hallways and cellblocks as if they are walking in slow motion. There are some here at Phoenix. It's common practice in federal prisons to heavily medicate those who are perceived as a threat to staff.

But, as I and other prisoners can attest, there are even more violent men who regularly kill fellow convicts. These types are transferred to another prison after they kill someone, and they often do it again. Many of them aren't ever medicated with psychotropic drugs. As long as they are no threat to staff, they continue their murderous sprees. This sends us convicts a pretty clear message.

The people who are medicated become defenseless in the convict community and are often seriously abused by predatory fellow convicts. They are physically unable to defend themselves, and that fact increases their paranoia manyfold.

A little-acknowledged aspect of chemical straitjackets is the direct threat they pose to law-abiding society.

A violent man at Lompoc who was nearing the end of a 10-year-sentence was kept heavily dosed with antipsychotic drugs. He'd done every day of his sentence because of lost good time. I used to watch him trying to run the track. He ran as if he were under water. It took him fifteen minutes to complete a lap that I ran in three minutes, and I'm no speed demon.

He was so disagreeable, paranoid, and violent that no one wanted to approach him. When his sentence was finished, the guards walked him to the front gate and shoved him out into the free world—no halfway house, no parole—and I doubt he went off to a psychiatrist and got a prescription to continue on psychotropic drugs. I've often wondered what happened when he regained his physical momentum after ten years of suppression by disabling chemicals. . . .

SOURCE: Martin, D. *Committing Journalism: The Prison Writings of Red Hog* (New York: Norton, 1993): 225–227. Article originally appeared in the *San Francisco Chronicle*.

---

involved in administering unwanted mind-altering medication? That is a question that many prison psychiatrists will have to answer for themselves.

Psychologists have their own ethical code, and some principles seem especially relevant to corrections. For instance, under the principle of responsibility, psychologists are instructed to prevent the distortion, misuse, or suppression of their psychological findings by the institution or agency by which they are employed. This obviously affects institutional psychologists, who may feel that their findings are compromised by custody concerns. For instance, something confessed to in a counseling session may be used in parole reports to prevent release, findings may be used to block transfer, behavior brought out in psychological testing may be punished, and so on ("Ethical Principles," 1981: 633).

Other principles involve the treatment of clients: "In their professional roles, psychologists avoid any action that will violate or diminish the legal and civil rights of clients or of others who may be affected by their actions" ("Ethical Principles," 1981: 634). This principle may be applicable to certain treat-

ETHICS FOR CORRECTIONAL PROFESSIONALS

ment programs in prison that restrict inmates' liberty or choice—for instance, some of the behavior modification programs have been questioned legally and ethically. Many treatment professionals feel behavior modification has been subverted by the prison environment. Although it is extremely effective in inducing behavioral change, some professionals feel uneasy participating in a punishment-oriented program in an environment that is already one of deprivation. The coercive power inherent in the prison setting creates the potential for unethical practices by treatment personnel. The fact that prisoners are captive audiences makes them attractive subjects for experimentation of all kinds. Most programs ask for volunteers rather than force participation, but in a prison environment the assumption is always there that release is tied to compliance, so what may appear as voluntary action may be the result of no choice at all.

The psychologist's or psychiatrist's responsibility to innocent victims is being scrutinized more closely today. What is the ethical responsibility of a counselor when an offender threatens future violence toward a particular victim? As in the legal profession, confidentiality is an issue for psychologists. As their ethical principles state,

> Psychologists have a primary obligation to respect the confidentiality of information obtained from persons in the course of their work as psychologists. They reveal such information to others only with the consent of the person or the person's legal representative, except in those unusual circumstances in which not to do so would result in clear danger to the person or to others. Where appropriate, psychologists inform their clients of the legal limits of confidentiality. ("Ethical Principles," 1981: 636)

Some psychiatrists find it hard to be associated with something as damaging as prison and feel a moral resistance to involvement with prison treatment efforts, given the negative effects that are inevitable. As Thomas (quoted in Tanay, 1982: 386) writes,

> The length of sentences and the nature of maximum security prisons combine to damage the personalities of the prisoners to such a degree as to make it especially difficult for them to function as autonomous and independent individuals in a free society following their release. I believe that whenever a man serves three or more years in a maximum security prison, the experience will usually have a lasting deleterious effect on his personality.

Even for those who feel comfortable working in prison, treatment and security concerns clash in many instances. The treatment professional must choose between two value systems. To emphasize security concerns puts the psychiatrist or counselor in a role of a custodian with professional training used only to better control inmate behavior. To emphasize treatment concerns puts the professional in an antagonistic role *vis-à-vis* the security staff, and they may find themselves in situations where these concerns directly conflict. For instance, if the superintendent demands to see a client's file to support a disciplinary committee's decision, should the psychiatrist surrender the information that was given in confidence? In answer to this dilemma, the psychiatrist or psychologist should probably have never allowed the inmate to assume that information regarding rule infractions or potential wrongdoing could ever be confidential. On the other hand, if inmates believe that counselors and psychologists can offer no confidentiality protections, then is there any possibility of a trusting relationship? The issues that confront treatment personnel in prison seem to always involve the conflicting goals of punishment and treatment.

Although religion has always had a role in corrections, the separation of church and state has relegated religion to a separate element, unsanctioned while not necessarily unsupported by prison officials. This may change if a program in Texas becomes popular. Newspaper reports indicate that Texas will allow a faith-based pre-release program to run in Texas prisons and will provide security staff for the program. Prison Fellowship Ministries, Inc., a Washington, D.C., group headed by Watergate figure Charles Colson, will start a special center in one Texas prison. The program will run all the programming in that unit. The program staff promise they won't be involved in any "proselytizing." However, the program is Christ-centered, biblically rooted, and values-based, and will emphasize family, community, and Jesus Christ. The group will provide staff and run free of charge for two years, but then expect to seek funding from the state. Inmates in the program are all volunteers (Ward, 1996). The existence of such a program raises several issues. First is the worry that some inmates will have their freedom of religion impaired—if the program offers hope for early release or other advantages, Muslims may take advantage of such elements only if they also compromise their faith. However, another element of the program is a return to an ethics-based approach (specifically using a religious ethical system) for correctional programming. It will be interesting to watch and see if the program has any greater success than secular attempts to change offenders' value systems.

PROBATION AND PAROLE OFFICERS

Formal ethical guidelines for probation and parole officers are provided by the ACA code previously presented, as well as their own codes. Probation and parole officers are considered more professional than correctional officers: they typically have at least a bachelor's degree if not a graduate degree, they are subject to fewer organizational controls in the form of rule books and policies, and they have a great deal of discretion. The formal ethics of the profession is summarized by the ideal of service—to the community and to the offender—and herein lies the crux of most of the ethical issues that present themselves. Whether to favor meeting offenders' needs over community needs or vice versa is at the heart of a number of different ethical dilemmas for the probation and parole officer. Other ethical issues are more similar to those encountered in the other subsystems discussed; they primarily revolve around decisions to substitute personal values and goals for organizational values.

In the next several sections we will touch on some of the themes of previous chapters—the use of discretion, officer subcultures, and relationships with clients. Although our treatment of these subjects may be more cursory than what has been accorded to other criminal justice professionals in this text, this by no means implies that these issues are less important.

Use of Discretion

Discretion in probation exists at the point of sentencing: probation officers make recommendations to judges concerning sentences. Discretion also exists during supervision, as probation officers decide when to file violation reports, decide what recommendation to make to the judge during revocation hearings, and make numerous decisions along the way regarding the people on their caseload. Parole boards also make decisions regarding release, and parole officers have the same discretion in managing their caseload that probation officers do. What are the criteria used for these decisions? Usually, the risk to the public is the primary factor, but other considerations also intrude. Some of these other considerations may be ethical; some may not. How would one evaluate the criteria of race, crime, family ties, the crowding in institutions, the status of the victim, the judge's preference, or the publicity of the crime? Are these ethical criteria or not?

Federal Probation Officers' Association

As a Federal Probation Officer, I am dedicated to rendering professional service to the courts, the parole authorities, and the community at large in effecting the social adjustment of the offender.

I will conduct my personal life with decorum, will neither accept nor grant favors in connection with my office, and will put loyalty to moral principles above personal consideration.

I will uphold the law with dignity and with complete awareness of the prestige and stature of the judicial system of which I am a part. I will be ever cognizant of my responsibility to the community which I serve.

I will strive to be objective in the performance of my duties, respect the inalienable rights of all persons, appreciate the inherent worth of the individual, and hold inviolate those confidences which can be reposed in me.

I will cooperate with my fellow workers and related agencies and will continually attempt to improve my professional standards through the seeking of knowledge and understanding.

I recognize my office as a symbol of public faith and I accept it as a public trust to be held as long as I am true to the ethics of the Federal Probation Service. I will constantly strive to achieve these objectives and ideals, dedicating myself to my chosen profession.

SOURCE: Adopted September 1960. Federal Probation Officers' Association, Washington, D.C. Revised March 1993. The Federal Probation Pretrial Officers Association. Reprinted with permission. All rights reserved.

Probation Officers' Dilemmas—What Would You Do?

- A judge directed me to change my negative recommendation for probation to a favorable recommendation.
- I found out that my supervisor changed a negative recommendation I had to a positive recommendation.
- A judge instructed us that if we can convince [female] defendants to get Norplant he will waive court costs and fines.

Probation officers write presentence reports to help judges decide sentences, but research has found that there may be errors in the information presented and that some officers are not as thorough as others in gathering information. This may not make much difference if it is true, as some have found, that probation officers' recommendations and judges' decisions are almost completely determined by the present offense and prior record (Whitehead, 1991).

Some practices in decision making are clearly unethical and illegal. Peter Maas's (1983) book, *Marie,* details a scheme in Tennessee that involved "selling" paroles to convicts (this will be discussed in more detail in a later section); however, other situations are perhaps more difficult to judge as unethical or not. In a controversy in Texas, ex-parole board members were found to have sold their services as "parole consultants" to inmates and inmates' families in order to help them obtain a favorable release decision. Although the practice evidently was not against any state law and those who participated described their help as simply explaining the process and helping the inmate prepare a presentation to the board, many viewed it as unethical. There is at least the possibility that what the inmate was buying was an ex-parole board member's influence. Anytime government officials go into the private sector and trade on their status as ex-officials, we feel uncomfortable. There are specific laws against influence peddling at some levels of government reflecting this discomfort. In some situations, the possibility of private gain may influence how the official performs his or her job while in office, as in the case of military leaders who decide on contracts with private vendors (such as Lockheed) and then end up in highly paid, visible positions with the company immediately upon retirement. In other instances, the ability to provide an open door or inside information is considered unfair when used only for those who are willing to pay, as in the case of ex–White House staff who sell their services as consultants to foreign countries or corporations. The situation with ex-parole officials in Texas was brought to light when a serial killer was arrested for yet another murder while out on parole; when how he obtained parole was investigated, it was discovered that one of these ex-parole board members/"parole consultants" had been hired by the inmate. Whether or not that had anything to do with a favorable parole decision will never be known, but many allege there is at least the appearance of impropriety in the arrangement, and steps were taken to eliminate the practice.

Officer Subculture

The subculture of probation and parole officers has never been as extensively documented as that of police and correctional officers. Due to differences between these professions, the subculture of the former is not as pervasive or strong as that of the latter. First, probation and parole officers do not feel as isolated as police or correctional officers do. They experience no stigmatization, they have normal working hours, they do not wear a depersonalizing uniform, and they have a less obviously coercive relationship with their clients. These factors reduce the need for a subculture. On the other hand, one can probably identify some norms that might be found in any probation or parole office. First, there is a norm of cynicism toward clients. The subculture promotes the idea that clients are inept, deviant, and irredeemable. Probation and parole professionals who express positive attitudes toward clients' capacity for change are kidded as naive and guileless. Second, there is a pervasive subcultural norm of lethargy or minimal work output. This norm is supported by the view that officers are underpaid and overworked. Third, a norm of individualism can be identified. This relates to the idea that while parole and probation officers may seek opinions from other professionals in the office, there is an unspoken rule that each runs his or her own caseload; to offer unsolicited opinions about decisions another person makes about his or her client violates this norm of autonomy.

Although there does not seem to be the "blue curtain of secrecy" to the same extent as found in policing, there is no doubt a norm against informing on fellow officers for unethical or illegal behaviors. This relates somewhat to the norm of individualism, but is also part of the pervasive occupational subculture against informing on the wrongdoing of colleagues. Probation and parole officers may see and hear unethical behaviors and not feel comfortable in coming forward with such information. If they work in an office where the norm against exposing such wrongdoing is strong, they may indeed suffer similar sanctions as police and correctional officers for exposing others' wrongdoing.

Probation and parole officers have been described as adapting different roles on the job. In the same way that police have been described by the watchman, caretaker, and law enforcer typology, probation and parole officers have been described by their orientation to the job and individual adaptation

---

Probation Officers' Dilemmas—What Would You Do?

- One morning a fellow officer was meeting with a probationer. This officer was yelling profanities and was very rude to this probationer, for whatever reasons.
- A close colleague at work was dating a probationer and they were planning to move in together. The close colleague told me about it. What should be done?

to organizational goals. For instance, Souryal (1992) summarizes other litera-ture in his description of the following types: the punitive law enforcer, the welfare/therapeutic practitioner, the passive time server, and the combined model.

Different ethical issues can be discussed in relation to each of these types. For instance, the punitive law enforcer may need to examine his or her use of authority. This officer may have a tendency to use illegal threats and violate the due-process protections that each client deserves. The welfare/therapeutic worker may need to think about natural law rights of privacy and autonomy. These officers have a tendency to infringe on clients' privacy more because of their mindset that they are helping the client, and indeed they may be, but the client may prefer less help and more privacy. The passive time server needs to be aware of ethical formalism and concerns of duty. All of us may have some tendency to be a time server in our respective professions. It is important to continue to take personal inventories and ask whether we are still putting in a "day's work for a day's pay."

As is the case for many of the other criminal justice professionals we have discussed in this book, parole and probation officers often have a great deal of flexibility in their day. They leave the office to make field contacts; they often "trade" weekdays for weekend days, since weekends are more conducive to home visits. This flexibility is necessary if they are to do the job, but some abuse it and use the freedom to accomplish personal tasks or spend time at home. Some offices have attempted to prevent this behavior by instituting measures such as time clocks and strict controls on movements, but these con-trols are inconsistent with professionalism and not conducive to the nature of the task. Other offices develop norms that accept unethical practices and lethargy. Once this occurs, it becomes a difficult pattern to change. If it is al-ready present, a single officer will have a hard time not falling into the pattern. If all officers feel overwhelmed by their caseloads and the relative lack of power they have to do anything about failure, then the result may be that they throw up their hands and adapt a "who cares?" attitude. If the supervisor does not exhibit a commitment to the goal of the organization, does not encourage workers, treats certain officers with favoritism, or seems more concerned with his or her personal career than with the needs of the office, then there is an inevitable deterioration of morale.

Probation Officers' Dilemmas—What Would You Do?

- I took a supervisor's job and had an officer that didn't do anything—all day. Read magazines at her desk. The thing was, I was told I couldn't fire her, she had already been transferred around, and now I was stuck with her.
- In one office I worked, there was an officer who took naps in the afternoon. It was well known. He would close his door and lie down on the floor. After a couple hours he would open his door again and go on. No one did any-thing about it.

Whitehead (1991) discusses workers' frustration over incompetents being promoted, low wages, and high caseloads that lead to burnout. Souryal (1992) notes that low pay, a public view that probation and parole are ineffective, and the politicization of parole and probation are factors in professionals' feeling that their role is ambiguous, contradictory, and politically vulnerable. Disillusionment becomes almost inevitable. Although these issues exist in many organizations, they are especially problematic in a profession that requires a great deal of emotional investment on the part of the practitioner. If the organization does not encourage and support good workers, then it is no wonder that what develops is an informal subculture that encourages minimum effort and treats organizational goals with sarcasm and cynicism.

Caseload Supervision

Discretion exists not only at the recommendation to release stage, but also throughout supervision. Officers do not make the decision to revoke, but they do make the decision to file a violation report and make a recommendation to the judge or the parole hearing examiner as to whether to continue on supervision status with perhaps new conditions, or revocation and a prison sentence. Many do not submit violation reports automatically upon discovery of every offender infraction—in this way they are like police officers who practice selective enforcement of the laws. And, like police officers, some of their criteria for decision making are ethical, and some are not. Also, like police officers, many report ethical dilemmas when the law doesn't seem to be able to take into account social realities, such as poverty.

The discretion to decide when to write a violation report is a powerful element in the control the officer has over the offender, but it obviously can be a difficult decision to make sometimes. If the officer excuses serious violations,

---

Probation Officers' Dilemmas—What Would You Do?

- I discovered that the applicant was an illegal alien but had a family of four with a baby who was born with a defect. His wife did not work and he was the sole provider of the family. The dilemma was that if INS was contacted, the individual would be deported while his family stayed in [city] with no support.
- Do I collect fees from a client who is a single mother with three children and take the money out of her budget and allow the single mother to neglect the needs of her children, or do I collect the fees and disregard the problems the client is struggling with, and alienate the client more?
- I had a single parent with three hyperactive attention deficit disorder young children. She receives no support from ex-husband. Her mother wants nothing to do with her or the children as Mother believes God is punishing her. She works as a topless dancer but hates it. She continues dancing because it pays the bills so well. In an effort to deal with stress she smokes marijuana on a fairly regular basis. Clearly a violation of probation. If I file on her, she will either go into long-term treatment or prison. What happens to the kids?

such as possessing a firearm or continuing drug use, and the decision to do so is based on personal favoritism, fear, or bribery, then that officer is putting the community at risk unethically. Those situations in which the officer sincerely believes the offender made a mistake, has extraordinary excuses for such misbehavior, and is a good risk still present a danger to the community. Is the decision any more ethical because of the officer's belief in the offender? Would it be more ethical to conduct oneself "by the book" and always submit violation reports when the offender committed any violation, including a purely technical one?

Probation and parole officers are presented with other dilemmas in their supervision of offenders. For instance, the offender often acquires a job without the employer's knowledge of his or her previous criminality. Is it the duty of the officer to inform the employer and thereby imperil the continued employment of the offender? What about when offenders become personally involved with others and refuse to tell them about their past history? Does the probation or parole officer have a duty to the unwary party? Recently, the issue of confidentiality *vis-à-vis* AIDS has emerged. If the probation or parole officer knows or suspects that the offender is HIV positive and the offender begins an intimate relationship with someone, does the officer have a duty to warn the other party? Most states protect the confidentiality of victims of AIDS, and in these cases the officer has a legal duty *not to* disclose. This issue is extremely problematic, and the rights of the offender, the rights of unwary innocents, and the responsibilities of society are not well sorted out at this point.

What is the probation or parole officer's responsibility to the offender's family? If they are unwilling to help the offender and perhaps fear his or her presence, should the officer find a reason for revocation? Again, these questions revolve around competing loyalties to public and client. The correctional professional must balance these interests in every decision, and these decisions are often not easy to make.

There are other issues regarding family. Again, very similar to the police officer, at times the probation officer's role as a family member, or friend, conflicts with the professional role. Family members and/or friends may expect special treatment or expect that the officer will use his or her powers for unethical purposes. These are always difficult dilemmas because family and friends may not be sympathetic to the individual's ethical responsibilities to the organization and to society at large.

Probation Officers' Dilemmas—What Would You Do?

- I had a cousin on probation for his second DWI. No one in the family knows he is on probation. At a family gathering I see the probationer drinking (more than one). What do I do?
- A friend from high school has a boyfriend on probation. The boyfriend has violated his conditions of probation and an mtrp is being filed in his case. The girlfriend wants you to give her confidential information out of the file.

Probation Officers' Dilemmas—What Would You Do?

- I was having dinner at a nice restaurant and the manager on duty happened to be on my caseload and offers me a free dinner and gives me [basketball] tickets to five games.

The officer also has the issue of gratuities to contend with. Again, similar to the police officer, probation or parole officers may be offered special treatment, material goods, or other items of value because of their profession. In most cases, the situation is even more clearly unethical for probation and parole officers because the gift is offered by a client over whom decisions are made, as opposed to police officers who may or may not ever be in a position to make a decision regarding a restaurant or convenience store manager. Probation departments have clear rules against any "business relationships" with probationers, and this makes sense, but probation officers in very small towns ask, "How can I avoid a business relationship with a client when the only coffee shop in town is run by one of my clients? Am I never to go there during the years he is on probation?" In the same manner as police, some probation and parole officers feel that the gifts offered are given in the spirit of gratitude or generosity and not to influence decision making.

Because probationers and parolees may appear to be more similar to the probation or parole officer in socioeconomic status, family background, lifestyle, or personal value systems, there is a greater tendency to feel affinity and friendship for some clients. Some probation officers have been known to have clients baby-sit for them, to rent a room in their house, or to socialize with them and their families. Obviously, these personal relationships cause problems in the ability to perform one's official function as a protector of the community and enforcer for the legal system. Personal relationships of any type—romantic, platonic, or financial—are simply not appropriate or ethical for the probation and parole professional.

Corruption

Peter Maas (1983) describes a case of high-level corruption in Tennessee where parole releases were being sold and traded for political favors. Each individual who learned of such corruption had to decide whether to participate or expose the corruption, and the decision was often life changing.

There may indeed come a time when a correctional professional runs across a scheme such as the one described in *Marie: A True Story* or the one described in the following personal vignette. Both involve a type of corruption, although perhaps of a different level. No doubt, there are schemes in existence where probation recommendations are made based on bribery or favoritism, or decisions not to violate are made unethically. Sexual coercion of clients may exist, and certain officers may be known to coerce female clients. Urinalysis testing may be subverted by some corrupt scheme to switch test

Literary Perspective

She'd had about enough of this, Marie thought. But she had to hand it to Rose Lee Cooper. For a downtrodden lady, she sure could turn out the troops.

"Ben, I really appreciate how you feel. I've gotten quite a few calls on her. She's a fortunate woman. A lot of people are interested in her welfare. I'm sure you've talked to Charlie Benson, though. I'm afraid it isn't a good case."

"Oh," said Haynes, his voice getting hard, "you've already decided against this poor creature. Marie, I thought you were my friend, *our* friend."

"You know I'm your friend, Ben. I hope you're my friend. I'm trying to do what's best for the Governor."

"Is that it? Case closed, or what?"

"Ben," Marie said sweetly, "no case is ever closed. We're just now making a decision about a hearing. I'll let you know." She was about to broach the possibility of work release when Haynes hung up.

A week later, in Nashville, Benson called. "Goddamnit, Marie, schedule Rose Lee Cooper."

"Charlie, you know as well as I do I talked to Eddie and he said never mind."

"Well, I just talked to him and he said never mind what he said. Do it!" . . .

She searched her soul. Where did her loyalty lie? To Eddie? He could be maimed by this. To the people of Tennessee, however grandiose that sounded? Didn't she owe them? Or how about an inmate who knew the guy in the next cell was buying his way out?

Loyalty, Marie discovered, wasn't so simple. But she had to act. By not acting, she was being cowardly. So, of course, it was loyalty to her conscience that finally counted, and if it cut across a friendship, well then, the friendship was no longer viable.

SOURCE: Maas, Peter. *Marie: A True Story* (New York: Random House, 1983): 189, 190–191. Copyright © 1983 by JMM Productions, Inc. Reprinted by permission of Random House, Inc.

results. One should not be surprised if these practices exist, although they are not widespread and many people will complete their careers and retire without having heard about or being involved in any of them. However, it would be a wise approach to consider what one would do in a situation similar to the dilemmas described in this section, or similar to any of the others in this book. Corrupt practices exist because honest people allow them to. Organizations experience corruption because they do not support and nurture ethical workers. Hopefully, the increasing professionalization of each of the subsystems of the criminal justice system will create a situation in which "rabble-rousers" don't have to lose careers and suffer subcultural sanctions because of standing up for what is ethical.

Probation Officers' Dilemmas—What Would You Do?

■ Had a guy on my caseload that had not been reporting for any of the court sanctioned programs and a Motion to Revoke was to be filed. However, a very high-ranking administrator told me to not file an M.T.R. nor take any negative actions as this person was a personal friend.

MANAGEMENT ISSUES

Administrators are removed from day-to-day contact with inmates, but their power over decision making may actually be greater than that of line staff. Administrators emphasize the goal of control—that is, keeping the organization out of the newspapers and minimizing negative publicity. Because of this emphasis, administrators may be faced with difficult choices. For instance, in prisons or jails all treatment programs using outside people are potential security risks. An easy solution would be to prohibit all outsiders from entering the prison. Obviously, few prison administrators are this stringent in their control, but the choice may be made in specific instances to limit entry based on convenience and security. The decision to limit entry could probably be justified under a utilitarian framework, but other ethical systems may not support it.

Another dilemma that decision makers face is the balance between cost and inmate or officer need. If inmates' programming is sparse, clothing is minimal, or medical care is inadequate, or if officers' safety and efficiency are compromised because too few are employed or too much overtime is required, a decision maker must, at some point, determine priorities. Obviously, administrators often have no choice since they can work only within the budget given. However, situations do arise in governmental agencies where workers are told there is no money in the budget for needed items such as office supplies and equipment or overtime pay, yet at the same time administrators manage to find the money to order expensive new office furniture for themselves or go on expensive training weekends. This discrepancy between what administrators say and what workers see is demoralizing to those in the helping professions who try to make do with increasingly smaller budgets. Moral leadership is exhibited by those administrators who share the sacrifices. Ethical decisions for administrators arise when budget allocations are made, when program futures are decided, and when rules and procedures are developed.

Administrators have found themselves forced to change after prisoners' rights suits have resulted in court mandates to change. The implementation of court-ordered changes has often been halting and superficial, showing that compliance to the letter of a court ruling may be different from compliance to the spirit of one. Is this response to court-ordered change an ethical one? *Cruz v. Beto* (Civil No. 71-H-1371 [S.D. Tex. 1976]) was a case dealing with the actions of administrators in the Texas system in response to a particularly active prisoners' rights attorney who was taking on cases *pro bono* that challenged the practices of the Texas Department of Corrections. First, the director barred her from all prisons in the state, and then, when forced to allow her back into the prison because the ban was an unconstitutional infringement on the inmates' right to legal assistance, transferred all inmates who were her clients to one unit, deprived them of good behavior points that were necessary for higher security classifications and favorable parole decisions, and evidently subjected the inmates to a barrage of pressure indicating that if they dropped her as their lawyer they would have all privileges reinstated. Not surprisingly, the court took a dim view of these actions, and they could be scrutinized under an ethics microscope as well. What ethical system would justify such behavior?

Administrators have also found themselves in the position of testifying in court about conditions or the actions of their employees. Their testimony may be perjured to protect themselves or others; in this situation, their ethical dilemma is similar to that of police officers testifying about undercover activities. However, an issue more specific to administrators is pleading ignorance of activities for which they arguably should be held responsible.

A rabble-rouser can be defined as someone who finds it impossible to live with knowledge of corruption without doing something about it—usually creating a scandal that exposes the corruption. The term has negative connotations, but it actually describes someone who is typically responding to a higher ethical code than those whose behavior is exposed. Tom Murton found his career dramatically altered when he was hired by the Arkansas Department of Correction. Upon arriving in the Arkansas system he discovered abuses and inhumane conditions, documented later in several writings and immortalized in the movie *Brubaker*. The Supreme Court case of *Holt v. Sarver*, 442 F.2d 304 (8th Cir. 1971), also documented the abuses. In addition to extreme physical treatment, including the "Tucker Telephone"—an electrical apparatus used to shock inmates—Murton had information that there were hundred of inmates listed as escapees who had evidently disappeared. Acting on the information of one informant, he dug up on the grounds of the prison two bodies that had injuries exactly as the inmate described—one had been decapitated, and one had a crushed skull. Opposing testimony at the legislative hearing called in response proposed that the bodies were from an old church cemetery. Instead of pursuing the matter further and digging up more bodies or testing them in any way for age and other identifying marks, state officials fired Murton and threatened him with prosecution as a "graverobber" (Murton, 1976).

Individuals are often forced to make a choice between their career and challenging unethical or illegal practices. For administrators, this dilemma may appear more often since their scope of knowledge is broader than that of line staff. Often the career path of an administrator, with its investment of time and energy and the mandate to be a "company man," creates an immersion in bureaucratic thinking to the point that an individual loses sight of ethical issues. For instance, protecting the department or the director from scandal becomes more important than analyzing the behavior that created the potential for scandal in the first place. When decision making becomes influenced solely by short-term gains or avoidance of scandal, then decisions may be unsupported by the ethical systems discussed previously.

Another issue for correctional managers is what to do when faced with a worker alleging sexual harassment. The type of behavior defined as constituting a "hostile work environment" was common when women first entered as officers in prisons for males. Women officers reported behavior such as C.O.'s making sexual references and disparaging comments to them in front of inmates, "setting them up" by having inmates masturbate when they were sent down the tier, putting up posters with naked women and sexual messages, and even more serious behaviors such as assaults and attempted rapes. Today, the behavior that women experience is usually not so blatant, but some still do experience problems. When a correctional manager is approached by a female subordinate who is being subjected to a work environment where other officers or workers conduct themselves in a manner that makes her uncomfortable, there is a tendency to encourage her to handle it herself and not rock the boat. All administrators fear negative publicity and lawsuits, and if a problem such as sexual harassment can be swept under the rug, there is a great temptation to do so. Even ethical administrators face conflicting duties. They have a duty to the organization—to keep from having to defend it against a lawsuit—but also to the employee—to help the employee undertake the best course of action, and that might be to pursue charges. Possible ethical resolutions to the problem may be to talk to the individuals involved, punish the wrongdoers, or encourage the complainant to pursue internal or external sanctions. Obviously, administrators and managers themselves should take pains to avoid behavior that may be misconstrued as sexual coercion or be perceived by their employees as offensive. Managers have a higher duty than co-workers to set a tone for an office free from sexual innuendo that may lead to a description of the workplace as a hostile work environment. They have an ethical and legal affirmative duty to stop sexual humor, inappropriate touching, and inappropriate behavior before there is a complaint.

Administrators are in a difficult position when officers under their command have been accused of (and are guilty of) wrongs against inmates or probationers or parolees, such as brutality or harassment. If the administrator supports the officer (publicly or privately), he or she is in effect condoning that behavior and allowing it to continue. If the administrator exposes the officer and subjects him or her to punishment, then there is a possibility that the administrator will lose the trust and allegiance of other officers who feel betrayed. Of course, the ideal situation would be one where everyone involved would not condone such behavior and would resolve it satisfactorily. Realistically, this is usually not the case. Probably the best an administrator can do is to make clear to all what will not be tolerated and serve as a role model; when wrongdoing is exposed, to treat the individuals involved fairly, with due process and offering them an opportunity to change; and if sanctions are deemed necessary, to administer them fairly and without favoritism.

CONCLUSION

In this chapter we have touched on some of the ethical issues that correctional personnel face. These individuals have much in common with other criminal justice practitioners, especially in the area of discretion, but they are also in a unique position in that they hold power over the most basic aspects of life for confined inmates or over the freedom of those in community corrections. This position allows correctional officers either to intensify the humiliation

---

QUOTATION

*It seemed to me, just as it usually seems to my kind, that society was simply
trying to strip or rip off my shield, that it was willing to do so ruthlessly, that it
didn't care about me personally, or the amount of humiliation or degradation
it might inflict in the process. I stubbornly balked at being manipulated, regulated, or being compelled to conform blindly through fear or threat or punishment, however severe. Indeed, I came to question the validity of a society that
appeared more concerned with imposing its will than in inspiring respect. There
seemed to me something grossly wrong with this. "We'll make you be good!" I
was told, and I told myself nobody should, would or could make me anything.
And I proved it.*

SOURCE: Caryl Chessman (executed on May 2, 1960). Quoted in "Special Section: Inside Looking Out,"
Time, 13 Sept. 1982: 42.

---

that incarcerated offenders feel or to make the prison experience more tolera-
ble for those who serve time. The difficult decisions for correctional officers
arise from the personal relationships that develop with inmates, the trust that
is sometimes betrayed, the favors that seem harmless, and the coercive environment that makes violence normal and humanity abnormal. Correctional
treatment personnel have their own problems in resolving conflicts between
loyalty toward clients and toward the system. To be in a helping profession in
a system geared for punishment is a difficult challenge for anyone, and the
temptation to retreat into bureaucratic compliance is ever present. Probation
and parole personnel face similar issues to the ones described, as well as unique
dilemmas related to their power over offenders' freedom.

One final note: although this chapter has discussed officers mistreating inmates and correctional professionals engaging in other unethical conduct, we
do not mean to imply that criminal justice workers are blatantly or pervasively
unethical. Arguably, the criminal justice system operates only as well as it does
because of the caring, committed, honest people who choose it as a career.

REVIEW QUESTIONS

1. Describe the C.O. subculture.
2. Describe the formal ethical code for correctional personnel.
3. Choose three ethical issues of C.O.'s and analyze them by using the ethical
   frameworks.
4. Discuss the differences between guarding jail inmates and guarding state
   prison inmates.
5. What are the two interests that treatment staff have to balance? Give examples.

6. Choose and discuss three ethical issues of managers.
7. Describe the probation officer subculture.
8. Discuss ethical issues for probation and parole officers.

ETHICAL DILEMMAS

Situation 1

You are a prison guard supervising a tier. One of the inmates comes to you and asks a favor. Because he is a troublemaker, his mail privileges have been taken away. He wants you to mail a letter for him. You figure it's not such a big deal; besides, you know he could make your job easier by keeping the other inmates on the tier in line. What would you tell him?

Situation 2

As a new C.O. you soon realize that there is a great deal of corruption and graft taking place in the prison. Guards routinely bring in contraband for inmates in return for money, food bought for the inmates' mess hall finds its way into the trunks of staff cars, and money is being siphoned from inmate accounts. You are not sure how far up the corruption goes. Would you keep your mouth shut? They're just inmates anyway. Would you go to your supervisors? What if, in exposing the corruption, you implicated yourself? What if you implicated a friend?

Situation 3

You are a prison psychologist, and during the course of your counseling session with one drug offender, he confessed he has been using drugs. Obviously, this is a serious violation of prison rules. Should you report him? What if he told you of an impending escape plan?

Situation 4

You are a probation officer and have a specialized sex-offender caseload. The judge disagrees with a recommendation for a prison sentence and places an offender on probation. This man was convicted of molesting his four-year-old niece. One of the conditions of his probation is that he notify you whenever he is around children. He becomes engaged and moves in with a woman who has three children under the age of twelve. You believe that the man is not repentant and that there is a good chance he will molest these children. Although the woman knows his criminal history, she does not seem to care and, in fact, allows him to baby-sit the young girls. The judge has indicated that he will not entertain new conditions or a revocation unless there is evidence of a crime, but you understand from the offender's counselor that he continues to be sexually aroused by children. What can you do?

SUGGESTED READINGS

Crouch, B. (Ed.). 1980. *Keepers: Prison Guards and Contemporary Corrections*. Springfield, IL: Charles C. Thomas.

Johnson, R. 1987/1995. *Hard Time: Understanding and Reforming the Prison*. Pacific Grove, CA: Brooks/Cole.

Kauffman, K. 1988. *Prison Officers and Their World*. Cambridge, MA: Harvard University Press.

Martin, D. 1993. *Committing Journalism: The Prison Writings of Red Hog*. New York: Norton.

Murton, T. 1976. *The Dilemmas of Prison Reform*. New York: Irvington Publications.

Staples, W. 1997. *The Culture of Surveillance*. New York: St. Martin's.

11

Policy Making and Ethical Decision Making in Criminal Justice

Chapter Objectives

Become familiar with the ways that paradigms and ideologies shape our beliefs about crime and how to control criminals.

Understand that the fundamental nature of crime control in a democracy includes respect for individual liberties.

Understand how criminal justice policies are formed by belief systems.

Know the elements of good, ethical leadership.

Review procedures for individual ethical decision making.

Be able to discuss this question: Why be ethical?

In this book we have explored ethical issues in each of the subsystems of the criminal justice system. We have discovered that some themes run through all of these subsystems—the ethical use of authority, power, force, and discretion; subcultural barriers to ethical decision making; and the importance of ethical leadership. In this final chapter we will reiterate these themes. We start with a discussion of how ideologies (albeit somewhat stereotypical) have the power to shape our thinking about crime and social control. We explore the "myths" of crime and criminal justice that continue to influence policy making, as well as the role of research in creating these myths. Next, we revisit the concepts of ethical leadership. Finally, we will offer some final thoughts on how to decide what is ethical and address the more basic question: "Why be ethical?"

ETHICS AND CRIMINAL JUSTICE

As stated before, professionals in all areas of criminal justice have awesome power over people's lives. Criminal law and the system to implement it deal with all the fundamental questions that have concerned philosophers down through the ages. In criminal justice we must wrestle with questions of responsibility and excuse, the limits of the state's right to control the individual, the ethical use of force, and the appropriate use of discretion. Murphy (1985) summarizes a description of the connections between philosophy and criminal justice (see box).

Philosophy and Criminal Justice

1. *The intersection of law and morals:* Criminal law deals with issues that are at the heart of morality; excuse and justification, responsibility, duty and obligation, good and evil, right and wrong. A study of the legal use of a certain concept will also illuminate the moral use of that concept.
2. *The moral centrality of the topic of punishment:* The concept of punishment affects and is affected by a number of other moral concepts: blame, praise, reward, responsibility, mercy, forgiveness, justice, charity, obligation, and rights.
3. *Metaphysical involvement:* It is impossible to discuss the nature of a just system of responsibility and excuse without also discussing the mind–body problem, the problem of free will and determinism, and other metaphysical issues.
4. *Political philosophy:* If the central problem of political philosophy is coming to terms with the nature and justification of coercion, the punishment is state coercion in its most obvious form. Thus, political philosophy must come to terms with punishment.
5. *Philosophy and empirical science:* While philosophical theories are not themselves empirical, and philosophers are not usually engaged in assessing the confirmation of empirical claims, falsity may undercut their own theories. Therefore, they have an obligation to keep informed of relevant work in the scientific community.
6. *Practical urgency:* If philosophy is to be socially useful, then the issues of punishment and responsibility seem to provide an area in which philosophical work can have practical social utility.

SOURCE: Murphy, 1985: 4.

Although professionals and practitioners may get bogged down with day-to-day problems and bureaucratic agendas may cause them to lose sight of larger goals, foremost in their minds should be the true scope and meaning of the power inherent in the criminal justice system. That power depends on each person's maintaining high standards of ethical behavior. It is the people within a justice system who make it just or corrupt.

To protect citizenry from any misuse and abuse of the power inherent in a justice system, personnel in the system must have a strong professional identity. There is a continuing debate over whether police officers can be described as professionals; there is even more question of whether correctional officers can be described as such. These arguments miss a central point. Whether one calls the men and women who wear these uniforms professionals, practitioners, or some other term, the fact is that they have immense power over other people's lives. This power must be recognized for what it is and held as a sacred trust.

Criminal justice professionals are public servants and, as such, have a higher standard of behavior than and a duty to the citizenry they serve, but even more than that, they must possess the moral and ethical sense to prevent the power inherent in their positions from being used for tyranny. Education isn't enough. Learning a body of knowledge and acquiring essential skills do not give individuals the moral sense necessary to use those skills wisely. Witness the recurring scandals involving lawyers and business professionals—a highly educated group does not necessarily mean that the group is free from corruption.

The greatest protection against corruption of power is a belief in and commitment to the democratic process and all it entails. If one desires a career in criminal justice, one must ask these questions: "Do I love the Constitution?" "Do I believe in the Bill of Rights" "Do I truly believe in the sanctity and natural right of due process?" If these are viewed as impediments, nuisances, or irrelevant to today's problems of crime control, the individual should seriously question accepting the role of public servant.

The Bill of Rights (Selected Amendments)

Article I. Congress shall make no law respecting an establishment of religion, or prohibiting the free exercise thereof; or abridging the freedom of speech, or of the press; or the right of the people peaceably to assemble, and to petition the Government for a redress of grievance.

Article II. A well regulated militia, being necessary to the security of a free State, the right of the people to keep and bear arms, shall not be infringed.

Article III. No Soldier shall, in time of peace be quartered in any house, without the consent of the owner, nor in time of war, but in a manner to be prescribed by law.

Article IV. The right of the people to be secure in their persons, houses, papers, and effects, against unreasonable searches and seizures, shall not be violated, and no warrants shall issue, but upon probable cause, supported by oath or affirmation, and particularly describing the place to be searched, and the persons or things to be seized.

Article V. No person shall be held to answer for a capital, or otherwise infamous crime, unless on a presentment or indictment of a Grand Jury, except in cases arising in the land or naval forces, or in the militia, when in actual service in time of war or public danger; nor shall any person be subject for the same offense to be twice put in jeopardy of life or limb; nor shall be compelled in any criminal case to be a witness against himself, nor be deprived of life, liberty, or property, without due process of law; nor shall private property be taken for public use, without just compensation.

Article VI. In all criminal prosecutions, the accused shall enjoy the right to a speedy and public trial, by an impartial jury of the State and district wherein the crime shall have been committed, which district shall have been previously ascertained by law, and to be informed of the nature and cause of the accusation; to be confronted with the witnesses against him; to have compulsory process for obtaining witnesses in his favor, and to have the assistance of counsel for his defense.

POLICY MAKING IN CRIMINAL JUSTICE

Professionals in criminal justice are called upon to enforce laws and also to implement policies. Policy making is undertaken by the executive and legislative branches of the government, as well as by agencies in the criminal justice system. Policies can be formal or informal. They have tremendous influence on people's lives. For instance, the policy of "zero tolerance" has meant that many individuals who hold mostly pro-social values and follow law-abiding lifestyles—except for some amount of drug use—may have become entangled in the criminal justice system. Another example of a law enforcement policy might have just the opposite effect—e.g., an informal policy of ignoring prostitutes unless business owners or residents in the area complain. If laws are the skeleton of the system, then policies are the muscles—they influence the way that the laws are enforced.

The Bill of Rights (Selected Amendments) *(continued)*

Article VII. In Suits at common law, where the value in controversy shall exceed twenty dollars, the right of trial by jury shall be preserved, and no fact tried by a jury, shall be otherwise reexamined in any Court of the United States, than according to the rules of the common law.

Article VIII. Excessive bail shall not be required, nor excessive fines imposed, nor cruel and unusual punishments inflicted.

Article IX. The enumeration in the Constitution, of certain rights, shall not be construed to deny or disparage others retained by the people.

Article X. The powers not delegated to the United States by the Constitution, nor prohibited by it to the States, are reserved to the States respectively, or to the people.

Article XIII. Section 1. Neither the slavery nor involuntary servitude, except as a punishment for crime whereof the party shall have been duly convicted shall exist within the United States, or any place subject to their jurisdiction. Section 2. Congress shall have power to enforce this article by appropriate legislation.

Article XIV. Section 1. All persons born or naturalized to the United States, and subject to the jurisdiction thereof, are citizens of the United States and of the State wherein they reside. No State shall make or enforce any law which shall abridge the privileges or immunities of citizens of the United States; nor shall any State deprive any person of life, liberty, or property, without due process of law; nor deny to any person within its jurisdiction the equal protection of the laws. . . .

Article XV. Section 1. The right of citizens of the United States to vote shall not be denied or abridged by the United States or by any State on account of race, color, or previous condition of servitude. . . .

Article XIX. The right of citizens of the United States to vote shall not be denied or abridged by the United States or by any State on account of sex. . . .

Policies sometimes have more to do with belief systems than with empirical reality. In the next section we present an extended discussion of liberalism and conservatism. Although these descriptions are stereotypical, they are so powerful in our thought processes and so often used that a great deal of meaning is transmitted by their use. The label of "liberal" or "conservative" communicates definitional elements about what is right and wrong and good and bad in social control that, if not universally agreed upon, at least provide a basis of comparison. So, with apologies to those who dislike broad generalizations, we begin.

Ideologies of Liberalism and Conservatism

An *ideology* is "a set of general and abstract beliefs or assumptions about the correct or proper state of things, particularly with respect to the moral order and political arrangements, which serve to shape one's positions on specific issues" (Hornum and Stavish, 1978: 143). Two opposing ideologies regarding crime and criminals are the *liberal* versus the *conservative* view. Although these are broad-brush categorizations, they provide illumination of basic values and important issues in social control and crime. Both the liberal perspective and the conservative perspective are primarily operating under the consensus paradigm in that they accept the basic definitions of crime as given by law.

The Liberal Perspective   The liberal perspective explains criminal behavior and deviance through reference to psychological, social, or biological causation. Because individuals are seen as influenced by factors outside their control, they are not completely culpable for their crimes. Rather, explanations are developed to explain behavior, including psychological, sociological, and other definitions of "why" behavior occurs.

In policing, the liberal perspective is manifested by attempts of police departments to make themselves more accessible to the population and departmental approval for informal means of resolving disputes. Innovations such as neighborhood policing, team policing, and youth groups attempt to help the police understand and empathize with certain groups they come into contact with. The liberal ideology would endorse police officers as a positive social control tool in their provision of services to the community that would, in turn, influence pro-social values. For instance, "Officer Friendly" programs in schools not only teach bicycle safety tips but also give the message that the police officer is a friend and that the child should look up to him or her as a role model. "Storefront" police stations transmit the message that the police are a part of the community, and neighborhood policing allows the police officer to become involved in noncrime issues in the community, creating and cementing relational ties to the community that is being policed.

In courts, the liberal perspective is seen in individualized justice—the preference to consider the offender rather than the offense. This would involve the acceptance of reasons or rationales for unlawful behavior. For instance, the burglar who had lost his job and had bills to pay, the enraged wife who killed her husband because he left her for another woman, or the ghetto youth whose father turned him on to drugs would all have their individual backgrounds considered in decisions regarding responsibility and punishment. The liberal perspective perceives that law cannot easily define wrongdoing and set punishment for human behavior that is complex, not categorical. Thus, the courts, and their human representatives in the legal system, must use discretion to administer "individual justice."

In corrections, the liberal ideology supports most correctional programming. Attempts to make criminals more like us, by vocational training, education, and social skills training, are based on the idea that the criminal could change given a different environment, different influences, or given solutions to problems such as illiteracy or addiction. Correctional programs target biological problems (addiction), social problems (negative role models), or psychological problems (weak ego state), and all are based on the assumption that if the problem is corrected, the criminal would no longer commit crime.

The liberal perspective may identify as unethical any treatment of the offender by the system that does not take into account individual factors. For instance, it would be considered unethical to ignore the fact that an individual was coerced into an illegal action. It would be unethical to ignore a prisoner's need for special attention or medical care. It would be unethical to prosecute a very young offender in the same way that one would a more culpable older offender. It would be unethical to ignore evidence that an individual was mentally ill when committing an offense. Basically, the liberal is concerned when the law tries to uphold some unrealistic standard of objective justice, since that is not possible.

The Conservative Perspective The conservative, in general, agrees with the liberal that the legal code is a true representation of society's morals and values, but differs in the perception of the offender. Rather than influenced by forces beyond their control, offenders are seen as evil persons who freely choose actions and must be held accountable for them. Criminals are different from their victims and law-abiding people and, thus, not worthy of the same protections that the law provides to the rest of us.

The conservative perspective views the police as enforcers of society's morality, and any attempts to weaken that role are to be resisted. Court restrictions against police power or police actions should be limited since criminals must be caught and punished in whatever way is most effective. Police are seen as becoming "soft" or bureaucratized in recent years, and there may be a wistful element in the popularity of such fictional characters as "Dirty Harry," who bypasses due process to get criminals off the streets.

In the conservative perspective, courts are the worst threat to society, because they allow criminals to go free. Only the most punitively oriented judges achieve conservative approval, and the majority of judges are seen as do-gooders who do not give criminals the prison sentences they deserve. Conservatives believe the death penalty is justified and not used often enough. Criminals are believed to have too many rights and victims none in the court system.

Under the conservative perspective, correctional facilities have too many programs; these programs only coddle the criminals and teach them that they will be rewarded and excused for criminal behavior. Old-fashioned punishments, such as chain gangs and rock piles, are seen as appropriate and worthy. Although prisons should satisfy basic needs, anything beyond what is absolutely necessary for survival is considered a luxury and decreases the effectiveness of prison as a deterrent.

The conservative concern for ethics involves criminal justice practitioners who may use their powers of discretion too freely. It is unethical to let criminals off because of courtroom deals or because of some error in the proceedings. It is unethical for police to ignore wrongdoing when it is done by informants, especially if it is someone who will continue the behavior. It is unethical for criminal justice practitioners to give special privileges to criminals because of status or money—for instance, to give special favors to mobsters in prison. Whenever the system is less than objective in meting out punishment, the conservatives' concern for ethics is aroused, and that would also include disparate sentencing based on offender characteristics. For instance, it is unethical if two defendants had committed the same crime for one defendant to get more years in prison than the other due to different circumstances.

In the following excerpt, Smith (1982: 137) uses the terms *right* and *left* instead of our terms *conservative* and *liberal,* and presents additional definitional elements of the two ideologies. If disorder is feared, social control becomes more acceptable. The left's concern for justice includes distributive justice, and that is why offenders' backgrounds are considered in the equation.

> For the right, the paramount value is order—an ordered society based on a pervasive and binding morality—and the paramount danger is disorder—social, moral and political. For the left, the paramount value is justice—a just society based on a fair and equitable distribution of power, wealth, prestige and privilege—and the paramount evil is injustice.

Although many people would associate the liberal (or left) viewpoint with due process (as does Smith), it might also be true that the liberal ideology does not necessarily or even logically imply a due-process position. The liberal support of treatment implies that one may go beyond what even conservative, retributive ends would dictate. The justice perspective described in the last chapter was largely developed as a backlash to perceptions of due-process violations in the name of treatment.

Of course, these descriptions are fairly simplistic. Most people hate to be labeled as conservative or liberal, probably because it denies the presence of more complicated views of humanity and human relationships. Despite the obvious generalizations apparent in these characterizations, however, they can be detected in news coverage or political speeches and are useful to understand the development of policy. The conservative position is obviously more popular today than the liberal perspective, which might explain the greater emphasis on accountability and punitiveness in discussions about crime and social control.

Myths and Reality in Criminal Justice

What we believe about crime and criminals is partially influenced by our ideology, as described above, but it also is influenced by what we know about crime—or what we think we know. Several excellent sources have now become available that "debunk" some of the more standard myths in criminal justice. Walker (1994) was one of the first to address fundamental beliefs that influenced criminal justice policy—for example, that more police patrols would reduce crime. He also addressed fundamental beliefs that support liberal ideology—for example, that education reduces crime. Some of Walker's findings and use of empirical evidence may be criticized, but the approach of a "skeptic" is a necessary one if we want to avoid complacency and policy making influenced by unsupported truisms.

Others have continued this inquiry. For instance, Kappeler, Blumberg, and Potter (1996) present in their work a series of myths that influence criminal justice policy—the myth of crime waves, the myth of child abduction, the myth of the drug crisis, the myth of equal justice, the myth of the utility of punishment, and the myth of a lenient criminal justice system. Bohm (1996) also discusses myths—crime is a bad social problem, the criminal justice system enforces all laws, crime is primarily violent, and crime is increasing—and their influence on criminal justice policy. He also explains their function: they offer identities (good guy, bad guy), they aid comprehension by creating order out of the bombardment of information we experience today, and they help to form common bonds and reinforce a sense of community.

In Chapter 3 we illustrated an approach to resolve an ethical dilemma by first isolating the relevant factual issues, then the relevant concepts, and finally the relevant ethical issues. What we think we know has obvious implications for what we believe to be the right response to any particular dilemma. The sources above show us that what we think we know may not necessarily be accurate. If our beliefs about what should be done with criminals are based on the myth that the system is lenient and/or the myth that crime is increasing, then we are operating under faulty assumptions.

How do these myths develop? The media and government are obvious participants in creating and perpetuating false perceptions, but social science bears a great deal of responsibility as well. This book has not dealt with ethics in criminal justice research, and there are obvious issues relevant to the development and testing of hypotheses in this area.

Criminal Justice Researchers—
Participants in Myth Making?

The argument that social science can never be truly objective has been discussed in a variety of venues (Roberg, 1981). A social scientist is influenced by his or her value system, ideology, and perception of reality. What questions to ask may be more important than the answers one finds. Individual perceptions will always somewhat influence the research process; however, if hypothesis construction and methodology are tainted by special interest groups or political agendas, then one must question any results that emerge from such research. The most obvious example of this is research funded by the National Rifle Association on the impact of handguns on violent crime. There are serious questions about whether such research could ever be unbiased, given human inclinations not to "bite the hand that feeds." In less blatant ways, the research currently conducted and disseminated in criminal justice must be considered in light of funding priorities. One can assume that it would be difficult to secure public funding to study the criminal behavior of state or federal legislators, or corporate crime—does that mean such crime does not exist? Does all the research on drug use, the connection between drug use and criminality, and evaluations of drug treatment programs help our understanding of drug use patterns and governmental response patterns and the truth of the so-called drug epidemic, or actually obscure it?

In one study of criminal justice researchers' experiences with ethical dilemmas, it was found that the most common ethical dilemma was perceived pressure to study a certain topic, issue, or question, and/or pressure to influence the findings (Longmire, 1983). False research findings may occur because of laziness, incompetence, or political pressure. Recent exposés in the medical research field have called into question what we think we know about such things as heart disease; unethical researchers in criminal justice may also affect what we think we know about crime and criminals.

In addition to outside pressures that influence the selection of a research question or prompt improper influence over, improper use of, or outright falsification of research findings, other dilemmas in research exist, including the following:

1. protection of subject confidentiality
2. negative effects of the research on the client (e.g., the Milgram experiment and the Zimbardo experiment are the two best-known examples of research that had tremendously negative effects on subjects) and issues of privacy for subjects
3. deception of subjects in terms of what they will experience or the true focus of the research
4. related to the above, obtaining informed voluntary consent
5. withholding benefits or services to subjects for the purpose of research
6. use of research findings—either misinterpretation or overreaching, otherwise illegal, or unethical treatment based on findings

The interaction among ideology, knowledge acquisition, and policy formation is complicated. Policies may originate in ideology and then become supported by research, or research may influence a shift of ideology. The danger is that individual decision making may be subverted by myths and that individual ethics may be the victim of misguided ideologies. Since all criminal justice professionals have varying degrees of discretion to make decisions and these decisions affect the life and liberty of individuals, it is important to remember basic fundamental guidelines for the use of discretion. Discretion is influenced by an individual's value system, ethical system, and environmental factors such as ethical leadership.

ETHICAL LEADERSHIP

Most writers, theorists, and practitioners point out that ethical organizations must have ethical administrators and managers. Administrators and managers have duties that are different from those of subordinates. They are responsible not only for their personal conduct but also for the actions of those they supervise. In other countries and cultures, this responsibility seems to be more pronounced than in the United States. For instance, when the Falkland War occurred, the foreign minister in Great Britain resigned. He did so because the situation happened on "his watch." Even though he did nothing personally blameworthy, and he was not negligent in his duties and in all respects performed his job competently, he held himself personally responsible because he failed to know of and therefore warn or prepare for the threat that Argentina presented. Contrast this with the attitude of the captain of the *Exxon Valdez,* responsible for the largest oil spill in history, who professed innocence because he wasn't the one on the bridge at the time of the incident, or Darryl Gates, the Los Angeles police chief, who insisted that the problem of brutal officers was an individual problem and not one for which he should be held responsible. Of course, the explanation that one was "unaware" of wrongful behavior has been used by the highest office in the country, so it should not be surprising that it is frequently heard from administrators when faced with the wrongdoing of their subordinates.

What does it mean to be an ethical leader? Obviously, one first needs to be sure that one is not engaged in unethical and corrupt behaviors oneself. In addition, one has to take responsibility for the larger role responsibilities of a leader position. Standards applied to public administrators can be helpful to this discussion. The American Society for Public Administration (1979) has promulgated standards that can be applied to all administrators if they aspire to be good leaders. The standards include the following:

Responsibility and Accountability: Measures of quality service delivery should be developed and implemented to enable the administrator to identify strengths and weaknesses.

Commitment: Leaders should be dedicated and enthusiastic about the role of the organization, as well as have a commitment to the law, codes, regulations, and professional standards of behavior.

Responsiveness: Leaders should be sensitive to changing circumstances and evolving demands and needs of the public. Good leadership exhibits flexibility in the face of social change.

Knowledge and Skills: Technology is dynamic, and leadership must keep abreast of better ways of accomplishing its mission, as well as possess the understanding to interpret data that are relevant to the mission of the organization. Training—both upon entry and in-service—is a necessity in order to have an effective workforce.

Conflicts of Interest: Since there will always be conflicts, the administrator should be sensitive to them, especially when personal needs conflict with organizational needs.

Professional Ethics: Administrators should practice self-reflection and continually check their decision making against some ethical standard.

Administrators and managers do not necessarily ensure an organization free from corruption merely by avoiding engagement of corrupt practices themselves; they must take affirmative steps to encourage ethical actions. Issues that could be examined in a discussion of ethical leadership include the practice of recruitment, training, discipline and reward structures, and evaluation of performance. Souryal (1992: 307) offers advice to leaders who would like to advance ethical decision making and emphasizes the importance of organizational support for ethical actions. Ethical leaders should

- Create an environment that is conducive to dignified treatment on the job.
- Increase ethical awareness among the ranks through formal and informal socialization.
- Avoid deception and manipulation in the way officers are assigned, rewarded, or promoted.
- Allow for openness and the free flow of unclassified information.
- Foster a sense of shared values and incorporate such values in the subculture of the agency.
- Demonstrate an obligation to honesty, fairness, and decency by example.
- Discuss the issue of corruption publicly, expose corrupt behavior, and reward ethical behavior.

Metz (1990) offers a similar set of advice. He proposes that ethical administrators

- Establish realistic goals and objectives.
- Provide ethical leadership (meaning set a moral tone by actions).
- Establish formal written codes of ethics.
- Provide a whistleblowing mechanism.
- Discipline violators of ethical standards.
- Train all personnel in . . . ethics.

The common administrative reaction to unethical practices is to institute even more rules covering a greater range of behavior. As discussed in previous chapters, extensive rules seem to be present in inverse proportion to high ethical standards; what often occurs is as more rules are written, more creative ways are found to get around them. Rules are not ethical standards, and without a commitment and belief in the legitimacy of the rules, there is no way that more rules will affect the ethics of an organization.

When top leaders take responsible for their subordinates' behavior, they will lead and administer with greater awareness, interaction, and responsibility. Because of this responsibility, a supervisor or administrator must be concerned with how the workplace treats the worker, how the worker views the mission, and how the public views the organization. Concern for public image may be shared by ethical leaders and egoistic bureaucrats, but the first group has a sincere desire to understand the public's complaints and respond to them, and the second group is concerned solely with protecting the image of the organization—a stand that may mean whistleblowers are punished rather than appreciated for bringing problems out in the open.

A strong ethical leader would have a personal relationship with subordinates—without showing favoritism. This personal relationship is the building block of modeling, identification, and persuasive authority. Strong leadership involves caring and commitment to the organization. A strong leader is someone who is connected with others but also has a larger vision, if you will, of goals and mission. Delattre (1989) discusses a realistic idealist—it's possible he would also be content with the phrase "an idealistic realist." What he was referring to was the capacity for good leaders to understand social realities but avoid cynicism in the face of such social realities—for instance, in the use of force, a realistic idealist would understand that force is necessary at times but attempt every alternative means to protect all human life, including the offender's life. Leaders must never lose sight of the organizational mission—for public servants this means public service. Souryal also describes ethical leaders as those with "a mental state that is characterized by vision, enlightened reasoning, and moral responsibility" (1992: 186).

Good leaders must recognize and relay the idea that public service applies to all, not just a favored few. Criminals are also part of the public that the criminal justice system serves. This means that they deserve the same civility, protections, and services as the rest of us unless such is prohibited by law or personal safety is threatened. When the protections represented by our Bill of Rights and democratic process become reserved for certain groups, the rights of all are threatened.

INDIVIDUAL DECISION MAKING

In these final sections, we revisit the question discussed in the first several chapters of this book—how to make an ethical decision. John Rawls (1957) presents a somewhat abstract procedure for deciding moral issues. He explains that moral principles can be developed through inductive logic. The method to discover these moral principles is through the considered moral judgments of a number of cases by a number of moral judges. These individuals would have the following characteristics:

- They would possess common sense—they would not intellectualize the problem but apply common reason to arrive at a resolution.
- They would have open minds.
- They would know their own emotions.
- They would have a sympathetic knowledge of humans.

The cases given them to decide would be such that the judges would not be harmed or benefited in any way by their decision in order to ensure neutrality. The cases would present real conflicts of interest, but conflicts that were not too difficult and that were likely to present themselves in ordinary life. The judges would be presented with all relevant facts in the matter so that they could make a reasoned judgment. The judgments should be certain, and they should be stable; that is, other judges at other times should also arrive at the same judgments. Finally, the judgments should be intuitive. The reason for this is that ethical principles are to be derived from a series of judgments, and if judges were already using predetermined rules, there would be no way to derive general rules from the judgments. Rawls (1957: 180) describes the procedure in the following way:

> Up to this point I have defined, first a class of competent judges, and, second, a class of considered judgments. If competent judges are those persons most likely to make correct decisions, then we should take care to abstract those judgments of theirs which, from the conditions and circumstances under which they are made, are most likely to be correct.

The next step is to formulate an explication of the total range of judgments. An *explication* is a set of principles described as follows (Rawls, 1957: 182):

> [I]f any competent man were to apply them intelligently and consistently to the same cases under review, his judgments, made systematically nonintuitive by the explicit and conscious use of the principles, would be, nevertheless identical, case by case, with the considered judgments of the group of competent judges.

These explications must be written in ordinary language, be written in the form of principles, and be comprehensive in solving the range of moral judgments. In other words, common principles are extrapolated from the decisions of the moral judges, and these common principles are then used by the rest of us in decision making (Rawls, 1957).

Obviously, Rawls's proposal is more rhetorical device than useful tool for deciding ethical issues. However, the basic premise of this exercise is to discover common principles that can be used to decide moral questions. This is fundamental to any logical solution to moral dilemmas. The ethical systems we have discussed throughout this book present principles similar to the explications Rawls seeks through moral judges. For instance, ethical formalism presents basic principles for moral decision making in the form of the categorical imperative. The rules of the categorical imperative match some of the definitional components of Rawls's explications, since they are in the form of principles and are comprehensive.

Although Rawls's effort to delineate the steps needed to arrive at moral principles is logically appealing, it does not help an individual make personal decisions when confronted with ethical dilemmas. Other writers have attempted to provide more pragmatic guidelines for use in decision making. A method proposed by Laura Nash (1981) helps individuals make business decisions, and these same questions seem applicable to those situations faced by criminal justice professionals (see box).

Although Nash's guidelines are obviously directed to business decisions, they have applicability to other fields. Basically, the questions are designed to lead individuals to analyze their behavior and its implications. There is an assumption that exposure of unethical conduct will make the individual feel uneasy. To some extent, there is an assumption that a commonly agreed–upon definition of right and wrong exists. The general principles that can be drawn from these questions are obvious. First, we are interested in attaining all the facts of the situation; this includes the effects of the decision on oneself and others. It is important to understand hidden motivations and indirect effects. Second, the concept of scrutiny works well to evaluate the decision taken; one must be comfortable with public disclosure. Along with this concept goes the notion that others should be able to make the same decision and have it

---

How to Make an Ethical Decision

1. Have you defined the problem accurately?
2. How would you define the problem if you stood on the other side of the fence?
3. How did the situation occur in the first place?
4. To whom and to what do you give your loyalty as a person and as a member of the corporation?
5. What is your intention in making this decision?
6. How does this intention compare with the probable result?
7. Whom could your decision or action injure?
8. Can you discuss the problem with the affected parties before you make your decision?
9. Are you confident that your position will be as valid over a long period of time as it seems now?
10. Could you disclose without qualm your decision or action to your boss, your CEO, the board of directors, your family, your society as a whole?
11. What is the symbolic potential of your action if understood? If misunderstood?
12. Under what conditions would you allow exceptions to your stand?

SOURCE: Nash, 1981: 81.

judged acceptable. Finally, the concept of rationale or reason implies that the individual decision is based on a larger set of moral or ethical principles.

Let us apply these guidelines to a criminal justice example. If a police officer were confronted with an opportunity to accept some type of gratuity, either a dinner or a more expensive present, the officer should first evaluate all facts. Is anything expected in return? Is the gift really a gift, or a payment for some service? Would the officer be comfortable if others knew of the gift or gratuity? Could the officer reconcile the decision to take the gratuity with a larger set of moral principles, such as the Law Enforcement Code of Ethics?

Krogstand and Robertson (1979) describe three principles of ethical decision making. The first is the *imperative principle,* which directs a decision maker to act according to a specific, unbending rule. The second is the *utilitarian principle,* which determines the ethics of conduct by the good or bad consequences of the action. The third is the *generalization principle,* which is based on this question: "What would happen if all similar persons acted this way under similar circumstances?" These should sound familiar because they are, respectively, religious or absolutist ethics, utilitarianism, and ethical formalism. Ethical frameworks, if recognized, can be a great aid in individual decision making. If one is familiar with these ethical principles, then any specific dilemma can be analyzed using an ethical framework as a guideline.

To question one's general ethical behavior is a challenging self-survey. The boxed set of questions takes a general approach to evaluating one's ethics. It comes from the American Society for Public Administration (1979: 22–23) but has been adapted where necessary to apply to those who work in the criminal justice field.

Close and Meier (1995: 130) provide a set of questions more specific to criminal justice professionals and sensitive to the due-process protections that are often discarded in a decision to commit an unethical act. They propose that the individual decision maker should ask the following:

1. Does the action violate another person's constitutional rights, including the right of due process?

2. Does the action involve treating another person only as a means to an end?

3. Is the action under consideration illegal?

4. Do you predict that your action will produce more bad than good for all persons affected?

5. Does the action violate department procedure or professional duty?

The simplest formulation of questions on which to base an ethical decision is as follows: Does it affect others? Does it hurt others? Would I want it done if I were on the other side? Would I be proud of the decision? These four simple questions may be sufficient to address most ethical dilemmas.

Chapter 2 of this book discussed the ethics of virtue. Part of this ethical framework is the idea that one's character is most relevant to ethical decision making. That is, good character comprises virtues such as honesty, trustworthiness, and generosity. Bad character, obviously, would be the absence or

---

Ethics Self-Survey

1. Do I confront difficult ethical decisions directly and attempt to think through the alternatives and the principles involved? Am I inclined to make decisions on grounds of convenience, expediency, pressure, impulse, or inertia?
2. Do I systematically review my behavior as an administrator and question whether what I do is consistent with my professional values?
3. If someone asked me to explain my professional ethics, what would I say?
4. Have my values and ethics changed since I began working as a public administrator? If so, why and how have they changed? What are the primary influences that have changed my thinking?
5. Looking ahead to the remainder of my career, are there particular areas of my ethical conduct to which I would like to pay closer attention?
6. Do I ever find myself in situations in which providing equitable treatment to clients, members of my organization, or members of other organizations creates ethical conflicts? How do I handle such dilemmas? Can I perceive any consistent pattern in my behavior?
7. Where do my professional loyalties ultimately lie? With the Constitution? The law? My organization? My superiors? My clients? The general public? Do I feel torn by these loyalties? How do I deal with the conflicts?
8. Do I ever confront situations in which I feel that it is unfair to treat everyone in the same way? How do I determine what to do in those cases? How do I decide what is fair?
9. When I am responsible for some activity that turns out to be inappropriate or undesirable, do I accept full responsibility for it? Why? How?
10. Do I ever dismiss criticism of my actions with the explanation that I am only "following orders"? Do I accept any responsibility for what happens in these circumstances?

SOURCE: Adapted from American Society of Public Administrators, 1979: 22–23.

---

opposite of these traits. If one has a bad character, then one is unlikely to perceive ethical dilemmas, since one will go through life in essence an egoist, making choices influenced by one's negative character traits. If one has a good character, then one does not perceive ethical dilemmas in some situations either, since it is second nature for one to do the honorable thing, whether it be not steal or tell the truth or whatever. Most people in the criminal justice field (or indeed any profession) have basically good characters; some do not. In some situations, even those who have formed habits of honesty, truthfulness, and integrity are sincerely perplexed as to the correct course of behavior. These situations occur because the behavior choice seems so innocuous or trivial (for example, whether to accept free coffee) or seems so difficult (for example, how to reconcile demands of loyalty to friends versus loyalty to the organization or society). In these instances where basically good people have trouble deciding what to do, the ethical frameworks provided in this volume might help them analyze their choices. It must also be accepted that in some dilemmas, there are going to be sacrifices for making the right decision.

In any organization, there are those who will almost always make ethical choices, those who will usually make unethical ones, and those who can be influenced one way or the other. The best course of action is to identify those in the second group and encourage them to find other employment or at least remove them from temptation. Then organizational leaders must create an atmosphere for the third group that encourages ethical decision making. This can be done by promoting ethical administrators, rewarding morally courageous behavior, and providing clear and powerful organizational policies that emphasize worthwhile goals and honest means.

For criminal justice practitioners, ethical decisions arise from the exercise of discretion and the use of power. Criminal justice practitioners find themselves faced with ethical choices when balancing friendship against institutional integrity—that is, when friends and colleagues engage in inappropriate or illegal behavior or rule breaking. There are also ethical choices to be made when balancing client (offender) needs against bureaucratic efficiency and institutional goals. Ethics are at issue when the individual professional has personal goals or biases that conflict with fair and impartial treatment of the public and the clients served. The inappropriate use of discretion occurs when the professional uses unethical criteria to resolve decisions.

In conclusion, the individual should become aware of the implications of day-to-day choices—sharpen his or her ethical antennae, so to speak. Small decisions become larger life positions in a slow, cumulative way. When faced with a choice of behavior, one should first examine all possible solutions to the problem and be aware of the direct and indirect effects of each response. Often, ethical issues arise and are not recognized for what they are. The individual may limit analysis of a problem to finding a short-term solution or making a quick decision, in which case the larger issues or the situation's ethical implications are never addressed. It becomes easy to rationalize unethical behavior in this way by the explanation that it only happened once, or it was the easiest way, or there was no intention to do wrong.

Then one should determine whether any solutions would be viewed as unacceptable if made public, and for what reason. If an individual would be uncomfortable talking about an action, then chances are it is questionable. Too often, unethical decisions are protected by a shroud of secrecy, and then the secrecy is defended by pleading institutional or agency confidentiality. On an individual level, unethical behavior is almost always hidden, and further unethical behavior may follow to cover up what has already been done. Probably the best signal that something is wrong is when a person hesitates to make it public knowledge.

Finally, the individual must be able to reconcile the decision with his or her personal set of values or ethical system. Hopefully, the ethical concepts, discussions, and issues we have presented in this book have helped clarify these decision processes. When one has to make a difficult decision about a moral issue, although one has recourse to value systems passed on by family and advice and counsel from friends and colleagues, ultimately the decision made should be one the individual is willing to take responsibility for and be proud of.

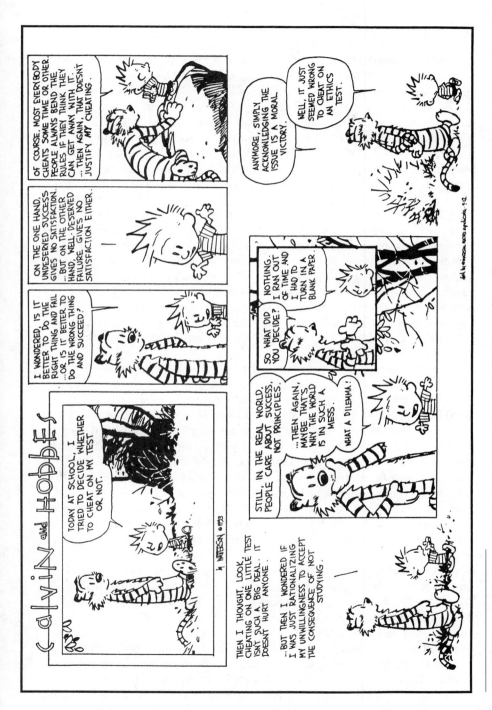

WHY BE ETHICAL?

After completing a class on ethics that involved detailed explanations and applications of the ethical systems discussed in this book, an individual responded with the question "Why should we?" The student was really asking why anyone should be ethical or moral. There is a long version and a short version of the answer to this question. The long version is that philosophers down through the ages have examined, debated, and analyzed this same question. The ethical systems can be seen as not only answering the question "What is good?" but also the question "Why be good?" Under ethical formalism the answer is that the world works better, and it is rational to do one's duty and live up to the categorical imperative. Under utilitarianism, the answer is that it is better for everyone, including the individual, to do what benefits the majority. Under the ethics of care, the answer is that we naturally and instinctively have the capacity to care and to be concerned about others. Each of the other frameworks also provides answers. One dominant theme emerges from all the ethical systems—that we are connected to each other in fundamental and emotional ways. The golden rule, the universalism principle under the categorical imperative, rule utilitarianism, and even enlightened egoism recognize this connection. The theme running through all these ethical systems is empathy and caring for one another. The reason we should act ethically can be explained rationally (ethical formalism and utilitarianism) or intuitively (ethics of care and religion).

A similar question was asked by Tyler (1990) in a book titled *Why People Obey the Law.* The answers found in his research may shed light on this discussion. He found that people obey the law not because of fear of being punished but rather because of a fundamental belief in the goodness of law. If they believe that the system is fair, that their rights are protected, and that they are treated with dignity and respect, then they typically believe in and abide by the law. Arguably, the converse is that if people do not trust that the process is fair, that rights are protected, or they do not receive dignity and respect, then they have no normative controls on their behavior and the only thing left is deterrence. Tyler's findings present an interesting commentary on what effect the criminal justice system has on citizens. One obvious conclusion is that unethical behavior that ignores rights creates the very behavior that one is trying to prevent.

Professional ethics is merely an application of moral systems to a particular set of questions or a specific environment. The basis of all professional ethical codes is the same: to be a good professional, one must be a good person. Many of the ethical choices one will make throughout the course of a career are easy: no one needs to tell a police officer that bribery is wrong, or correctional officers that hitting a shackled and helpless inmate is wrong. These actions occur because individuals have chosen to take the path of least resistance, or they pursue personal interests over organizational values. For those choices that are truly difficult, people of goodwill, using rationality and sensitivity, can apply any ethical system and come up with an ethical solution. It may not be one that everyone will agree upon, but it will allow the individual to make the decision public and will allow the person to be satisfied that his or her choice was based on ethics rather than egoism. Finally, why be ethical? The short answer was given by someone in the class who responded to the question with "So you can sleep at night." Simplistic, perhaps, but no less accurate.

Two of the greatest dangers in criminal justice are cynicism and burnout. Cynical leadership, cynical instructors, and overwhelming evidence that we live in an imperfect world create the all-too-common occurrence of workers who are cynical, who are burned out, and who have abandoned the ideals that led them to the profession in the first place. As mentioned before, ethical leaders should be able to transmit a vision and be committed to the mission of the organization, but many administrators and managers exhibit only pessimistic cynicism over the potential for change, the worth of humanity, and the importance of doing what is right.

How does one avoid cynicism and burnout? First, by adopting realistic goals before entering the profession. A police officer cannot expect to save the world, and a treatment professional should not expect to find success with every client. A more realistic career goal might be a resolution to do one's best and to always follow the law. Second, find and nurture a network of mentors and colleagues that promotes ethical values. In every department that has a corruption scandal, there are those who have managed to avoid participating in such activity. Cynical people are contagious, and cynicism breeds rationalizations for committing unethical behavior—from leaving work early or falsifying overtime records to violating the rights of suspects. Third, seek self-fulfillment and personal enrichment. This could be higher education, reading self-help books, attending church, joining interest clubs, participating in charitable activities, volunteering to coach community sport teams, or becoming involved in the PTA. Note that such activities all have the element of communication and interaction with others. Such activities promote connectedness with the community at large and counteract the negativity that pervades the criminal justice field. Unfortunately, criminal justice professionals see humanity at its worst, and we all need to provide for ourselves the opportunity to see the best of the human spirit as well.

REVIEW QUESTIONS

1. Select the most difficult ethical dilemma in the previous chapters and try to answer it again, using the questions posed by Laura Nash.

2. Now select an ethical or moral dilemma from your own life and try to solve it by using any guidelines derived from this book. Be explicit about the procedure that you used to arrive at a decision and about the decision itself.

ETHICAL DILEMMAS

Situation 1

You are a criminal justice student who is serving as an intern in a police department, attached to a narcotics squad. During one raid, all suspects in a house were lined up on a long couch, and one of the detectives hit each one of the African American men hard on the back of the head, but avoided hitting the sole white man. What would you do?

Situation 2

You obtain a job as a probation officer upon graduation and quickly realize that several probation officers in your office make things extremely difficult for you because of their racial humor and sexist remarks. They swear at clients and act inappropriately toward the female secretaries. One has been making suggestive comments to you, and you dread getting caught alone with him in the coffee room. You don't want to make waves because you have been there only a month, but what can you do?

Situation 3

You are a criminal justice student and have become friendly with another student named Joe. You are both nearing graduation, and Joe has told you that he will start work as a constable in a small town. The problem is that you believe Joe is a bigot and a bully who shows entirely too much interest in guns. He brags about how he's going to "teach people a lesson" and that he can match anyone in "firepower." You truly believe that someone is going to get hurt. What can you do?

Glossary

act utilitarianism type of utilitarianism that determines goodness of a particular act by measuring the utility for all, but only on that act and without regard for future actions

age of reason legal age at which a person is said to have the capacity to reason and thus to understand the consequences of her or his action

bureaucratic justice concept referring to the goal of efficiency over justice; policy of assuming guilt and moving cases through the system quickly with the least amount of work

categorical imperative part of ethical formalism as formulated by Kant; states that one should act in such a way that one wills it to be a universal law and should treat each person as an ends and not as a means

civil disobedience voluntary, nonviolent disobedience of established laws based on moral beliefs

cognitive dissonance psychological term referring to the discomfort that is created when behavior and attitude or belief are inconsistent; the inclination is to change one or the other to achieve congruence

concept idea or notion that cannot be proven

crime control model Packer's concept of a criminal justice system that maximizes crime control at the expense of personal liberties or due process

cultural relativism ideas that many values and behaviors differ from culture to culture, but are functional to the culture that holds them

deontological study of duty or moral obligation emphasizing the intent of the actor or goodwill as the element of morality; character of the person (as in virtue-based ethics) or consequences of the action (as in utilitarianism) are not seen as important

deterrence (general) an attempt to discourage or prevent some group or nonspecific individual from committing an act; for instance, to do something to one offender that should discourage the rest of society from committing any crime

deterrence (specific) an attempt to discourage or prevent a particular individual from committing an act; for instance, to deter a criminal offender from committing any more crime

discretion the power to make a decision or a choice

distributive justice component of justice concerned with the allocation of the goods and burdens of society to its respective members

due process constitutionally mandated (Sixth and Fourteenth Amendments) procedural steps designed to eliminate error in governmental deprivation of protected liberty, life, or property; that is, right to a neutral hearing body, presentation of evidence, cross-examination and confrontation of accusers, appeal, and so on

due-process model Packer's concept of a criminal justice system that emphasizes procedural protections (see *due process*) over crime control

egoism ethical system that claims that good results from pursuing self-interest (see also *psychological egoism*)

enlightened egoism concept that egoism may look altruistic since it is in one's long-term best interest to help others (since then they will help one)

entrapment legal term referring to police misconduct that results in a crime being committed that would not otherwise have occurred but for the police conduct

ethical formalism ethical system espoused by Kant that depends on duty; holds that the only thing truly good is a goodwill, and that what is good is that which conforms to the categorical imperative

ethical system systematic ordering of moral principles, also called moral theory or moral philosophy

ethics study of what constitutes good or bad conduct

ethics of care ethical system that defines good as meeting needs and preserving and enriching relationships

ethics of virtue ethical system that bases ethics largely on character and possession of virtues

exclusionary rule court-created rule of evidence that excludes evidence obtained through illegal means

expiation atonement

free will freedom of choice or freedom to make individual decisions without external forces influencing decisions

gratuities gifts given because of occupation or role of the recipient

group think psychological term referring to the tendency of a group that works together and develops a common mind-set to agree on ideas that are problematic or even irrational using objective evaluation

halo effect psychological term referring to the tendency to believe a person who is an expert in one area is knowledgeable about other areas as well; giving greater weight to opinion because of irrelevant expertise

hedonistic calculus Bentham's formulation of the amount of punishment (pain) necessary to outweigh the anticipated profit (pleasure) of a criminal act; using this calculus, the state should be able to deter crime

hypothetical imperative a statement of contingent demand: *if* I want something, *then* I must work for it; contrasted with the categorical imperative, which states that one must conform to the imperative with no "ifs"

imperfect duties general moral values that do not specify acts; for instance, to be charitable

incapacitate to make incapable; in corrections, to hold someone for any length of time in order to prevent him or her from committing crime

just deserts model model of punishment advocated by von Hirsh that states that the only appropriate punishment is proportional to the seriousness of the crime and rejects treatment as a correctional policy related to sentencing

justice   the quality of being just, impartial, or fair; the principle or ideal of just dealing or right action

justice model   model of punishment advocated by Fogel that is similar to the just deserts model and states that treatment can be made available but should not influence sentence

lex salica   compensation-based justice; payment or atonement

lex talionis   vengeance-oriented justice concerned with equal retaliation (an eye for an eye . . .)

mala in se   wrong in itself; refers to natural crimes or acts that are condemned by all cultures through all time

mechanical solidarity   Durkheim's concept of societal solidarity as arising from similarities among its members

mens rea   legal concept meaning guilty mind, the mental state necessary for culpability

meta-ethics   discipline investigating the meaning of ethical terms

modeling   learning theory concept that people learn behaviors, values, and attitudes through relationships; they identify with another person and want to be like that other person and so pattern their behavior, expressions, beliefs after that person; transitory to the extent that the relationship is transitory

morals   judgment of good and bad conduct

natural law   concept of the laws of nature such as gravity; such laws are discovered by reason but exist apart from humankind; natural laws also govern morality and human nature

normative ethics   study of what is right and wrong in particular situations

order maintenance   type of police work not related to crime control; such as responding to family disturbance, neighbor dispute, lost child, health problem, traffic, and such

organic solidarity   Durkheim's concept of societal solidarity as arising from differences among people, as exemplified by the division of labor

pantheism   view that all existence is made up of attributes of God; God is everything

paternalistic laws   those laws that protect the individual against the dangers of his or her own actions; seat belt laws, helmet laws, and such

plea bargaining   practice of exchanging promises to recommend reduced sentence, reduced charge, or dropping some charges in return for a guilty plea

pluralism   idea that power groups form and reform coalitions, which in turn affect the social and political structure of society

pluralistic ignorance   idea that in any occupational subculture or group of people, the vocal minority appear to represent the beliefs of the majority and the majority believe that they do, but when polled, private beliefs are different and opposite from what the majority believe everyone believes; for instance, prison correctional officers privately believe in more treatment principles than what they express or what they believe others agree with

positive law   laws written and enforced by society (contrasted to *natural law*)

principle of forfeiture   states that one gives up one's right to be treated under the principles of respect for persons to the extent that one has abrogated someone else's rights; for instance, self-defense is acceptable according to the principle of forfeiture

principle of the golden mean   Aristotle's concept of moderation, that one should not err toward excess or deficiency; associated with the ethics of virtue

procedural justice   component of justice that concerns the steps taken (due process) to reach a determination of guilt and punishment

psychological egoism   concept that humans naturally and inherently seek self-interest, and that they can do nothing else because it is their nature

quid pro quo   something for something

rationality   the quality or state of being rational (having reason or understanding); ability to judge the consequences of one's action

rectificatory (or commutative) justice   component of justice concerning business dealings where unfair advantage or undeserved harm has occurred and justice is the recompense or righting of such a wrong

reinforcement   reward

religious ethics   ethical system that is based on religious concepts of good and evil; what is good is that which is God's will

retributive justice   concerns the determination and methods of punishments

rule utilitarianism   type of utilitarianism that determines the goodness of an action by measuring the utility of that action made into a rule for behavior

selective incapacitation   policy of identifying high-risk offenders and incarcerating them for longer periods of time based on perceived risk

social contract theory   concept developed by Hobbes, Rousseau, and Locke, stating that the state of nature is a "war of all against all" in which life is nasty, brutish, and short; to protect being victimized by those who are stronger, each member gives up some liberties in return for protections; the contract is between society, which promises protection, and the individual, who promises to abide by laws and punishments if laws are broken

substantive justice   concept of just deserts; appropriate amount of punishment for the crime

supererogatories   actions that are commendable but not considered moral duties required to be a moral person

teleological   study of ends; teleological system is one concerned with consequences or ends of an action to determine goodness

treatment (correctional)   that which constitutes accepted and standard practice and could reasonably result in cure

treatment ethic   the idea that crime is a symptom of an underlying pathology that can be treated (also *rehabilitative ethic*)

universalism   concept of absolute truths or truths that hold for all people over all time

utilitarianism   ethical system that claims that the greatest good is that which results in the greatest happiness for the greatest number; major proponents are Bentham and Mill (see also *act utilitarianism* and *rule utilitarianism*)

utility   good or benefit

values   measure of worth or priority

veil of ignorance   John Rawls's heuristic device used to determine justice: if one were ignorant of one's position in society—i.e., whether one was born to a wealthy or poor family—then one's ideas of just distribution of resources would be more objective and truthful

victim precipitation   concept related to victim's participation in the criminal act; victim plays a role and is not a passive object to the criminal's action; precipitation can range from instigating the victimization to merely making it possible—i.e., being an attractive target

Bibliography

Adams, Virginia. 1981. "How to Keep 'Em Honest." *Psychology Today* (Nov.): 52–53.

Albert, Ethel, Denise, Theodore, and Peterfreund, Sheldon. 1984. *Great Traditions in Ethics.* Belmont, CA: Wadsworth.

Allen, H., and Simonsen, C. 1986. *Corrections in America: An Introduction.* New York: Macmillan.

American Bar Association. 1979. *Annotated Code of Professional Responsibility.* Chicago: American Bar Association.

American Bar Association. 1986. *Informal Opinions, Committee on Ethics and Professional Responsibility.* Chicago: American Bar Association.

American Society for Public Administration. 1979. *Professional Standards and Ethics: A Workbook for Public Administrators.* Washington, DC: American Society for Public Administration.

Anderson, C. 1989. "DNA Evidence Questioned." *American Bar Association Journal* (Oct.): 18–19.

Arafat, Ibtihaj, and McCahery, Kathleen. 1978. "The Relationship Between Lawyers and Their Clients." In *Essays on the Theory and Practice of Criminal Justice,* ed. R. Rich, 193–219. Washington, DC: University Press.

Arboleda-Florez, J. 1983. "The Ethics of Psychiatry in Prison Society." *Canadian Journal of Criminology* 25(1): 47–54.

Arbuthnot, J. 1984. "Moral Reasoning Development Programmes in Prison: Cognitive-Developmental and Critical Reasoning Approaches." *Journal of Moral Education* 13(2): 112–113.

Arbuthnot, J., and Gordon, D. 1988. "Crime and Cognition: Community Applications of Sociomoral Reasoning Development." *Criminal Justice and Behavior* 15(3): 379–393.

Aronson, Robert. 1977. "Toward a Rational Resolution of Ethical Dilemmas in the Criminal Justice System." In *Criminal Justice Planning and Development,* ed. A. Cohn, 57–71. Beverly Hills, CA: Sage.

Attorney General's Commission on Pornography. 1986. *Final Report.* Washington, DC: U.S. Government Printing Office.

Aubert, Vilhelm. *Sociology of Law.* London: Penguin.

Baelz, Peter. 1977. *Ethics and Beliefs.* New York: Seabury Press.

Baier, Annette. 1987. "Hume, the Women's Moral Theorist." In *Women and Moral Theory,* ed. E. F. Kittay and D. Meyers, 37–51. Totawa, NJ: Rowman, Littlefield.

Barker, T., and Carter, D. 1991. *Police Lies and Perjury: A Motivation Based Taxonomy in Police Deviance,* 2d ed. Cincinnati: Anderson.

Baro, Agnes. 1995. "Tolerating Illegal Use of Force Against Inmates." In *Morality in Criminal Justice,* eds. D. Close and N. Meier, 380–396. Belmont, CA: Wadsworth.

Barry, Vincent. 1985. *Applying Ethics: A Text with Readings.* Belmont, CA: Wadsworth.

Bazemore, G., and Maloney, D. 1994. "Rehabilitating Community Service Toward Restorative Service Sanctions in a Balanced Justice System." *Federal Probation* 58(1): 24–35.

Beauchamp, Tom. 1982. *Philosophical Ethics.* New York: McGraw-Hill.

Beccaria, Cesare. 1977. *On Crimes and Punishment,* 6th ed. Trans. Henry Paolucci. Indianapolis: Bobbs-Merrill.

Bedau, Hugo. 1982. "Prisoners' Rights." *Criminal Justice Ethics* 1(1): 26–41.

Bedau, Hugo. 1991. "How to Argue About the Death Penalty." *Israel Law Review* 25: 466–480.

Bem, D. J. 1970. *Beliefs, Attitudes and Human Affairs.* Belmont, CA: Brooks/Cole.

Bentham, Jeremy. 1970. "The Rationale of Punishment." In *Ethical Choice: A Case Study Approach,* eds. R. Beck and J. Orr. New York: Free Press (original work published 1843).

Blumberg, Abraham. 1969. "The Practice of Law as a Confidence Game." In *Sociology of Law,* ed. V. Aubert, 321–331. London: Penguin.

Bohm, R. 1996. "Crime, Criminal, and Crime Control Policy Myths." In *Justice, Crime, and Ethics,* eds. M. Braswell, B. McCarthy, and B. McCarthy, 341–363. Cincinnati: Anderson.

Borchert, Donald, and Stewart, David. 1986. *Exploring Ethics.* New York: Macmillan.

Bossard, Andre. 1981. "Police Ethics and International Police Cooperation." In *The Social Basis of Criminal Justice: Ethical Issues for the 80's,* eds. F. Schamalleger and R. Gustafson, 23–38. Washington, DC: University Press.

Bowhee, L. 1980. *Prison Victimization.* New York: Elsevier.

Bowie, Norman. 1985. *Making Ethical Decisions.* New York: McGraw-Hill.

Boyce, William, and Jensen, Larry. 1978. *Moral Reasoning: A Psychological–Philosophical Integration.* Lincoln: University of Nebraska Press.

Braswell, M. 1996. "Ethics, Crime, and Justice: An Introductory Note to Students." In *Justice, Crime, and Ethics,* eds. M. Braswell, B. McCarthy, and B. McCarthy, 3–9. Cincinnati: Anderson.

Braswell, M., and Gold, J. 1996. "Peacemaking, Justice, and Ethics." In *Justice, Crime, and Ethics,* eds. M. Braswell, B. McCarthy, and B. McCarthy, 23–39. Cincinnati: Anderson.

Brehm, J. W., and Cohen, A. R. 1982. *Explorations in Cognitive Dissonance.* New York: Wiley.

Brown, Michael. 1981. *Working the Street.* New York: Russell Sage Foundation.

Bureau of Justice Statistics. 1992. *Prosecutors in State Courts, 1990.* Washington, DC: U.S. Department of Justice.

Bureau of Justice Statistics. 1996. *Capital Punishment, 1996.* Washington, DC: U.S. Department of Justice.

Callahan, Daniel. 1982. "Applied Ethics in Criminal Justice." *Criminal Justice Ethics* 1(1): 1, 64.

Casey, R. 1996. "Cop Wins One Million in Whistleblower Appeal." In *The Ethics Roll Call* (Fall) 4(6).

Cheek, F., and Miller, M. D. 1983. "The Experience of Stress for Correctional Officers." *Journal of Criminal Justice* (11): 105–120.

Clinard, Marshall, et al. 1985. "Illegal Corporate Behavior." In *Exploring Crime,* ed. J. Sheley, 205–218. Belmont, CA: Wadsworth.

Close, D., and Meier, N. 1995. *Morality in Criminal Justice.* Belmont, CA: Wadsworth.

Cohen, Elliott. 1991. "Pure Legal Advocates and Moral Agents: Two Concepts of a Lawyer in an Adversary System." In *Justice, Crime, and Ethics,* eds. M. Braswell, B. McCarthy, and B. McCarthy, 123–163. Cincinnati: Anderson.

Cohen, Howard. 1983. "Searching Police Ethics." *Teaching Philosophy* 6(3): 231–242.

Cohen, Howard. 1985. "A Dilemma for Discretion." In *Police Ethics: Hard Choices in Law Enforcement,* eds. W. Heffernan and T. Stroup, 69–83. New York: John Jay Press.

Cohen, Howard. 1986. "Exploiting Police Authority." *Criminal Justice Ethics* 5(2): 23–31.

Cohen, Howard. 1987. "Overstepping Police Authority." *Criminal Justice Ethics* (Summer/Fall): 52–60.

Cohen, Howard, and Feldberg, Michael. 1991. *Power and Restraint: The Moral Dimension of Police Work.* New York: Praeger.

Cole, George. 1970. "The Decision to Prosecute." *Law and Society Review* 4 (Feb.): 313–343.

Collins English Dictionary. 1979. London: Collins.

Commission on Obscenity and Pornography. 1970. *Report of the Commission on Obscenity and Pornography.* New York: Random House.

Corey, G., Corey, M., and Callanan, P. 1988. *Issues and Ethics in Helping Professions.* Pacific Grove, CA: Brooks/Cole.

Crouch, Ben, ed. 1980. *Keepers: Prison Guards and Contemporary Corrections.* Springfield, IL: Charles C. Thomas.

Crouch, Ben. 1986. *The Dilemmas of Punishment,* eds. K. Haus and G. Alpert. Prospect Heights, IL: Waveland.

Crouch, Ben, and Marquart, J. 1989. *An Appeal to Justice: Litigated Reform in Texas Prisons.* Austin: University of Texas Press.

Curridan, M. 1991. "Indigent Defense in the South: Begging for Justice." *American Bar Association Journal* (Jan.): 64–67.

Daley, Robert. 1984. *Prince of the City.* New York: Berkley.

Daly, Kathleen. 1989. "Criminal Justice Ideologies and Practices in Different Voices: Some Feminist Questions About Justice." *International Journal of the Sociology of Law* (17): 1–18.

Davis, Michael. 1991. "Do Cops Really Need a Code of Ethics?" *Criminal Justice Ethics* 10(2): 14–28.

Davis, Michael, and Elliston, Frederick. 1986. *Ethics and the Legal Profession.* Buffalo: Prometheus Books.

Dawson, J. 1992. "Prosecutors in State Courts." In *Bureau of Justice Statistics Bulletin.* U.S. Department of Justice.

Delaney, H. R. 1990. "Toward a Police Professional Ethic." In *Ethics in Criminal Justice,* ed. F. Schmalleger, 78–95. Bristol, IN: Wyndham Hall Press.

Delattre, Edwin. 1989a. *Character and Cops: Ethics in Policing.* Washington, DC: American Enterprise Institute for Public Policy Research.

Delattre, Edwin. 1989b. "Ethics in Public Service: Higher Standards and Double Standards." *Criminal Justice Ethics* 8(2): 79–83.

DiIulio, J. 1987. *Governing Prisons: A Comparative Study of Correctional Management.* New York: Free Press.

Dorschner, J. 1989. "The Dark Side of the Force." In *Critical Issues in Policing,* 2d ed., 254–274. Prospect Heights, IL: Waveland.

Douglass, John Jay. 1981. "Prosecutorial Ethics." In *The Social Basis of Criminal Justice: Ethical Issues for the 80's,* eds. F. Schmalleger and R. Gustafson, 109–171. Washington, DC: University Press.

Dror, Yehezkel. 1969. "Law and Social Change." In *Sociology of Law,* ed. V. Aubert, 90–100. London: Penguin.

Dunham, R., and Alpert, G. 1989. *Critical Issues in Policing,* 2d ed. Prospect Heights, IL: Waveland.

Durkheim, Emile. 1969. "Types of Law in Relation to Types of Social Solidarity." In *Sociology of Law,* ed. V. Aubert, 17–29. London: Penguin.

Elias, Robert. 1986. *The Politics of Victimization.* New York: Oxford University Press.

Ellis, L., and Pontius, A. 1989. *The Frontal-Limbic-Reticular Network and Variations in Pro-antisociality: A Neurological Based Model of Moral Reasoning and Criminality.* Reno, NV: Paper presented at the 1989 ASC conference.

Elliston, Frederick. 1986. "The Ethics of Ethics Tests for Lawyers." In *Ethics and the Legal Profession,* eds. M. Davis and F. Elliston, 50–61. Buffalo, NY: Prometheus Books.

Elliston, Frederick, and Bowie, Norman. 1982. *Ethics, Public Policy and Criminal Justice.* Cambridge, MA: Oelgeschlager, Gunn and Hain.

Elliston, F., and Feldberg, M. 1985. *Moral Issues in Police Work.* Totawa, NJ: Rowman & Allanheld.

"Ethical Principles for Psychologists." 1981. *American Psychologist* 36 (June): 633–638.

Ewin, R. E. 1990. "Loyalty and the Police." *Criminal Justice Ethics* 9(2): 3–15.

"FBI, Media Could Face Lawsuit in Jewell Case." *Austin American-Statesman,* 27 Oct. 1996: A1, A8.

Feibleman, James. 1985. *Justice, Law and Culture.* Boston: Martinus Nijhoff.

Feinberg, Joel, and Gross, Hyman. 1977. *Justice: Selected Readings.* Princeton, NJ: Princeton University Press.

Felkenes, G. 1987. "Ethics in the Graduate Criminal Justice Curriculum." *Teaching Philosophy* 10(1): 23–36.

Felkenes, George. 1984. "Attitudes of Police Officers Towards Their Professional Ethics." *Journal of Criminal Justice* (12): 211–220.

Fink, Paul. 1977. *Moral Philosophy.* Encino, CA: Dickinson.

Flanagan, D., and Jackson, K. 1987. "Justice, Care, and Gender: The Kohlberg–Gilligan Debate Revisited." *Ethics* (97): 622–637.

Fogel, David. 1975. *We Are the Living Proof.* Cincinnati: Anderson.

Fogel, David, and Hudson, Joe. 1981. *Justice as Fairness.* Cincinnati: Anderson.

Foot, P. 1982. "Moral Relativism." In *Relativism: Cognitive and Moral,* eds. J. Meiland and M. Krausz, 152–167. Notre Dame, IN: University of Notre Dame Press.

Freedman, Monroe. 1986. "Professional Responsibility of the Criminal Defense Lawyer: The Three Hardest Questions." In *Ethics and the Legal Profession,* eds. M. Davis and F. Elliston, 328–339. Buffalo, NY: Prometheus Books.

Fried, Charles. 1986. "The Lawyer as Friend." In *Ethics and the Legal Profession,* eds. M. Davis and F. Elliston, 132–157. Buffalo, NY: Prometheus Books.

Fuller, Lon. 1969. *The Morality of Law.* New Haven, CT: Yale University Press.

Galston, William. 1980. *Justice and the Human Good.* Chicago: University of Chicago Press.

Garland, David. 1990. *Punishment and Modern Society.* Chicago: University of Chicago Press.

Gavaghan, M., Arnold, K., and Gibbs, J. 1983. "Moral Judgement in Delinquents and Nondelinquents: Recognition Versus Production Measures." *The Journal of Psychology* (114): 267–274.

Gerber, R., and McAnany, P. 1972. *Contemporary Punishment: Views, Explanations, and Justifications.* Notre Dame, IN: University of Notre Dame Press.

Gershman, Bennet. 1991. "Why Prosecutors Misbehave." In *Justice, Crime, and Ethics,* eds. M. Braswell, B. McCarthy, and B. McCarthy, 163–177. Cincinnati: Anderson.

Gibbs, J., Arnold, K., Ahlborn, H., and Cheesman, F. 1984. "Facilitation of Sociomoral Reasoning in Delinquents." *Journal of Consulting and Clinical Psychology* 52(1): 37–45.

Gilligan, Carol. 1982. *In a Different Voice: Psychological Theory and Women's Development.* Cambridge, MA: Harvard University Press.

Gilligan, Carol. 1987. "Moral Orientation and Moral Development." In *Women and Moral Theory,* eds. E. F. Kittay and D. Meyers, 19–37. Totawa, NJ: Rowman, Littlefield.

Glendon, M. 1994. *A Nation Under Lawyers.* New York: Farrar, Straus and Giroux.

Gold, J. 1996. "Utilitarianism and Deontological Approaches to Criminal Justice Ethics." In *Justice, Crime, and Ethics,* eds. M. Braswell, B. McCarthy, and B. McCarthy, 9–23. Cincinnati: Anderson.

Gold, Jeffery, Braswell, Michael, and McCarthy, Belinda. 1991. "Criminal Justice Ethics: A Survey of Philosophical Theories." In *Justice, Crime, and Ethics,* eds. M. Braswell, B. McCarthy, and B. McCarthy, 3–25. Cincinnati: Anderson.

Gottfredson, Michael, and Hirschi, Travis. 1990. *A General Theory of Crime.* Stanford, CA: Stanford University Press.

Greenwood, Peter. 1982. *Selective Incapacitation.* Santa Monica, CA: Rand Institute.

Gushman, B. 1990. *Prosecutorial Misconduct.* New York: Clark Boardman.

Hamm, M. 1995. *The Abandoned Ones.* Boston: Northeastern University Press.

Harper, J. 1992. "Local Judge on Hot Seat Over Conduct." *Houston Post,* 6 July: A9.

Harris, C. E. 1986. *Applying Moral Theories.* Belmont, CA: Wadsworth.

Hassine, V. 1996. *Life Without Parole: Living in Prison Today.* Los Angeles: Roxbury.

Heffernan, W. 1982. "Two Approaches to Police Ethics." *Criminal Justice Review* (7): 28–35.

Heffernan, W., and Stroup, T. 1985. *Police Ethics: Hard Choices in Law Enforcement.* New York: John Jay Press.

Heidensohn, Francis. 1986. "Models of Justice: Portia or Persephone? Some Thoughts on Equality, Fairness and Gender in the Field of Criminal Justice." *International Journal of the Sociology of Law* (14): 287–298.

Hersh, F., et al. 1979. *Developing Moral Growth: From Piaget to Kohlberg.* New York: Longman.

Hickey, Joseph, and Scharf, Peter. 1980. *Toward a Just Correctional System.* San Francisco: Jossey-Bass.

Hook, Sidney. 1977. "Social Protest and Civil Disobedience." In *Moral Philosophy,* 122–130. Encino, CA: Dickinson.

Hopfe, Lewis. 1983. *Religions of the World.* New York: Macmillan.

Hornum, Finn, and Stavish, Frank. 1978. "Criminology Theory and Ideology: Four Analytical Perspectives in the Study of Crime and the Criminal Justice System." In *Essays on the Theory and Practice of Criminal Justice,* ed. R. Rich, 143–161. Washington, DC: University Press.

Jaccoby, Joan, Mellon, Leonard, and Smith, Walter. 1980. *Policy and Prosecution.* Washington, DC: Bureau of Social Science Research.

Jenson, E., and Gerber, J. 1996. "The Civil Forfeiture of Assets and the War on Drugs: Expanding Criminal Sanctions While Reducing Due Process Protection." *Crime and Delinquency* 42(3): 421–434.

Johnson, Charles, and Copus, Gary. 1981. "Law Enforcement Ethics: A Theoretical Analysis." In *The Social Basis of Criminal Justice: Ethical Issues for the 80's,* eds. F. Schmalleger and R. Gustafson, 39–83. Washington, DC: University Press.

Johnson, Deborah. 1982. "Morality and Police Harm." In *Ethics, Public Policy, and Criminal Justice,* eds. F. Elliston and N. Bowie, 79–92. Cambridge, MA: Oelgeschlager, Gunn and Hain.

Johnson, Leslie. 1982. "Frustration: The Mold of Judicial Philosophy." *Criminal Justice Ethics* 1(1): 20–26.

Johnson, Robert. 1987. *Hard Time: Understanding and Reforming the Prison.* Pacific Grove, CA: Brooks/Cole.

Johnson, Robert. 1991. "A Life for a Life? Opinion and Debate." In *Justice, Crime, and Ethics,* eds. M. Braswell, B. McCarthy, and B. McCarthy, 199–210. Cincinnati: Anderson.

Johnston, M. 1995. "Police Corruption." In *Morality in Criminal Justice,* eds. D. Close and N. Meier. Belmont, CA: Wadsworth.

Kamisar, Yale, LeFave, Wayne, and Israel, Jerold. 1980. *Modern Criminal Procedure: Cases, Comments and Questions.* St. Paul, MN: West Publishing.

Kania, Richard. 1988. "Police Acceptance of Gratuities." *Criminal Justice Ethics* 7(2): 37–49.

Kant, Immanuel. 1949. *Critique of Practical Reason,* trans. Lewis White Beck. Chicago: University of Chicago Press.

Kant, Immanuel. 1981. "Ethical Duties to Others: Truthfulness." In *Lectures on Ethics,* ed. L. Infield, 224–232. Indianapolis: Hackett.

Kaplan, Morton. 1976. *Justice, Human Nature and Political Obligation.* New York: Free Press.

Kappeler, V., and Potter, G. 1996. *The Mythology of Crime and Justice.* Prospect Heights, IL: Waveland.

Kappeler, V., Sluder, K., and Alpert, G. 1984. *Forces of Deviance: Understanding the Dark Side of Policing.* Prospect Heights, IL: Waveland.

Karmen, Andrew. 1984. *Crime Victims: An Introduction to Victimology.* Pacific Grove, CA: Brooks/Cole.

Kauffman, Kelsey. 1988. *Prison Officers and Their World.* Cambridge, MA: Harvard University Press.

Kelly, Orr. 1982. "Corporate Crime: The Untold Story." *U.S. News & World Report* (Sept. 6): 25–30.

Kessler, Gary. 1992. *Voices of Wisdom: A Multicultural Philosophy Reader.* Belmont, CA: Wadsworth.

Kittel, Norman. 1990. "Criminal Defense Attorneys: Bottom of the Legal Profession's Class." In *Ethics in Criminal Justice,* ed. F. Schmalleger, 42–62. Bristol, IN: Wyndam Hall Press.

Kleinig, John. 1986. "The Conscientious Advocate and Client Perjury." *Criminal Justice Ethics* 5(2): 3–15.

Kleinig, John. 1990. "Teaching and Learning Police Ethics: Competing and Complementary Approaches." *Journal of Criminal Justice* (18): 1–18.

Klockars, Carl. 1983. "The Dirty Harry Problem." In *Thinking About Police: Contemporary Readings,* ed. C. Klockars, 428–438. New York: McGraw-Hill.

Klockars, Carl. 1984. "Blue Lies and Police Placebos." *American Behavioral Scientist* 27(4): 529–544.

Knudten, Mary. 1978. "The Prosecutor's Role in Plea Bargaining: Reasons Related to Actions." In *Essays on the Theory and Practice of Criminal Justice,* ed. R. Rich, 275–295. Washington, DC: University Press.

Kohlberg, Lawrence. 1976. "Moral Stages and Moralization." In *Moral Development and Behavior: Theory, Research and Social Issues,* ed. T. Lickona, 31–53. New York: Holt, Rinehart and Winston.

Kohlberg, Lawrence. 1983. *Essays in Moral Development, Vol. 2. The Psychology of Moral Development.* New York: Harper & Row.

Kohlberg, Lawrence. 1984. *The Psychology of Moral Development.* San Francisco: Harper & Row.

Kohlberg, L., and Candel, D. 1984. "The Relationship of Moral Judgment to Moral Action." In *The Psychology of Moral Development,* ed. L. Kohlberg, 498–582. San Francisco: Harper & Row.

Kottak, Conrad Philip. 1974. *Anthropology: The Exploration of Human Diversity.* New York: Random House.

Kramer, Ronald. 1982. "The Debate Over the Definition of Crime: Paradigms, Value Judgments, and Criminological Work." In *Ethics, Public*

Policy and Criminal Justice, eds.
F. Elliston and N. Bowie, 33–59.
Cambridge, MA: Oelgeschlager,
Gunn and Hain.

Krisberg, Barry. 1975. *Crime and Privilege:
Toward a New Criminology.* Englewood
Cliffs, NJ: Prentice-Hall.

Krogstand, Jack, and Robertson, Jack.
1979. "Moral Principles for Ethical
Conduct." *Management Horizons*
10(1): 13–24.

Kronenwerter, M. 1993. *Capital Punishment: A Reference Handbook.* Santa
Barbara, CA: ABC-CLIO.

Leahy, R. 1981. "Parental Practices and
the Development of Moral Judgment
and Self Image Disparity During
Adolescence." *Developmental Psychology* 17(5): 580–594.

Leiser, Burton. 1986. *Liberty, Justice and
Morals.* New York: Macmillan.

Levine, C., Kohlberg, L., and Hewer, A.
1985. "The Current Formulation of
Kohlberg's Theory and Response to
Critics." *Human Development* (28):
94–100.

Lickona, T., ed. 1976. *Moral Development
and Behavior: Theory, Research and
Social Issues.* New York: Holt, Rinehart and Winston.

Lombardo, Lucien. 1981. *Guards Imprisoned: Correctional Officers at Work.* New
York: Elsevier.

Lombardo, Lucien. 1997. "Guards Imprisoned: Correctional Officers at Work."
In *Correctional Contexts,* eds. J. Marquart and J. Sorensen, 189–203. Los
Angeles: Roxbury.

Longuire, D. 1983. "Ethical Dilemmas in
the Research Setting." *Criminology*
21(3): 333–348.

Louthan, William. 1985. "The Politics of
Discretionary Justice Among Criminal
Justice Agencies." In *Discretion, Justice,
and Democracy: A Public Policy Perspective,* eds. C. Pinkele and W. Louthan,
13–19. Ames: Iowa State University
Press.

Lucas, J. R. 1980. *On Justice.* Oxford:
Oxford University Press.

Lutwak, N., and Hennessy, J. 1985. "Interpreting Measures of Moral Development to Individuals." *Measurement*

*and Evaluation in Counseling and Devel-
opment* 18(1): 26–31.

Maas, Peter. 1973. *Serpico.* New York:
Viking Press.

Maas, Peter. 1983. *Marie.* New York:
Random House.

MacIntyre, Alasdair. 1991. *After Virtue.*
South Bend, IN: University of Notre
Dame Press.

Mackie, J. L. 1977. *Ethics: Inventing Right
and Wrong.* New York: Penguin.

Mackie, J. L. 1982. "Morality and the
Retributive Emotions." *Criminal
Justice Ethics* 1(1): 3–10.

Maestri, William. 1982. *Basic Ethics for the
Health Care Professional.* Washington,
DC: University Press.

Malloy, Edward. 1982. *The Ethics of Law
Enforcement and Criminal Punishment.*
Lanham, NY: University Press.

Mappes, Thomas. 1982. *Social Ethics.* New
York: McGraw-Hill.

Margolis, Joseph. 1971. *Values and Conduct.* New York: Oxford University
Press.

Marks, F. Raymond, and Cathcart, Dar-
lene. 1986. "Discipline Within the
Legal Profession." In *Ethics and the
Legal Profession,* eds. M. Davis and
F. Elliston, 62–105. Buffalo, NY:
Prometheus Books.

Marquart, J., and Roebuck, J. 1986.
"Prison Guards and Snitches." In *The
Dilemmas of Corrections: Contemporary
Readings,* eds. K. Haus and G. Alpert,
158–176. Prospect Heights, IL:
Waveland.

Martin, D. 1993. *Committing Journalism:
The Writings of Red Hog.* New York:
Norton.

Marx, Gary. 1985a. "Police Undercover
Work: Ethical Deception or Decep-
tive Ethics?" In *Police Ethics: Hard
Choices in Law Enforcement,* eds.
W. Heffernan and T. Stroup, 83–117.
New York: John Jay Press.

Marx, Gary. 1985b. "Who Really Gets
Stung? Some Issues Raised by the
New Police Undercover Work."
In *Moral Issues in Police Work,* eds.
F. Elliston and M. Feldberg, 99–129.
Totawa, NJ: Rowman & Allanheld.

Marx, Gary. 1992. "Under-the-Covers Undercover Investigations: Some Reflections on the State's Use of Deception." *Criminal Justice Ethics* 11(1): 13–25.

Matthews, John, and Marshall, Ralph. 1981. "Some Constraints on Ethical Behavior in Criminal Justice Organizations." In *The Social Basis of Criminal Justice: Ethical Issues for the 80's,* eds. F. Schmalleger and R. Gustafson, 9–22. Washington, DC: University Press.

McAnany, Patrick. 1981. "Justice in Search of Fairness." In *Justice as Fairness,* eds. D. Fogel and J. Hudson, 22–51. Cincinnati: Anderson.

McAnany, Patrick, Thomas, Doug, and Fogel, David, eds. 1984. *Probation and Justice: A Reconsideration of Mission.* Cambridge, MA: Oegeschlager, Gunn and Hain.

McCarthy, Bernard. 1991. "Keeping an Eye on the Keeper: Prison Corruption and Its Control." In *Justice, Crime, and Ethics,* eds. M. Braswell, B. McCarthy, and B. McCarthy, 239–253. Cincinnati: Anderson.

McCarthy, Bernard. 1995. "Patterns of Prison Corruption." In *Morality in Criminal Justice,* eds. D. Close and N. Meier, 280–285. Belmont, CA: Wadsworth.

Merlo, Alida. 1992. "Ethical Issues in the Private Sector." In *Corrections: Dilemmas and Directions,* eds. P. Benekos and A. Merlo, 23–27. Cincinnati: Anderson.

Metz, Harol. 1990. "An Ethical Model for Law Enforcement Administrators." In *Ethics in Criminal Justice,* ed. F. Schmalleger, 95–103. Bristol, IN: Wyndam Hall Press.

Milgram, Stanley. 1963. "Behavioral Study of Obedience." *Journal of Abnormal and Social Psychology* (67): 371–378.

Miller, K., and Radelet, M. 1993. *Executing the Mentally Ill.* Newbury Park, CA: Sage.

Mitchell, J., and Banks, S. 1996. "Once Again Americans Fall into Racial Rut." *Austin American-Statesman,* 9 Feb. 1996.

Mitford, Jessica. 1971. *Kind and Usual Punishment.* New York: Vintage Books.

Morris, T., and Morris, P. 1980. "Where Staff and Prisoners Meet." In *Keepers: Prison Guards and Contemporary Corrections,* ed. B. Crouch, 247–273. Springfield, IL: Charles C. Thomas.

Muir, William. 1977. *Police: Streetcorner Politicians.* Chicago: University of Chicago Press.

Murphy, Jeffrie. 1985. *Punishment and Rehabilitation.* Belmont, CA: Wadsworth.

Murphy, Jeffrie. 1995. *Punishment and Rehabilitation.* Belmont, CA: Wadsworth.

Murphy, P., and Caplan, D. 1989. "Conditions That Breed Corruption." In *Critical Issues in Policing,* eds. R. Dunham and G. Alpert, 304–324. Prospect Heights, IL: Waveland.

Murphy, Paul, and Moran, Kenneth T. 1981. "The Continuing Cycle of Systemic Police Corruption." In *The Social Basis of Criminal Justice: Ethical Issues for the 80's,* eds. F. Schmalleger and R. Gustafson, 87–101. Washington, DC: University Press.

Murton, T., and Hyams, J. 1969. *Accomplices to the Crime: The Arkansas Prison Scandal.* New York: Grove.

Murton, Thomas. 1976. *The Dilemma of Prison Reform.* New York: Irvington.

Nash, Laura. 1981. "Ethics Without the Sermon." *Harvard Business Review* (Nov.–Dec.): 81.

National Institute of Justice. 1992. "Community Policing in the 1990's." *National Institute of Justice* (Aug.): 2–9.

Nettler, Gwen. 1978. *Explaining Crime.* New York: McGraw-Hill.

Newman, Graeme. 1978. *The Punishment Response.* New York: J. B. Lippincott.

Noddings, Nel. 1986. *Caring: A Feminine Approach to Ethics and Moral Education.* Berkeley: University of California Press.

Papke, David. 1986. "The Legal Profession and Its Ethical Responsibilities: A

History." In *Ethics and the Legal Profession,* eds. M. Davis and F. Elliston, 29–49. Buffalo, NY: Prometheus.

Pellicciotti, Joseph. 1990. "Ethics and the Criminal Defense: A Client's Desire to Testify Untruthfully." In *Ethics and Criminal Justice,* ed. F. Schmalleger, 67–78. Bristol, IN: Wyndam Hall Press.

Pinkele, Carl, and Louthan, William. 1985. *Discretion, Justice and Democracy: A Public Policy Perspective.* Ames: Iowa State University Press.

Platt, Anthony. 1977. *The Child Savers.* Chicago: University of Chicago Press.

Postema, Gerald. 1986. "Moral Responsibility in Professional Ethics." In *Ethics and the Legal Profession,* eds. M. Davis and F. Elliston, 158–179. Buffalo, NY: Prometheus.

Power, C., and Kohlberg, L. 1980. "Faith, Morality, and Ego Development." In *Toward Moral and Religious Maturity,* eds. J. Fowler and C. Bursselmans, 311–372. Morristown, NJ: Silver Burdett.

Prior, W. 1991. "Aristotle's Nicomanchean Ethics." In *From Virtue and Knowledge: An Introduction to Ancient Greek Ethics,* ed. W. Prior, 144–193. New York: Routledge, Kegan Paul.

Quetelet, L. J. 1969. *A Treatise on Man and the Development of His Faculties.* Gainesville, FL: Scholars, Facsimiles and Reprints.

Quinney, Richard. 1969. *Crime and Justice in America.* New York: Little, Brown.

Quinney, Richard. 1974. *Critique of the Legal Order.* New York: Little, Brown.

Radelet, M., Bedau, H., and Putnam, C. 1992. *In Spite of Innocence: Erroneous Convictions in Capital Cases.* Boston: Northeastern University Press.

Raphael, D. D. 1980. *Justice and Liberty.* London: Athlone Press.

Rawls, J. 1995. "Two Concepts of Rules." In *Morality in Criminal Justice,* eds. D. Close and N. Meier, 439–450. Belmont, CA: Wadsworth.

Rawls, John. 1957. "Outline of a Decision Procedure for Ethics." *Philosophical Review* (66): 177–197.

Rawls, John. 1971. *A Theory of Justice.* Cambridge, MA: Belknap Press.

Reasons, Charles. 1973. "The Politicalization of Crime, the Criminal and the Criminologist." *Journal of Criminal Law, Criminology and Police Science* 64 (March): 471–477.

Reichel, P. 1997. *Corrections.* Minneapolis: West.

Reiman, Jeffrey. 1990. *Justice and Modern Moral Philosophy.* New Haven, CT: Yale University Press.

Report of the Commission on Obscenity and Pornography. 1970. *Final Report.* New York: Random House.

Rich, Robert. 1978. *Essays on the Theory and Practice of Criminal Justice.* Washington, DC: University Press.

Roberg, K. 1981. "Management Research in Criminal Justice: Exploring Ethical Issues." *Journal of Criminal Justice* (9): 41–49.

Rothbart, M., Hanley, D., and Albert, M. 1986. "Differences in Moral Reasoning." *Sex Roles* 15(11/12): 645–653.

Rutherford, Andrew. 1984. *Prisons and the Process of Justice.* London: Heinemann.

Scheingold, Stuart. 1984. *The Politics of Law and Order.* New York: Longman.

Schmalleger, F., and McKendrick, R. 1991. *Criminal Justice Ethics: An Annotated Bibliography.* Westport, CT: Greenwood.

Schmalleger, Frank, and Gustafson, Robert, eds. 1981. *The Social Basis of Criminal Justice: Ethical Issues for the 80's.* Washington, DC: University Press.

Schoeman, Ferdinand. 1982. "Friendship and Testimonial Privileges." In *Ethics, Public Policy and Criminal Justice,* eds. F. Elliston and N. Bowie, 257–272. Cambridge, MA: Oelgeschlager, Gunn and Hain.

Schoeman, Ferdinand, 1985. "Privacy and Police Undercover Work." In *Police Ethics: Hard Choices in Law Enforcement,* eds. W. Heffernan and

T. Stroup, 133–153. New York: John Jay Press.

Schoeman, Ferdinand. 1986. "Undercover Operations: Some Moral Questions About S.804." *Criminal Justice Ethics* 5(2): 16–22.

Sellin, Thorsten. 1970. "The Conflict of Conduct Norms." In *The Sociology of Crime and Delinquency,* eds. M. Wolfgang, L. Savitz, and N. Johnston, 186–189. New York: Wiley.

Senna, Joseph, and Siegel, Larry. 1984. *Introduction to Criminal Justice.* St. Paul, MN: West.

Sheley, Joseph, ed. 1985. *Exploring Crime.* Belmont, CA: Wadsworth.

Sherman, Lawrence. 1981. *The Teaching of Ethics in Criminology and Criminal Justice.* Washington, DC: Joint Commission on Criminology and Criminal Justice Education and Standards, LEAA.

Sherman, Lawrence. 1982. "Learning Police Ethics." *Criminal Justice Ethics* 1(1): 10–19.

Sherman, Lawrence. 1985a. "Becoming Bent: Moral Careers of Corrupt Policemen." In *Moral Issues in Police Work,* eds. F. Elliston and M. Feldberg, 253–273. Totawa, NJ: Rowman & Allanheld.

Sherman, Lawrence. 1985b. "Equity Against Truth: Value Choices in Deceptive Investigations." In *Police Ethics: Hard Choices in Law Enforcement,* eds. W. Heffernan and T. Stroup, 117–133. New York: John Jay Press.

Skolnick, Jerome. 1982. "Deception by Police." *Criminal Justice Ethics* 1(2): 40–54.

Skolnick, Jerome, and Leo, Richard. 1992. "Ideology and the Ethics of Crime Control." *Criminal Justice Ethics* 11(1): 3–13.

Smith, Dwight. 1982. "Ideology and the Ethics of Economic Crime Control." In *Ethics, Public Policy and Criminal Justice,* eds. F. Elliston and N. Bowie, 133–156. Cambridge, MA: Oelgeschlager, Gunn and Hain.

Smith, Steven, and Meyer, Robert. 1987. *Law, Behavior, and Mental Health.* New York: New York University Press.

Snider, L. 1995. *Towards Safer Societies.* Unpublished manuscript. Department of Sociology, Queen's University, Kingston, Ontario.

Souryal, S., and Potts, D. 1996. "What Am I Supposed to Fall Back On? Cultural Literacy in Criminal Justice Ethics." *Journal of Criminal Justice Education* (4): 15–41.

Souryal, Sam. 1992. *Ethics in Criminal Justice: In Search of the Truth.* Cincinnati: Anderson.

Spader, D. 1984. "Rule of Law v. Rule of Man: The Search for the Golden Zigzag Between Conflicting Fundamental Values," *Journal of Criminal Justice* (12): 379–394.

Spence, Gerry. 1989. *With Justice for None.* New York: Penguin.

Stace, W. 1995. "Ethical Relativity and Ethical Absolutism." In *Morality and Criminal Justice,* eds. D. Close and N. Meier, 25–32. Cincinnati: Anderson.

Staples, W. 1977. *The Culture of Surveillance.* New York: St. Martin's.

Stefanic, Martin. 1981. "Police Ethics in a Changing Society." *The Police Chief* (May): 62–64.

Sterba, James. 1980. *The Demands of Justice.* Notre Dame, IN: University of Notre Dame Press.

Stitt, B. Grant, and James, Gene. 1985. "Entrapment: An Ethical Analysis." In *Moral Issues in Police Work,* eds. F. Elliston and M. Feldberg, 129–147. Totawa, NJ: Rowman and Allanheld.

Stover, Robert. 1989. *Making It and Breaking It: The Fate of Public Interest Commitment During Law School,* ed. H. Erlanger. Urbana: University of Illinois Press.

Sykes, Gresham. 1980. "The Defects of Total Power." In *Keepers: Prison Guards and Contemporary Corrections,* ed. B. Crouch. Springfield, IL: Charles C. Thomas.

Sykes, Gresham. 1989. "The Functional Nature of Police Reform: The Myth of Controlling the Police." In *Critical Issues in Policing,* eds. R. Dunham and G. Alpert, 292–304. Prospect Heights, IL: Waveland.

Tanay, E. 1982. "Psychiatry and the Prison System." *Journal of Forensic Sciences* 27(2): 385–392.

Taylor, W. B. 1993. *Brokered Justice: Race Politics and Mississippi Prisons 1798–1992.* Columbus: Ohio State University Press.

Thoma, S. 1986. "Estimating Gender Differences in the Comprehension and Preference of Moral Issues." *Developmental Review* (6): 165–180.

Thompson, Dennis. 1980. "Paternalism in Medicine, Law and Public Policy." In *Ethics Teaching in Higher Education,* eds. D. Callahan and S. Bok, 3–20. Hastings, NY: Hastings Center.

Toch, Hans. 1977. *Living in Prison.* New York: Free Press.

Toch, Hans, and Grant, J. Douglas. 1991. *Police as Problem Solvers.* New York: Plenum.

Toch, Hans, Grant, J. Douglas, and Galvin, Raymond. 1975. *Agents of Change: A Study in Police Reform.* New York: Wiley.

Tonry, Michael, Ohlin, Lloyd, and Farrington, David. 1991. *Human Development and Criminal Behavior.* New York: Springer Verlag.

Turk, Austin. 1982. "Legal, Polemical and Empirical Definitions of Criminality." In *Ethics, Public Policy and Criminal Justice,* eds. F. Elliston and N. Bowie, 5–18. Cambridge, MA: Oelgeschlager, Gunn and Hain.

Tyler, T. 1990. *Why People Obey the Law.* New Haven, CT: Yale University Press.

Umbreit, M. S. 1994. *Victim Meets Offender: The Impact of Restorative Justice and Mediation.* Monsey, NY: Criminal Justice Press.

Umbreit, M. S., and Carey, M. 1995. "Restorative Justice Implications for Organizational Change." *Federal Probation* 59(1): 47–54.

Van Ness, D., and Heetderks Strong, K. 1997. *Restoring Justice.* Cincinnati: Anderson.

von Hirsch, Andrew. 1976. *Doing Justice.* New York: Hill and Wang.

von Hirsch, Andrew. 1985. *Past or Future Crimes.* New Brunswick, NJ: Rutgers University Press.

von Hirsch, Andrew, and Maher, Lisa. 1992. "Can Penal Rehabilitation Be Revived?" *Criminal Justice Ethics* 11(1): 25–31.

Walker, L. J. 1986. "Sex Difference in the Development of Moral Reasoning." *Child Development* (57): 522–526.

Walker, S. 1994. *Sense and Nonsense About Crime and Drugs.* Belmont, CA: Wadsworth.

Walker, Samuel. 1985. *Sense and Nonsense About Crime.* Monterey, CA: Brooks/Cole.

Ward, M. 1996. "State Approves Faith-Based Pre-Release Program for Texas Inmates." *Austin American-Statesman,* 16 Nov.: B12.

Wasserman, Richard. 1985. "Lawyers as Professionals: Some Moral Issues." In *Ethics and the Legal Profession,* eds. M. Davis and F. Elliston, 114–131. Totawa, NJ: Rowman & Allanheld.

Weber, D. 1987. "Still in Good Standing. The Crisis in Attorney Discipline." *American Bar Association Journal* (Nov.): 58–63.

Webster's Ninth New Collegiate Dictionary. 1984. Springfield, MA: Merriam-Webster.

Whitehead, John. 1991. "Ethical Issues in Probation and Parole." In *Justice, Crime, and Ethics,* eds. M. Braswell, B. McCarthy, and B. McCarthy, 253–273. Cincinnati: Anderson.

Wiley, L. 1988. "Moral Education in a Correctional Setting: Reaching the Goal by a Different Road." *Journal of Offender Services and Rehabilitation* 12(2): 161–174.

Williams, Gregory. 1984. *The Law and Politics of Police Discretion.* Westport, CT: Greenwood.

Williams, H. 1992. "Reconciling Higher Educational Standards and Minority Recruitment: New York City Model." *Police Foundations Reports* (Sept.): 1–2.

Wilson, James Q. 1976. *Varieties of Police Behavior.* New York: Atheneum.

Wolff, Robert. 1977. *Understanding Rawls.* Princeton, NJ: Princeton University Press.

Wozencraft, Kim. 1990. *Rush.* New York: Random House.

Wren, Thomas. 1985. "Whistle-blowing and Loyalty to One's Friends." In *Police Ethics: Hard Choices in Law Enforcement,* eds. W. Heffernan and T. Stroup, 25–47. New York: John Jay Press.

Name Index

Adams, V., 69
Adler, M., 78
Albert, E., 43, 78
Albert, M., 63
Allen, H., 99
Alpert, G., 137, 154, 155, 161, 166, 190, 191, 192, 201, 203
Amin, I., 29
Anacharsis, 15
Aquinas, T., 39
Arafat, I., 213
Arboleda-Florez, J., 307
Arbuthnot, J., 81, 84
Aristotle, 43, 87, 88, 95, 196, 206
Armani, F., 223
Arnold, K., 69, 83
Aronson, R., 232
Aubert, V., 118

Baelz, P., 27
Baier, H., 43
Baker, M., 75, 178, 191
Bandura, A., 66
Barker, T., 138, 161, 174, 175, 203
Barry, M., 176
Barry, V., 6, 33, 38, 60, 126
Bazemore, G., 271
Beauchamp, T., 79, 90, 118
Beccaria, C., 36, 103, 114

Bedau, H., 234, 243, 244, 245, 256, 278, 286
Belge, F. 223
Bennett, R., 70
Bentham, J., 32, 33, 43, 67, 103, 114
Beto, G., 294
Bloom, A., 78
Blumberg, A., 208
Bohm, R., 333
Bok, S., 79
Bonger, 116
Borchert, D., 31, 32, 33, 38, 39, 78
Bossard, A., 142, 151
Bowie, N., 30, 79
Boyce, W., 59, 62, 66, 67, 72
Braithwaite, J., 47
Brandley, C., 244
Braswell, M., 6, 23, 29, 32, 47, 56, 79
Brink, D., 78
Brooks, W. M., 210
Brown, M., 146, 150, 152, 153, 157
Buro, A., 298

Callahan, D., 127
Campbell, K., 78
Candel, D., 69
Capone, A., 18
Carroll, L., 301
Carson, T., 78

Subject Index